P, control of, 19
P.S., to indicate postscript, 162, 172, 349
Page-end reminder, 152, 195
Page numbers of manuscripts, 192, 352
Paper, assembling for carbon pack, 115, 145, 165, 357; facts about, 116, 118, 346; horizontal centre of, vii; inserting, vii; size of, 116, 118, 346
Paper guide, setting the, vii
Paper guide placement, vii
Paragraph headings, 192, 200, 352
"Paragraph" symbol, 151, 217, 358
Paragraphs, block, 37; handwritten, 46; indented, 43; number and symbol, 99; speed escalator, 58
Parentheses, control of, 85
Parenthetic source notations, 207, 353
Per cent sign (%), 83
Percentages, expressing, 73, 341
Period (.), after abbreviations, 17; after initials, 17; at end of sentence, 9; control of, 9; in exclamation mark, 92; placement with quotation mark, 91; spacing after, 9; use as decimal point, 75; with initials, 17; with quotation mark, 91
Periodicals, titles of, 144, 339
Personal data sheet, 177, 350
Personal letter, complimentary close, 174; definition, 135; illustrated, 350; notes on, 173
Personal notation, on envelope, 142, 351
Personal/business letter, definition, 135; illustrated, 349; notes on, 169
Pica type, vii, 346
Pivoting, 126
Plays, titles of, 144, 339
Plus symbol (+), 92, 345
Poems, titles of, 144, 339
Points of compass, 339
Postal cards, 264, 352; form message on, 266
Postal Codes, 74, 342; exercises, 98
Postscript, 162, 172, 349
Posture, ix
Pound Sterling symbol, 345
Professional titles without name of person, 339
Program of a meeting, 274
Proofreaders' marks, 217, 358
Proofreading, 138, 335
Punctuation, styles, 136, 347
Purchase orders, 280

Q, control of, 23
Question mark, after direct question, 31; control of, 31; placement with quotation mark, 91; spacing after, 31
Quotation marks (''), 91
Quotations, capitalization in, 91; colon before long, direct, 168, 207; fragments of, 91, 352; long, in manuscript, 207, 352
Quoted material in manuscripts, 207, 352, 353

R, control of, 16
Ratchet release, See Automatic line finder
Reference initials, 135, 348
Reports, See Manuscripts
Return address, envelopes, 142, 351; personal/business letter, 169, 349; postal card, 265
Ribbon, changing, 334; control, v, vi
Right parenthesis ()), control of, 85
Right shift key, control of, 13
Roman numerals, aligning, 188; in topic outline, 188
Rough draft, 108, 217, 358
Ruled lines, drawing on the typewriter, 335; typed and nontyped, 280

S, control of, 2
Salutation, business letter, 135, 348; notes on, 154; personal/business letter, 169, 349; personal letter, 173, 350; placement of, 135, 348; postal card, 264
Seasons of the year, 339
Second-page heading for letter, 152, 349
Semicolon, control of, 2; spacing after, 6
Sentences, alphabetic, 53; difficult reach, 67; error-elimination, 63; speed escalator, 57
Seven (7), control of, 74
Shift key, control of left, 8; control of right, 13
Shift lock, use in typing ALL-CAP words, 119; use in underlining several words, 89
Side headings, 192, 199, 352
Signature, business letter, 135, 348; personal/business letter, 169, 349; personal letter, 173, 350; postal card, 264; simplified letter, 158, 348
Signer's name on letter, 135, 348
Simplified letter, 158, 348; illustrated, 160
Simplified style, 136
Six (6), control of, 73
Space bar, control of, 4
"Space" symbol, 217, 358
Spaces (horizontal), to a full line of elite type, vii; to a full line of pica type, vii; to 25.4 mm of elite type, 137, 346; to 25.4 mm of pica type, 137, 346
Spaces (vertical), on P4 paper, 118, 232, 346; on P5 paper, 118, 231, 233, 346; to 25.4 mm, 137, 346
Spacing, bibliography, 205, 353, 354, 356; envelope addresses, 138, 142, 351; footnotes, 211, 212, 353, 354, 355; letters, 137, 348; manuscripts, 192, 352, 355, 356; outlines, 187, 354, 356; summary of paper, 116, 346; table of contents, 214, 353, 355; title page, 215, 353, 355
Spacing (horizontal), above and below divider line for footnote, 211, 353, 355; after comma in sentence, 22; after colon, 32; after exclamation mark, 36, 92; after period at end of abbreviation, 17; after period at end of sentence, 9; after period used with an initial,

17; after period within an abbreviation, 17; after question mark, 31; after semicolon, 6; before and after "at" sign, 90; before and after "cent" sign, 90; in Postal Codes, 74; in serial, patent, and policy numbers, 77, 342; to indicate thousands (000's), 69; with cent sign, 90; with dollar sign, 82; with metric symbols, 70, 344; with number sign, 86
Spacing, summary of rules, 338, 339
Spacing (variable), between lines, 121; between words, 122
Spacing (vertical), after heading lines, 120, 192, 352; after main heading, 120, 192, 352; between headings and columns, 234; between lines of title page, 215, 353, 355; between main and columnar headings, 234; between main and side headings, 192, 352; between main, side, and paragraph headings, 192, 352; double, 3, 347; single, 3, 347; triple, 3, 347
Special characters and symbols, 345
Spread headings, 125, 346
Spreading letters, 125, 346
Squeezing letters, 143, 337
Statements, 283; income, 286
Street names, abbreviations in, 342
Subject, in simplified letter, 158, 348
Subject line, in letter, 163, 348
Subtitles, 242; spacing between columnar headings and, 242; two-line, 247
Superior figures, 95, 353
Superscript, 95, 353
Syllable intensity (SI), 38

T, control of, 7
Tab stops, clearing, 334; in columnar material, 199, 231, 237, 239, 240; setting, 43; setting for columns, 231, 237, 239, 240; use in paragraph indentions, 43; use in typing date and closing lines of letters, 139; use in typing outlines, 188; use in typing invoices, 281
Table of contents, 214, 353, 355
Tables, aligning figures, 199; centring by columnar headings or entries, 242; dollar sign in, 199; five-column, 247; four-column, 238; grouped data, 241; in manuscripts, 199; three-column, 232; with footnotes, 246; with subtitles and columnar headings, 242; with titles, 233; with titles and columnar headings, 234
Tabulation summary, 358, 359
Telegrams, 278; notes on, 279
Three (3), control of, 69
Three-column tables, 232
Time, how to express, 94
Title page, 215, 353, 355
Titles, articles, 144, 339; books, 144, 339; magazines, 144, 339; manuscripts, 192, 352; newspapers, 144, 339; plays, 144, 339; poems, 144, 339; of signer of letter, 135, 348; solid underline for, 89; two-line, 243

"Transpose" symbol, 217, 358
Twenty-four hour clock, 94
Two (2), control of, 75
Two-letter abbreviations, provincial and territory, 144, 343; state, district, and territory, 343
Two-page letters, 151, 349; heading for second page, 152, 349; second page paper, 152
Two-point punctuation, 136, 347
Typewriters, facts about, 334, 335
Typing position, ix

U, control of, 14
Unbound manuscript style, outline of, 192, 352, 353
Unbroken line, shift lock used to type, 89, 335
Underline, continuous for series of words, 89, 335; solid, under several words, 89, 335; symbol, 217, 358; to introduce footnotes, 211, 353, 354; unbroken, below several words, 89; use with columnar headings, 234
Underlining, bibliography, 204, 353, 354; in footnotes, 211, 353, 354; paragraph headings, 192, 200, 352; side headings, 192, 199, 352; titles of books, 144, 211, 339; titles of magazines, newspapers, and periodicals, 144, 339
Underscore, control of, 89

V, control of, 24
Variable line spacer, v, vii, 335
Vertical centring, See Centring (vertical)
Vertical ruled lines, drawing, 335

W, control of, 20
Word counts, in copy, 38
Word division, exercises, 56; hints on, 33, 46, 340
Words, average length of (AWL), 38; counting typewritten, 10; high-frequency (HFW), 38
Wrist position, 3
Writer, name of, on business letter, 135, 348

X, control of, 29
x, symbol for multiplication, 345

Y, control of, 27

Z, control of, 30
Zero (0), control of, 78; before a decimal, 78
ZIP Code, 163, 342, 343

"The SI units and symbols used in the text of Business Applications in Typewriting have been reviewed by the Canadian Government Specifications Board and are found to comply with the requirements of the two National Standards of Canada — the International System of Units (SI) CAN3-Z234.2-73 and the Canadian Metric Practice Guide, CAN3-Z234.1-76".
1976 06 11

"The Metric Commission has granted use of the National Symbol for Metric Conversion."   1977 03 25

BUSINESS APPLICATIONS IN TYPEWRITING

Geraldine M. Farmer, Ph.D.
Elizabeth J. Graham, M.Ed.
Lois M. Jenkins, B.Ed.

gage PUBLISHING LIMITED
TORONTO ONTARIO CANADA

Mathematical Method

1. Follow steps 1 and 2 above for determining vertical placement and for typing the headings.
2. Count the number of strokes in the longest item of each column or column heading. Add these numbers.
3. Subtract the resulting figure from the available horizontal strokes on the paper.
4. Divide the remainder by the number of columns plus one, to determine the spaces to leave between columns and for the left and right margins.
5. Set margins and tab stops.
6. Follow steps 10 - 13 above to centre and type column headings and body.

Mathematical Example

Horizontally centre a line with four columns on a sheet of P4 paper. Column 1 has 12 strokes; column 2, 14 strokes; column 3, 16 strokes; and column 4, 18 strokes.

Step 2: Total number of column strokes = 60

Step 3: Pica Type — 85 − 60 = 25
        Elite Type — 102 − 60 = 42

Step 4: Pica Type — 25 ÷ (4 + 1) = 5
        Elite Type — 42 ÷ (4 + 1) = 8 and 2 extra strokes

Step 5: With the left edge of the paper at "0" on the paper-guide scale, set margins and tabs as follows:
        Pica Type — Left margin at 5, second column at 22, third column at 41, and fourth column at 62.
        Elite Type — Left margin at 9, second column at 29, third column at 51, and fourth column at 75.

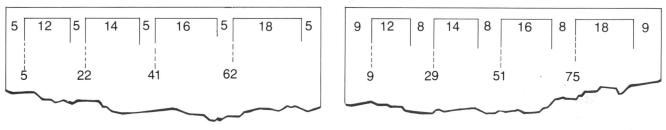

BUSINESS APPLICATIONS IN TYPEWRITING

Farmer, Graham, Jenkins

ISBN: 7715-0878-6

7 8 9 10 11   BP   84 83 82 81

Printed and Bound in Canada

PROOFREADERS' MARKS

Revisions that should be made in rough draft copy are indicated by proofreader's marks. The following proofreaders' marks may be encountered when re-typing edited rough draft copy.

⌒	Close up	⅃	Delete
∧	Insert	⩛	Insert space
⋏	Insert comma	ⱽ	Insert apostrophe
ⱽ ⱽ	Insert quotation marks	⊙	Insert period
⅂	Move right	⌐	Move left
⊔	Move down	⊓	Move up
lc	Lower case	¶	New paragraph
Cap or ≡	Capitalize	*stet*	Let it stand
∿	Transpose	⎯⎯	Underline

TABULATION

<u>Backspace From Centre Method</u>

1. Determine the vertical placement of the tabulation to be centred. Count the total number of lines to be used (including any blank spaces between lines of type); subtract this from the total lines available for typing; divide the remainder by 2. Leave this number of blank lines at the top of the sheet of paper.
2. Centre and type the main heading in ALL CAPITALS. If there is no subheading, triple-space. If there is a subheading, centre and type it capitalizing the important words. Triple-space.
3. Clear margins and tab stops.
4. Position print point at the centre of the paper.
5. Determine the number of spaces to leave between the columns.
6. From centre, backspace once for every two strokes (letters, numbers, symbols, punctuation marks, and spaces) in the longest item in each column or column heading. Backspace once for every two spaces to be left between columns. Ignore single leftover strokes.
7. Set the left margin stop.
8. Space ahead once for each stroke in the longest item of the first column, and once for each space to be left between columns. Set the second column tab stop. Repeat for all columns.
9. Re-position the carriage at the left margin.
10. To type the column headings, space forward once for every two strokes of the longest item in the column. Backspace once from this point for every two strokes in the column heading. Type and underscore the column heading.
11. Tab to the next column and repeat the process until the headings for all columns have been typed. Double space.
12. If the column headings are longer than the column items, re-adjust the tab stops so that the column items will be centred under the heading.
13. Type the body of the tabulation.

PREFACE   BUSINESS APPLICATIONS IN TYPEWRITING provides for the development of typewriting skills by combining copy from our physical, social, and economic environment with the best instructional practices and preferences as determined by verifiable research.

Component I is designed to introduce the student to the alphabetic keyboard by the sight method. You will notice that the flow charts instruct the student to look at the keyboard, to find the location of the key to be learned, to trace the path of the movement from the guide row to that key, to vocalize or spell aloud as he strikes, and to use the letter as soon as possible in words and sentences. Sight typing in keyboard learning, high speed of stroking, rapid coverage of the keyboard, and immediate typing of words and sentences are basic constituents of the learning process.

The words for alphabetic letter practice have been carefully selected so that the letter to be learned appears at the beginning of words, within words, and where possible, at the end of words.

Component II is comprised of sentences and paragraphs carefully chosen from Canadian written materials. Accordingly, they present the student with regular language material for reinforcing the keyboard learning to which he was exposed in *Component I*. Balanced-hand words and other contrived artificial materials are not included in the book because they do not represent regular language material which will build associations between letters and digraphs appearing in the English language.

Component III is designed to introduce the student to the figure and symbol keys, again by the sight method. The flow chart approach is the same as used in *Component I*.

Components IV through *IX* introduce the student to a variety of realistic typing tasks. Procedures have been streamlined to promote speed of performance and transfer of learning from one task to another.

Individualized Typewriting Applications (ITA's) accompany all *Components* except *I* and *II* to give the student an opportunity to extend his skill and knowledge by completing imaginative and creative assignments.

The *Appendix* is organized into two sections: *Timed Writings*, and *Typing Facts and Tips*. The *Timed Writings* have been carefully selected for wide appeal and for extensiveness of vocabulary. They supplement the paragraphs included in *Component II* by providing a rich source of materials for class or individual practice on speed and accuracy. *Typing Facts and Tips* assembles in convenient form and for quick reference, valuable and frequently used typing information.

BUSINESS APPLICATIONS IN TYPEWRITING is adaptable to any classroom schedule. The material is not presented in daily time segments. It is designed to accommodate abbreviated or extended instructional periods, and continuous progress or independent study classes.

MANUSCRIPT FRAME

			66
		Number of lines remaining on the page →	65
	Title of essay for second and subsequent pages		64
		Page No.	63
			62
	First typed line on second and subsequent pages		61
			60
	←Left margin when essay is unbound	*Right margin for all essays →*	59
	←Left margin when essay is bound on left		58

TITLE OF ESSAY ON FIRST PAGE

←Centre point when essay is unbound

←Centre point when essay is bound on left

Warning line — You can type three more lines before starting a fresh page

Last line of page should be typed here

A manuscript frame, when used as a backing sheet, can assist you in allowing sufficient space for a 25 mm bottom margin and footnote notations.

The illustration to the left can be used as a guide when preparing your manuscript frame.

Similar frames can be prepared for the outside margins of letters.

ASSEMBLING A CARBON PACK

1. Place copy sheet on desk.
2. Place carbon paper (carbon side down) on copy sheet.
3. Add an additional copy sheet and carbon sheet for each extra carbon copy required.
4. Place sheet for original copy on top of last sheet of carbon.
5. Insert carbon pack so that the original is in typing position. (When inserting, hold the carbon pack with one hand to prevent slippage; turn the cylinder with the other.)

145

ACKNOWLEDGMENTS

Many teachers and students have helped the authors in collecting and organizing the materials for this book. To them we are indebted. In particular we acknowledge the contributions made by those groups of teachers who met with our editors; Mrs. Virginia Julson, North Vancouver; classes at the University of Alberta; Mr. Julius Bell, Eastern High School of Commerce, Toronto, Mrs. A. Rae Weist, Grand Trunk High School, Evansburg, and Mrs. Doris Holdaway for the initial piloting of *Components I* through *III*; Helen Verdin, Marjorie Cook, Neville World Travel Service Ltd., and Mr. Ronald J. Young, Barrister for the provision of sample business forms; The Royal Bank of Canada for selections extracted from The Monthly Letters; Mr. Melvin R. Bakken, Iris Dmytryshyn, Gwendolyn S. Newsham, Mrs. Anne-Marie Stacey, Lynda Pyrch, Brian Taylor, and Judi, Jim, and Margie Gilholme; and Mrs. Sylvia Gilchrist for the numerous hours spent in reading and typing the many drafts of the manuscript.

G. M. Farmer
E. J. Graham
L. M. Jenkins

TABLE OF CONTENTS

			Page
		Preface	iii
		Acknowledgments	iv
		Parts of the Typewriter	v
		Adjusting the Typewriter	vii
		Posture	ix
COMPONENT	I:	Operating the Alphabetic Keyboard	1
COMPONENT	II:	Developing Alphabetic Keyboard Continuity	35
COMPONENT	III:	Operating the Non-Alphabetic Keyboard	68
COMPONENT	IV:	Centring Typewritten Material	112
COMPONENT	V:	Business Letters	132
COMPONENT	VI:	Outlines, Reports, and Manuscripts	185
COMPONENT	VII:	Tables	228
COMPONENT	VIII:	Business Forms	251
COMPONENT	IX:	Masters for Duplicating	289
APPENDIX	A:	Timed Writings	293
APPENDIX	B:	Typing Facts and Tips	333

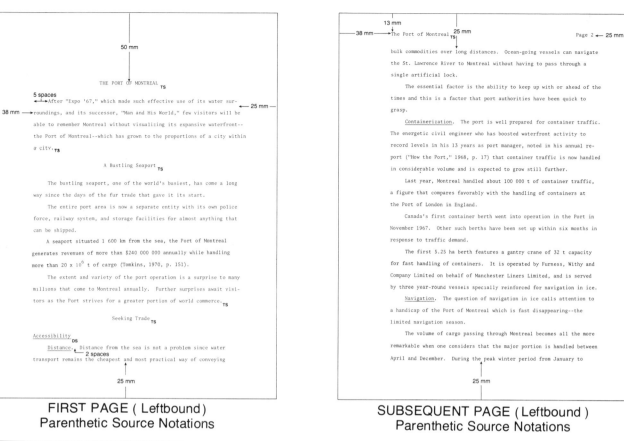

FIRST PAGE (Leftbound)
Parenthetic Source Notations

50 mm

THE PORT OF MONTREAL ₜₛ

5 spaces
After "Expo '67," which made such effective use of its water surroundings, and its successor, "Man and His World," few visitors will be
able to remember Montreal without visualizing its expansive waterfront--
the Port of Montreal--which has grown to the proportions of a city within
a city. ₜₛ

A Bustling Seaport ₜₛ

The bustling seaport, one of the world's busiest, has come a long
way since the days of the fur trade that gave it its start.

The entire port area is now a separate entity with its own police
force, railway system, and storage facilities for almost anything that
can be shipped.

A seaport situated 1 600 km from the sea, the Port of Montreal
generates revenues of more than \$240 000 000 annually while handling
more than 20 x 10^6 t of cargo (Tomkins, 1970, p. 151).

The extent and variety of the port operation is a surprise to many
millions that come to Montreal annually. Further surprises await visitors as the Port strives for a greater portion of world commerce. ₜₛ

Seeking Trade ₜₛ

Accessibility DS

Distance. Distance from the sea is not a problem since water
2 spaces
transport remains the cheapest and most practical way of conveying

25 mm

38 mm   25 mm

SUBSEQUENT PAGE (Leftbound)
Parenthetic Source Notations

13 mm
38 mm   The Port of Montreal ₜₛ 25 mm   Page 2   25 mm

bulk commodities over long distances. Ocean-going vessels can navigate
the St. Lawrence River to Montreal without having to pass through a
single artificial lock.

The essential factor is the ability to keep up with or ahead of the
times and this is a factor that port authorities have been quick to
grasp.

Containerization. The port is well prepared for container traffic.
The energetic civil engineer who has boosted waterfront activity to
record levels in his 13 years as port manager, noted in his annual report ("How the Port," 1968, p. 17) that container traffic is now handled
in considerable volume and is expected to grow still further.

Last year, Montreal handled about 100 000 t of container traffic,
a figure that compares favorably with the handling of containers at
the Port of London in England.

Canada's first container berth went into operation in the Port in
November 1967. Other such berths have been set up within six months in
response to traffic demand.

The first 5.25 ha berth features a gantry crane of 32 t capacity
for fast handling of containers. It is operated by Furness, Withy and
Company Limited on behalf of Manchester Liners Limited, and is served
by three year-round vessels specially reinforced for navigation in ice.

Navigation. The question of navigation in ice calls attention to
a handicap of the Port of Montreal which is fast disappearing--the
limited navigation season.

The volume of cargo passing through Montreal becomes all the more
remarkable when one considers that the major portion is handled between
April and December. During the peak winter period from January to

25 mm

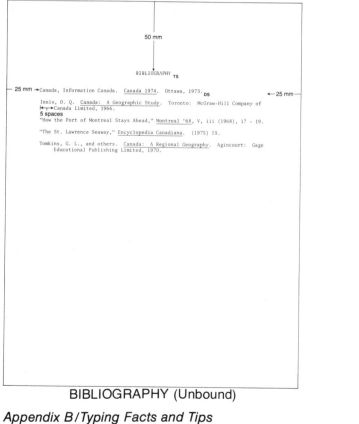

BIBLIOGRAPHY (Unbound)

50 mm

BIBLIOGRAPHY ₜₛ

25 mm   Canada, Information Canada. Canada 1974. Ottawa, 1973. DS   25 mm

Innis, D. Q. Canada: A Geographic Study. Toronto: McGraw-Hill Company of
Canada Limited, 1966.
5 spaces
"How the Port of Montreal Stays Ahead," Montreal '68, V, iii (1968), 17 - 19.

"The St. Lawrence Seaway," Encyclopedia Canadiana. (1975) IX.

Tomkins, G. L., and others. Canada: A Regional Geography. Agincourt: Gage
Educational Publishing Limited, 1970.

OUTLINE

INSTRUCTION ON BASIC SWIMMING ₜₛ

I. Swimming Strokes DS

A. Breast Stroke
1. Legs
2. Arms
3. Coordination DS
2 spaces
B. Side Stroke
1. Legs
2. Arms
3. Coordination

C. Elementary Back Stroke
1. Legs
2. Arms
3. Coordination

D. Trudgen
1. Legs
2. Arms
3. Coordination

E. Front Crawl
1. Legs
2. Arms
3. Coordination ₜₛ

II. Life Saving Strokes and Kicks

A. Inverted Scissors Kick

B. Regular Scissors Kick

C. Frog/Rotary Broad Kick

PARTS OF THE TYPEWRITER

Typewriters have similar operative parts, the names of which may vary somewhat from typewriter to typewriter. These similar operative parts are identified in the four composite diagrams of a typewriter given below and on page vi. The exact location of a part identified in the diagrams may be slightly different from that on your typewriter. Extra parts that are peculiar to your typewriter can be identified by reference to the manufacturer's guide.

Top *Left* Segment of a Typewriter

Top *Right* Segment of a Typewriter

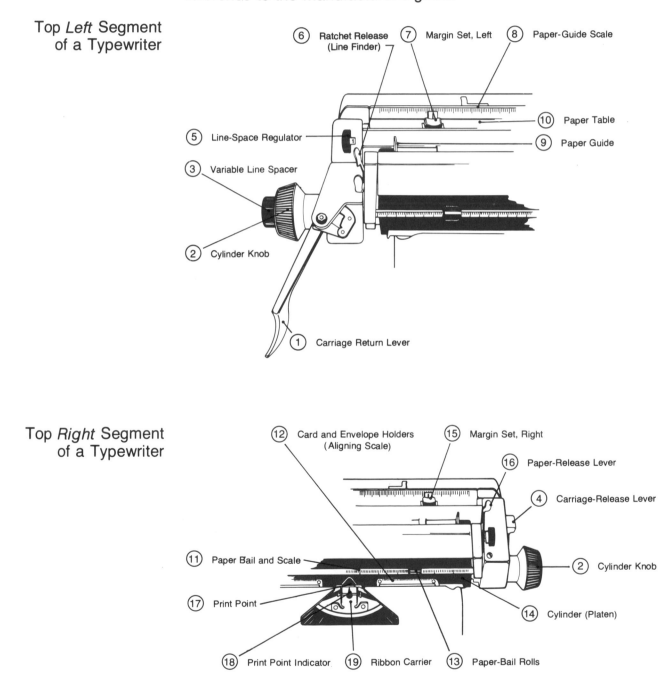

Top Left Segment labels:
- 6 Ratchet Release (Line Finder)
- 7 Margin Set, Left
- 8 Paper-Guide Scale
- 10 Paper Table
- 9 Paper Guide
- 5 Line-Space Regulator
- 3 Variable Line Spacer
- 2 Cylinder Knob
- 1 Carriage Return Lever

Top Right Segment labels:
- 12 Card and Envelope Holders (Aligning Scale)
- 15 Margin Set, Right
- 16 Paper-Release Lever
- 4 Carriage-Release Lever
- 11 Paper Bail and Scale
- 2 Cylinder Knob
- 17 Print Point
- 14 Cylinder (Platen)
- 18 Print Point Indicator
- 19 Ribbon Carrier
- 13 Paper-Bail Rolls

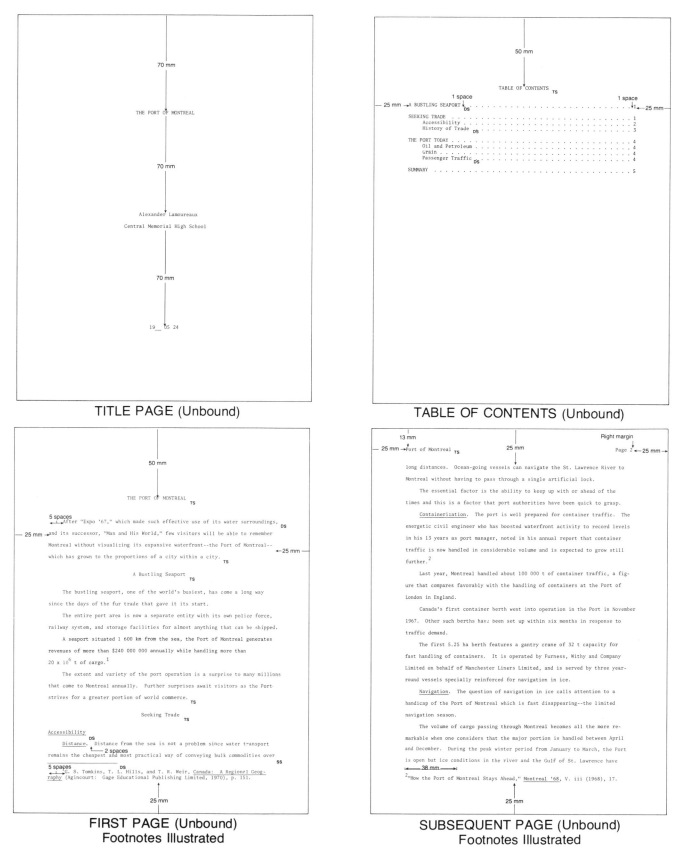

TITLE PAGE (Unbound)

TABLE OF CONTENTS (Unbound)

FIRST PAGE (Unbound)
Footnotes Illustrated

SUBSEQUENT PAGE (Unbound)
Footnotes Illustrated

Lower Segment of a
Manual Typewriter

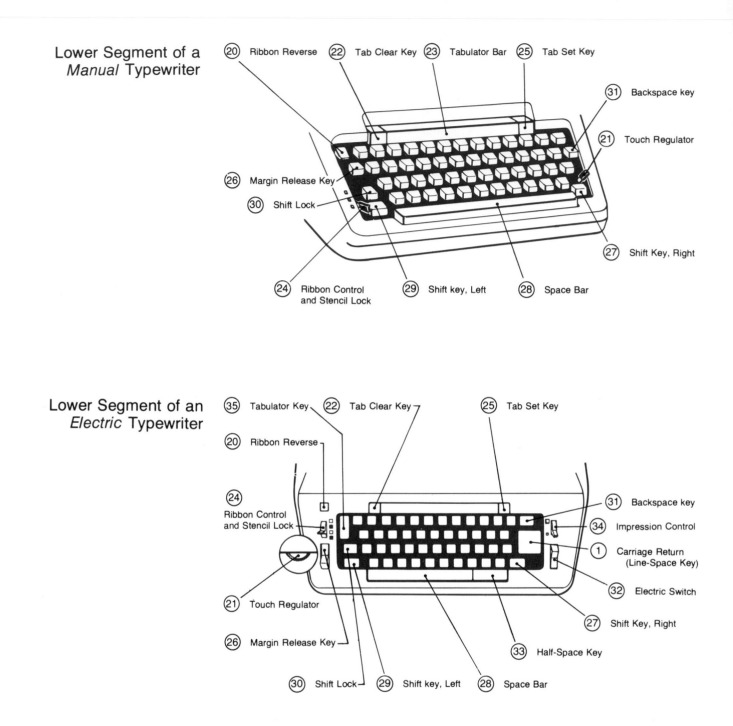

20 Ribbon Reverse   22 Tab Clear Key   23 Tabulator Bar   25 Tab Set Key

31 Backspace key

21 Touch Regulator

26 Margin Release Key

30 Shift Lock

27 Shift Key, Right

24 Ribbon Control and Stencil Lock   29 Shift key, Left   28 Space Bar

Lower Segment of an
Electric Typewriter

35 Tabulator Key   22 Tab Clear Key   25 Tab Set Key

20 Ribbon Reverse

24 Ribbon Control and Stencil Lock

31 Backspace key

34 Impression Control

1 Carriage Return (Line-Space Key)

32 Electric Switch

21 Touch Regulator

27 Shift Key, Right

26 Margin Release Key

33 Half-Space Key

30 Shift Lock   29 Shift key, Left   28 Space Bar

TYPING OUTLINES

Centre an outline vertically and horizontally. Include the first Roman numeral when centring the longest line. *187*
Set the left margin at the first Roman numeral.

Centre and type the title in ALL CAPITALS. Triple-space after the title.

Identify main headings by Roman numerals; side headings by capital letters; paragraph headings by Arabic numerals; and further subdivisions by small letters.

Triple-space before and double-space after main headings. Double-space before and after side headings, except when the side heading has a further subdivision. In this instance, single-space after the side heading and double-space after the last division line. Other subdivisions are single spaced. All Roman and Arabic numerals, and capital and lower case letters are followed by a period and two spaces.

Align columns of numerals (Roman and Arabic) and columns of letters at the right. Use the margin release and backspace key to type outside the left margin.

TYPING FOOTNOTES

The typographical form to follow is this: *211*

212

1. the author's name first, with his given names or initials preceding the surname, and with a comma following it;
2. the title of the book, underlined and followed by a space;
3. within parentheses the details of publication: the place, followed by a colon; the publisher followed by a comma; followed in turn by the date; the whole parenthesis being followed by a comma;
4. the page number(s) in Arabic numerals, preceded by "p." (or "pp." if more than one) and followed by a period.

For complete footnoting instructions refer to <u>Form and Substance</u> by W.K. Thomas, Gage Educational Publishing Limited, 1963.

TYPING BIBLIOGRAPHIES

The typographical form to follow is this: *204*

1. the author's name, reversed (i.e., surname first, comma, initials or given names), followed by a period and two spaces;
2. the title of the book, underlined, followed by a period and two spaces;
3. place of publication, followed by a colon and the publisher followed by a comma and one space;
4. date of publication, followed by a period.

For complete instructions on typing bibliographies refer to <u>Form and Substance</u> by W.K. Thomas, Gage Educational Publishing Limited, 1963 or <u>WEP: A Handbook for Writing, Editing, and Polishing</u> by E. Plattor and P. Drysdale, Gage Educational Publishing Limited, 1975.

TYPING LEADERS

Leaders are used when typing a table of contents and in some statistical material as a guide for reading from *214* column to column. Leaders (....) are made by typing a series of periods or by alternating the period and the space bar. Leaders should align vertically, and should be preceded and followed by a space.

(e.g. 25 cartons .... 200 kg)
25 boxes .... 20 kg)

ADJUSTING THE TYPEWRITER

Setting The Paper Guide

If your paper-guide scale does not start with a "0" reading at the left, your instructor will assist you in inserting the paper and determining the centre point.

Inserting The Paper

When the paper is inserted its left edge should be at zero on the paper-guide scale. (If you are not familiar with your typewriter, examine the illustrations on page v. The zero can be located on either the paper-guide scale ⑧ or the cylinder scale ⑫ .) Move the paper guide ⑨ to the left edge of the paper.

For P4 stationery (21.5 cm x 28 cm) the centring point is at 51 (or 50) for machines with elite type, and at 42 for machines with pica type.

1. Position paper on the desk to the left of the typewriter.

2. Set the paper guide ⑨ .

3. Pull the paper bail ⑪ forward or up with your right hand.

4. Grasp the paper in the left hand.

5. Drop the paper behind the cylinder ⑭ and against the paper guide ⑨ .

6. Twirl the right hand cylinder knob ② with a quick movement of the fingers and thumb. If the paper is not straight, pull the paper-release lever ⑯ forward and adjust.

7. Return the paper bail ⑪ .

References to a Bibliography

Parenthetical source notations appear in the text and include the author's name, year of publication, and *207*
page or pages references. Examples:

A recent study (MacDonald, 1972) . . .
Saunders (1970) claimed . . .
The statement made by Green (1973, p. 10) . . .

When a quotation is typed, the page number is placed at the end of the quotation. It precedes the period and the quotation marks when used. Example:

Jacobs (1974) referred to his invention as "the greatest
accomplishment of the century (p. 68)."

Superscripts

A superscript is a numeral or symbol placed above the line of writing to indicate a notation. A superscript *95*
within the body of a manuscript is typed a half space above the line immediately following the statement or punctuation mark. No space precedes the superscript.

A superscript introducing a footnote is raised a half space above the typewritten line. No space follows the superscript.

To type a superscript move the ratchet release forward. Turn the cylinder to position a half space above the typewritten line. Type the superscript. Return the ratchet release. Return the cylinder to the original typewritten line.

Footnotes

Place footnotes on the same page as their related superscripts — above the bottom margin of the page. *211*
Starting at the left margin, type a 38 mm line a single space below the last line of the text. Double space. *212*
Indent five spaces, type the superscript, and without spacing type the first line of the footnote. Begin the second and subsequent lines at the left margin. Single space the footnote. Double-space between footnotes.

Each footnote usually requires three lines for typing.

Bibliography

At the end of the manuscript, list all references alphabetically by the author's surname. Each entry is single *204*
spaced and begins even with the left margin. Subsequent lines are indented five spaces. Double space between entries. The title is centred and typed in ALL CAPITALS. The margins are the same as those used on page one of the manuscript.

Title Page

A title page usually contains the title of the manuscript, the name of the author and his/her institution · *215*
affiliation, and the date. A great deal of flexibility is allowed in typing a title page, but usually the three required parts are centred horizontally and vertically dividing the page into quarters.

Table of Contents

A table of contents is prepared when a manuscript is lengthy or if it contains many divisions. *214*
The main divisions of the manuscript and the appropriate page numbers are shown and separated by leaders.

The margins for a table of contents are the same as those used on page one of the manuscript.

Planning The Margin Stops

1. Determine the length of line to be typed (number of spaces).

2. Divide the number of spaces by two. Subtract this amount from the centre point. Set the left margin stop. Set the right margin stop approximately five spaces beyond the desired length of line. Since mechanical adjustments vary from typewriter to typewriter, determine the number of spaces after the bell rings before the carriage locks. The bell is a cue for carriage return.

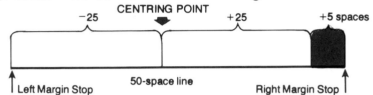

Setting The Margin Stops

Below are instructions for setting the margin stops on the machines most frequently found in typewriting classrooms. If the instructions given do not apply to your typewriter, consult the manufacturer's guide which illustrates the particular mechanics for your machine.

Set By Hand

The margins on the **Underwood**, **Selectric**, **Olympia**, and **Remington** machines are set by hand.

1. Press the margin set.

2. Slide the set to the desired position.

3. Release the margin set.

Spring Set

The margins on the **Royal** and **Smith-Corona** are spring set.

1. Pull forward the left margin set and hold while moving the carriage to the desired position.

2. Release the margin set.

3. Pull forward the right margin set and hold while moving the carriage to the desired position.

4. Release the margin set.

Hook-on Device

The **IBM** and **Underwood electrics** use a hook-on device.

1. Return the carriage to the left margin.

2. Hook onto the margin set by depressing the margin set key.

3. While holding down the margin set key, engage the carriage-release lever and move the carriage to the desired position. Disengage the carriage-release lever.

4. Release the margin set key.

5. Move the carriage to the right margin.

POSTAL CARDS

Postal cards (89 mm x 140 mm) are often used by organizations to send invitations or announcements of a non-confidential nature. Because the return and letter addresses are typed on the "address side" of the postal card, they are eliminated from the "message side."

When typing the "message side" of a postal card leave top and side margins of 13 mm.

The typing of addresses on postal cards follows the same procedures and spacing requirements as for the typing of addresses on envelopes.

264

MANUSCRIPT TYPING

Paper

192

Use standard P4 paper, 21.5 cm x 28 cm.

Margins for Unbound Manuscripts

192

Use 25 mm left, right, and bottom margins. Use a 50 mm top margin for the first page and a 25 mm top margin for subsequent pages.

Margins for Leftbound Manuscripts

192

Use 25 mm right and bottom margins; a 38 mm left margin. Use a 50 mm top margin for the first page and a 25 mm top margin for subsequent pages.

Page Numbers

192

Page numbers are placed on the second and subsequent pages 13 mm from the top edge and even with the right margin.

Spacing

192

Double-space the body of the manuscript. Use a five-space paragraph indention.

Title

192

Centre and type the title in ALL CAPITALS. Triple-space after the title.

Headings

192

Centre and capitalize the important words in all main headings. Triple-space before and after the main centred headings. (If a main heading follows the title, double-space before and triple-space after.)

Side headings are typed even with the left margin. Capitalize the important words and underscore the heading. Triple-space before and double-space after the side heading.

Paragraph headings are indented five spaces from the left margin. Capitalize the important words and underscore the heading. The heading is separated from the rest of the paragraph by a period followed by two spaces.

Quotations

207

Place in a separate paragraph quoted information which exceeds three lines. Such quotations are indented five spaces from the left and right margins, and are single spaced.

Acknowledge the source of quotations and paraphrased information by using footnotes or references to a bibliography. Use parenthetical source notations to designate reference to a bibliography or use consecutive superscripts to designate footnotes.

6. Hook onto the margin set by depressing the same margin set key.

7. While holding down the margin set key, move the carriage to the desired position.

8. Release the margin set key.

TYPING POSTURE   Study the good typing posture illustration below. Check your own position.

1. Adjust the posture chair so that the back is straight.

2. Lean forward slightly from the waist with the body centred opposite the "J" key, 150-200 mm from the typewriter.

3. Elbows should be held loosely at the sides of the body.

4. Adjust the table or chair so that your hands are parallel to the slant of the keyboard.

5. Feet should be flat on the floor with one slightly in front of the other.

6. Copy should be at the right of the machine.

10 mm   30 mm

40 mm

ENVELOPES

Envelope Sizes

Only standard letter size envelopes can be machine sorted. They measure approximately:

89 mm x 140 mm
105 mm x 241 mm
121 mm x 235 mm
152 mm x 254 mm

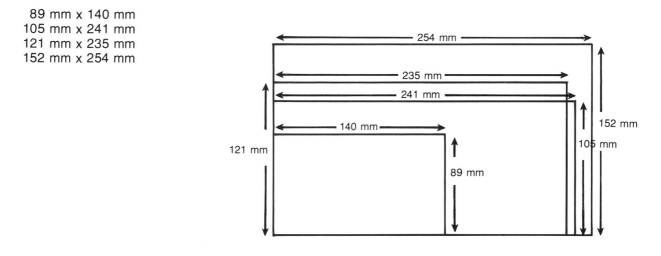

Addressing Envelopes

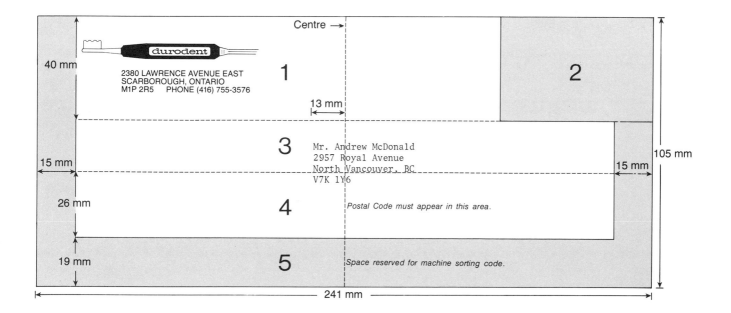

Area 1 is for the return address and Post Office stickers (e.g. Special Delivery). Area 2 is for postage stamps. Area 3 is for the letter address. The letter address may overflow into Area 4. (Any special notations, e.g., PERSONAL AND CONFIDENTIAL, will also appear in Area 3 to the left of the letter address.) The depth of Area 3 will increase as the depth of the envelope increases. Area 4 must contain the Postal Code. Area 5 must be left entirely blank. It is the machine sorting code band.

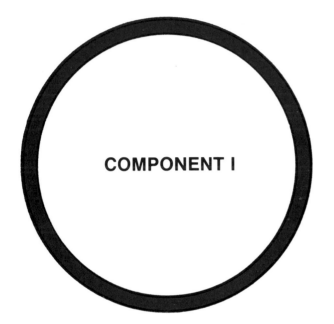

COMPONENT I

OPERATING THE ALPHABETIC KEYBOARD

STUDENT OBJECTIVES

1. To establish typing patterns for the alphabet, the hyphen, and common punctuation symbols.

2. To use correct techniques in striking keys; i.e., quick, sharp finger movements.

3. To use correct techniques in operating the typewriter parts.

4. To use correct spacing with punctuation marks.

5. To develop confidence in locating keys and in typing words and sentences.

6. To increase stroking speed on practised materials.

DAILY ACTIVITIES

1. Adjust the margins for a 50-space line.

2. Review selected exercises.

3. Proceed through the Component according to flow chart instructions.

CONTENTS

Component I introduces the student to the alphabetic keyboard, the hyphen, common punctuation symbols, and basic machine operations. The practice material is designed for early introduction of words, phrases, and sentences.

Each new letter of the alphabet appears at the beginning of words, within words, and where possible, at the end of words.

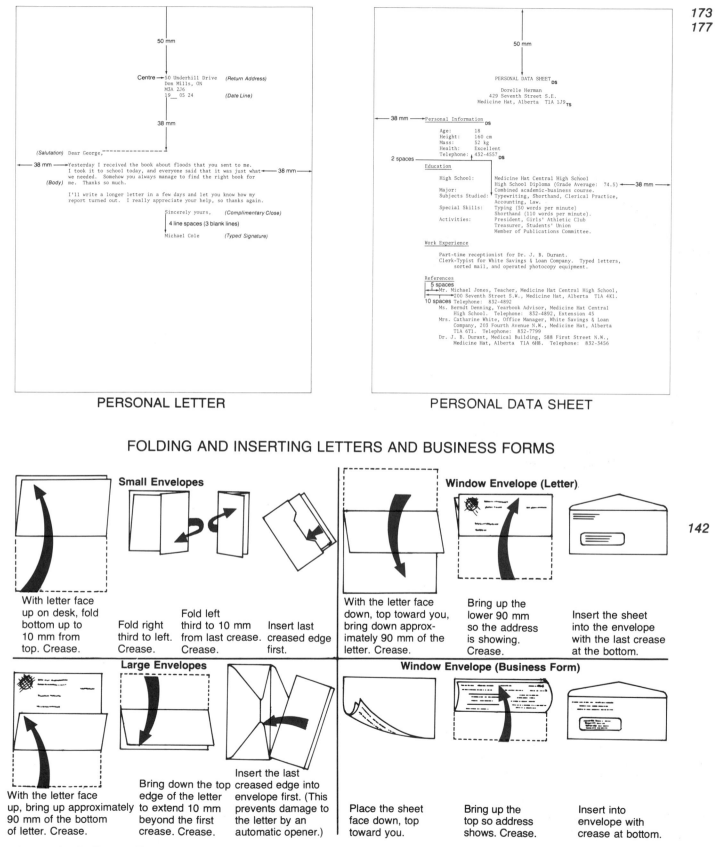

Centre→ 50 Underhill Drive   (Return Address)
Don Mills, ON
M3A 2J6
19___ 05 24   (Date Line)

(Salutation) Dear George,

←—38 mm—→ Yesterday I received the book about floods that you sent to me.
I took it to school today, and everyone said that it was just what ←—38 mm—→
we needed. Somehow you always manage to find the right book for
(Body)   me. Thanks so much.

I'll write a longer letter in a few days and let you know how my
report turned out. I really appreciate your help, so thanks again.

Sincerely yours,   (Complimentary Close)

4 line spaces (3 blank lines)

Michael Cole   (Typed Signature)

PERSONAL LETTER

PERSONAL DATA SHEET DS

Dorelle Herman
429 Seventh Street S.E.
Medicine Hat, Alberta T1A 1J9 TS

Personal Information DS

Age: 18
Height: 160 cm
Mass: 52 kg
Health: Excellent
Telephone: 432-4557 DS

Education

High School: Medicine Hat Central High School
                   High School Diploma (Grade Average: 74.5)
Major: Combined academic-business course.
Subjects Studied: Typewriting, Shorthand, Clerical Practice,
                   Accounting, Law.
Special Skills: Typing (50 words per minute).
                   Shorthand (110 words per minute).
Activities: President, Girls' Athletic Club
                   Treasurer, Students' Union
                   Member of Publications Committee.

Work Experience

Part-time receptionist for Dr. J. B. Durant.
Clerk-Typist for White Savings & Loan Company. Typed letters,
   sorted mail, and operated photocopy equipment.

References
5 spaces
Mr. Michael Jones, Teacher, Medicine Hat Central High School,
200 Seventh Street S.W., Medicine Hat, Alberta T1A 4K1.
10 spaces Telephone: 832-4892
Ms. Berndt Denning, Yearbook Advisor, Medicine Hat Central
   High School. Telephone: 832-4892, Extension 45
Mrs. Catharine White, Office Manager, White Savings & Loan
   Company, 203 Fourth Avenue N.W., Medicine Hat, Alberta
   T1A 6T1. Telephone: 832-7799
Dr. J. B. Durant, Medical Building, 588 First Street N.W.,
   Medicine Hat, Alberta T1A 6H8. Telephone: 832-3456

PERSONAL DATA SHEET

FOLDING AND INSERTING LETTERS AND BUSINESS FORMS

Small Envelopes

With letter face up on desk, fold bottom up to 10 mm from top. Crease.

Fold right third to left. Crease.

Fold left third to 10 mm from last crease. Crease.

Insert last creased edge first.

Window Envelope (Letter)

With the letter face down, top toward you, bring down approximately 90 mm of the letter. Crease.

Bring up the lower 90 mm so the address is showing. Crease.

Insert the sheet into the envelope with the last crease at the bottom.

Large Envelopes

With the letter face up, bring up approximately 90 mm of the bottom of letter. Crease.

Bring down the top edge of the letter to extend 10 mm beyond the first crease. Crease.

Insert the last creased edge into envelope first. (This prevents damage to the letter by an automatic opener.)

Window Envelope (Business Form)

Place the sheet face down, top toward you.

Bring up the top so address shows. Crease.

Insert into envelope with crease at bottom.

**GETTING READY
TO TYPE:**

1. Insert the paper.

2. Adjust the margins for a 50-space line. (If you have not learned how to do this, refer to page viii.)

3. Set the line-space regulator for single spacing.

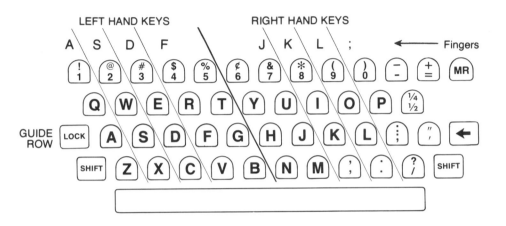

STRIKING THE KEYS:

I.1 USING THE GUIDE ROW

Curve your fingers and place them on the guide row so that your left index finger rests lightly on Ⓕ and your right index finger rests lightly on Ⓙ .

LEFT HAND   RIGHT HAND

Using a quick, sharp motion of the right index finger, strike the Ⓙ . As you strike, SAY ALOUD with your instructor:

j j j

> *Your copy will look like this:* j j j

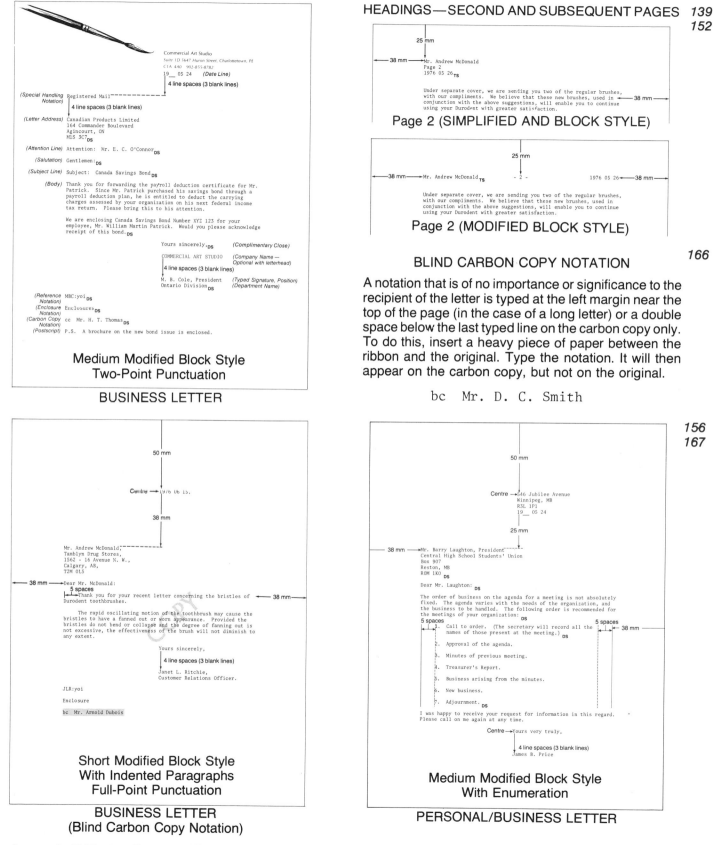

Commercial Art Studio
Suite 1D 5647 Huron Street, Charlottetown, PE
C1A 4A0 902-855-8782
19__ 05 24 *(Date Line)*
4 line spaces (3 blank lines)

(Special Handling Notation) Registered Mail

4 line spaces (3 blank lines)

(Letter Address) Canadian Products Limited
164 Commander Boulevard
Agincourt, ON
M1S 3C7 DS

(Attention Line) Attention: Mr. E. C. O'Connor DS

(Salutation) Gentlemen: DS

(Subject Line) Subject: Canada Savings Bond DS

(Body) Thank you for forwarding the payroll deduction certificate for Mr.
Patrick. Since Mr. Patrick purchased his savings bond through a
payroll deduction plan, he is entitled to deduct the carrying
charges assessed by your organization on his next federal income
tax return. Please bring this to his attention.

We are enclosing Canada Savings Bond Number XYZ 123 for your
employee, Mr. William Martin Patrick. Would you please acknowledge
receipt of this bond. DS

Yours sincerely, DS *(Complimentary Close)*

COMMERCIAL ART STUDIO *(Company Name — Optional with letterhead)*
4 line spaces (3 blank lines)

M. B. Cole, President *(Typed Signature, Position)*
Ontario Division DS *(Department Name)*

(Reference Notation) MBC:yoi DS
(Enclosure Notation) Enclosures DS
(Carbon Copy Notation) cc Mr. H. T. Thomas DS
(Postscript) P.S. A brochure on the new bond issue is enclosed.

**Medium Modified Block Style
Two-Point Punctuation**

BUSINESS LETTER

---

25 mm

38 mm → Mr. Andrew McDonald
Page 2
1976 05 26 TS

Under separate cover, we are sending you two of the regular brushes,
with our compliments. We believe that these new brushes, used in ← 38 mm
conjunction with the above suggestions, will enable you to continue
using your Durodent with greater satisfaction.

Page 2 (SIMPLIFIED AND BLOCK STYLE)

25 mm

← 38 mm → Mr. Andrew McDonald TS - 2 - 1976 05 26 TS ← 38 mm →

Under separate cover, we are sending you two of the regular brushes,
with our compliments. We believe that these new brushes, used in
conjunction with the above suggestions, will enable you to continue
using your Durodent with greater satisfaction.

Page 2 (MODIFIED BLOCK STYLE)

BLIND CARBON COPY NOTATION *166*

A notation that is of no importance or significance to the
recipient of the letter is typed at the left margin near the
top of the page (in the case of a long letter) or a double
space below the last typed line on the carbon copy only.
To do this, insert a heavy piece of paper between the
ribbon and the original. Type the notation. It will then
appear on the carbon copy, but not on the original.

bc Mr. D. C. Smith

---

50 mm

Centre → 1976 06 15.

38 mm

Mr. Andrew McDonald
Tamblyn Drug Stores,
1562 - 16 Avenue N. W.,
Calgary, AB,
T2M 0L5

← 38 mm → Dear Mr. McDonald:
5 spaces
Thank you for your recent letter concerning the bristles of ← 38 mm →
Durodent toothbrushes.

The rapid oscillating motion of the toothbrush may cause the
bristles to have a fanned out or worn appearance. Provided the
bristles do not bend or collapse and the degree of fanning out is
not excessive, the effectiveness of the brush will not diminish to
any extent.

Yours sincerely,

4 line spaces (3 blank lines)

Janet L. Ritchie,
Customer Relations Officer.

JLR:yoi

Enclosure

bc Mr. Arnold Dubois

**Short Modified Block Style
With Indented Paragraphs
Full-Point Punctuation**

BUSINESS LETTER
(Blind Carbon Copy Notation)

---

50 mm

Centre → 546 Jubilee Avenue
Winnipeg, MB
R3L 1P1
19__ 05 24

25 mm

← 38 mm → Mr. Barry Laughton, President
Central High School Students' Union
Box 907
Reston, MB
R0M 1K0 DS

Dear Mr. Laughton: DS

The order of business on the agenda for a meeting is not absolutely
fixed. The agenda varies with the needs of the organization, and
the business to be handled. The following order is recommended for
the meetings of your organization: DS
5 spaces
1. Call to order. (The secretary will record all the 5 spaces
names of those present at the meeting.) DS ← → 38 mm

2. Approval of the agenda.

3. Minutes of previous meeting.

4. Treasurer's Report.

5. Business arising from the minutes.

6. New business.

7. Adjournment. DS

I was happy to receive your request for information in this regard.
Please call on me again at any time.

Centre → Yours very truly,

4 line spaces (3 blank lines)
James B. Price

**Medium Modified Block Style
With Enumeration**

PERSONAL/BUSINESS LETTER

156
167

Using a quick, sharp motion of the left index finger, strike the Ⓕ . As you strike, SAY ALOUD with your instructor:

f f f

Your copy will look like this: jjjfff

Strike each of the guide keys as you SAY ALOUD with your instructor:

k k k d d d l l l s s s ; ; ; a a a j j j

RETURNING THE CARRIAGE:

On the manual or non-electric typewriter:

1. Brace the fingers of the left hand.
2. Move the left hand to the return lever.
3. Take up the slack.
4. With a flick of the wrist return the carriage.

On the electric typewriter:

1. Keep the right index finger anchored on Ⓙ .
2. Depress the RETURN key with the little finger of the right hand.
3. Bring the little finger back to the guide key Ⓙ .

With hands on guide row, strike sharply and SPELL ALOUD the following lines. This will give you practice in returning the carriage.

Your copy will look like this:

jjjfffkkkddd111
jjjfffkkkddd111

1   j j j f f f k k k d d d l l l s s s ; ; ; a a a

2   j j j f f f k k k d d d l l l s s s ; ; ; a a a

3   j j j f f f k k k d d d l l l s s s ; ; ; a a a
                                                    ← Double-Space (DS)

To double-space between groups of lines, operate the carriage return twice. To triple-space, operate the return three times.

separate title line. A period is used at the end of the date line and at the end of a typed signature line which is not followed by a separate title line. A colon is used after the salutation.

Regardless of punctuation style, punctuation is not used after attention or subject lines; after the company name (unless part of the company name); or after reference, enclosure, and copy notations. Punctuation within the body of the letter follows normal punctuation practices.

Letter Placement

137

PLACEMENT CHART
BUSINESS, PERSONAL/BUSINESS, AND PERSONAL LETTERS
(P4 Stationery: 21.5 cm x 28 cm)

LENGTH OF LETTER	APPROXIMATE NUMBER OF PARAGRAPHS	RETURN ADDRESS OR DATE LINE* (From Top of Page)	SIDE MARGINS	SPACE BETWEEN DATE AND LETTER ADDRESS
Short	3 or fewer	50 mm	38 mm	38 mm
Medium	3 - 5	50 mm	38 mm	25 mm
Long	5 or more	50 mm	38 mm	13 mm

*Because a business letter is usually typed on letterhead, type the date line 50 mm from top of page or two blank lines below the letterhead. Because personal and usually personal/business letters are typed on plain stationery, the first line of the return address begins 50 mm from top of page. The date line follows immediately the last line of the return address.

Parts of the Letter

Letter parts vary according to the type of letter (simplified, business, personal/business, and personal) and to the content of the letter. The following three illustrations will assist you in determining the position of all letter parts.

135
158
169
173

INDEPENDENT
fish company limited

11 SEA AVENUE NORTH . BURNABY BC V5B 1K4 /TELEPHONE (604) 431-5678

(Date Line) 1976 06 15

38 mm

(Letter Address) R. B. Seafoods Ltd.
P. O. Box 4500
Sydney, NS
B1P 6L1 TS

(Subject) PROPOSED PLANT TS

38 mm — (Body) Your proposal appears to be worth our consideration. A good place — 38 mm
to start might be for you to send us more detailed information on
the proposed operation. Since you have been contemplating the
project for some time, you no doubt have this information readily
available. We should be interested in the following details:

1. Peak daily fish deliveries.
2. Landed cost of fish.
3. Location of plant.
4. Estimated cost of plant.
5. Labor costs.
6. Sales value of production.
7. Projected markets.

It was a pleasure to see you on your brief visit to Vancouver. You
must have had a very interesting trip. I look forward to hearing
about it sometime.

4 line spaces (3 blank lines)

(Typed Signature) LAWRENCE R. GREENLEESE, PRESIDENT DS
(Reference
Notation) yoi

SIMPLIFIED LETTER

durodent

2380 LAWRENCE AVENUE EAST
SCARBOROUGH, ONTARIO
M1P 2R5   PHONE (416) 755-3576

50 mm

(Date Line) 1976 06 15
13 mm

(Letter Address) Tamblyn Drug Stores
1562 - 16 Avenue N. W.
Calgary, AB
T2M 0L5 DS

(Attention Line) Attention: Mr. Andrew McDonald DS

(Salutation) Gentlemen DS

(Subject Line) Subject: Durodent Bristles DS

(Body) Thank you for your recent letter concerning the bristles of
Durodent toothbrushes. May we make the following comments which
we hope you will find helpful. DS

38 mm — The rapid oscillating motion of the toothbrush may cause the
bristles to have a fanned out or worn appearance. Provided the
bristles do not bend or collapse and the degree of fanning out is
not excessive, the effectiveness of the brush will not diminish to
any extent.

For many years before purchasing a Durodent, your customers were — 38 mm
accustomed to using a manual toothbrush and the cleaning and
massaging results depended entirely on the amount of energy they
supplied. Now we have an instrument to do this work for them. It
is no longer necessary to press or scrub as the built-in, controlled
action of Durodent provides all the energy required to produce a
thorough job. They just have to guide the brush allowing only the
bristle tips to contact the dental surfaces. Excessive pressure
tends to flatten the bristles and hinder their action.

We realize that automatic brushing represents a distinct change in
dental hygiene habits and it may require more time for some users
to adapt to this new technique. However, the enclosed reports
from clinical trials show that, if allowed to do the job properly,
the brush will give good service for a long period of time. DS

(Complimentary Yours sincerely
Close)
4 line spaces (3 blank lines)

(Typed Signature, Janet L. Ritchie
Position) Customer Relations Officer DS

(Reference JLR:yoi DS
Notation)
(Enclosure Enclosure
Notation)

Long Block Style
No-Point Punctuation

BUSINESS LETTER

DAILY ACTIVITY

If you are beginning a new class period:

1. Adjust the margins for a 50-space line, and
2. Review selected exercises from previous pages.

THE SPACE BAR

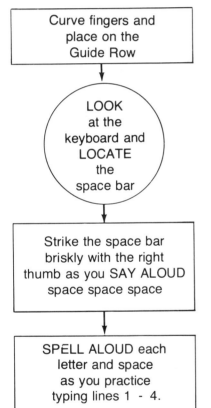

I.2 USING THE SPACE BAR

```
1  jj ff jj ff jj kk ff jj kk ff dd jj ss jj ss aa jj
2  jj kk ll ff ll ff jj ff jj dd aa jj kk ll ss dd jj
```
← Double-Space (DS)

```
3  lad lad fad fad all all ask ask lads lads falls
4  sad sad all all dad dad fad fad asks asks falls
```

Vertical Spacing

In tables, letters, and memoranda, typewritten material is most frequently single spaced. In the case of reports and news releases, such material is most often double spaced (one blank line between typewritten lines). For special effects, such as headings, triple spacing (two blank lines between typewritten lines) is sometimes used.

```
0 This passage in      0 This passage in      0 This passage in
0 elite type is        1                      1
0 single spaced.       0 elite type is        2
                       1                      0 elite type is
                       0 double spaced.       1
                                              2
                                              0 triple spaced.
```

Vertical Centring

1. Count all the lines required to type the problem. Include headings, subheadings, and all blank lines.
2. Subtract the total lines required for the problem from the number of vertical lines available on the size of paper being used for the problem.
3. Divide the figure obtained by 2 to determine the number of blank lines for the top margin. Ignore a fraction.
4. Space down to this position and type the problem following horizontal centring techniques.

LETTERS

Paper Sizes

Most letters are typed on P4 paper. However, if the correspondence is particularly short, P5 paper may be used.

If a second sheet of paper is required for a very long letter, the second sheet should be the same size as the first sheet.

Letter Styles

Three letter styles are common—block style (all lines flush with the left margin), modified block style (return address—if used, date line, complimentary close, and typed signature are typed from the centre point), modified block style with indented paragraphs (as for modified block style, except that the first line of each paragraph is usually indented five strokes).

A fourth letter style — simplified — is increasing in popularity. The salutation, complimentary close, and company name are omitted from the letter. No-point punctuation is used, and all lines except unnumbered enumerated items (which are indented five spaces) begin flush with the left margin. A subject line follows the letter address and is typed in ALL CAPITALS with a triple space above and below it. The typed signature and title is typed in ALL CAPITALS at least three blank lines below the body.

Punctuation Styles

Two types of punctuation are widely used—no-point and two-point. A third style—full-point—is sometimes used. With no-point punctuation, punctuation is omitted from the ends of special letter part lines. With two-point punctuation, a colon (in the case of business or personal/business letters) or a comma (in the case of personal letters) follows the salutation; and a comma follows the complimentary close.

With full-point, commas are used at the end of all lines in the return and letter addresses (except when the line ends with a Postal Code); after the complimentary close; and after the typed signature line if it is followed by a

DAILY ACTIVITY

If you are beginning a new class period:

1. Adjust the margins for a 50-space line, and
2. Review selected exercises from previous pages.

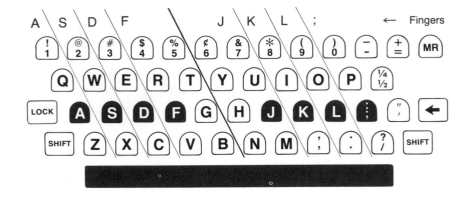

THE LETTER ⓘ

Curve fingers and place on the Guide Row

↓

LOOK at the keyboard and LOCATE the ⓘ

↓

Trace the reach to ⓘ and back to **K**. Keep the little finger of the right hand on the guide key **J**.

↓

Strike briskly as you SAY ALOUD

ik
space
ik
space
ik

↓

SPELL ALOUD each letter and space as you practice typing lines 1 - 4.

I.3 USING THE ⓘ

1 ik ik ik if if is is if if is is ik ik if if is is
2 kid kid lid lid dill dill did did aid aid lid lid **DS**

3 skill skill skill slid slid slid lid lid kid kid
4 disks disks disks sail sail sail ill ill ail aid

CENTRING

Type Face

There are two common sizes of typewriter type — elite and pica. On a pica machine 10 horizontal spaces require 25.4 mm; 6 vertical lines require 25.4 mm. On an elite machine 12 horizontal spaces require 25.4 mm; 6 vertical lines require 25.4 mm.

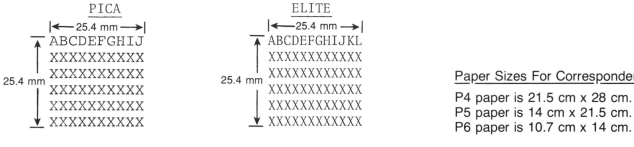

Paper Sizes For Correspondence

P4 paper is 21.5 cm x 28 cm.
P5 paper is 14 cm x 21.5 cm.
P6 paper is 10.7 cm x 14 cm.

LINES AND SPACES

	Horizontal Spaces		Vertical
	Elite	Pica	Lines
P4 (short edge inserted)	102	85	66
P4 (wide edge inserted)	132	110	51
P5 (short edge inserted)	66	55	51
P5 (wide edge inserted)	102	85	33
P6 (short edge inserted)	51	42	33
P6 (wide edge inserted)	66	55	26

Remember: 10.7 cm = 107 mm
14 cm   = 140 mm
21.5 cm = 215 mm
28 cm   = 280 mm

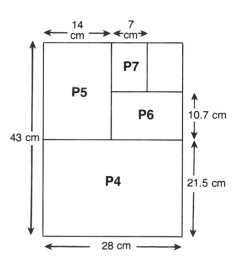

Centring Lines, Titles, Headings

1. Clear margins and tab stops.
2. Position print point at the centre of the paper. Set a tab stop at this point.
3. From the centre, backspace once for every two strokes (letters, numbers, symbols, punctuation marks, and spaces) in the line to be centred. Ignore single leftover strokes.
4. Type the line at the point where the backspacing is completed.
5. Repeat steps 3 and 4 until all lines are centred.

To Centre a "S p r e a d" Heading

1. Backspace from the centre point once for each letter, except the last one in a line, and once for each space between words.
2. Type the heading spacing once between letters and three times between words.

DAILY ACTIVITY

If you are beginning a new class period:

1. Adjust the margins for a 50-space line, and
2. Review selected exercises from previous pages.

THE LETTER ⓞ

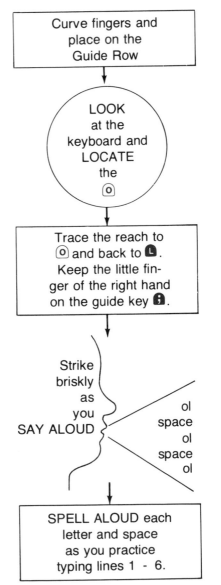

Curve fingers and place on the Guide Row

↓

LOOK at the keyboard and LOCATE the ⓞ

↓

Trace the reach to ⓞ and back to **L**. Keep the little finger of the right hand on the guide key **;**.

↓

Strike briskly as you SAY ALOUD

ol
space
ol
space
ol

↓

SPELL ALOUD each letter and space as you practice typing lines 1 - 6.

I.4   USING THE ⓞ

```
1   ol ol ol do do do so so so lo lo lo do do do ol
2   old old old aid aid aid ado ado ado old old old  DS

3   fold fold fold sold sold sold load load load foil
4   all aid all loads so all is sold all skills of old
```

Basic typewriting style rules are presented in italic type within boxes. These rules should be learned and applied as necessary when preparing typewritten copy.

> *Space once after a semicolon.*

```
5   aid dad; ask a lad; all sails fail; of a load; do
6   if all is sold dads of a skill all of a lid is off
```

12. Do not capitalize metric terms when typed in words as part of a heading, title, or subtitle.

Measured in square kilometres.   *246*
                    not
Measured in Square Kilometres.

13. Metric symbols are used when associated with a number. However, when no number is used the unit should be spelled out.

16 mm^2 *not* 16 square millimetres.   *73*
                                                  127

TYPING SYMBOLS NOT ON THE KEYBOARD

Symbol	Letters to Use	Example
Caret	Underscore and diagonal	red the/dress
Dash	One hyphen with space before and after	Now - not tomorrow.
	or	
	Two hyphens without spacing	Now--not tomorrow.
Degree	Lower case "o" as a superscript	22°C
Ditto	Quotation mark	''
Division sign	Hyphen and periods. (Use the ratchet release.)	÷
Divide into	Right bracket and underscore	$45\overline{)56.80}$
Equal sign	Two hyphens one above the other. (Use the ratchet release.)	=
Exclamation point	Apostrophe with period below	!
Left brace	Two left parentheses	((all present
Minus sign	Hyphen with space before and after	6 - 5 = 1
Multiplication sign	Lower case "x" with space before and after	6 x 5 = 30
Plus sign	Diagonal with hyphen through it	6 ≠ 5 = 11
Pound Sterling	Upper case "L" with hyphen through it	£400
Right brace	Two right parentheses	))
Square brackets	Underscore and diagonal	⌊ ⌋
Square root	Lower case "v", diagonal, and underscore	$\sqrt{144.00}$

DAILY ACTIVITY

If you are beginning a new class period:

1. Adjust the margins for a 50-space line, and
2. Review selected exercises from previous pages.

THE LETTER Ⓣ

```
┌─────────────────────────┐
│    Curve fingers and    │
│      place on the       │
│       Guide Row         │
└─────────────────────────┘
            │
            ▼
        ╭───────╮
        │ LOOK  │
        │ at the│
        │keyboard and│
        │ LOCATE │
        │ the   │
        │  Ⓣ   │
        ╰───────╯
            │
            ▼
┌─────────────────────────┐
│    Trace the reach to   │
│   Ⓣ and back to Ⓕ .   │
│  Keep the little fin-   │
│  ger of the left hand   │
│  on the guide key Ⓐ .  │
└─────────────────────────┘
            │
            ▼
```

Strike briskly as you SAY ALOUD

tf
space
tf
space
tf

```
┌─────────────────────────┐
│   SPELL ALOUD each      │
│    letter and space     │
│     as you practice     │
│   typing lines 1 - 6.   │
└─────────────────────────┘
```

I.5 USING THE Ⓣ

1 tf tf to to it it at at it it to to at at it it
2 tot tot tot jot jot jot too too too dot dot dot **DS**

3 sat sat fat fat kit kit kit tot tot tot too too
4 told told told total total total told told told

5 all loads; so all is sold; all aid; if all skills;
6 a fad; a sad fall; so do all lads; ask all lads;

TYPING METRIC TERMS

1. Spaces are used to separate long lines of digits into easily-readable blocks of three digits with respect to the decimal marker.

   The exact measure is 10 345.686 22 m.   69

2. Use a decimal to express partial units. A zero is always placed before the decimal marker.

   0.75 kg *not* 3/4 kg   78

   0.75 kg *not* .75 kg

3. When symbols consist of letters, there is always a full space between the quantity and the symbols.

   0.75 kg *not* 0.75kg   70

4. When the first character of a symbol is not a letter, no space is left.

   $32^{o}C$ *not* 32° C or 32 ^{o}C

5. A full stop after a symbol is not used, except when the symbol occurs at the end of a sentence.

   Buy 2.5 kg of coffee today.   73
   He bought 2.5 kg.

6. Symbols are never pluralized.

   45 kg *not* 45 kgs *or* 45 kg's   73

7. All symbols are written in lower case, except when the unit is derived from a proper name.

   m for metre   297
   A for ampere
   N for newton
   W for watt

8. Square and cubic unit symbols are expressed using exponents.

   The area of a carpet is 16 m^2.   95

   Carpet is sold by the square metre.

9. Common use values should be rounded off rather than expressed in precise figures.

   Montreal is 563 km from Toronto.   73

   not

   Montreal is 563.458 km from Toronto.

10. Symbols are always printed in roman type, regardless of the type face used in the rest of the text.
    Note: the symbol for litre is the upper case L, both when used alone and when used with a prefix.

    How much will 0.5 L of milk cost next   78
    year?

    not

    How much will 0.5 L of milk cost next
    year?

    or

    The recipe calls for 4 L of milk and
    6 mL of salt.

11. The year, month, and day, in descending order of magnitude, are expressed with eight digits: four for the year, followed by a space or hyphen, two for the month, followed by a space or hyphen, and two for the day.

    September 1, 1977 is correctly   138
    expressed as either 1977 09 01 *or*
    1977-09-01.

DAILY ACTIVITY
If you are beginning a new class period:
1. Adjust the margins for a 50-space line, and
2. Review selected exercises from previous pages.

THE LEFT SHIFT KEY

I.6 TYPING CAPITAL LETTERS USING THE LEFT SHIFT KEY

To type capital letters that are located on the right half of the keyboard:

1. Use the **F** finger as an anchor.

2. Depress the left shift key with the **A** finger.

3. Hold the left shift key down as you strike the desired key with the appropriate finger of the right hand.

4. Release the shift key and return the **A** finger to the guide row.

5. SPELL ALOUD each letter and space as you practice typing lines 1 - 5 below. SAY ALOUD

shift I release f space shift I release f space

```
1   If If If Is Is Is It It It If If If Is Is If It
2   Jill Jill Jo Jo Jill Jill It It Is Is If If Jill
                                                    DS
3   It is It is If it If it It is It is Is it Is it
4   I said so; I said so; I said so; I said so; I do

5   Jill is old; Jo is old; Jill is old; Jo is old;
```

Alberta	AB	Nova Scotia	NS
British Columbia	BC	Ontario	ON
Labrador	LB	Prince Edward Island	PE
Manitoba	MB	Quebec	PQ
New Brunswick	NB	Saskatchewan	SK
Newfoundland	NF	Yukon Territory	YT
Northwest Territories	NT		

American States, Districts, and Territories

Alabama	AL	Kentucky	KY	Ohio	OH
Alaska	AK	Louisiana	LA	Oklahoma	OK
Arizona	AZ	Maine	ME	Oregon	OR
Arkansas	AR	Maryland	MD	Pennsylvania	PA
California	CA	Massachusetts	MA	Puerto Rico	PR
Canal Zone	CZ	Michigan	MI	Rhode Island	RI
Colorado	CO	Minnesota	MN	South Carolina	SC
Connecticut	CT	Mississippi	MS	South Dakota	SD
Delaware	DE	Missouri	MO	Tennessee	TN
District of Columbia	DC	Montana	MT	Texas	TX
Florida	FL	Nebraska	NE	Utah	UT
Georgia	GA	Nevada	NV	Vermont	VT
Guam	GU	New Hampshire	NH	Virgin Islands	VI
Hawaii	HI	New Jersey	NJ	Virginia	VA
Idaho	ID	New Mexico	NM	Washington	WA
Illinois	IL	New York	NY	West Virginia	WV
Indiana	IN	North Carolina	NC	Wisconsin	WI
Iowa	IA	North Dakota	ND	Wyoming	WY
Kansas	KS				

METRIC SYMBOLS

Units   ## Prefixes

ampere	A	exa	E
candela	cd	peta	P
day	d	tera	T
degree Celsius	°C	giga	G
gram	g	mega	M
hectare	ha	kilo	k
hour	h	hecto	h
kelvin	K	deca	da
kilogram	kg	deci	d
litre	l or ℓ	centi	c
metre	m	milli	m
minute	min	micro	μ
mole	mol	nano	n
pascal	Pa	pico	p
radian	rad	femto	f
second	s	atto	a
steradian	sr		
tonne	t		
volt	V		
year	a		

DAILY ACTIVITY

If you are beginning a new class period:

1. Adjust the margins for a 50-space line, and
2. Review selected exercises from previous pages.

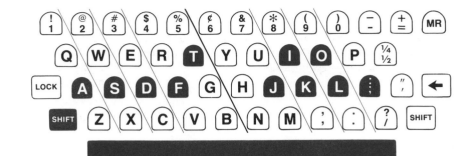

THE PERIOD ⊡

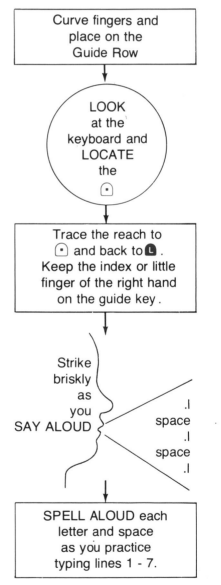

Curve fingers and place on the Guide Row

LOOK at the keyboard and LOCATE the ⊡

Trace the reach to ⊡ and back to **L**. Keep the index or little finger of the right hand on the guide key.

Strike briskly as you SAY ALOUD

.l space .l space .l

SPELL ALOUD each letter and space as you practice typing lines 1 - 7.

I.7 USING THE ⊡

1 .1 .1 .1 .1. .1. .1.**DS**

Space twice after a period that ends a sentence. If a line ends with a period, return the carriage without spacing.

---

2 I did. I did. I do. I do. I did it. I did it.
3 It is I. It is I. It is I. It is a doll. I do.**DS**

4 It is a doll. It is a doll. It is old. It is.
5 sat sat tot tot told told too old load lid kid aid

6 I said so; I said so; lad dad slid slid do do kit
7 I sold it. I sold it. fat fat to to it it totals

13. In typewritten copy use the word "cents" instead of the "¢" symbol.	The stock is quoted at 22 cents.	75
14. Serial, policy, year, telephone, invoice, order, room, and page numbers are typed in figures according to the style of the original source.	Serial .... GA6910368 Policy .... 861794031 Year .... 1975 Telephone .... 449-8828 Invoice .... #63345A Order .... #B-21 Room .... 1014 Page 1321	77
15. Use numbers to indicate time. Hours and minutes are separated by a colon.	16:00	94
16. Express measures, mass, dimensions, and distances in figures.	He drove 68 km on his way to work each day.	73
17. Roman and Arabic numerals are aligned on the right.	X 16 XVI 8 LX 432	187

Addresses

1. A space appears before and after the hyphen separating building and street numbers.	Mr. J. W. Smith 9227 - 98 Avenue Grande Prairie, AB T8V 3X7	272
2. The Postal Code is typed directly below the line containing the city and province. A space separates the second letter from the second number.	Mr. W. J. Gage P. O. Box 498 Agincourt, ON M1S 3C5	74 142
3. The American ZIP Code begins two spaces after the two-letter state abbreviation.	Mrs. Catherine Johansen 206 Front Street Poulsbo, WA 98370	163
4. When a house or building number consists of a single number "1", write the number in full.	One Hillspring Avenue *but* 7 Hillspring Avenue	71

PERMISSIBLE ABBREVIATIONS

Addresses

Apartment	Apt.	Drive	Dr.
Avenue	Ave.	Heights	Hts.
Boulevard	Blvd.	Road	Rd.
Building	Bldg.	Rural Route	R. R.
Corner	Cor.	Street	St.
Crescent	Cresc.		

DAILY ACTIVITY

If you are beginning a new class period:

1. Adjust the margins for a 50-space line, and
2. Review selected exercises from previous pages.

THE LETTER H

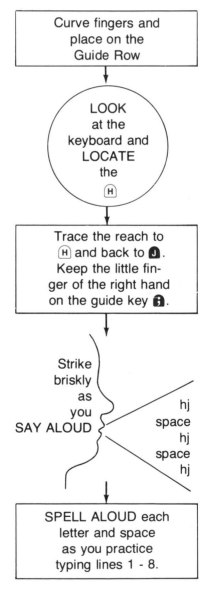

Curve fingers and place on the Guide Row

↓

LOOK at the keyboard and LOCATE the H

↓

Trace the reach to H and back to J. Keep the little finger of the right hand on the guide key ;.

↓

Strike briskly as you SAY ALOUD
hj
space
hj
space
hj

↓

SPELL ALOUD each letter and space as you practice typing lines 1 - 8.

I.8 USING THE H

```
1  hj hj hj ha ha ha hj hj hj ho ho ho hi hi hi hj
2  had had had hat hat hat hit hit hit has has has
                                                    DS
3  aha aha aha ash ash ash had had had has has has hi
4  dish dish dish hall hall hall hill hill hill hills

5  I hit it.  I hit it.  It is hot.  It is hot.
6  I had a hat.  I had a hat.  I hid a hat.  Jill is.

7  too old; so sold; I said so too.  so sad; to do it;
8  It is a hit.  Hal hid it.  Hal hid that hat too.
```

TIMED WRITING

Type the following sentence as many times as you can in one minute. If you type it once you will be typing at four (4) words per minute. If you type it one and one-half times, you will be typing at six words per minute. If you type it twice you will be typing at eight words per minute.

```
9  I sold a hat to Hal.      ←— Return carriage; begin again.

   | 1 | 2 | 3 | 4 |
```

> *In typewriting, five strokes (spaces or letters) are counted as one word.*
>
> *For example:* as at *is one word*
> a boy *is one word*
> there *is one word*
> typewriter *is two words.*

TYPING NUMBERS

<u>General Rules</u>

1. Numbers ten and under are spelled out.

> There were three accidents in January.   *69*

2. Numbers above ten are written in figures.

> At least 3 333 people will attend.   *69*

3. If several numbers both over and under ten are used in a sentence, all the numbers should be typed in figures *or* spelled out.

> Send 3 to John, 33 to Mary, and 333 to Joseph.   *69*
>
> *or*
>
> Send three to John, thirty-three to Mary, and three hundred thirty-three to Joseph.

4. Numbers that begin a sentence are written as words.

> Thirty-six members attended the meeting.   *94*

5. When adjacent unrelated numbers follow one another, the smaller number is expressed in words.

> Buy 75 eight-cent stamps today.

6. Express percentage and decimals in figures.

> He will pay 6 per cent interest.   *73*
>
> *or*
>
> He will pay 6% interest.

7. When a decimal fraction of a unit is used, a zero is always placed before the decimal.

> Buy 2.5 kg of butter.   *78*
>
> He could only buy 0.75 kg of butter.

8. A space should be used to indicate groups of three digits before or after the decimal.

> The exact measure is 10 346.456 81 m.   *69*

9. Express in figures numbers that follow a noun.

> Table 6 may be used in solving the problem.   *73*

10. When numbers are used before other words to form compound adjectives, a hyphen is used. When numbers are used before metric symbols to form compound adjectives, the use of the hyphen is optional.

> He took a 24-week course on insurance. *77*
> He took a 99-d note for the loan.
>
> *or*
>
> He took a 99 d note for the loan.   *102*

11. Use a comma to separate unrelated groups of numbers which come together.

> During 1975, 3 248 cars were damaged in accidents each week.

12. Express sums of money in figures. Even sums are written without decimals and zeros.

> Pay $64.57 for the canoe.   *75*
>   *82*
>
> He paid $35 for a pair of shore anchors.

Appendix B/Typing Facts and Tips   *341*

DAILY ACTIVITY

If you are beginning a new class period:

1. Adjust the margins for a 50-space line, and
2. Review selected exercises from previous pages.

DEVELOPING TYPING CONTINUITY

Continuity means continuous keystroking—no pauses or breaks in typing. Stroking should be smooth and fluent, the speed varying with copy difficulty.

I.9　REVIEWING ALL PREVIOUSLY LEARNED KEYS

SPELL ALOUD each letter and space as you practice typing lines 1 - 16. When confident that you know the location of all keys, proceed to the next page.

```
1    lad lad fad fad dad dad all all lad lad lid lid
2    old old aid aid ado ado old old lid lid did did   DS

3    fold sold load Jill Jill tot tot jot jot too to
4    told told sold sold kit kit total total told it

5    I did it.  I did it.  I said it is old.  I said.
6    I hit it.  I hit it.  It is a hit.  It is a hit.

7    It is a hill.  It is a hill.  Hal did it.  I did.
8    Jo sold a hat.  Jo sold a hat.  Jill sold a doll.

9    total total jot jot too too I sold sold old old to
10   It is a hit.  aid aid did did tot tot old old doll

11   fad fad lads lads aids aids so so folds folds load
12   I hid a hat.  said said fat fat totals totals doll

13   It is a hit; it is a hit.  Hal sold a kit.  I did.
14   I sold a kit of tools.  Hal sold a kit of tools.

15   Look at it.  It is a kit of tools.  Hal has tools.
16   I did it as fast as dad.  I hit it.  It is a hill.
```

9. Capitalize words such as street, avenue, boulevard, and company when used with a proper noun.

This book is not published by Bonner and Company whose offices are located on Commander Street. *71*

The people down the street make good company.

10. Capitalize only the first word of the complimentary close in a letter.

Yours very sincerely *145*
Sincerely yours
Cordially

11. Capitalize the names of school subjects when they are languages or when they precede a course number.

We study French and mathematics. *175*

Next year we will study French 20 and Mathematics 21.

12. Capitalize trade names.

We use a Xerox machine for photocopying. *35*

WORD DIVISION

When words are written or printed, the longer ones must sometimes be broken to equalize the length of lines, and thereby to improve the appearance of the page. In such cases, these principles apply: *33* *46* *56*
  1. Word division in print is undesirable. When it occurs, the division should be that which least interferes with the reader's comprehension.
  2. Words are pronounced in syllables, or units of sound. These oral breaks are the most significant factor in determining points of division for the printed word.

From these principles, certain guides to practice may be set down:
  1. Monosyllables, however long, may not be divided.
  2. One-letter syllables
      a. at the beginning or end of a word, may not stand alone, e.g., emergency, flat-ter*y*.
      b. within a word, should join the preceding syllable, e.g., cat*a*-logue, unless followed by -*ble*, -*bly*, -*cal*, *cle*, as terminal syllables, e.g. envi-*able*, mir-*acle*, or by a two-letter terminal syllable, e.g., stead-*ily*.
      c. if consecutive within a word, should be separated, e.g., rad*i*-ator.
  3. Two-letter terminal syllables should not be carried over, e.g., gra-cious*ly* rather than gracious-*ly*.
  4. Doubled consonants before a suffix are divided, e.g., pla*n-n*ing, unless the double consonant forms part of the root word, e.g., ca*ll*-ing.
  5. Five-letter words should not be divided. Division of six-letter words should be avoided, e.g., *basket* rather than *bas-ket*.
  6. Compound words and hyphenated words should be divided only between the components.
  7. Personal names, foreign words, abbreviations, trade names, numerals, and place names should not be divided. Dates and addresses should be divided only between their major elements, e.g., *January 1,/1968* and *Saint John,/New Brunswick* rather than *January /1, 1968* and *Saint John, New /Brunswick*.
  8. Breaks at the ends of more than two consecutive lines should be avoided.
  9. The last word in a paragraph or on a page should not be divided.
  10. All things considered, a word is best divided to achieve a balance of letters, e.g., *accom-modate* rather than *accommo-date*.

DAILY ACTIVITY

If you are beginning a new class period:

1. Adjust the margins for a 50-space line, and
2. Review selected exercises.

THE LETTER E

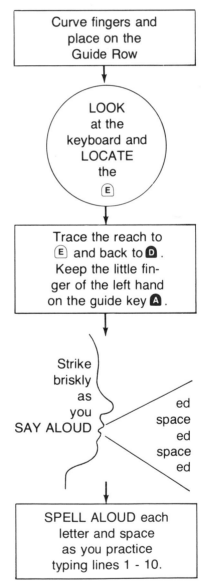

Curve fingers and place on the Guide Row

↓

LOOK at the keyboard and LOCATE the E

↓

Trace the reach to E and back to D. Keep the little finger of the left hand on the guide key A.

↓

Strike briskly as you SAY ALOUD

ed
space
ed
space
ed

↓

SPELL ALOUD each letter and space as you practice typing lines 1 - 10.

I.10 USING THE E

1 ed ed eh eh edit edit edit elf elf elf elk elk led
2 led led let let fed fed jet jet lee lee fee fee **DS**

3 see see tee tee fed fed tea tea jet jet edit edits
4 sea sea led led heed heed lead lead deed deed like

5 I see it. I see it. I see the jet. I see it.
6 He fed the elk. He fed the elk. Kit feeds it.

7 did dish to to had had sat sat told told lid slid
8 told told lids kid sold it; Lee said hello to Hal.

9 He has the last old desk. Let Jill ·see the total.
10 Joe feeds the seals. He has the lead. I sold it.

g. before or after the apostrophe.	Gerry's car has new snow tires.	88
h. before or after the colon when indicating hours and minutes.	Meet me at 18:00.	94
i. between parentheses and the words they enclose.	Mrs. D. Johnson (Paraplegic Society representative) presented a brief.	85
j. between quotation marks and the words they enclose.	Winston Churchill said: "We have nothing to offer but blood, sweat, and tears."	91
k. between the # symbol and numerals.	Cheque #36 is drawn for $604.35.	86

CAPITALIZATION

1. Capitalize the first word of every sentence and the first word of every complete direct quotation.	He said, "Civil strife is now a thing of the past."	8 91
2. Capitalize an official title immediately preceding a name. Titles elsewhere in a sentence may be typed without a capital.	On Wednesday, Prime Minister Trudeau will address the Empire Club. Susan Hilmer is the president of the club.	
3. Business and professional titles used without a name are not capitalized.	The solicitor will issue the mortgage documents.	84
4. Capitalize the first word and all important words in titles of books, booklets, newspapers, articles, periodicals, magazines, plays, poems, and operas. (The title may be typed in ALL CAPITALS or underscored.)	<u>Jogfree of Canda</u> by Don Harron was a best seller in 1974.	144 204
5. Capitalize all proper nouns and words derived from them.	The report on bilingualism and biculturalism deals with Canadian and French-Canadian cultures.	79
6. Capitalize seasons of the year when they are personified.	April usually marks the beginning of spring. The fresh breath of Spring is delightful.	
7. Capitalize geographic names, names of geographic regions, and localities. The compass points are not capitalized.	We are going East for a holiday this summer. We shall drive east on Highway 17.	163
8. Capitalize the names of clubs, organizations, and buildings.	He spoke at the meeting of the Empire Club.	34

DAILY ACTIVITY

If you are beginning a new class period:

1. Adjust the margins for a 50-space line, and
2. Review selected exercises from previous pages.

THE RIGHT SHIFT KEY

I.11 TYPING CAPITAL LETTERS USING THE RIGHT SHIFT KEY

To type capital letters that are located on the left half of the keyboard:

1. Use the 🄹 finger as an anchor.

2. Depress the right shift key with the 🄰 finger.

3. Hold the right shift key down as you strike the desired key with the appropriate finger of the left hand.

4. Release the shift key and return the 🄰 finger to the guide row.

5. SPELL ALOUD each letter and space as you practice typing lines 1 - 10. SAY ALOUD

shift A release s space shift A release s space

```
1    As As Ed Ed Sod Sod Dale Dale Foot Foot Test Test
2    Do Do Fed Fed Alf Alf That That Ease Ease Sid Sid DS

3    See the jet.  See the jet.  Dad sees it.  See it.
4    This is a hit.  This is a hit.  This is the hill.

5    Alf asks.  Ted fell.  Ed told.  Dale sees it.
6    Kit asks.  Ike fell.  Jo told.  Otto sees it.

7    She told the little tot.  The tot likes Joe.
8    I told Hal to hold the kites.  I see a lake.

9    It is a lake.  It is a little lake.  I see it.
10   Elk feed at the lake.  Look at the little lake.
```

SPACING

1. Space once:

   a. after a comma.   We will mail staples, paper, and   22
                                                        string.

   b. after a semicolon.   Think about it; you may agree.   6

   c. after a period in an abbreviation.   Mr. T. R. Gelmici will speak.   17

   d. after an exclamation mark within a sentence.   What! late again?   92

   e. after the second alpha character in a Postal Code.   M1S 3C7   142

   f. before and after the ampersand.   Mr. & Mrs. Benson were late.   84

   g. before and after a single hyphen dash.   Don't wait for spring - do it now!   81

   h. to indicate thousands when grouping numbers of   The exact measure was   69
      four or more digits.   10 123.386 42 cm.

   i. between a number and the associated metric sym-   Buy 50 kg of flour.   70
      bol.

2. Space twice:

   a. after punctuation at the end of a sentence.   Canada celebrated its centennial in   9
                                                        1967. It was a spectacular birthday
                                                        party.

   b. after a colon.   The preacher said: "Get to church   32
                                                        on time."

   c. after a figure or a letter in an enumeration.   A.   Annual Reports   167
                                                             1.   Northern Region
                                                                  a.   Workshop
                                                                  b.   Seminar

3. Do NOT space:

   a. after the $ symbol.   They will pay $63.40 this year.   82

   b. before the % symbol.   Long-term bonds yield 7.5% interest.   83

   c. before a subscript, superscript, or exponent.   We produced $21.2 \times 10^6 \ m^3$ of crude   95
                                                        oil.

   d. before or after the hyphen in compound words.   His sister-in-law sells flowers.   33

   e. before or after the double hyphen dash.   Don't wait for spring--do it now!   81

   f. before or after a decimal point.   The company paid a 4.5% dividend.   75

DAILY ACTIVITY

If you are beginning a new class period:

1. Adjust the margins for a 50-space line, and
2. Review selected exercises.

THE LETTER ⓊU

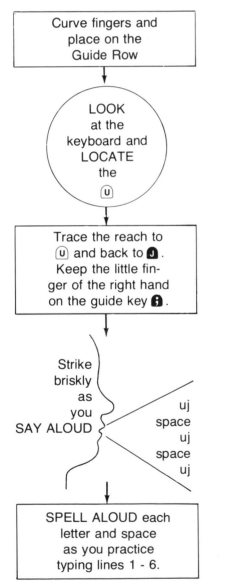

Curve fingers and place on the Guide Row

↓

LOOK at the keyboard and LOCATE the ⓊU

↓

Trace the reach to ⓊU and back to Ⓙ. Keep the little finger of the right hand on the guide key Ⓚ.

↓

Strike briskly as you SAY ALOUD

uj
space
uj
space
uj

↓

SPELL ALOUD each letter and space as you practice typing lines 1 - 6.

I.12 USING THE ⓊU

1 uj uj uj us us us use use use used used used used
2 out out out due due due use use use sue sue sue **DS**

3 Hal is out. Hal is out. He is out. He is out.
4 It is due. It is due. Use it all. Use it all.

5 The food is so old. The lease is out at the lake.
6 He used it all. She used it all. It is a duet.

CORRECTING ERRORS AFTER THE PAPER HAS BEEN REMOVED

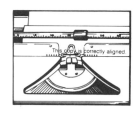

1. Erase the error.
2. Re-insert the paper in the typewriter.
3. Use the variable line spacer to position the paper so that the bottoms of the typewritten letters are slightly above the aligning scale.
4. Use the paper release to move the paper to left or right so that the letter "i" or "l" is lined up with a vertical line scale.
5. Test the position of the printing point by locating a typewritten period, setting the ribbon on stencil position, and typing over the period. Make any needed adjustments.
6. Return the ribbon to type position and type the correction.
7. While some typists attempt to re-insert carbon copies with the original for correction, it is recommended that errors on carbons be corrected individually. Follow the procedures as outlined above, but do not type directly onto the carbon copy. Insert a piece of carbon between the ribbon and the copy. Then, type the corrections.

"SQUEEZING IN" AND "OMITTING" LETTERS

"Squeezing In" at the Beginning or End of a Word

Machines with a half-space mechanism:
1. Move the carriage to the last space before the omitted letter.
2. Depress and hold down the space bar.
3. Type the omitted letter.

Machines without a half-space mechanism:
1. Move the carriage to the space following the place for "squeezing in" the letter.
2. Depress the backspace key halfway and hold it.
3. Type the omitted letter.

Electric machines:
1. Push the carriage backward or forward a half space by hand.
2. Type the omitted letter.

"Squeezing In" Within a Word

1. Erase the word to be corrected.
2. Position the carriage to type correctly the first letter of the word.
3. Press down and hold the space bar. Strike the first letter.
4. Release the space bar, then press down again. Hold it as you type the second letter.
5. Repeat the procedure for all the letters to be typed.

"Omitting" a Letter Within a Word

1. Erase the word to be corrected.
2. Position the carriage to type correctly the first letter of the word.
3. Press down and hold the space bar. Type the first letter.
4. Release the space bar.
5. Repeat the procedure for all the letters to be typed.

DAILY ACTIVITY

If you are beginning a new class period:
1. Adjust the margins for a 50-space line, and
2. Review selected exercises.

THE LETTER G

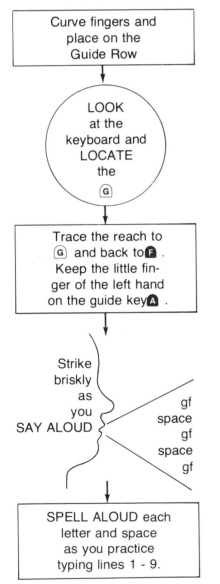

Curve fingers and place on the Guide Row

↓

LOOK at the keyboard and LOCATE the G

↓

Trace the reach to G and back to F. Keep the little finger of the left hand on the guide key A.

↓

Strike briskly as you SAY ALOUD
gf space gf space gf

↓

SPELL ALOUD each letter and space as you practice typing lines 1 - 9.

I.13 USING THE G

1 gf gf gf go go go got got got get get get ago ago

DS

2 keg keg keg glad glad glad good good good glass
3 gas gas gas egg egg egg glue glue glue ego ego ego

4 tugs tugs tugs ages ages ages eagle eagle eagle
5 joke joke joke glass glass glass joke age age age

6 The glass is hot. The glass is old. It is good.
7 He is good. Gus is good. I see the eagle.

8 It is good glue. The glue held. Jill is good.
9 Joe is good. Joe told a joke. Jill told a joke.

CORRECTING ERRORS

TYPEWRITER ERASER

1. Choose a hard or soft eraser to match the grade of paper. The eraser chosen may be a wheel type with or without a brush; a pencil type with an eraser on one end and a brush on the other; or a pencil type with a coarse eraser on one end and a softer eraser (for carbon copies) on the other end. *114* *115*
2. Turn the paper up a few spaces so that the error will be at the top of the cylinder. (If the error is at the bottom of the page, roll <u>back</u> the paper until the bottom of the paper can be rested on the top of the cylinder. This prevents paper slippage.)
3. Move the carriage to the extreme right or left (use margin release) to prevent eraser crumbs from falling into the machine.
4. Position the eraser shield so that one of the holes exposes the error to be corrected. This allows you to erase only the error — not the surrounding copy. If you do not have an eraser shield, one can easily be made by punching a hole in a piece of cardboard or heavy paper.
5. Remove the error using light strokes of the eraser directed away from the mechanical parts of the typewriter. Brush crumbs from the paper.
6. Re-position to type the correction.
7. Insert correct letter by striking lightly. Backspace and re-strike if necessary.

CORRECTION PAPER

1. Backspace to the beginning of error.
2. Insert the correction paper (available in a variety of colors to match paper color) behind the ribbon and in front of the copy to be corrected.
3. Re-type the error exactly as you made it. Remove the correction paper.
4. Backspace to the beginning of correction and type the correction.

CORRECTION FLUID

1. Turn the paper up a few spaces. (If error is near the bottom of the page, turn the paper <u>back</u> several spaces.)
2. Move the carriage to the extreme right or left (use margin release). This will prevent any fluid from falling into the machine.
3. Select a fluid to match the color of paper and shake the bottle. Then remove the applicator brush and daub off any excess fluid on the inside of the bottle opening.
4. Apply the fluid lightly and quickly to the outline of the stroke or strokes to be corrected. Do not "paint" the fluid onto the paper.
5. Replace the applicator brush and tighten cap.
6. Re-position paper and type correction.

CORRECTING ERRORS ON CARBON COPIES

1. Errors on carbon copies should be corrected when the paper is still in the typewriter. Place a stiff card behind the sheet on which you are erasing, to prevent carbon marks from appearing on the remaining copies. Use a soft eraser. Blow eraser crumbs off the paper. When the error on all copies has been erased, remove the card. Re-position paper to type correction.
2. If you do not have a stiff card, use a sheet of paper, folded several times, behind the original; or a single sheet inserted behind the carbon paper.

DAILY ACTIVITY

If you are beginning a new class period:

1. Adjust the margins for a 50-space line, and
2. Review selected exercises.

THE LETTER ⓡ

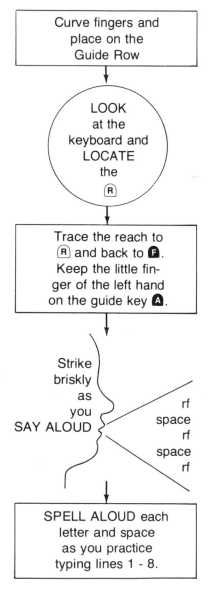

Curve fingers and place on the Guide Row

↓

LOOK at the keyboard and LOCATE the ⓡ

↓

Trace the reach to ⓡ and back to Ⓕ. Keep the little finger of the left hand on the guide key Ⓐ.

↓

Strike briskly as you SAY ALOUD

rf
space
rf
space
rf

↓

SPELL ALOUD each letter and space as you practice typing lines 1 - 8.

I.14 USING THE ⓡ

```
1  rf rf rf rod rod rod rid rid rid ride ride ride
2  ore ore ore for for for fair fair fair jar jar  DS

3  real real real rate rate rate order order order
4  after after after relate relate relate rule rule

5  Look for the rat.  The dog looked for the rat.
6  The real estate is sold.  He asked Ruth to go.

7  The girls tried to read the joke.  The glass fell.
8  The road to the lake has ruts.  He told it to all.
```

TIMED WRITING

Type the following sentence as many times as you can in one minute. If you type it once you will be typing at 6 words per minute. If you type it one and one-half times, you will be typing at 9 words per minute. If you type it twice, you will be typing at 12 words per minute.

```
9  A tall lad sold all the desks. ◄——— Return carriage; begin again

   |  1  |  2  |  3  |  4  |  5  |  6  |
```

> *In typewriting, five strokes are counted as one word.*

THE RATCHET RELEASE

The ratchet release allows you to type subscripts, superscripts, exponents, and double lines. Operate the ratchet release; roll the cylinder (platen) backward or forward; type the required subscript, superscript, exponent, or double line; return the ratchet release; and then the cylinder (platen) to the normal position. By following this procedure you will be able to complete an exercise without changing the normal spacing between continuing lines. **95**

THE VARIABLE LINE SPACER

The variable line spacer should be used for re-aligning type or for typing copy on a line. When used, the normal spacing between continuing lines of type, is changed. Unlike the ratchet release, the variable line spacer will not automatically return the cylinder to the line of writing, and should not be used for typing subscripts, superscripts, exponents, or double lines. **v** **vii**

UNDERLINING

To underline, depress the backspace key or move the carriage by hand to the first letter of the word to be underlined. Then strike the underscore once for each letter to be underlined. When underlining a group of letters or words, move the carriage to the required position. Then, depress the shift lock key and type an unbroken line using the underscore key. It is permissible and quicker to type an unbroken line than to omit the underscore for the space between words. **89**

RULING

Horizontal and vertical lines may be drawn while the paper is still in the typewriter. This is particularly useful in preparing invoices, purchase orders, and boxed tabular data.

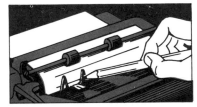

Horizontal Rules.
1. Place the pencil firmly against the card-holder or on the ribbon-carrier.
2. Depress the left carriage release while holding the left cylinder knob.
3. Move the carriage to the point at which the line ends.

Vertical Rules.
1. Place the pencil firmly against the card-holder or on the ribbon-carrier.
2. Operate the ratchet release.
3. Turn the left cylinder knob quickly and smoothly. (If left-handed, turn the right cylinder knob.)

GOOD TYPING HABITS

1. Keep the typewriter centred and covered when not in use.
2. Clean the typewriter regularly.
3. Always centre the paper on the cylinder by adjusting the position of the paper guide. This ensures even wear on the cylinder.
4. Always type on a double thickness of paper. This will improve the appearance of the typed copy and will prevent undue wear on the cylinder.
5. When typing on a manual typewriter, use an even touch. Strike punctuation marks lightly.
6. Do not over-use your typewriter ribbon. When the print becomes faint, replace the ribbon.
7. Be accurate in typing, punctuating, capitalizing, spelling, and dividing words.
8. Make neat corrections. A strike-over is not a correction!
9. Proofread all material before removing it from the typewriter.
10. Call a typewriter repairperson to make difficult machine repairs.

DAILY ACTIVITY

If you are beginning a new class period:

1. Adjust the margins for a 50-space line, and
2. Review selected exercises.

THE LETTER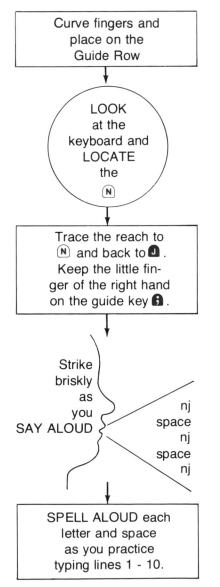

Curve fingers and place on the Guide Row

LOOK at the keyboard and LOCATE the N

Trace the reach to N and back to J. Keep the little finger of the right hand on the guide key J.

Strike briskly as you SAY ALOUD

nj space nj space nj

SPELL ALOUD each letter and space as you practice typing lines 1 - 10.

I.15 USING THE N

```
1   nj nj nj an an an and and and no no no note note
2   fern fern tone tone tone than than than in in in  DS

3   thank thank thank think think think inner inner
4   He hit the nail.  He hit the nail on the head.

5   Nothing is done right.  I think there is a loss.
6   I shall thank John.  Joe thinks the note is due.
```

> *Space once after a period that follows an abbreviation or an initial.*

```
7   Dr. Ash is old.  Dr. Ash has a jet.  He likes it.
8   Dr. D. K. Ash likes tea.  Dr. J. T. Lee likes tea.

9   Ask Ted to see Dr. Hill.  He is old.  He fell.
10  Dr. Lee and Dr. Ash said so.  He hit the tree.
```

GENERAL MACHINE INFORMATION

CARE AND MAINTENANCE OF YOUR TYPEWRITER

Your typewriter, whether it be a portable, manual, or electric, will give you many years of good service if you take the time to regularly remove the dust, dirt, and eraser crumbs that may clog the machine. The following list of cleaning equipment and supplies may be purchased from any local stationery store:

— a long handled brush for cleaning the machine
— a short, stiff brush or "putty" substance for cleaning the type face
— fluid, such as carbon tetrachloride or methylated spirits, for cleaning the cylinder (platen) and type face
— a soft cloth for dusting the machine.

CLEANING THE TYPEWRITER

1. Dust your typewriter daily.
2. Use the long handled brush to remove dust from areas which you cannot reach with the cloth.
3. Use the stiff brush or "putty" to regularly clean the type face. If your type face is clogged with grime, use the brush or "putty" and the fluid.
4. Once a week, clean the cylinder (platen) by rubbing it lightly with a cloth slightly dampened by the cleaning fluid.

NOTE: Eraser crumbs are enemies of your typewriter! Avoid letting them clog your machine by moving the cylinder to the extreme left or right before erasing.

CHANGING TYPEWRITER RIBBONS

The method of changing typewriter ribbons varies from machine to machine. If a manufacturer's guide is available for your typewriter, follow the instructions provided. If a manufacturer's guide is not available, refer to the following general instructions:

1. Observe carefully how the old ribbon is mounted, the direction in which it unwinds from one spool and rewinds on the other spool, and the system of threading the ribbon through the ribbon-carrier mechanism.
2. Locate the ribbon reverse mechanism. If necessary, adjust the ribbon reverse so that the ribbon is winding toward the spool with the most ribbon on it.
3. Wind the entire ribbon onto one spool.
4. Observe carefully the method of attaching the ribbon to the empty spool. Detach the ribbon from the empty spool and discard.
5. Attach the free end of the new ribbon to the empty spool.
6. Mount the spools containing the new ribbon.
7. Thread the ribbon exactly as the old ribbon was thread.
8. Check the direction of ribbon travel. If necessary, operate the ribbon reverse to cause the ribbon to wind onto the empty spool.

CLEARING TABULATOR STOPS

The method of clearing tabulator stops varies from machine to machine. If a manufacturer's guide is available for your typewriter, follow the instructions provided. If a manufacturer's guide is not available, one of the following methods may be used:

1. Clear individual tab stops by tabbing to the stop and depressing the tab clear key.
2. Depress the total clear key. (This key, available on some machines, clears all tab stops.)
3. Move the carriage all the way to the right, holding the tab clear key down and returning the carriage its full length.

DAILY ACTIVITY

If you are beginning a new class period:

1. Adjust the margins for a 50-space line, and
2. Review selected exercises.

THE LETTER Ⓒ

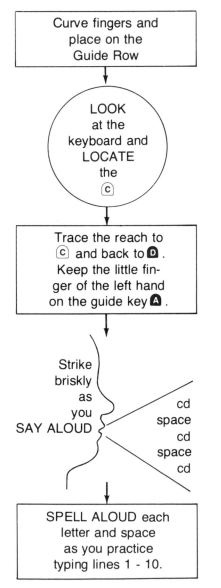

Curve fingers and place on the Guide Row

↓

LOOK at the keyboard and LOCATE the Ⓒ

↓

Trace the reach to Ⓒ and back to Ⓓ. Keep the little finger of the left hand on the guide key Ⓐ.

↓

Strike briskly as you SAY ALOUD

cd
space
cd
space
cd

↓

SPELL ALOUD each letter and space as you practice typing lines 1 - 10.

I.16 USING THE Ⓒ

1 cd cd cd cod cod cod code code code cold cold cold
2 can can cane cane critic critic critic cling cling **DS**

3 since since since office office office color color
4 enclose enclose enclose credit credit credit chart

5 coin coin coin chart chart chart contract contract
6 letter letter letter thick thick thick thicket

7 He is in the office. His jacket is clean. I can.
8 The color is red. Jack signs contracts. Read it.

9 He can read the old letter. It is fun to read it.
10 Cancel all the old contracts. Run to the house.

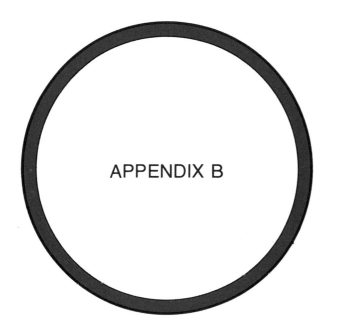

APPENDIX B

TYPING FACTS AND TIPS

The purpose of this appendix is to summarize in convenient form and location, the theory presented in BUSINESS APPLICATIONS IN TYPEWRITING.

The only information not summarized is that relating to the various formats used in the typing of news releases, agenda, minutes of meeting, financial reports, business forms, et cetera; and the information on typing masters.

If you are beginning a new class period:

1. Adjust the margins for a 50-space line, and
2. Review selected exercises.

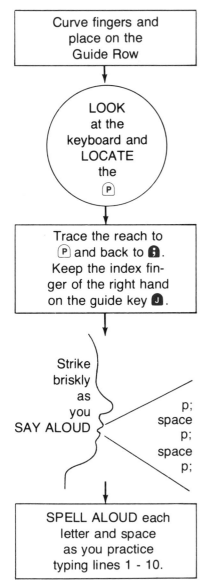

THE LETTER P

Curve fingers and place on the Guide Row

↓

LOOK at the keyboard and LOCATE the P

↓

Trace the reach to P and back to *f*. Keep the index finger of the right hand on the guide key J.

↓

Strike briskly as you SAY ALOUD

p;
space
p;
space
p;

↓

SPELL ALOUD each letter and space as you practice typing lines 1 - 10.

I.17 USING THE P

1   p; p; p; pep pep pep pet pet pet put put put pass
2   pass pass pad pad pad cap cap cap pick pick pick   DS

3   up up up upper upper upper supper supper supper
4   lip lip lip tip tip sip sip top top julep julep

5   spill spill spill spell spell spell help help help
6   press press press pole pole pole surprise surprise

7   She put it in the pail. Keep it for supper.
8   Peter put the apples in the pail. Dan ate grapes.

9   Please pass the pepper. Pass the peas to Paul.
10 Pencil and paper are all he needs. Place it here.

	SI	1.69
	HFW	56%
	AWL	5.8
	TW	44

One of the most crucial elements of economic development is population. It is known that Antarctica has extensive mineral resources, but there are no permanent settlements there; hence the continent remains undeveloped.

	SI	1.41
	HFW	75%
	AWL	4.6
	TW	59

Too much population may be more dangerous than too little. Sri Lanka is an example of this: the population is growing rapidly but production and sales of the chief export—tea—are not enough to support the increasing numbers, and Sri Lanka has had to introduce rationing of food and clothes.

	SI	1.52
	HFW	71%
	AWL	5.2
	TW	27

Nor is development encouraged by a static population. A country with a static population has little room for flexibility and change.

	SI	1.43
	HFW	79%
	AWL	4.8
	TW	132

If a country is to develop economically it should have a population which is neither too small nor too large: one which is growing, but not faster than the country's industry. This turns out to be rather an exacting requirement for economic growth and development. Most of the underdeveloped countries do not meet this requirement. As a rule, their populations are too large for their resources and industry, and their numbers are increasing so rapidly that new jobs cannot be created fast enough. Over-population or the threat of it is one of the most serious of today's economic problems, not only for the developing countries but for the world as a whole.

	SI	1.39
	HFW	84%
	AWL	4.6
	TW	64

Besides being the right size, a country's population should be as healthy and well educated as possible. The age distribution of the population is important too: there should be more people of working age (say 20-65) than there are children and old people who cannot work and must be supported by those who are working.

The numbers down the right margin of the passage:

11	4	2
23	8	5
34	11	7
44	15	9
54	18	11
67	22	13
80	27	16
92	31	18
102	34	21
11	38	23
25	42	26
26	43	26
37	46	28
51	51	31
64	55	34
76	59	36
88	63	38
101	66	41
	72	43
	76	46
	80	48
	84	51
	86	52
10	90	54
22	94	57
35	98	59
48	102	62
59		64
63		65

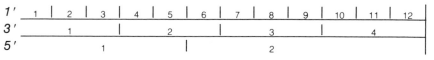

1' | 1 | 2 | 3 | 4 | 5 | 6 | 7 | 8 | 9 | 10 | 11 | 12
3' | 1 | 2 | 3 | 4
5' | 1 | 2

DAILY ACTIVITY

If you are beginning a new class period:

1. Adjust the margins for a 50-space line, and
2. Review selected exercises.

THE LETTER W

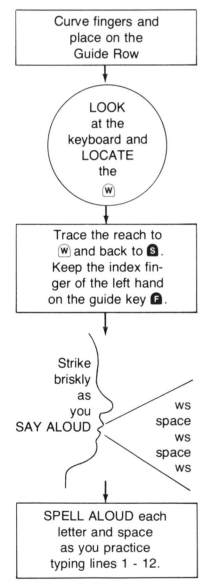

Curve fingers and place on the Guide Row

↓

LOOK at the keyboard and LOCATE the W

↓

Trace the reach to W and back to S. Keep the index finger of the left hand on the guide key F.

↓

Strike briskly as you SAY ALOUD

ws space ws space ws

↓

SPELL ALOUD each letter and space as you practice typing lines 1 - 12.

I.18 USING THE W

```
1   ws ws ws who who who what what what when when when
2   wit wit wit walk walk walk will will will was was  DS

3   wet wet wet wheat wheat wheat week week week win
4   wink wink wink were were were was was was saw saw

5   awe awe awe while while awhile awhile awful awful
6   await await await awake awake awake aware aware

7   Write the letter now.  She will wear a new dress.
8   Water the plants while she is gone.  Walk on now.

9   We hope Pat will win the race.  Follow a recipe.
10  We went to the park.  We all went for a picnic.

11  The water was cold.  He will sail on the water.
12  Jack thinks we can win the race.  He thinks so.
```

TIMED WRITING

Type the following sentence as many times as you can in one minute. If you type it once you will be typing at 8 words per minute. If you type it one and one-half times, you will be typing at 12 words per minute. If you type it twice, you will be typing at 16 words per minute.

```
13  We see the coins that fell on the paper.  ⟵— Begin Again

    |   1   |   2   |   3   |   4   |   5   |   6   |   7   |   8   |
```

America and Western Europe, have developed only in the temperate zones of the world.

Natural resources are distributed throughout the world apparently at random. England has the coal and iron which made the industrial revolution possible. Among its extensive mineral riches, Canada has the world's largest discovered reserves of uranium, nickel, and asbestos. The little countries of Jamaica and Surinam have been the world's major sources of bauxite—the ore from which aluminum is made—but neither of them has enough available cheap electric power to process the bauxite and produce aluminum. Because it has this power, Canada imported the bauxite and became one of the world's largest producers of aluminum. The discovery of enormous reserves of oil in the Middle Eastern countries, especially Kuwait, has radically changed life in these desert economies. People from countries with the skills, money, and materials to develop these resources have moved in; this has affected not only the economy but the political climate as well. Other countries, like Austria, are short of minerals, but have valuable forest resources from which can be developed lumber, pulp and paper, and synthetic textile industries. Still other countries have limited resources but are particularly suited to the growing of certain crops: cloves in Tanzania, tea in Sri Lanka, sugar in Cuba, and cocoa in Ghana. And there are many countries in the world with no known resources, or at least none worth exploiting at present. Some of the developing countries of Africa and Asia are in this group, but so are older countries like Italy and Greece. If Italy had more natural resources on which to base economic development, its people might not have turned to fascism in the twenties.

SI	1.40
HFW	66%
AWL	5.1
TW	339

DAILY ACTIVITY

If you are beginning a new class period:
1. Adjust the margins for a 50-space line, and
2. Review selected exercises.

THE LETTER Ⓜ

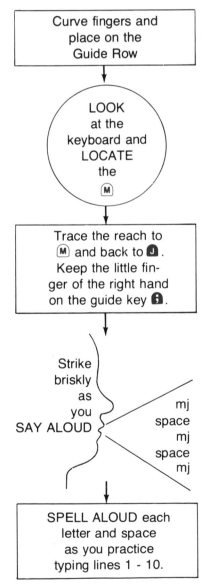

I.19 USING THE Ⓜ

1 mj mj mj me me me mad mad mad made made made make
2 home home home foam foam foam some some some gum **DS**

3 sum sum sum from from from much much much man man
4 palm palm palm poem poem poem slump slump slump

5 Pam purchased a trumpet. Norm wrote memoranda.
6 She sent a credit memo. He forgot to warn them.

7 Madge has measles. Mike has mumps. Make a cake.
8 Jim went to the market to get some meat and eggs.

9 Mr. and Mrs. J. T. Doe are here. Miss Lee is not.
10 Ms. Grant is planning to attend. Mr. Rand is ill.

Buildings. <u>Freedom of assembly</u> permits people to gather together in public, but not to cause a riot or damage property.

| | 71 |
| | 74 |

SI	1.46
HFW	71%
AWL	5.0
TW	984

SI	1.56
HFW	76%
AWL	5.1
TW	51

SI	1.66
HFW	72%
AWL	5.6
TW	44

SI	1.54
HFW	63%
AWL	5.1
TW	70

SI	1.44
HFW	74%
AWL	5.0
TW	154

GEOGRAPHY, CLIMATE, AND POPULATION

	1'	3'	5'

When we come to examine the more developed nations, · 10 · 3 · 2
we find an extraordinary variation in standards of living and · 22 · 7 · 4
types of economic activity. International co-operation could · 34 · 11 · 7
probably be improved if we had a clear explanation of how this · 47 · 16 · 9
has come about. · 50 · 17 · 10

Some of the factors which contribute to a country's de- · 61 · 20 · 12
velopment are rather obvious. First there are natural factors, · 73 · 24 · 15
such as geography, climate, natural resources, and population, · 86 · 29 · 17
which are important in every country. · 93 · 31 · 19

Geography has been hostile to economic development · 10 · 34 · 21
in Canada: constructing a railway to link east and west was a · 22 · 39 · 23
tremendous task, and, although there now seem to be too many · 34 · 43 · 26
railways, settlement is still largely confined to a 160 km strip · 47 · 47 · 28
along the southern border. In countries such as Tibet, geog- · 63 · 51 · 31
raphy has almost prevented settlement altogether. · 69 · 54 · 32

Tropical climates make it possible for people to live and · 11 · 58 · 35
to maintain large families relatively easily, since they can gather · 25 · 62 · 37
enough food to survive and no one needs much in the way of · 36 · 66 · 40
clothing or housing. Unfortunately, hot humid climates also en- · 49 · 71 · 42
courage diseases such as sleeping sickness which reduce the · 61 · 74 · 45
energy needed for any sort of work. In desert regions too much · 74 · 79 · 47
time must be spent in looking for and conserving supplies of · 86 · 83 · 50
water. Arctic climates also require the inhabitants to lead limited · 99 · 87 · 52
and carefully planned lives and severely restrict the range of · 111 · 91 · 55
possible occupations. Up to the present time, advanced indus- · · 95 · 57
trial economies, such as those we are familiar with in North · · 99 · 60

```
1'   1 | 2 | 3 | 4 | 5 | 6 | 7 | 8 | 9 | 10 | 11 | 12
3'       1      |     2      |     3      |     4
5'           1              |          2
```

DAILY ACTIVITY

If you are beginning a new class period:

1. Adjust the margins for a 50-space line, and
2. Review selected exercises.

THE COMMA ⟨,⟩

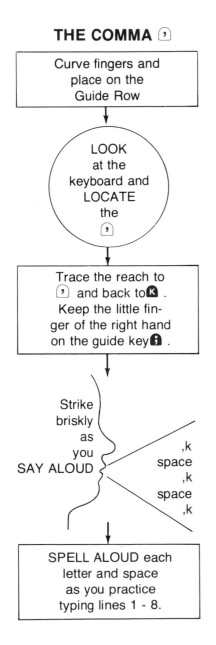

Curve fingers and place on the Guide Row

↓

LOOK at the keyboard and LOCATE the ⟨,⟩

↓

Trace the reach to ⟨,⟩ and back to **K**. Keep the little finger of the right hand on the guide key **;**.

↓

Strike briskly as you SAY ALOUD

,k space ,k space ,k

↓

SPELL ALOUD each letter and space as you practice typing lines 1 - 8.

I.20 USING THE ⟨,⟩

> *Leave one space after a comma.*

1 ,k ,k ,k one, two, three, four; one, two, three,
2 Frank, John, and Alec will go. Well, sir, I won**DS**

3 When I get it, I will pass it on to him.
4 John left his home town of Orillia, Ontario.

5 His original order, he recalled, was confirmed.
6 Mr. Jonas, who called on our friends, went home.

7 Leo Chan, the doctor, is retiring this month too.
8 The sale of suits, coats, and hats will start now.

with that expressed in other political and economic theories. | 98 | 84

SI	1.55
HFW	68%
AWL	5.0
TW	143

The political philosophy of the western democracies assumes that society exists for the benefit of the individuals living in it. Considerable restriction of individual freedom exists, but it is supposed to be limited to preventing some individuals from harming other individuals. Since it is very easy to harm others, even unintentionally, we need many restrictive laws. We have laws against making too much noise, or using blasphemous language in a public place, or selling food which has gone bad, just as we have laws against deliberate acts like murder, arson, and theft. As long as the purpose and effect of restrictive laws is the protection of individuals, such laws are not out of place in a democracy.

SI	1.50
HFW	75%
AWL	4.9
TW	229

Certain rights are considered so important in our kind of democracy that they are put in a special category and called the civil liberties. But these fundamental rights cannot be exercised without regard for the rights of others. It is comparatively easy to explain how and why a democratic society must put up with a certain amount of restriction of its civil liberties. Fortunately, freedom of opinion, the basis of all the others, is not restricted by law today. Freedom of speech (the public expression of opinion) must be limited to prevent some people from telling harmful lies about others. Thus we have laws against libel and slander. Freedom of the press is also subject to the libel laws, and certain secrets vital to national defence cannot be published. Freedom of association allows people to join whatever organizations they wish, as long as these organizations are not of an illegal nature. A bank-robbing gang would be considered an illegal association, and so would a conspiracy to blow up the Parliament

Right margin numbers (per line):
11 3 2
24 8 5
38 12 8
50 17 10
63 21 13
76 25 15
87 29 17
99 33 20
112 37 22
42 25
46 28
47 28
11 51 30
14 55 33
37 59 36
51 64 38
63 68 41
76 71 43
90 77 46
103 81 49
86 51
90 54
94 56
98 59
102 61
64
66
69

1' | 1 | 2 | 3 | 4 | 5 | 6 | 7 | 8 | 9 | 10 | 11 | 12
3' | 1 | 2 | 3 | 4
5' | 1 | 2

DAILY ACTIVITY

If you are beginning a new class period:
1. Adjust the margins for a 50-space line, and
2. Review selected exercises.

THE LETTER Ⓠ

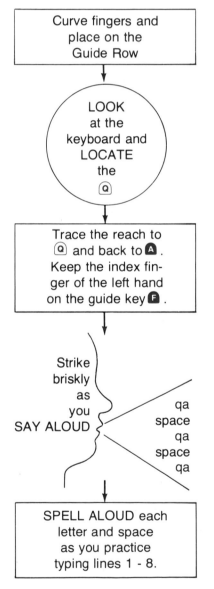

Curve fingers and place on the Guide Row

↓

LOOK at the keyboard and LOCATE the Ⓠ

↓

Trace the reach to Ⓠ and back to Ⓐ. Keep the index finger of the left hand on the guide key Ⓕ.

↓

Strike briskly as you SAY ALOUD

qa space qa space qa

↓

SPELL ALOUD each letter and space as you practice typing lines 1 - 8.

I.21 USING THE Ⓠ

1   qa qa qa quit quit quit quote quote quote quip
2   pique pique pique aqua aqua aqua enquire enquire **DS**

3   acquire acquire acquire acquit acquit acquit quest
4   quest question question quota quota quell quell

5   All office work is done in sequence. He is quick.
6   Sara quilted quicker. There was a quota on grain.

7   The quick question made him stop. He almost quit.
8   Ken enquired if he had a quarter section. He had.

TIMED WRITING

Type the following sentence as many times as you can in one minute. If you type it once you will be typing at 8 words per minute. If you type it one and one-half times, you will be typing at 12 words per minute. If you type it twice, you will be typing at 16 words per minute.

9   A sale of shirts, coats, and hats is on.

| 1 | 2 | 3 | 4 | 5 | 6 | 7 | 8 |

fidelity set which will not play tapes, you might decide to buy a

great many records now while you can still get them, so that your

machine will continue to be useful. If you think that clothing

prices are likely to go down, or that there will be a major change

in fashions next fall, you might think it wise to make your last

year's spring wardrobe do for another season. A person who is

able to adjust spending to economic trends will usually have a

higher standard of living than one who drifts along, buying on

impulse.

SI	1.32
HFW	78%
AWL	4.5
TW	155

Personal decisions, whether made deliberately or un-

consciously, influence the economy. When you put salt on your

potatoes (which you may do without consciously thinking about

it) you affect the national consumption of salt, though by an

amount so small that it is not worth measuring. If you decide to

drink skim instead of whole milk because you want to lose

weight, you will save a few cents a week, because skim milk is

cheaper. At the end of a year you will have saved several dollars,

perhaps without realizing it. If many people do the same thing

the effect on the economy over a period of time will be very

significant. The whole dairy industry will have to adjust to the

change in consumption, and the change in spending patterns

will be felt all over the country.

SI	1.54
HFW	65%
AWL	5.1
TW	99

"Society" and "the economy" are abstract terms, but it

should not be forgotten that societies and economies are made

up of separate and unique human beings. The degree of free-

dom which individuals have in making decisions, either trivial

(like using salt) or serious (like selecting a career), varies from

country to country. In theory, our society is based on a very

special attitude to individual freedom, which contrasts sharply

49	79	47
62	83	50
74	87	52
88	92	55
100	96	58
	100	60
		63
		65
		65
10	3	67
23	8	70
35	12	72
47	16	75
60	20	77
72	24	80
84	28	82
97	32	85
110	37	87
	41	90
	45	92
	49	95
	51	96
11	55	98
23	59	101
35	63	103
47	67	
61	71	
73	75	
86	80	

1' 1 | 2 | 3 | 4 | 5 | 6 | 7 | 8 | 9 | 10 | 11 | 12

3'   1 | 2 | 3 | 4

5'   1 | 2

DAILY ACTIVITY

If you are beginning a new class period:

1. Adjust the margins for a 50-space line, and
2. Review selected exercises.

THE LETTER (V)

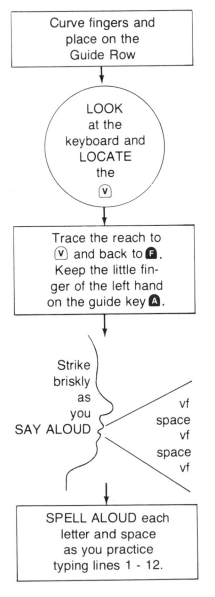

I.22 USING THE (V)

1   vf vf vf vie vie vie van van van vital vital vital
2   solve solve oven oven vigor vigor vim vim various **DS**

3   visa visa visa viper viper viper vice vice vice
4   via via via wives wives lives lives lives waves

5   liver liver liver ever ever seven seven even even
6   vs. vs. vs. vs. quiver quiver quiver view view

7   Please open the oven. The liver is on fire.
8   The review was helpful. It was done with vim.

> *When typing the next four sentences listen for your typewriter bell. When you hear the bell, complete the word you are typing and then return the carriage.*

9   I informed the superintendent in charge of repairs to have the case solved as soon as he can.

10 There is evidence that the oldest stock is not shipped out first.

11 I have reviewed the figures contained in the data sheet Victor provided.

12 At present, a valid method of evaluating our needs is still missing.

Increases in sales and excise taxes mean increased costs for manufacturers, but it is difficult for the government to know in advance whether the burden of the increase will fall on the producer, on the consumer, or on one of the intervening links in the distribution process; or whether it will be shared by all of these. Such uncertainty as to what action producers will take in response to cost changes sometimes has implications for government tax policy.

95	74	44
108	78	47
	82	49
	87	52
	91	54
	95	57
	99	59
	101	60

Timed Writing No. 23

EXERCISING INDIVIDUAL FREEDOMS

An understanding of the economic system — the mechanisms of production, distribution, and exchange — is useful to individual citizens, not only in interpreting the news and deciding how to vote, but in planning their lives. Choosing a career, for example, is an economic as well as a personal decision. You must consider how you would like to earn your living, but you must also take into account the possibility that the job that suits your inclinations will disappear in five or ten years. There is no point in preparing yourself for such a job, unless you are willing to undergo complete retraining at that time. As things are now, it is estimated that most employed persons will have to take some retraining two or three times in their lives, and so will need to keep their ideas flexible. Those who are aware of economic trends are better able to figure out what the new opportunities are likely to be, and can prepare to take advantage of them.

Ordinary household purchasing is also affected by economic trends. If you think that records will be totally replaced by tapes in a few years, and you already have an expensive high

1'	3'	5'
9	3	2
20	7	4
34	11	7
46	15	9
57	19	11
69	23	14
82	27	16
95	32	19
108	36	22
	40	24
	44	26
	48	29
	53	32
	57	34
	61	37
	63	38
10	66	39
23	70	42
36	74	45

1'	1	2	3	4	5	6	7	8	9	10	11	12
3'		1		2		3		4				
5'		1			2							

DAILY ACTIVITY

If you are beginning a new class period:

1. Adjust the margins for a 50-space line, and
2. Review selected exercises from previous pages.

DEVELOPING TYPING CONTINUITY

I.23 REVIEWING ALL PREVIOUSLY LEARNED KEYS

SPELL ALOUD each letter and space as you practice typing lines 1 - 30. When confident that you know the location of all keys, proceed to Exercise I.24.

```
 1   Jim and Carol have entered the competition.
 2   The woman fell as she stepped off the train.  DS

 3   She has asked for our help; we have complied.
 4   I have no talent for, nor interest in, weaving.

 5   The motion was defeated; therefore, we resigned.
 6   Quarrels are often started when people disagree.

 7   Mark has practised the skill for several months.
 8   The train for London leaves at seven each night.

 9   Just then Norman heard a loud crash at the door.
10   Rick Staples scored all the other Winnipeg goals.

11   We must prepare our lunch for the picnic at once.
12   Mr. and Mrs. Charles Cook are going to the movie.

13   Glen sprang to his feet and ran towards the door.
14   Dr. Wild was pleased with our good work, I think.

15   We shall travel to England, Scotland, and France.
16   D. F. Scott reported increases in oats and wheat.

17   The talk, free to students, will include a movie.
18   Mrs. Finn, the author, left for Europe last week.

19   The perfume has a high percentage of perfume oil.
20   Janice was quite willing to assist; Hilda was not.

21   Ann Lim, Kim Price, and Sam Sears were there, too.
22   If he wins this game, he will join the other team.
```

offered for sale. If some of the costs subsequently change, the producer must decide whether or not the changes should be passed on to the consumer. Sometimes a small increase in costs will be absorbed for the time being by the producer, if it is thought that a rise in price is likely to damage sales. One may simply postpone the price rise, but warn consumers that it will take place after; this may have the effect of boosting sales in the meantime. The producer may absorb an increased cost if the volume of sales is large enough to give a satisfactory profit, or may be able to replace the more expensive component with a cheaper substitute.

48	54	95
60	58	97
71	62	99
84	66	102
97	71	105
110	75	
	79	
	83	
	87	
	91	
	93	

SI	1.36
HFW	93%
AWL	4.6
TW	126

Reductions in costs are much less frequent than increases. Where they do occur, the producer may pass them on to the consumer in the form of lower prices. Sometimes, however, if the product has a good market at the established price, the producer may not lower prices immediately. One may not be anxious to stimulate demand: perhaps it would be difficult to increase production. Or one may take the opportunity of a cut in costs to improve quality while maintaining prices. Of course, if competitors cut the prices of very similar products, one will probably have to cut prices too, in order to maintain a share of the market.

10	3	2
22	7	4
34	11	7
47	16	9
60	20	12
72	24	14
85	28	17
98	33	20
110	37	22
	41	25
	42	25

SI	1.41
HFW	82%
AWL	4.9
TW	85

Sometimes a producer uses increased costs as an excuse for raising prices when the costs are not actually increased. For example, reports of snowstorms in Florida have been followed immediately by increases in the price of frozen orange juice, even though it is clear that the producer is continuing to make sales from existing stocks and it will be some time before the smaller crops actually increase the price of oranges.

10	45	27
22	49	29
34	53	32
46	57	34
60	62	37
72	66	39
85	70	42

I.23 REVIEW (Con't)

23 I shovelled the wet snow for two hours last night.
24 Lorraine Hunt will discuss nutrition for children.

> *When the typewriter bell rings, complete the word you are typing and then return the carriage.*

25 The teachers, as well as the students, like the arrangement.

26 Mr. Jensen, the principal, will retire the first of August.

27 The victims of the accident were David W. Ware, Ottawa; U. V. Repper, Toronto; and P. R. Smith, Clinton.

28 When I returned home that night, there was a huge pile of logs near the gate. I was to cut them for firewood.

29 Letters were sent to our friends in Eskasoni, Nova Scotia; Prescott, Ontario; and Chatham, Ontario.

30 For more than a decade Ottawa has given aid to the project.

depend on the level of output. These include the materials used and wages for the number of people employed.

| | 46 | 28 |
| | 49 | 29 |

Although prices are closely related to costs, it is not true to say that costs completely determine prices. In the modern economy, prices for most products tend to be determined in advance. The first step in planning a new product is to decide what kind of product consumers might be interested in buying and what they might be prepared to pay for it—on the basis of the existing prices of products already available. The producer knows that consumers are likely to buy "leather-look" armchairs at a hundred dollars each, but not at five hundred dollars, plans to upholster them in plastic rather than in real leather will be made. If one wants to open a restaurant in an expensive neighborhood, one will plan to charge high prices and budget for prime grades of meat and produce; for a snack bar one would probably buy cheaper goods.

12	53	32
24	57	34
36	61	36
48	65	39
60	69	41
73	73	44
86	77	46
98	82	49
111	86	52
	90	54
	94	56
	98	59
	102	61
		62

Such decisions are immensely complex and must be weighed separately for every stage of the production process, including its final packaging as well as its actual components. In what circumstances will an expensive package add to the "sales appeal" of a product? In what circumstances will it simply raise the overall price to a point where the consumer may refuse to buy, or may buy a rival product instead? Such considerations also extend to service. A shop offering expensive clothes has an expert sales staff; a budget clothes department may be run on a self-service basis.

10	3	64
22	7	67
35	12	69
46	15	72
59	20	74
72	24	77
85	28	79
98	33	82
111	37	84
	38	85

Once a price range is chosen and a cost structure is worked out, production is begun, the market is prepared for the introduction of the new item, and in due course the product is

10	42	87
23	46	90
35	50	92

SI	1.28
HFW	86%
AWL	4.5
TW	183

SI	1.45
HFW	82%
AWL	4.9
TW	117

SI	1.26
HFW	87%
AWL	4.5
TW	169

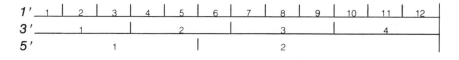

DAILY ACTIVITY

If you are beginning a new class period:

1. Adjust the margins for a 50-space line, and
2. Review selected exercises

THE LETTER Ⓨ

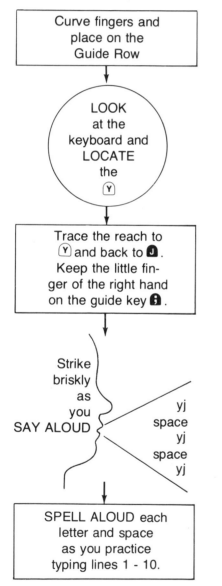

Curve fingers and place on the Guide Row

↓

LOOK at the keyboard and LOCATE the Ⓨ

↓

Trace the reach to Ⓨ and back to Ⓙ. Keep the little finger of the right hand on the guide key Ⓙ.

↓

Strike briskly as you SAY ALOUD

yj space yj space yj

↓

SPELL ALOUD each letter and space as you practice typing lines 1 - 10.

1.24 USING THE Ⓨ

```
 1  yj yj yj yell yell yell yellow yellow yellow yes
 2  my my you you your your any any day day already DS

 3  yard yard yard year year year yet yet yet you you
 4  your your your youth youth youth they they they

 5  loyal loyal query query royal royal key key key
 6  joys joys joys eye eye eye fry fry fry gray gray

 7  They had no idea why this item was not included.
 8  Many decisions made from day to day are routine.

 9  It is part of his duty to help those in need.
10  Every voter should demand a statement of policy.
```

when water melting on the roof over the heated part of the house | 77 | 26 | 39
runs down onto the cold eaves and refreezes. The same hap- | 89 | 30 | 42
pens again when the slope of the roof forms a valley which | 101 | 34 | 44
retains the water behind the dam and allows it to infiltrate under | | 38 | 47
the shingles and drip into the house. Do not wait for this to | | 42 | 49
happen. Anticipate the formation of these ice barriers. Remove | | 46 | 52
the leaves which have become stuck in the eavestroughs during | | 50 | 54
the fall and which prevent the water from going on its way. If you | | 55 | 57
have ice dams forming due to melting water refreezing at the | | 59 | 59
eaves, ask an expert for help. There are a number of solutions. | | 63 | 62

One of these solutions, and a way to save yourself work, | 11 | 67 | 64
is to install a heated electric wire along the edge of the roof. This | 25 | 72 | 67
will melt the ice or melt channels through the ice so the | 37 | 75 | 69
dammed-up water can drain away. This type of insulation is | 48 | 79 | 72
expensive and will make the monthly electricity bill go up. Do not | 62 | 84 | 74
do anything until you have consulted an electrician. | 72 | 87 | 76

Now it's your turn to shout advice from all the rooftops. | 83 | 91 | 79

SI	1.25
HFW	79%
AWL	4.3
TW	74

SI	1.18
HFW	73%
AWL	4.2
TW	11

Timed Writing
No. 22

SI	1.35
HFW	87%
AWL	4.7
TW	921

SI	1.36
HFW	88%
AWL	4.7
TW	149

PRICES IN THE MODERN ECONOMY

	1'	3'	5'
The price of any given product reflects the cost of making	12	4	2
it. Costs in turn are determined by the prices of the various	24	8	5
goods and services required in the production process. There	36	12	7
are the initial research costs, as the producer investigates the	49	16	10
market and decides what to produce and how to do it. There are	62	21	12
capital costs for acquiring land and buildings and equipping a	74	25	15
factory; these costs are amortized in equal payments over a	86	29	17
period of years. There are fixed or overhead costs—the factory	99	33	20
must be lighted and heated whether it is operating at full capac-	112	37	22
ity or at half that rate. Finally, there are variable costs which		42	25

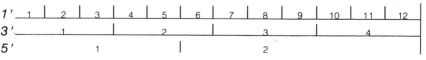

DAILY ACTIVITY

If you are beginning a new class period:

1. Adjust the margins for a 50-space line, and
2. Review selected exercises.

THE LETTER Ⓑ

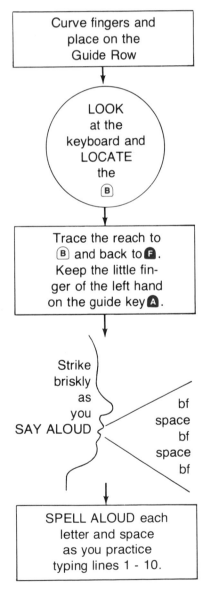

I.25 USING THE Ⓑ

```
1   bf bf bf buff buff buff bus bus bus bill bill bill
2   ball ball ball but but but by by by bit bit bit
```
DS

```
3   balance balance balance back back back buy buy buy
4   bank bank bank tub tub tub stub stub stub be be be

5   been been been before before before brave brave
6   quibble quibble quibble rib rib rib crib crib crib

7   The new way is not said to be better, but easier.
8   A blue ribbon was used to tie the big parcel.

9   She will be busy planning the breakfast or brunch.
10  He feels much better because he has a good job.
```

TIMED WRITING

Type the following sentence as many times as you can in one minute. If you type it once you will be typing at 8 words per minute. If you type it one and one-half times, you will be typing at 12 words per minute. If you type it twice, you will be typing at 16 words per minute.

```
11  She feels so happy because he has a job.

   |   1   |   2   |   3   |   4   |   5   |   6   |   7   |   8   |
```

from poorly insulated buildings. This loss of heat can be reduced if the amount of insulation material in the attic is increased. In addition, to prevent condensation and frost formation in the attic which will melt in hot days and drip onto your ceiling, there should be adequate ventilation between the insulation which is lying on the top of the ceiling and the roof. There should be at least a one square metre opening for every 300 m² of insulated ceiling. These openings, or vents, can be placed on the roof, or in the gables, or under the eaves, or in all these places. Make sure they are placed in such a way as to ensure that there is cross ventilation in the attic and that no obstacle stops the air from getting through.

While examining the roof ventilation see how much insulation you have. In moderately cold regions, there should be 10 cm of soft insulation; in colder areas, 15 cm (make inquiries about this through the local building service of the Central Mortgage and Housing Corporation or your municipal building inspector and also ask about vapor barriers).

With regard to snow on your roof, you can call on expert snow removal services; but because of the demand these are sometimes difficult to obtain. Check the amount of snow on the roof of your house frequently. Removal can then be carried out regularly.

To remove ice, proceed very carefully in order not to damage the roof. Use a shovel or the blunt end of an axe on a mild day, if possible, when the ice will come off more easily and with less effort on your part.

Eavestroughs are places where miniature dams form and allow ice or water to accumulate. These ice dams also occur

SI	1.55
HFW	65%
AWL	5.2
TW	70

SI	1.31
HFW	80%
AWL	4.5
TW	51

SI	1.18
HFW	82%
AWL	3.7
TW	43

SI	1.30
HFW	70%
AWL	4.4
TW	149

57	19	71
69	23	74
82	27	76
95	32	79
107	36	81
	40	84
	44	86
	48	89
	53	91
	57	94
	61	96
	64	98
11	67	2
23	71	5
36	76	7
48	80	10
60	84	12
69	87	14
80	90	16
92	94	19
104	98	21
	103	24
		24
11	4	26
23	8	29
36	12	31
42	14	32
53	18	35
65	22	37

1' 1 2 3 4 5 6 7 8 9 10 11 12
3'   1   2   3   4
5'   1   2

DAILY ACTIVITY

If you are beginning a new class period:
1. Adjust the margins for a 50-space line, and
2. Review selected exercises.

THE LETTER ⓧ

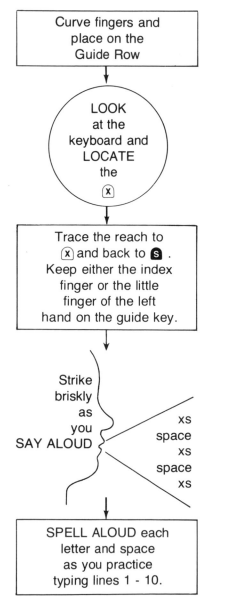

Curve fingers and place on the Guide Row

LOOK at the keyboard and LOCATE the ⓧ

Trace the reach to ⓧ and back to Ⓢ. Keep either the index finger or the little finger of the left hand on the guide key.

Strike briskly as you SAY ALOUD

xs
space
xs
space
xs

SPELL ALOUD each letter and space as you practice typing lines 1 - 10.

I.26 USING THE ⓧ

1 xs xs xs ox ox ox fox fox fox box box box tax tax
2 express express express extra extra extra six six   **DS**

3 expire expire expire expell expell expell axe axe
4 exact exact exact executive executive executive

5 expert expert expert expense expense expense jinx
6 index index index fix fix fix lax lax lax sax sax

7 exam exam exam exit exit exit external externally
8 We are quite sure the schedule will extend to May.

Listen for the bell.

9 It changes the typing of letters from a dull grind to an exciting exercise.

10 If you have been lax in recent years, the time has come for you to get out the books again.

Component I/The Alphabetic Keyboard

SI	1.18
HFW	82%
AWL	4.2
TW	35

SI	1.38
HFW	81%
AWL	4.7
TW	43

SI	1.20
HFW	61%
AWL	4.7
TW	69

SI	1.34
HFW	80%
AWL	4.1
TW	46

SI	1.59
HFW	60%
AWL	5.6
TW	36

SI	1.31
HFW	64%
AWL	4.6
TW	48

SI	1.14
HFW	62%
AWL	4.8
TW	24

SI	1.47
HFW	83%
AWL	4.6
TW	34

SI	1.31
HFW	75%
AWL	4.3
TW	155

The roof is probably the most important part of a building. In addition to protecting the building against bad weather, it must ensure the comfort of the occupants and protect their goods. And that's no mean feat!

In Canada roofs have to carry heavy snow loads. Freshly fallen snow is usually loose and fluffy. Soon after it lands, the snow crystals are changed into small irregularly shaped grains which pack together more easily. A period of mild weather and rain falling into the snow, makes it sodden and very heavy and increases its density even further.

The accumulation of snow on a roof naturally varies from one winter to the next, but it also depends to a great extent on the climate, orientation of the dwelling-place, its exposure to wind, and on the form and type of its roof.

Roofs situated below an adjacent higher roof are particularly susceptible to heavy drift loads caused by the wind. The same accumulations occur on awnings, canopies, and balconies.

Flat roofs with projections often accumulate snow in the form of cone shaped "dunes" which can reach the height of the projection on the building, but ordinarily, the mass of these drifts is less than on low roofs adjacent to higher roofs.

Pointed or sloping roofs exposed to the wind, produce poorly balanced loads that are often higher than those on the ground.

In general, building standards have been developed so as to determine the mass a roof can bear and to reduce to a minimum the accident hazards its collapse could provoke.

Snow melts due to radiation from the sun and heat loss

47	16	9
59	20	12
71	24	14
77	26	15
88	29	18
102	34	20
	38	23
	42	25
	46	28
	49	29
11	52	31
25	57	34
38	61	37
45	64	38
57	67	40
69	72	43
80	75	45
82	76	45
11	80	48
23	84	50
37	88	53
47	92	55
58	95	57
70	99	59
71	100	60
11	4	62
22	7	64
34	11	66
44	15	69

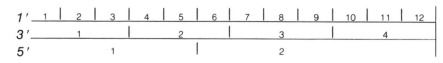

DAILY ACTIVITY

If you are beginning a new class period:

1. Adjust the margins for a 50-space line, and
2. Review selected exercises.

THE LETTER Z

```
┌─────────────────────────┐
│    Curve fingers and    │
│    place on the         │
│    Guide Row            │
└─────────────────────────┘
            │
            ▼
      ╭───────────╮
      │   LOOK    │
      │  at the   │
      │ keyboard and │
      │  LOCATE   │
      │   the     │
      │    Z      │
      ╰───────────╯
            │
            ▼
┌─────────────────────────┐
│  Trace the reach to     │
│  Z and back to A .      │
│  Keep the index fin-    │
│  ger of the left hand   │
│  on the guide key F .   │
└─────────────────────────┘
            │
            ▼
    Strike
    briskly
      as              za
      you           space
    SAY ALOUD         za
                    space
                      za
            │
            ▼
┌─────────────────────────┐
│  SPELL ALOUD each       │
│  letter and space       │
│  as you practice        │
│  typing lines 1 - 6.    │
└─────────────────────────┘
```

I.27 USING THE Z

1 za za za zone zone zone zoo zoo zoo zero zero zero
2 prize prize zoom zoom ozone ozone zeal zeal zeal **DS**

3 Voting is not the only duty of a citizen.
4 One should minimize the chance of failure.

┌─────────────────────────┐
│ *Listen for the bell.* │
└─────────────────────────┘

5 One youth who was undecided about his proper field
   held a half dozen jobs while attending school.

6 We have an attitude toward life demanding fairness
   toward all citizens. Let us recognize this.

are infringed upon, shareholders may apply for a court order obliging the company to comply with the law.

Whereas the bondholder can expect regular payment of interest, the common shareholder cannot. Many companies do, however, make a habit of paying a regular dividend, no matter how small, because it enhances the prestige of the particular issue and of the corporation. The decision whether to pay a dividend, when to pay it, and for what amount, is made by the board of directors, who in turn have been elected by the shareholders.

Sometimes an extra dividend may be declared by the board of directors to pass on to shareholders the increased earnings of a particular period. By declaring it an "extra" dividend they are telling the investor that it is not to be expected as a regular thing, but there is some reason to think it may happen again.

Dividend cheques are mailed directly to the holder as of the dividend record date, which is usually two to four weeks ahead of the payment date. If the stock is a "street certificate" (registered in the name of a stockbroker rather than of a private individual), the dividend will be paid to the broker or dealer whose name appears on the certificate. The broker will send the client a cheque for the amount owing. On the other hand, the broker may simply enter the amount of the dividend in the account of the shareholder.

73	97	15
82	100	16
10	3	18
22	7	21
35	12	23
47	16	26
59	20	28
71	24	31
84	28	33
85	28	33
10	32	35
22	36	38
35	40	40
48	45	43
61	49	46
62	49	46
74	53	48
86	57	51
99	61	53
112	66	56
	70	58
	74	61
	78	63
	82	65
	84	67

SI	1.42
HFW	92%
AWL	4.7
TW	86

SI	1.37
HFW	89%
AWL	4.4
TW	63

SI	1.31
HFW	93%
AWL	4.5
TW	105

Timed Writing No. 21

SI	1.32
HFW	73%
AWL	4.5
TW	888

KEEP AN EYE ON YOUR ROOF

Enough advice has been shouted from the rooftops, now it's time to talk about the roof itself. What can you do to protect the roof of your house, perhaps even prolong its life?

1'	3'	5'
11	4	2
24	8	5
35	12	7

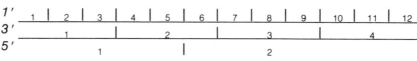

DAILY ACTIVITY
If you are beginning a new class period:
1. Adjust the margins for a 50-space line, and
2. Review selected exercises.

THE QUESTION MARK ⟨?⟩

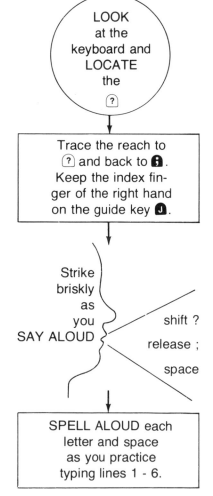

Curve fingers and place on the Guide Row

LOOK at the keyboard and LOCATE the ⟨?⟩

Trace the reach to ⟨?⟩ and back to ⟨;⟩. Keep the index finger of the right hand on the guide key ⟨J⟩.

Strike briskly as you SAY ALOUD
shift ?
release ;
space

SPELL ALOUD each letter and space as you practice typing lines 1 - 6.

I.28 USING THE ⟨?⟩

> *Leave two spaces after the question mark.*

1 ?; ?; ?; Who? What? Where? When? Why?
2 Is it? Who is it? What is it? Is it you? **DS**

3 What is being done by whom? Is it necessary?
4 Are we ready for the next upturn?

5 Who is to say when the end of progress may be?
6 Are we getting our share of the current market?

TIMED WRITING

Type the following sentence as many times as you can in one minute. If you type it once you will be typing at 10 words per minute. If you type it one and one-half times, you will be typing at 15 words per minute. If you type it twice, you will be typing at 20 words per minute.

7 The water is not used for drinking or for cooking.

| 1 | 2 | 3 | 4 | 5 | 6 | 7 | 8 | 9 | 10 |

pute will then canvass the other shareholders asking for their votes. Thus one or a few shareholders, quite insignificant in terms of the number of shares represented, might be able to muster enough support to effectively oppose the directors and carry the vote.

SI	1.44
HFW	97%
AWL	4.9
TW	48

If enough shareholders demand it, a special shareholders' meeting must be called. This does not replace the annual meeting, which must be called by the board of directors; rather, it is an occasion to air special problems or grievances.

SI	1.58
HFW	94%
AWL	4.9
TW	60

Sometimes an investment dealer who has underwritten some or all of the securities of the corporation in question may take the necessary action to have a special meeting if the situation warrants it. He has a responsibility, both to the corporation and to the public who have bought the securities.

SI	1.54
HFW	82%
AWL	5.3
TW	115

It is not always possible for shareholders to attend the annual meeting. By signing a proxy, shareholders can give their votes to another shareholder. Before doing so, one would think a shareholder would seriously consider the issues involved. In practice, however, the majority of shareholders are apathetic about the corporation's affairs. One result of the combination of apathy and the proxy system is that huge corporations are often managed by directors whose combined ownership of common stock may be a very small percentage of the total shares outstanding.

SI	1.25
HFW	88%
AWL	4.6
TW	83

The right to vote for and elect directors and to share in the growth of the company places the holder of common shares in a very different position from the person who holds bonds or preferred shares. But many shareholders do not understand their rights and privileges. Nor do they know that if their rights

87	52	
91	55	
95	57	
99	60	
100	60	
11	4	62
23	8	65
36	12	67
47	16	70
58	19	72
70	23	74
82	27	77
96	32	79
107	36	82
11	40	84
24	44	86
37	48	89
49	52	91
62	56	94
75	60	97
87	65	99
98	68	101
111	72	
	73	
12	77	2
24	81	5
36	85	7
48	89	10
61	93	12

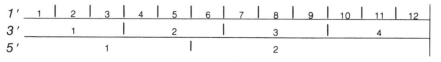

1′ | 1 | 2 | 3 | 4 | 5 | 6 | 7 | 8 | 9 | 10 | 11 | 12
3′ | 1 | 2 | 3 | 4
5′ | 1 | 2

DAILY ACTIVITY
If you are beginning a new class period:
1. Adjust the margins for a 50-space line, and
2. Review selected exercises.

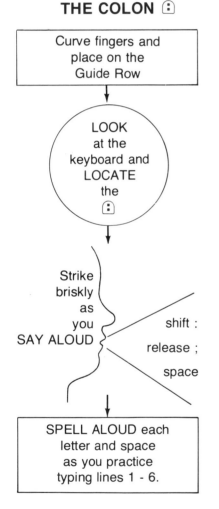

THE COLON :

Curve fingers and place on the Guide Row

↓

LOOK at the keyboard and LOCATE the :

↓

Strike briskly as you SAY ALOUD

shift :

release ;

space

↓

SPELL ALOUD each letter and space as you practice typing lines 1 - 6.

I.29 USING THE :

Leave two spaces after a colon that appears within a typewritten line.

1   :; :; :; To: From: Type: Date: Gentlemen:
2   Dear Sir: Dear Joan: Dear Mr. Smith: Sir: Sir: **DS**

3   They began to ask: What do we want of life?
4   Have these girls do the work: Mae, Sue, and Jane.

5   How much of what we want of the good life can society give us? Even jesters ask that question.

6   I have the following items: staples, stapler box, scissors, tape, and ruler. Are you amazed?

thirty-five per cent. Or, when the supplier charges five per cent | 85 | 28 | 48
on all past due accounts — usually accounts that are owed for | 97 | 32 | 51
more than sixty days — the effective interest rate is slightly more | 110 | 37 | 53
than thirty per cent. In both instances it would make sense for the | | 41 | 56
entrepreneur to borrow money, if necessary, to pay the bill on | | 45 | 59
time. | | 46 | 59

THE CORPORATION AND THE SHAREHOLDER

	1′	3′	5′
Every incorporated company must have at least three	10	3	2
common shareholders. They are the legal owners and they elect	23	8	5
the directors, who run the company, from among themselves.	34	11	7
One vote is usually allowed for each share held, although be-	46	15	9
cause of share splits, the voting power may be differently ar-	59	20	12
ranged. Management is responsible to the common sharehold-	71	24	14
ers and must report to them at least once a year. Copies of the	83	28	17
company's annual report must be sent to all shareholders. Cer-	96	32	19
tain of the company's books — for example, the register of	107	36	21
shareholders — must be made available to a shareholder if he		40	24
asks for it.		41	24
In a private company there may be only a small number of	11	44	27
common shareholders, each of whom can exercise a significant	23	48	29
influence. But the large public corporation has hundreds of	35	52	31
common shareholders, who may seem very remote from man-	46	56	34
agement. Does this mean that the individual shareholder has no	59	60	36
real voice in the affairs of the company?	67	63	38
It may and it may not. Take, for example, a situation where	79	67	40
a small shareholder holds views strongly opposed to those of	91	71	42
the present board of directors. He is aware of a certain sym-	103	75	45
pathy for his views among the other shareholders, and he pro-		79	47
ceeds to organize an opposition group. Both sides in the dis-		83	50

Timed Writing
No. 20

SI	1.33
HFW	89%
AWL	4.8
TW	864

SI	1.47
HFW	91%
AWL	4.9
TW	123

SI	1.51
HFW	86%
AWL	4.9
TW	68

SI	1.39
HFW	81%
AWL	4.8
TW	113

1′ | 1 | 2 | 3 | 4 | 5 | 6 | 7 | 8 | 9 | 10 | 11 | 12
3′ | | 1 | | 2 | | 3 | | 4
5′ | | 1 | | 2

DAILY ACTIVITY

If you are beginning a new class period:

1. Adjust the margins for a 50-space line, and
2. Review selected exercises.

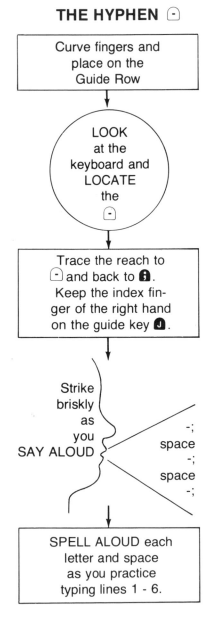

THE HYPHEN ⊙

Curve fingers and place on the Guide Row

↓

LOOK at the keyboard and LOCATE the ⊙

↓

Trace the reach to ⊙ and back to **J**. Keep the index finger of the right hand on the guide key **J**.

↓

Strike briskly as you SAY ALOUD

-;
space
-;
space
-;

↓

SPELL ALOUD each letter and space as you practice typing lines 1 - 6.

I.30 USING THE ⊙

In hyphenated words no space is left before or after the hyphen.

1   -; -; -; in-law non-stop co-trustee brother-in-law
2   co-operate in-law above-named non-stop co-ordinate **DS**

3   His brother-in-law is flying non-stop to Toronto.
4   The co-trustee must co-sign the above-noted form.

5   I hope he will co-operate with the vice-president.
6   He has fifty-two shares in the local co-operative.

WORD DIVISION

As a general rule, DON'T divide words. However, in order to make typewritten lines approximately equal in length, some words may have to be divided. Below are a few basic rules for dividing words in typewritten matter. For a complete listing of rules refer to Appendix B, page 340.

1. *Divide words only between syllables, such as* <u>accom-modate</u>.
2. *Divide compound hyphenated words at the hyphen, such as* <u>non-stop</u>.
3. *Do not divide one syllable words, such as* <u>through</u>.
4. *Do not divide four or five letter words, such as* <u>also</u> *and* <u>alone</u>.
5. *Do not divide a word unless you can type three strokes before the division (one of which may be the hyphen), and three strokes after the division; such as* <u>let-ter</u>.

---

shares—in other words, by increasing the risk capital, or equity. It can also increase its risk capital by putting earnings, or profits, back into the business, or by making leasing or franchising arrangements for certain long-term needs such as equipment or advertising.

Generally, the same companies and institutions that make loans to individuals are also in the business of extending short-term loans, or loans for working capital purposes, to businesses.

Businesses make use of many of the forms of service credit extended to individuals—for light, heat, telephones, and all those services and utilities which are paid for once a month or every few months.

In addition to these forms of service credit, most businesses benefit from the regular use of credit extended by suppliers of all kinds. Goods not paid for on delivery are, in effect, "borrowed" until the invoice is paid. The terms of repayment may vary with the supplier and the borrower's reputation.

It is the practice of some suppliers to offer a cash discount for prompt payment. The individual may come across this in the form of a discount on a utility bill, such as hydro, if payment is made by a certain date. Alternatively, a service charge is levied on overdue accounts.

For a business with many expenses it may become quite significant to be able to take proper advantage of any discounts and avoid any unnecessary charges. For instance, when the supplier allows a one per cent cash discount if payment is made within ten days after the invoice or the goods are received, computed on an annual basis the effective interest is more than

SI	1.53	
HFW	71%	
AWL	5.6	
TW	37	

SI	1.25	
HFW	89%	
AWL	4.7	
TW	41	

SI	1.39	
HFW	86%	
AWL	4.8	
TW	61	

SI	1.39	
HFW	92%	
AWL	4.4	
TW	56	

SI	1.36	
HFW	91%	
AWL	4.8	
TW	1.39	

73	24	85
87	29	88
98	33	90
111	37	92
113	38	93
10	41	95
23	45	97
35	49	100
37	50	
47	53	2
60	58	5
73	62	7
77	63	8
11	67	10
24	71	13
37	76	15
49	80	18
61	83	20
72	87	22
85	91	25
99	96	28
111	100	30
116	102	31
11	4	33
23	8	36
35	12	38
48	16	41
60	20	43
72	24	46

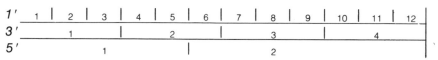

1' 1 | 2 | 3 | 4 | 5 | 6 | 7 | 8 | 9 | 10 | 11 | 12
3'   1 | 2 | 3 | 4
5'   1 | 2

If you are beginning a new class period:

1. Adjust the margins for a 50-space line, and
2. Review selected exercises.

THE MARGIN RELEASE KEY (MR)

If your MR key is not located as illustrated, your instructor will assist you in locating the key and in selecting the appropriate finger to use.

Listen for the typewriter bell. It alerts you to three possible courses of action:

1. *carriage-return at end of word,*
2. *selection of a suitable word division, or*
3. *use of the (MR) without dividing the word.*

I.31 USING THE (MR)

The margin-release key (MR) allows you to type beyond the margin. On some machines the (MR) is operated by the little finger of the right hand — the (A) finger. To type outside the right margin after the carriage is locked, depress the (MR) key and continue typing.

The following lines will give you practise in using the (MR) key.

1   His eyelids closed; his head dropped; and he was fast asleep. **DS**

2   How much are these shoes? What did the class decide to do?

3   Naturally, my project had to be one that I could do after school. I could see it; I could hardly wait to draw it.

4   The Canadian Consumer Council is an independent group appointed to advise the Minister of Consumer and Corporate Affairs.

5   It was a grimy, dusty, antique piano. First, it took me a lot longer to get ready that afternoon than I thought it would.

SI	1.39
HFW	91%
AWL	4.8
TW	76

SI	1.67
HFW	77%
AWL	5.9
TW	87

SI	1.48
HFW	91%
AWL	5.1
TW	70

SI	1.51
HFW	77%
AWL	4.9
TW	115

business. For a business to run smoothly, the owners or managers should be able to anticipate that current assets will sufficiently exceed current liabilities to meet these operating costs.

Working capital needs are usually considered in terms of the length of the operating cycle of the business. Sometimes, though, a certain amount of money may be needed for a week, or for a few months, to maintain the business during a slack period. This requires short-term financing. Short-term funds may be required for other reasons, perhaps to carry out a change of ownership.

Short-term funds are usually obtained from one or more of the following sources of credit: merchants and dealers who extend "open account" privileges, generally known as trade or service credit, to their customers; chartered banks and other financial institutions, such as acceptance companies; and discounting and factoring companies. Leasing and franchising agreements can also be significant in maintaining working capital needs.

Normally, when the owners of a business decide they need additional funds, they anticipate that an increase in profits will follow. Conditions might be such that expansion would be a wise move. Perhaps the plant or store building needs thorough renovation. It may be desirable to buy a related business. All of these require long-term financing.

Long-term and medium-term funds can be obtained in a number of ways: by contracting debts in the form of medium or long-term loans or by issuing bonds or debentures. Alternatively, the company may choose to enlarge the ownership or the business, either by taking in new partners or by issuing more

Col 1	Col 2	Col 3
95	32	19
108	36	22
	40	24
11	44	26
23	48	29
35	52	31
47	56	34
60	60	36
71	64	38
75	65	39
86	69	41
98	73	44
110	77	46
	81	49
	85	51
	89	54
	93	56
	94	56
10	98	59
23	102	61
36		64
49		66
62		69
69		70
10	3	72
23	8	75
35	12	77
47	16	80
59	20	82

1' | 1 | 2 | 3 | 4 | 5 | 6 | 7 | 8 | 9 | 10 | 11 | 12

3' | 1 | 2 | 3 | 4

5' | 1 | 2

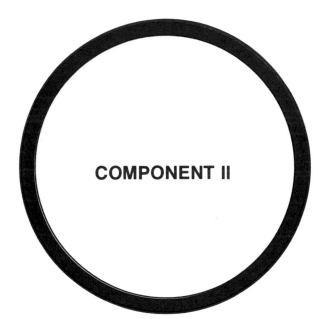

COMPONENT II

CONTENTS

Component II includes the following types of skill-development materials:

Paragraphs for reinforcing the location of the alphabetic keys and for developing continuity of typing.

Alphabetic sentences designed to provide daily practice on all letters of the alphabet.

Capitalization exercises.

Word division exercises.

Speed escalator sentences.

Speed escalator paragraphs.

Error-elimination sentences designed to overcome common letter substitution errors.

Difficult reach sentences.

DEVELOPING ALPHABETIC KEYBOARD CONTINUITY

STUDENT OBJECTIVES

1. To type with continuity.

2. To acquire a minimum speed of 25 words per minute.

3. To develop confidence in alphabetic key selection so that looking at the keyboard will become unnecessary.

DAILY ACTIVITIES

Preliminary:

1. Set your margins for a 60-space line.

2. Alphabetic sentence typing. Select and type several times an alphabetic sentence from pages 53 to 54.

Main:

Paragraph typing. Select and type a number of paragraphs to develop continuity. At least half of the class period should be devoted to the typing of paragraphs which appear on pages 37 to 52.

Supplementary:

1. Speed escalator practice. Select and type a sentence from page 57 or a paragraph from pages 58 to 62.

| | 111 | 62 | 100 |
to bid too low, the vendor might react negatively or insist upon

the full price. | 114 | 63 | |

A higher price might be grabbed immediately and then | 10 | 66 | 2 |

you will be left wondering if you could have purchased the realty | 23 | 70 | 5 |

for a bit less. You'll never be sure. | 30 | 73 | 6 |

Armed with all the information you can get about the sale, | 42 | 76 | 8 |

and considering what you can afford, make an offer that is a little | 55 | 81 | 11 |

lower than what you sincerely believe to be fair under the cir- | 68 | 85 | 14 |

cumstances. | 70 | 86 | 14 |

It may not be accepted, but if it is not an insulting offer, | 82 | 90 | 16 |

you will undoubtedly find it countersigned by the vendor with | 94 | 94 | 19 |

another price which you can accept, or negotiate further. And if | 107 | 98 | 21 |

by some chance your offer is accepted, you can smile and | | 102 | 24 |

consider yourself a shrewd buyer. | | | 25 |

Of course, there are cases where you will rightfully offer a | 12 | 4 | 27 |

full price (or even more) for a property you absolutely MUST | 24 | 8 | 30 |

have. | 25 | 8 | 30 |

But remember, an offer is the most important step in | 35 | 12 | 32 |

purchasing any real estate. Think it out well in advance, make a | 48 | 16 | 35 |

realistic offer, and you probably won't be sorry. | 58 | 19 | 37 |

Timed Writing No. 19

MANAGING CASH EFFECTIVELY

| | 1' | 3' | 5' |

Before a business commences operation the long-term | 10 | 3 | 2 |

capital needs of the business must be carefully assessed. This | 23 | 8 | 5 |

involves many things besides buildings and equipment or in- | 35 | 12 | 7 |

ventory. It also includes working capital—building maintenance | 47 | 16 | 9 |

and utilities, taxes, transportation and shipping costs, the | 59 | 20 | 12 |

wages paid out to hired personnel, and the many other ex- | 71 | 24 | 14 |

penses that are incurred in the day-to-day operation of the | 83 | 28 | 17 |

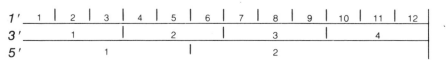

1' 1 2 3 4 5 6 7 8 9 10 11 12
3' 1 2 3 4
5' 1 2

2. Capitalization practice. Select and type one or two sentences from page 55.

3. Word division practice. Select and type one or two sentences from page 56.

4. Error-elimination practice. Select and type one or two error-elimination sentences from pages 63 to 66.

5. Difficult reach practice. Select and type one or two difficult reach sentences from page 67.

6. One-, three-, and five-minute timed writings. Select a practised sentence or paragraph from any of the pages in Component II. Some practice should be devoted to building speed; some to improving accuracy.

PUNCTUATION SPACING

<u>*Space twice after:*</u>
    a period at the end of a sentence
    a question mark at the end of a sentence
    an exclamation mark at the end of a sentence
    a colon

<u>*Space once after:*</u>
    a comma
    a period that follows an abbreviation or initial
    a semicolon

SI	1.18
HFW	86%
AWL	4.1
TW	93

SI	1.17
HFW	89%
AWL	4.1
TW	79

SI	1.30
HFW	80%
AWL	4.5
TW	46

SI	1.31
HFW	84%
AWL	4.3
TW	36

SI	1.13
HFW	85%
AWL	3.8
TW	39

SI	1.23
HFW	88%
AWL	4.2
TW	69

SI	1.24
HFW	94%
AWL	4.8
TW	19

SI	1.27
HFW	85%
AWL	4.3
TW	28

much would it take to get them out of there? Certainly a lot more than one would care to pay, and in isolated cases money would NEVER move them.

The next price tag down the scale is that of an owner who is "thinking of selling" but hasn't reached the point of making a firm decision about it. An offer could be made to this owner. The $75 000 home might be purchased for slightly more than its market value, but if one fails with such an offer, the result will be a "free appraisal" of the realty and inflation of the owner's ego.

Now we're approaching a more reasonable situation. The house that is on the market. (The overpriced listings can be flushed out with a bit of viewing, so we'll ignore them.) How much does one offer for property on the market?

Do a little probing. Reasons for selling can have a great bearing on price. Has the vendor bought another house? Is there a break-up in the family? Is the vendor leaving town?

This leads us to the lowest price tags of all: distress selling. The owner has to leave town in two weeks and wants the equity in cash right away. If you have the cash, you can get a bargain.

Another bargain could be the result of a feared final order of foreclosure. Time is running out and the vendor has taken no action to force a judicial sale of the property, which could leave some cash. A final order of foreclosure is a sad thing for the owner — everything is lost — unless a buyer can be found in a hurry who will close quickly.

Once you know the circumstances surrounding the sale, you are ready to make an offer. How much?

This calls for some calculations on your part. If you begin

76	59	35
88	63	38
91	64	38
11	68	41
24	72	43
38	76	46
49	80	48
64	85	51
76	89	54
87	93	56
100	97	58
	102	61
		63
11	4	65
23	8	67
35	12	70
46	15	72
59	20	74
72	24	77
73	24	77
12	28	80
25	33	82
38	37	85
50	41	87
62	45	90
68	47	91
78	50	93
87	53	95
99	57	97

1′ 1 | 2 | 3 | 4 | 5 | 6 | 7 | 8 | 9 | 10 | 11 | 12
3′   1 | 2 | 3 | 4
5′   1 | 2

PARAGRAPHS II.1 Your typewriter should be set for a 60-space line. Use single spacing but remember to double space between paragraphs.

Paragraph 1 We trust that our quotation meets with your approval. Should you require further information, please feel free to contact us.

Paragraph 2 Now that you are ready to look at houses, real estate agents and the local newspaper classified section will provide a great many leads.

Paragraph 3 You should protect your investment in your home and its contents from loss through fire, damage from the elements, theft, and other perils.

Paragraph 4 For additional information, a factory-trained sales representative is available to give you immediate service. His name is listed below.

Paragraph 5 It is your responsibility to see that this program is thoroughly and completely carried out in order that the information generated will be meaningful.

Paragraph 6 Sometimes just a small sticker, a simple notice, or a reminder placed or printed on the statement is all that is required to stimulate a customer who is tardy.

Paragraph 7 I am confident that there will be price increases in the very near future, and I would strongly urge you to consider your spring requirements now for immediate delivery.

Paragraph 8 There is no indication in the correspondence you attached to your letter that the proper gaskets and washers were used in the installation of these boards.

machinery, and other equipment, with which to carry out the technical process are required. As long as a person must catch, clean, and preserve one's own fish for sale, one's output will be limited by the amount of time and energy one has, and there will be no way one can increase it. If a large trawler is available with a freezing plant on board, the combined output of those working on the vessel will be far larger than the sum of what each could produce by oneself.

It is the existence of plant, machinery, and equipment (built with technical knowledge) which largely determines the growth potential of an economy.

36	89	7
49	93	10
62	97	12
75	102	15
89		18
101		20
		23
		23
11		26
23		28
29		29

SI	1.55
HFW	82%
AWL	5.5
TW	30

Timed Writing No. 18

SI	1.24
HFW	85%
AWL	4.3
TW	695

SI	1.20
HFW	60%
AWL	4.8
TW	23

SI	1.34
HFW	72%
AWL	4.8
TW	38

SI	1.05
HFW	91%
AWL	3.9
TW	23

SI	1.13
HFW	80%
AWL	4.5
TW	16

DON'T BE AFRAID TO MAKE AN OFFER

In 1867 the United States Government offered Russia $7 200 000 worth of 1867 gold for Alaska and the deal was sealed.

Later, it was discovered that Alaska could have been purchased for five million dollars (which, incidentally, is about the current value of a well-placed 75 by 30 m lot in downtown Toronto).

"Buy land, they're not making any more of it," said the late Will Rogers. Fine, but what about the offer? How much?

There are four basic price tags on every parcel of privately owned land in Canada.

The highest is on the land that is not for sale. Walk in cold on a family with a dream house, where they are comfortable, compatible with their neighbors, have a nice garden, are settled in the community, and are supremely happy with their home and life style. If that home has a current market value of $75 000, how

1'	3'	5'
10	3	2
22	7	4
23	8	5
33	11	7
46	15	9
59	20	12
60	20	12
71	24	14
84	28	17
95	32	19
100	33	20
12	38	23
24	41	25
37	46	27
49	50	30
63	54	33

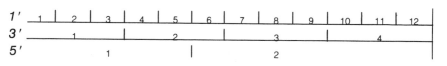

Paragraph   **9**   You will generally pay less for your car insurance if you do not have a bad claim or driving conviction record. Safe driving helps keep down your insurance rates.

Paragraph   **10**   We wish to thank you for the order received in the mail today. We are shipping the goods on open account with the understanding that the account will be paid in thirty days.

The ease with which a paragraph can be typed is influenced by syllable intensity (SI), percentage of high-frequency words (HFW), and by the average word length (AWL).

As SI and AWL increase, and as HFW decreases, the more difficult the material becomes.

DETERMINING WORDS PER MINUTE

1. *Read the scale at the right of the page opposite the last* <u>complete</u> *line typed. If the timing was for one minute, use the first column; if for three minutes, the second column; if for five minutes, the third column.*

2. *Read the scale at the bottom of the page below the last word of a* <u>partly</u> *finished line. Use the first row for one minute timings; the second row for three minute timings; the third row for five minute timings.*

3. *Add the extra words typed to the number of words typed at the end of the last* <u>complete</u> *line. The sum gives the number of words typed per minute.*

NOTE: If the length of the timed writing is other than one, three, or five minutes; follow the above procedure using the 1' scales. To calculate the number of words typed per minute, divide the total number of words typed by the number of minutes.

EXAMPLE: In a one-minute timed writing of Paragraph 11, the last word you typed was "the." By reading "11" in the first column opposite the last <u>complete</u> *line typed, and by reading "6" from the first row at the bottom of the page beneath "the," you will determine that the number of words per minute typed is "17."*

will plan to build a factory, and no institution will be willing to lend funds for this purpose if there is a general fear that the government may soon be overthrown and the enterprise either expropriated or destroyed. Even if violent revolution is not feared, funds for development will always tend to go to countries which are more rather than less stable. This is one reason why Canada has developed much further than Latin American countries.

SI 1.53
HFW 77%
AWL 5.4
TW 233

Supposing a country has a labor force and natural resources, what else does it need in order to develop its economy? First, it must have technical knowledge, sometimes called "know-how." The wheel and the steam engine are outstanding examples of basic inventions that have transformed economic life, but the whole process of scientific and technical discovery has been closely reflected in economic progress. In most of the advanced economies, technical knowledge is at roughly the same level: inventions do not remain secret for long, since engineers travel and share ideas, and reports in technical journals are translated into many languages. In the underdeveloped countries, however, there is often a serious lack of technical knowledge, usually because there is not enough money to provide adequate education. Under the Colombo Plan, sponsored by the Commonwealth, some of the industrial members, including Canada, are supplying technical experts who teach modern methods of farming, fishing, and processing of raw materials to people in the developing countries of Southeast Asia. Thus, they are helping these countries raise their levels of production.

SI 1.26
HFW 87%
AWL 4.3
TW 119

Knowledge of a certain process, such as the production of frozen fish sticks, is, of course, not enough in itself. Plant,

 **NOTE** IF YOU ARE STILL LOOKING AT THE KEYS, RE-TYPE PARAGRAPHS 1 TO 10 TRYING NOT TO LOOK AT THE KEYS.

	1'	3'	5'

Paragraph 11

SI	1.22
HFW	95%
AWL	4.1
TW	38

Will you be kind enough to let us have your comments and recommendations, and return the sketch, such as it is, when it has served its purpose. A copy of this letter is attached for your use.

11	4	2
24	8	5
37	12	7
38	13	8

Paragraph 12

SI	1.31
HFW	91%
AWL	4.4
TW	38

We certainly have a problem here and would appreciate any advice you might offer. We have put a fine screen on to keep any impurities from getting into the pump but still the wear persists.

11	4	2
24	8	5
37	12	7

Paragraph 13

SI	1.24
HFW	95%
AWL	4.0
TW	38

We do not send our accounts strictly to you on a test basis. This is one account on which we felt you could do the job for us better than having our representative try and trace the person.

13	4	3
26	9	5
38	13	8

Paragraph 14

SI	1.71
HFW	87%
AWL	5.4
TW	40

Your application has been circulated to the various interested department heads in our organization, but we have been informed there is no vacancy for a person of your qualifications and experience.

12	4	2
24	8	5
36	12	7
39	13	8

Paragraph 15

SI	1.27
HFW	88%
AWL	4.1
TW	43

In our opinion our visit was very worthwhile and may very well work toward our mutual advantage in the future. Needless to say, we would be pleased to have you drop in at the plant anytime you are in the vicinity.

12	4	2
24	8	5
36	12	7
42	14	8

Paragraph 16

SI	1.45
HFW	95%
AWL	4.5
TW	45

So far as this line is concerned, we do not anticipate any difficulties in delivering. However, we would appreciate it if you would tell us, as soon as you can, the approximate quantity you will require in the various shades.

15	5	3
27	9	5
39	13	8
45	15	9

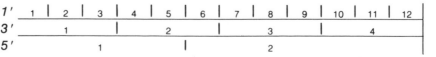

may also be made by telephone or by mail. You identify yourself | 113 | 92 | 23
to the store by quoting the number on your charge account card | | 96 | 25
or by presenting the card and having it processed. There is no | | 100 | 28
interest on an open charge, but some stores will levy a service | | 105 | 30
charge. If you are unnecessarily tardy about paying the balance | | 109 | 33
on the statement, interest may be charged. | | 112 | 34

ECONOMIC GROWTH

	1'	3'	5'

In a primitive agricultural economy each family grows its | 11 | 4 | 2
own food. This is usually a full-time job, and, moreover, every- | 24 | 8 | 5
thing that is produced is consumed by the family: there is | 36 | 12 | 7
nothing left over. As long as all the adults of the community are | 49 | 16 | 10
working in this way, it is never possible to keep some of the | 61 | 20 | 12
people out of the fields to make improved farm implements | 73 | 24 | 15
which would increase production and so reduce the number of | 85 | 28 | 17
people needed to raise the food the community requires. Nor | 97 | 32 | 19
will it ever be possible to spare enough of the community's time | 109 | 36 | 22
and resources to build a factory to produce farm machinery, | | 40 | 24
which would release still more workers for activities other than | | 45 | 27
farming and raise the whole level and variety of production. | | 49 | 29

In a modern economy some part of the national income is | 11 | 52 | 31
not spent on consumption, but is saved. The funds thus accumu- | 24 | 57 | 34
lated are lent, through banks and other financial institutions, to | 37 | 61 | 37
business people who will use them to finance the creation of new | 50 | 65 | 39
plants and equipment, which will increase future production. | 62 | 69 | 42
Thus part of the basis of economic growth is saving, which can | 74 | 73 | 44
take place only when there is a surplus of production over | 86 | 77 | 46
consumption. | 88 | 78 | 47

There are many other factors which contribute to growth. | 11 | 82 | 49
A very important one, not economic, is political stability. No one | 25 | 86 | 52

1'	1	2	3	4	5	6	7	8	9	10	11	12
3'		1		2		3		4				
5'		1			2							

			1'	3'	5'
Paragraph	17	Normally you ask us to return the building plans so, as usual,	12	4	2
		they are enclosed. Should you desire any further information	25	8	5
		concerning this contract, bear in mind that we will not be in a	37	12	7
		position to refer to the plan.	43	14	9

SI	1.35
HFW	98%
AWL	4.4
TW	44

			1'	3'	5'
Paragraph	18	It is company policy that at least two fire drills, which should	13	4	3
		include instruction to personnel on the handling of fire fighting	26	9	5
		equipment and their specific duties in the case of fire or other	39	13	8
		emergency, be held each year.	44	15	9

SI	1.05
HFW	92%
AWL	4.7
TW	45

			1'	3'	5'
Paragraph	19	The purpose of this letter is not to administer a fourth warning,	13	4	3
		after the three you have already received. Rather, it is to be sure	26	9	5
		that you understand the seriousness with which the company	38	13	8
		regards behavior of this type.	44	15	9

SI	1.38
HFW	85%
AWL	4.6
TW	45

			1'	3'	5'
Paragraph	20	The production supervisor estimates that the maximum over-	12	4	2
		time to be worked between now and the end of the year would	23	8	5
		be fifty hours for each person. There would be ten people	35	12	7
		involved and all of these would be production welders.	46	15	9

SI	1.40
HFW	93%
AWL	4.7
TW	46

TRY NOT TO LOOK AT THE KEYS.

			1'	3'	5'
Paragraph	21	Our visit with you impressed us with the work you have done,	12	4	2
		and with the results you have obviously been getting. Particu-	24	8	5
		larly interesting were the new approaches which you have taken	37	12	7
		to the subject of non-destructive testing of pipe and tubing.	49	16	10

SI	1.34
HFW	90%
AWL	5.0
TW	49

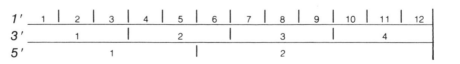

SI	1.38
HFW	92%
AWL	4.8
TW	77

Most people are familiar with the credit cards issued by oil and gas companies. These offer many goods and services other than oil and gas to holders of their cards. The all-purpose credit cards of the Diners' Club and American Express are also available, but are more difficult to obtain. Banks have developed credit card systems for their customers which are honored by many stores.

	11	81	48
	23	85	51
	36	89	53
	49	93	56
	62	97	58
	74	102	61
	78	103	62

SI	1.39
HFW	93%
AWL	4.9
TW	61

Payment on a credit card purchase is usually due on receipt of the monthly statement, with thirty days to pay, and there is no service charge. In this respect, though, a bank credit card operates more like a revolving charge account. Issuers of credit cards generally charge interest on overdue accounts.

	10	3	64
	23	8	66
	36	12	69
	49	16	72
	60	20	74

SI	1.44
HFW	81%
AWL	5.1
TW	33

Although the credit card makes travelling convenient for the cardholder, it can also make it easy for the dishonest person to abuse the privilege of extended credit.

	72	24	76
	85	28	79
	93	31	80

SI	1.30
HFW	93%
AWL	4.9
TW	72

Having a gas company credit card is, in effect, having a charge account with that company. Many retail stores provide charge accounts for which they issue some form of credit card. Shopping excursions are made simpler and more convenient when there is no need to carry cheques or cash. Some of the better-known types of charge accounts are described below.

	11	35	83
	23	39	85
	36	43	88
	47	47	90
	59	51	92
	71	55	95

SI	1.29
HFW	94%
AWL	4.4
TW	174

The most usual type of charge account and for some purposes the most desirable is the open charge. This is granted only after the retailer is satisfied that you are a good credit risk. It permits you to walk into the store, make your purchase, sign a sales slip as a record of the transaction, walk away with your purchase, and pay only upon presentation of a statement, usually monthly. The statement will include a record of all purchases made by you up to a given date. On an open charge, purchases

	10	58	2
	23	62	5
	37	67	7
	50	71	10
	62	75	12
	74	79	15
	88	84	18
	100	88	20

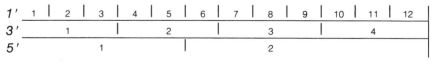

1' 1 | 2 | 3 | 4 | 5 | 6 | 7 | 8 | 9 | 10 | 11 | 12
3' 1 | 2 | 3 | 4
5' 1 | 2

Paragraph 22

SI	1.27
HFW	90%
AWL	4.1
TW	51

Therefore, the best thing we can do for you is recommend that you inquire at the various retail tire outlets in your area. In all likelihood one of them will have a set of used tires which will enable you to make your car operational at a very modest cost.

1'	3'	5'
12	4	2
26	9	5
38	13	8
51	17	10

Paragraph 23

SI	1.39
HFW	98%
AWL	4.5
TW	51

We present information, either in the form of news or advertising, when it is available to us. Since advertisers are paying more than half the total cost of service, it seems proper that they have some say as to when they make information available to us.

1'	3'	5'
13	4	3
27	9	5
40	13	8
51	17	10

Paragraph 24

SI	1.47
HFW	95%
AWL	5.0
TW	52

We know that our invoices are dated according to shipping date and that they do not reach you for perhaps three to seven days later. Our centralized billing procedure does not permit us to mail invoices daily without considerable disruption of our procedures.

1'	3'	5'
12	4	2
25	8	5
37	12	8
50	17	10
52	17	10

Paragraph 25

SI	1.34
HFW	98%
AWL	4.5
TW	56

With all equipment, as you know, there are times when machines become obsolete and it is difficult to assure that parts will be readily available. We do attempt to provide a parts replacement service, but will at no time guarantee that parts will be available for all time to come.

1'	3'	5'
12	4	2
25	8	5
38	13	8
51	17	10
55	18	11

Paragraph 26

SI	1.21
HFW	98%
AWL	4.1
TW	60

At the time you received your new price list, we sent you some order forms. If there is any equipment which you would like to pick up now, send your orders in to this office. On the other hand, you may want to contact your salesperson and discuss your orders personally. Do not hesitate to call.

1'	3'	5'
12	4	3
25	8	5
37	13	8
51	17	10
61	20	12

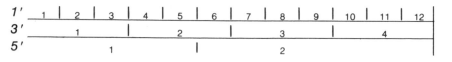

1'	1	2	3	4	5	6	7	8	9	10	11	12
3'		1		2		3		4
5'		1			2

have bumper crops there may be excess world supply and prices will tend to drop sharply; a coincidence of crop failures will raise prices for whatever output is available for sale. Many of these commodities, again unlike mineral or forest products, are extremely difficult to store, so that it is not easy to stabilize prices by withholding excess production in good years and saving it for poor ones.

58	86	12
71	91	14
85	95	17
97	99	19
112	104	22
	109	25
	109	25

TYPES OF RETAIL CREDIT

Timed Writing No. 16

SI	1.32
HFW	90%
AWL	4.7
TW	653

SI	1.35
HFW	82%
AWL	4.8
TW	81

SI	1.42
HFW	95%
AWL	5.1
TW	24

SI	1.26
HFW	85%
AWL	4.5
TW	131

Cash loans are the most obvious forms of credit. But the day may be approaching when credit will replace cash. Even today, to be able to say "charge it" has become a well-established tradition in merchandising. One prominent banker has predicted that in the near future loans will be arranged automatically by a computer each time you make a purchase and not only cash but cheques will be eliminated.

We are faced with a proliferation of credit cards, charge accounts, instalment plans, and other forms of retail credit.

The most common form of retail credit is what is known as "service credit." This is what enables you to telephone friends and relatives, to light your room, or to turn on a stove or a gas jet for cooking and heating, all without having to pay until your utility bills arrive. The convenience of service credit is also extended by doctors, clinics, dentists, and all who send out statements monthly. Most businesses send statements on the first or last of the month, but many of the larger firms practise "cycle billing" — that is, the statements they send out are "staggered," or sent at varying times during the month to avoid a heavy billing date.

1'	3'	5'
11	4	2
23	8	5
34	11	7
46	15	9
58	19	12
70	23	14
80	27	16
91	30	18
103	34	21
11	38	23
24	42	25
38	47	28
50	51	31
63	55	33
75	59	36
87	63	38
100	68	41
111	71	43
	76	45
	77	46

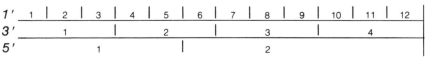

Paragraph 27

SI	1.35
HFW	93%
AWL	4.7
TW	63

You will recall that we have recently spoken about better methods of planning our sales attack for subsequent years. You have graciously accepted the information and suggestions that I have passed along to you, and I feel that you can set them into your program to assist in meeting our mutual goal of greater sales.

1'	3'	5'
12	4	2
24	8	5
36	12	7
49	16	10
61	20	12
62	21	13

Paragraph 28

SI	1.32
HFW	92%
AWL	4.4
TW	69

We wish to advise that we have already sent copies of both of your letters to our agents in Detroit with the request that they do everything possible to see that your application receives a quick reply. We might add that we drew special attention to the third paragraph of your letter suggesting the rate be extended for a period of one year.

1'	3'	5'
12	4	2
26	9	5
39	13	8
51	17	10
64	21	13
68	23	14

Paragraph 29

SI	1.24
HFW	85%
AWL	4.2
TW	70

Some will be content to be workers rather than leaders, but even if they have made up their minds not to be top dog they have decisions to make. If they are to serve others they should still have ambition; the ambition to serve the firm to which their service will be most useful. By advancing it and its interests they will expand their own lives.

1'	3'	5'
13	4	3
25	8	5
38	13	8
50	17	10
64	21	13
69	23	14

Paragraph 30

SI	1.41
HFW	98%
AWL	4.7
TW	71

To our knowledge, there is no reason for withholding payment of this account. However, if your records are not in agreement with ours, please advise so that necessary adjustments can be made. If your records are in agreement with ours, your remittance to cover by return mail will be much appreciated and will assure prompt shipment of orders now on hand.

1'	3'	5'
13	4	3
26	9	5
37	12	7
49	16	10
62	21	12
71	24	14

NOTE IF YOU ARE STILL LOOKING AT THE KEYS, RE-TYPE PARAGRAPHS 11 TO 30 TRYING NOT TO LOOK AT THE KEYS.

1'	1	2	3	4	5	6	7	8	9	10	11	12
3'		1		2		3		4				
5'		1			2							

small. The sale of these products abroad has generated employment and income far beyond what would have been possible in other circumstances.

Canada has been fortunate not only in the variety and extent of its resources, but also (in most cases) in their nature. World demand for mineral and forest products has been rising rapidly in the past century, as the process of industrialization has spread and accelerated.

Canada's exports of mineral and forest products have been a fundamental source of strength to the developing economy. They may be contrasted with the commodities produced and exported in certain other parts of the world. Countries which must rely on tropical commodities as their basic source of export revenue are often in a much more precarious position. Demand for commodities such as cocoa, coffee, cotton, rice, sugar, tea, or tobacco tends to grow at roughly the same rate as the population; it cannot usually be expected to accelerate with development as has demand for mineral and forest products. As per capita income rises, the consumption of these commodities will certainly go up a little, but there is a limit to how much coffee even a millionaire can drink. When it comes to sugar and cocoa, people may actually consume less rather than more as they become richer, because they begin to worry about their diets and to concentrate their purchases on foods which are more costly but less fattening.

Moreover, production of agricultural commodities depends largely on how good the annual harvest is—often beyond human control — in contrast with mineral production where the annual output can be planned. When all the producing countries

57	76	45
69	79	48
74	81	49
85	85	51
98	89	53
110	93	56
	97	58
	99	60
10	3	62
21	7	64
33	11	66
45	15	69
57	19	71
69	23	73
82	27	76
94	31	78
106	35	81
	39	83
44	86	
	48	88
	52	91
	56	93
	60	96
	64	98
	67	100
10	70	2
23	75	5
35	79	7
47	83	9

SI   1.48
HFW   74%
AWL   4.8
TW   55

SI   1.41
HFW   73%
AWL   4.9
TW   203

SI   1.47
HFW   74%
AWL   5.1
TW   129

1' 1 | 2 | 3 | 4 | 5 | 6 | 7 | 8 | 9 | 10 | 11 | 12
3'   1 | 2 | 3 | 4
5'   1 | 2

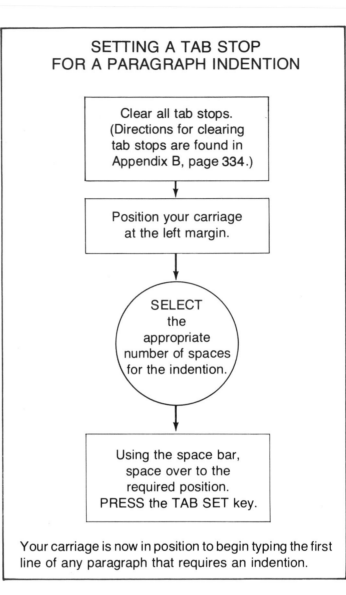

SETTING A TAB STOP
FOR A PARAGRAPH INDENTION

Clear all tab stops.
(Directions for clearing
tab stops are found in
Appendix B, page 334.)

Position your carriage
at the left margin.

SELECT
the
appropriate
number of spaces
for the indention.

Using the space bar,
space over to the
required position.
PRESS the TAB SET key.

Your carriage is now in position to begin typing the first
line of any paragraph that requires an indention.

NOTE

WHEN TYPING PARAGRAPHS 31-60 USE A 5-SPACE PARAGRAPH INDENTION. USE SINGLE SPACING BUT REMEMBER TO DOUBLE SPACE BETWEEN PARAGRAPHS.

	1'	3'	5'
It has rather concerned me that I have not heard a word	11	4	2
from you since talking to you last November. At that time you	23	8	5
were to read the chapters already written and give me a criti-	36	12	7
cism. As I still have not received a purchase order to cover the	49	16	10
project, I am left uncertain as to the correctness of my approach	62	21	12
to the subject.	65	22	13

Paragraph 31

SI	1.27
HFW	89%
AWL	4.1
TW	65

1' 1 2 3 4 5 6 7 8 9 10 11 12
3' 1 2 3 4
5' 1 2

became unfashionable and the skins were worth less, or more recently when people began to hoard silver coins because they could be melted down for industrial use at a price much higher than the face value of the original coins. The value of "fiat" money, on the other hand, is determined by the government which issues it and it commands confidence more or less as long as the economic system itself continues to do so.

72	64	101
84	68	103
97	72	106
109	76	108
	80	110
	84	113
	87	115

Timed Writing No. 15

SI	1.43
HFW	75%
AWL	5.0
TW	634

SI	1.44
HFW	74%
AWL	5.2
TW	172

SI	1.39
HFW	84%
AWL	5.0
TW	75

NATURAL RESOURCES IN ECONOMIC GROWTH

	1'	3'	5'

Canada's economic development began when people founded settlements on the Atlantic coast in the seventeenth and eighteenth centuries, using the proceeds from the sale of fish in Europe to purchase equipment and other necessities of life. Exports of timber provided a basis for the first development of Upper Canada, and the settlement of Western Canada in the late nineteenth and early twentieth centuries was made possible by large-scale exports of wheat. Without these export sales Canada's development would have been much slower. At the same time Canada began to sell large quantities of forest products: lumber, wood pulp, and newsprint — for many years the largest group of Canadian exports. Then came the discovery, production, and export of nickel, copper, and iron ore, followed by a whole range of other mineral products, including oil and gas.

Canada is one of the best examples of a country whose development has stemmed from the existence of rich natural resources which could be marketed in other parts of the world even though the domestic demand for them was relatively

1'	3'	5'
9	3	2
21	7	4
34	11	7
46	15	9
59	20	12
71	24	14
84	28	17
96	32	19
107	36	21
	40	24
	44	26
	48	29
	52	31
	56	34
	56	34
11	60	36
22	64	38
34	68	41
46	72	43

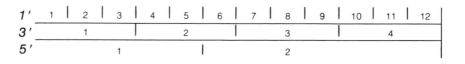

Paragraph	32		1'	3'	5'

The original request, you will remember, was a guaranteed supply of eight cars a year. We now know we could get by with a minimum of six cars yearly, but could not possibly go any lower. If you cannot guarantee to supply the six cars, we will have to look elsewhere for either a different supplier or a different product.

	1'	3'	5'
SI 1.38	11	4	2
HFW 95%	23	8	5
AWL 4.2	36	12	7
TW 66	49	16	10
	62	21	12
	65	22	13

Paragraph 33

It used to be the universal answer to a paperwork problem to hire more help. This has been outmoded by the high cost of office space, the difficulty of getting workers, and the high salaries needed to keep staff. The solution lies in improvement of procedures, updating of equipment, discrimination as to what is done, and checking of the output.

	1'	3'	5'
SI 1.43	11	4	2
HFW 82%	24	8	5
AWL 4.7	36	12	7
TW 70	49	16	10
	62	21	12
	69	23	14

Paragraph 34

If the foregoing does not meet with your approval, or is not understandable, would you please telephone the writer as soon as possible, so that we may get these matters cleared up in the shortest possible time. In the event that we do not hear from you we shall presume you concur with us, and we shall expect your cheque to bring your account into a nil position.

	1'	3'	5'
SI 1.26	11	4	2
HFW 94%	23	8	5
AWL 4.3	36	12	7
TW 73	49	16	10
	61	20	12
	72	24	14

Paragraph 35

We understand that several years ago you planned a new refinery in this region but your plans were shelved owing to changed conditions in the oil industry. In view of the changes that have occurred since then, we are wondering if you see any prospect for such a project being revived in the near future. If not, would you tell us under what conditions, if any, you might again consider expansion?

	1'	3'	5'
SI 1.31	11	4	2
HFW 93%	25	8	5
AWL 4.5	35	12	7
TW 80	48	16	10
	61	20	12
	73	24	15
	78	26	16

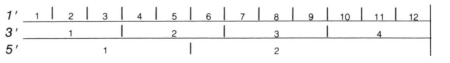

1' 1 | 2 | 3 | 4 | 5 | 6 | 7 | 8 | 9 | 10 | 11 | 12
3'   1 | 2 | 3 | 4
5'   1 | 2

fairly sure that it could be exchanged for something else. Beaver skins were useful in themselves for making hats. Moreover, they had the advantage of being small, lightweight, and durable, and reasonably uniform in size and quality, all desirable characteristics of any substance used as money.

Broadly speaking, money as a medium of exchange has taken two forms. The first includes, as well as beaver skins, such things as cattle, corn, tobacco, tea, coconuts, and coins made of gold, silver, or other precious metals—all objects with a use apart from their value as currency. These things could be used as money because their value was generally accepted. They were also relatively convenient to move around from one person to another, and in most cases could be easily used in different quantities.

The other kind of money consists of things which have no value in themselves, such as wampum, cowrie shells, or present-day currency, which basically consists of pieces of paper, coins made of rather inexpensive metals such as copper and nickel, and bank deposits—accounting entries transferable from one holder to another. The value of this kind of money depends entirely on the confidence it inspires: people holding it are confident that they will be able to exchange it for goods and services, or for other assets such as stocks and bonds, at any time. This implies confidence in the economy.

On the whole, the kind of money which has little or no value in itself has probably caused less trouble over the course of history than the kind which does have other uses. The value of the latter can be changed suddenly by circumstances which have nothing to do with its monetary use, as when beaver hats

SI	1.31
HFW	78%
AWL	4.7
TW	102

SI	1.36
HFW	79%
AWL	4.9
TW	120

SI	1.25
HFW	86%
AWL	4.4
TW	145

	56	33
	60	36
	64	39
	69	41
	71	43
10	74	45
24	79	47
36	83	50
49	87	52
62	91	55
73	95	57
86	99	60
98	104	62
100	104	63
11	4	65
25	7	67
34	11	69
46	15	72
58	19	74
71	24	77
84	28	79
97	32	82
109	36	85
	40	86
11	43	89
23	47	91
37	52	94
48	56	96
60	60	98

1' 1 2 3 4 5 6 7 8 9 10 11 12
3'   1   2   3   4
5'   1   2

	1'	3'	5'

Paragraph 36

SI	1.60		
HFW	93%		
AWL	5.6		
TW	77		

We are faced with the problem of life insurance coverage for these purchasers and note that your brochure does not cover either corporations or business partnerships for this type of life insurance and that there are certain specified limits concerning commercial vehicles, and agriculture equipment under your life insurance plan. These are not specifically stated in the brochure.

1'	3'	5'
11	4	2
24	8	5
37	12	7
50	17	10
62	21	12
74	24	15
75	25	15

Paragraph 37

SI	1.22
HFW	96%
AWL	4.2
TW	90

The matter in question is the continuing of extended benefits for a period after retirement for bills and costs in con-nection with an illness for which the worker was being treated at the time of leaving. It is known that there is such a clause in your standard major medical contract. It is not known why this item was not included in our plan when it first started, but there does not seem to be any good reason why it should not now be provided.

1'	3'	5'
10	3	2
24	8	5
36	12	7
50	17	10
63	21	13
76	25	15
87	29	17
89	30	18

Paragraph 38

SI	1.32
HFW	90%
AWL	4.7
TW	90

You cannot just pick up an incoming letter and start dictating a reply. Take a look at what you want to express and then think about how to put it down. Ask yourself what are your correspondent's interests, and write about them. You will be surprised to notice how few are the questions and how unpene-trating are the comments you receive about your own activities. Think what interesting things you could tell if someone pushed the proper button.

1'	3'	5'
10	3	2
23	8	5
36	12	7
48	16	10
60	20	12
73	24	15
85	28	17
89	30	18

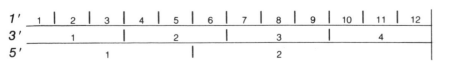

individual. And if each individual enjoys such a right, we will in effect have no laws at all and we will be back in the jungle conditions of "everyone for themselves." This does not mean that individuals should simply accept laws they think are wrong. On the contrary, it is one's right <u>and duty</u> to press for the reforms that one thinks are needed.

64	21	69
76	25	71
88	29	74
100	33	76
114	38	79
119	40	80

If a citizen deliberately refuses to obey a law, before doing so, one must consider the extent to which the action undermines the political and personal freedom of all Canadians, which rests on our system of justice. One must seriously ask if the political and legal systems that exist in Canada, compared with those in other countries, are worth supporting. Therefore, is the price of obedience not more than compensated for by the freedoms enjoyed?

11	43	82
23	47	84
35	52	87
48	56	89
60	60	92
74	64	95
86	68	97
89	70	98

SI	1.43
HFW	72%
AWL	4.9
TW	90

Timed Writing No. 14

SI	1.34
HFW	81%
AWL	4.7
TW	592

SI	1.40
HFW	81%
AWL	4.7
TW	225

TYPES OF MONEY

Many people have had the experience of having to sell one of their possessions in order to pay a bill or to make an essential purchase. In the modern economy, money is the accepted medium of exchange: you cannot pay your taxes by handing over your color television set to the government. At an earlier stage in economic development when assets were fewer and their value was more clearly established, it was possible to exchange one's assets for the assets of other people without making much use of money. For example, in the days of the fur trade, beaver skins had recognized value: trappers exchanged them for blankets and guns and the traders brought the skins back to the towns and exchanged them for food and other goods. Any person who acquired a beaver skin could be

1'	3'	5'
11	4	2
23	8	5
35	12	7
46	15	9
59	20	12
71	24	14
84	28	17
96	32	19
105	36	21
	39	24
	43	26
	47	28
	51	31

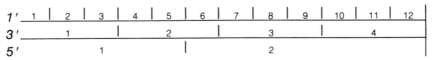

TYPING FROM HANDWRITTEN MATERIAL

Type the following handwritten paragraphs so that the right and left margins are approximately 25 mm.

1. *Set the left margin stop 25 mm from the left edge of the paper.*

2. *Set the right margin stop 20 mm from the right edge of the paper.*

3. *As you type, listen for the bell which rings several spaces from the right margin stop. (Check your machine to determine the exact number of spaces.)*

4. *End each typing line close to the right margin stop. Try to avoid dividing words.*

5. *If two or three strokes beyond the right margin stop will complete a word, use the MARGIN RELEASE key.*

6. *If a word must be divided, use the following rules:*
   — *divide words between syllables*
   — *do not divide one-syllable words*
   — *do not divide names, abbreviations, dates, or numerals*
   — *never carry less than three letters of a word to the next line.*

7. *For complete information on word division, refer to Appendix B, page 340.*

   EXAMPLE:

                                                        right margin stop
                                                              ↓

   It is not possible to plan too far in the future,
   but we are sure that the new schedule will extend
   to May when we normally reschedule for the summer
   operation. We cannot say if the frequency or service will be maintained beyond that date.

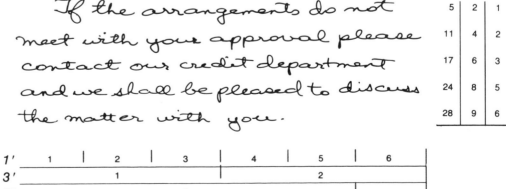

Paragraph 39

SI	1.32
HFW	100%
AWL	4.7
TW	29

Timed Writing No. 13

SI	1.37
HFW	80%
AWL	4.6
TW	495

SI	1.29
HFW	82%
AWL	4.2
TW	74

SI	1.42
HFW	81%
AWL	4.7
TW	129

SI	1.45
HFW	83%
AWL	4.7
TW	81

SI	1.27
HFW	80%
AWL	4.3
TW	121

OUR RESPONSIBILITY FOR LAW AND ORDER

	1'	3'	5'

In comparison with former times and in comparison with many other countries today, we in Canada are most fortunate in our system of justice. However, in a matter so vital to our whole way of life, it is up to each one of us to ensure that the system does not contain injustices. Times and people change, so much so that various laws can become restrictive and unfair.

Since Canada is a democracy, our laws are made by representatives of the people. If we do not like those laws, we can express our dissatisfaction directly to members of our legislative bodies at federal, provincial, and local levels. We can also express our opinions in the press, on radio and television, and through public meetings in an effort to gain support from other citizens. If our efforts to persuade government to make the desired changes do not succeed, we can try to elect representatives who do agree with our views. Therefore, this power to exercise our influence in the framing of laws imposes on us a commitment to obey them.

Now, seldom does everybody agree on any one matter, and law-making is no exception. When people disagree as to what our laws should do, the majority opinion has to prevail. This opinion may not always be right, but in a democracy it must always prevail. We must take care, however, that the majority opinion interferes with the activities of the minority only to the extent that public safety demands.

It has been argued that the individual should have the right to choose not to obey a particular law. But, individuals must remember that if they claim the right to select the laws they will and will not obey, they must give the same right to every other

(Marginal column figures)

1': 11, 23, 36, 49, 61, 72, 10, 23, 36, 49, 62, 74, 86, 99, 110, 10, 22, 35, 47, 60, 73, 80, 11, 24, 38, 50

3': 4, 8, 12, 16, 20, 24, 27, 32, 36, 41, 45, 49, 53, 57, 61, 65, 67, 70, 74, 79, 83, 87, 91, 93, 4, 8, 13, 17

5': 2, 5, 7, 10, 12, 14, 16, 19, 22, 24, 27, 29, 32, 34, 37, 39, 40, 42, 44, 47, 50, 52, 55, 56, 58, 61, 64, 66

1' 1 2 3 4 5 6 7 8 9 10 11 12
3' 1 2 3 4
5' 1 2

	1'	3'	5'

Paragraph 40

SI	1.48
HFW	96%
AWL	4.8
TW	29

We would appreciate it if you would send us details of the reports submitted by other dealers if the procedures differ from those outlined above.

	1'	3'	5'
	6	2	1
	13	4	3
	20	7	4
	27	9	5
	28	9	6

Paragraph 41

SI	1.39
HFW	82%
AWL	4.5
TW	32

While we feel confident that all of this will be resolved, we do wish to convey our impression of how the situation arose. We would appreciate your comments.

	6	2	1
	14	5	3
	20	7	4
	26	9	5
	31	10	6

Paragraph 42

SI	1.23
HFW	86%
AWL	4.1
TW	36

All office work is done in sequence and for this reason desks should be so placed as to facilitate the flow of work so that papers move as nearly as possible in a straight line.

	7	2	1
	14	5	3
	22	7	4
	28	9	6
	35	12	7

Paragraph 43

SI	1.19
HFW	97%
AWL	3.8
TW	35

The London Free Press has been working on a training program now for a number of years and we have asked them for information about it. When I get it, I will pass it on to you.

	7	2	1
	14	5	3
	21	7	4
	28	9	6
	35	12	7

Paragraph 44

SI	1.37
HFW	89%
AWL	4.1
TW	36

We hope you will be able to accept our apologies for the incident. Perhaps all that we can do now is to reassure you of our intentions to see that our customers are fully satisfied.

	7	2	1
	15	5	3
	22	7	4
	29	10	6
	35	12	7

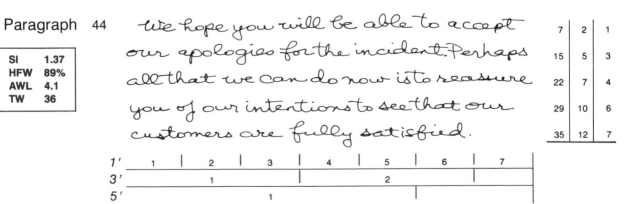

1'	1	2	3	4	5	6	7
3'		1			2		
5'			1				

creditor in the investigation of an applicant for credit, the expense of collection (which is directly proportionate to customer delinquency), and the losses experienced by the firm as a result of uncollectable accounts. The overhead expenses of any business — office space, heating, lighting, air conditioning, telephones, advertising — must also be taken into account.

But, to the borrower, a finance charge, to whatever attributed, is still a charge for credit. How can you determine for yourself just what this charge is and whether or not it is "reasonable" or if you could get better terms elsewhere?

To determine the cost of credit you need to know the amount of the principal, the period over which the principal is to be repaid and at what rate of interest, and the form of repayment. Usually interest is computed only on the amount of cash you actually have available for use; in other words, interest is charged on the outstanding balance. Since many loans are repaid in monthly instalments, this can make quite a difference. You must, of course, include all other charges, whatever called, and take into account the form of repayment.

Quite a few finance and other small loan companies deduct the total charge for the loan — usually called some combination of interest and service or carrying charge—before the money is turned over to you. This process is known as "discounting." If, for example, you borrow a hundred dollars for a period of a year at an interest rate of twelve per cent per annum, you would receive only eighty-eight dollars. You are, however, expected to repay the full hundred dollars when the loan is due, which means that you are paying more than thirteen and one-half per cent on the money you get.

SI	1.28
HFW	93%
AWL	4.4
TW	47

SI	1.36
HFW	93%
AWL	4.6
TW	109

SI	1.37
HFW	92%
AWL	4.6
TW	118

47	46	28
60	50	30
73	55	33
87	59	36
99	63	38
110	67	40
12	71	43
24	75	45
38	80	48
47	83	50
58	86	52
71	91	54
83	95	57
96	99	59
109	103	62
		64
		67
		69
		71
10	3	73
21	7	75
34	11	78
45	15	80
58	19	83
70	23	85
82	27	88
94	31	90
107	36	92
	39	94

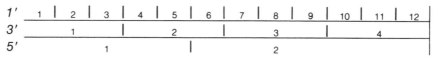

1' 1 | 2 | 3 | 4 | 5 | 6 | 7 | 8 | 9 | 10 | 11 | 12
3'   1 | 2 | 3 | 4
5'   1 | 2

	1'	3'	5'

Paragraph 45

SI	1.28
HFW	86%
AWL	4.1
TW	44

Many business decisions made from day to day are routine and repetitive to the manager, but one must bear patiently in mind that the problems are new to the staff and it is part of the duty of the manager to give guidance.

1'	3'	5'
6	2	1
12	4	2
19	6	4
25	8	5
31	10	6
38	13	8
43	14	9

Paragraph 46

SI	1.41
HFW	92%
AWL	4.6
TW	44

I was also advised by my solicitors that notwithstanding an option to purchase contained in a lease, the rental payments by a lessee are deductible as an expense of doing business and are not held to be capital payments.

1'	3'	5'
5	2	1
12	4	2
18	6	4
24	8	5
31	10	6
38	13	8
43	14	9

Paragraph 47

SI	1.43
HFW	83%
AWL	4.8
TW	48

Efficiency demands that the office manager be able to account for the time of secretaries, typists, filing clerks, and all other office workers who handle paper. What is being done by whom? Is it necessary? Is it being done efficiently?

1'	3'	5'
7	2	1
14	5	3
21	7	4
28	9	6
34	11	7
41	14	8
46	15	9

Paragraph 48

SI	1.37
HFW	88%
AWL	4.8
TW	51

The general attitude of the trade, as determined by these studies, was one of indifference. Store managers claimed they treated test products in the same manner as other new or

1'	3'	5'
7	2	1
14	5	3
21	7	4
28	9	6
35	12	7

1'	1	2	3	4	5	6	7
3'		1		2			
5'		1					

	SI	1.09
	HFW	78%
	AWL	3.2
	TW	19

As for cutting off that third prong of the plug of the mower cord, you're out of your skull. True, it's an expensive business to re-wire the place to accommodate the triple-pronged deal. But then, electric shock can be very serious, if not fatal at times. That third prong grounds the machine, and an amateur who tries to attach the cut wires into the plug has to know what he's doing, or there can be trouble afoot.

32	77	46
46	82	49
58	86	51
72	90	54
84	94	57
97	99	59
103	101	60

	SI	1.23
	HFW	74%
	AWL	4.3
	TW	84

New standards are being drafted by CSA for electric blankets. In fact, new standards are constantly appearing by the hundreds as times and models change and as new appliances and equipment appear on the scene.

10	3	62
23	8	65
35	12	67
41	14	69

	SI	1.37
	HFW	77%
	AWL	4.9
	TW	42

Children jumping on an electric blanket could damage the thermostats and wiring inside the blanket. Also, wires on the blanket can come loose, and form a spiral (unbroken) that creates a concentration of heat that could result in fire. You should read carefully and observe rigidly the instructions that come with electric blankets.

52	17	71
65	22	73
76	25	76
89	30	78
102	34	81
107	36	82

	SI	1.47
	HFW	72%
	AWL	5.2
	TW	67

Timed Writing No. 12

THE COST OF CREDIT

	1'	3'	5'

	SI	1.41
	HFW	90%
	AWL	4.8
	TW	473

Any business which extends credit has, of course, to meet the cost of offering that service. There is, first, the cost of having or making the money available. A business extending credit must either allocate a part of its working capital (which it could be using in other interest-bearing or profit-making ways) to do so, or, more usually, it obtains the necessary capital from banks or other financial institutions and pays interest on it.

10	3	2
24	8	5
36	12	7
51	17	10
64	21	13
77	26	15
91	30	18

	SI	1.45
	HFW	86%
	AWL	4.8
	TW	89

In addition, there are expenses that are not, strictly speaking, a charge for the rental of money. What are some of these "extras?" They are the time and money spent by the

11	34	20
23	38	23
34	42	25

	SI	1.51
	HFW	85%
	AWL	5.2
	TW	110

1'	1	2	3	4	5	6	7	8	9	10	11	12
3'		1		2		3		4				
5'		1			2							

regular products; they liked and
kept test products only when they
sold well.

	41	14	8
	48	16	10
	50	17	10

Paragraph 49

SI	1.44
HFW	95%
AWL	4.8
TW	50

I am anxious to proceed with
construction of the building as
soon as is conveniently possible. I
am quite prepared to meet with
you and members of your staff so
that we can finalize the plans
and specifications and discuss
proposed completion dates.

1'	3'	5'
6	2	1
13	4	3
20	7	4
26	9	5
32	11	6
38	13	8
44	15	9
49	16	10

Paragraph 50

SI	1.44
HFW	93%
AWL	4.7
TW	50

We appreciate having had the
opportunity of being of service to
you, and also the manner in
which you have discharged your
indebtedness. Should the occasion
again arise when a personal loan
would be the answer, please do
not hesitate to contact us.

6	2	1
12	4	2
18	6	4
24	8	5
31	10	6
37	12	7
43	14	9
48	16	10

Paragraph 51

SI	1.33
HFW	96%
AWL	4.6
TW	53

At this late date I can only apologize
to you for the inconvenience caused
you and for the unfair treatment for
which you have every right to blame
us. Should there be any further complaint against this firm, I would
appreciate your bringing it to my
personal attention.

8	3	2
15	5	3
22	7	4
29	10	6
36	12	7
43	14	9
49	16	10
53	18	11

1' 1 2 3 4 5 6 7
3'   1   2
5'   1

entire account in a single remittance. Usually an understanding

is reached that the customer will send a cheque for a portion of

the account by a certain date and additional remittances at one

or more future dates until the entire balance has been paid.

Immediately after the telephone conversation, the most impor-

tant points of the conversation should be confirmed in writing by

the creditor.

75	101	60
88	105	63
101	109	66
	113	68
	117	70
	118	71
	118	71

LET COMMON SENSE PREVAIL

	SI	1.26
	HFW	74%
	AWL	4.4
	TW	413

	SI	1.12
	HFW	74%
	AWL	3.8
	TW	48

	SI	1.19
	HFW	71%
	AWL	4.1
	TW	22

	SI	1.29
	HFW	71%
	AWL	4.2
	TW	32

	SI	1.28
	HFW	75%
	AWL	4.3
	TW	39

	SI	1.21
	HFW	89%
	AWL	3.6
	TW	17

	SI	1.15
	HFW	74%
	AWL	4.4
	TW	43

	1'	3'	5'
Tell me, does a child of yours take a radio into the bath-	12	4	2
room, plug it into an electric outlet, then put it on the edge of the	25	8	5
bath and proceed to step into the tub full of water, lie back and	38	13	8
soak up the music while soaking out the grime?	48	16	10
Are you given to plugging an electric kettle into an outlet	59	20	12
that is an arm's length away from a kitchen tap?	69	23	14
If when someone happens to run over the electric cord of	80	27	16
the lawn mower, do you immediately doctor up the break with	92	31	18
black tape, and let the mowing go merrily on?	101	33	20
And, still on the subject of those mowers, is anyone in	11	37	22
your house guilty of cutting off that third prong of the plug of the	25	42	25
cord because you don't have the three-holed outlet to accom-	37	46	27
modate it?	39	46	28
Do you permit children to jump up and down on a bed	49	50	30
that has an electric blanket on it?	56	52	31
That child with the plugged-in radio perched on the edge	67	56	34
of the bath is really inviting trouble, if not death. Should that radio	81	61	36
fall into the water, zing! — electric shock as soon as the water	94	65	39
seeps into the works.	98	66	40
The safest thing to do if the electric cord of the lawn	11	70	42
mower is cut in two is to buy a new cord.	19	73	44

```
1'    1 | 2 | 3 | 4 | 5 | 6 | 7 | 8 | 9 | 10 | 11 | 12
3'           1      |      2      |      3      |      4
5'              1            |            2
```

	1'	3'	5'

Paragraph 52

SI	1.32
HFW	90%
AWL	4.5
TW	56

We do not feel that you are being reasonable in this request. As at this date we have forwarded copies in triplicate of every invoice that has left this office, as well as further triplicate copies of invoices that have been lost or mislaid in your Edmonton or Winnipeg offices.

1'	3'	5'
7	2	1
13	4	3
20	7	4
27	9	5
35	12	7
43	14	9
50	17	10
54	18	11

Paragraph 53

SI	1.35
HFW	87%
AWL	4.4
TW	57

The world is full of people who shun this sort of responsibility. Only a few seek it, and they become leaders. They know that there is a possibility that a decision they reach may be wrong, but they know that this chance may be minimized by following some simple rules and procedures.

1'	3'	5'
6	2	1
13	4	3
20	7	4
27	9	5
33	11	7
40	13	8
46	15	9
53	18	11
55	18	11

Paragraph 54

SI	1.31
HFW	95%
AWL	4.1
TW	57

It is not possible to plan too far in the future, but we are sure that the new schedule will extend to May when we normally reschedule for the summer operation. We cannot say now if the same frequency of service will be provided beyond that date, but we are not hopeful that it will.

1'	3'	5'
7	2	1
14	5	3
21	7	4
27	9	5
33	11	7
40	13	8
46	15	9
53	18	11
55	18	11

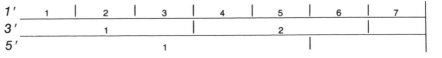

be converted to cash; liabilities—bank loans, charge accounts, mortgages, and instalment payments.

	1'	3'	5'
	72	112	67
	79	115	69

TELEPHONE CALLS

SI	1.46
HFW	91%
AWL	4.9
TW	372

SI	1.43
HFW	90%
AWL	4.9
TW	99

SI	1.44
HFW	90%
AWL	4.9
TW	131

SI	1.51
HFW	92%
AWL	4.8
TW	142

Text	1'	3'	5'
In modern practice, the telephone contact—as a collec-	11	4	2
tion technique—is generally considered as a means of achiev-	23	8	5
ing a change of pace which can return substantial dividends	35	12	7
both in the reduction of outstanding accounts and the building	47	16	9
of goodwill. When the account is not too long overdue, a gentle	60	20	12
reminder over the phone will often be all that is needed. The	72	24	14
small cost of a phone call frequently is repaid many times over	85	28	17
by additional orders obtained along with settlement of an ac-	97	32	19
count.	98	33	20
The telephone offers the advantage of personal contact	11	36	22
with the customer, but it must be used with great care. The	23	40	24
experience and skill of the collector are brought into play in the	36	45	27
course of the conversation in working out the best possible	48	47	29
arrangements, and at the same time making the customer feel	60	53	32
courteously and considerately treated. Most customers who	71	56	34
have difficulty in meeting terms of sale are faced with some kind	84	61	36
of business problem; and in a collection effort by phone, the	96	65	39
credit employee should be prepared to give a sympathetic ear	108	69	41
to the customer's problems. If any questions are in the custom-		73	44
er's mind, they can quickly be answered.		76	45
Besides learning the problems besetting the customer, it	11	79	48
must be the definite aim to wrap-up the situation or obtain an	24	84	50
understanding with regard to liquidation of the account. When	36	88	53
the size of the account and age of the obligation justify a long	49	92	55
distance call, it rarely will be possible for the customer to pay the	63	97	58

```
1'   1 | 2 | 3 | 4 | 5 | 6 | 7 | 8 | 9 | 10 | 11 | 12
3'        1    |    2    |    3    |    4
5'          1        |        2
```

Paragraph	55

SI	1.32
HFW	95%
AWL	4.4
TW	81

	1'	3'	5'

I think John makes a good point, but it seems to me to be carried a little too far. It makes one feel that he started with the assumption that fixed interest securities are preferable to common stock and then built up the reasons. In any event, it is certainly very interesting, particularly when one sees an article like this from a writer outside the life insurance industry. I hope you will keep me informed.

1'	3'	5'
6	2	1
13	4	3
21	7	4
28	9	6
36	12	7
43	14	9
50	17	10
58	19	12
64	21	13
72	24	14
79	26	16
81	27	16

Paragraph	56

SI	1.58
HFW	73%
AWL	5.5
TW	86

It is my intention to operate this apartment hotel for tourist accommodation, both summer and winter. Each unit will be completely furnished with top quality furniture, appliances, draperies, broadloom, and television. Daily maid service and linen change will be supplied. The kitchen will be equipped with all necessary dishes, cutlery, pots, pans, and appliances. Asphalt parking and plug-ins for winter use will be provided.

1'	3'	5'
7	2	1
14	5	3
21	7	4
29	10	6
37	12	7
44	15	9
51	17	10
59	20	12
66	22	13
73	24	15
79	26	16
85	28	17

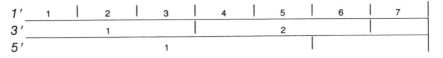

SAVINGS — A DAY-TO-DAY NECESSITY

	1'	3'	5'

SI	1.38
HFW	84%
AWL	4.9
TW	351

SI	1.37
HFW	91%
AWL	5.1
TW	53

SI	1.36
HFW	84%
AWL	4.8
TW	217

SI	1.42
HFW	79%
AWL	5.2
TW	81

Suppose that every person in the country had a guaranteed income, paid in small regular amounts daily, and that all commodities wanted or needed could be purchased on an instalment plan of equal daily payments. This would effectively eliminate the need for savings.

But the administrative nuisance and cost of paying everyone daily would be fantastic. Imagine making up pay envelopes, each for approximately one three-hundredth of the annual income, every working day of the week! Obviously this is not feasible. As soon as one can count on receiving money only every month, or every second Friday, or even every Friday, one is forced to save. The worker needs to save enough from payday to payday to be able to purchase those commodities that so far are available only for cash: streetcar or subway fare, coffee and cigarettes from the machine or the corner store, parking meter time, and most likely groceries. An individual must have enough on hand, or in the bank account, to cover the cost of goods and services that are purchased regularly but less frequently. Telephone and hydro bills fall due once a month, insurance premiums possibly every three months, licence fees and club memberships perhaps only once a year. If a person paid for everything in daily instalments one could easily be making fifty to a hundred payments every day.

There is no pat answer to the question of how much to save. It depends on a great many factors: age, health, and responsibilities; potential earning power and probably expenditures; assets — real estate, bonds, stocks, cars, insurance with loan value, and household effects — and how quickly these can

1'	3'	5'
11	4	2
23	8	5
33	11	7
46	15	9
51	17	10
11	21	12
22	25	15
33	28	17
46	32	19
58	37	22
71	41	24
83	45	27
95	49	29
108	53	32
	58	35
	62	37
	66	40
	70	42
	74	46
	78	47
	82	49
	86	52
	88	53
11	92	55
23	96	58
35	100	60
48	104	63
60	108	65

1'	1	2	3	4	5	6	7	8	9	10	11	12
3'		1		2		3		4				
5'			1			2						

	1'	3'	5'

Paragraph 57

SI	1.46
HFW	93%
AWL	4.9
TW	89

We have an extensive supply of descriptive and sales literature for our small group of friends and I have arranged to forward under separate cover a small supply of each of our brochures, including prospectus, quarterly reports, et cetera. Included in this shipment will be literature request cards on which appear a list of the literature which is available to dealers. I would suggest that you use this card in future when ordering more supplies.

	1'	3'	5'
	6	2	1
	13	4	3
	21	7	4
	27	9	5
	34	11	7
	41	14	8
	48	16	10
	55	18	11
	62	21	12
	69	23	14
	77	26	15
	83	28	17
	88	29	18

Paragraph 58

SI	1.32
HFW	97%
AWL	4.2
TW	93

We have a complete dealer sales meeting service including trained personnel and facilities to carry on formal sales meetings with you and your salespeople, which can be limited to one hour or may be extended through a full day, depending on your requirements. I am in your area from time to time and I would be delighted to include your office in my itinerary. My normal practice is to let dealers know a day or two in advance that I am going to be in their area.

	1'	3'	5'
	6	2	1
	13	4	3
	20	7	4
	27	9	5
	33	11	7
	39	13	8
	46	15	9
	53	18	11
	60	20	12
	66	22	13
	73	24	15
	81	27	16
	87	29	17
	91	30	18

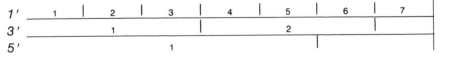

be cheaper to rent it. By next fall you may be tired of that new suit | 49 | 82 | 49
or coat you are thinking of buying on the instalment plan. Will you | 63 | 86 | 52
still be paying for it? | 67 | 88 | 53

PRODUCT CHANGE

	1'	3'	5'
While many products remain unchanged in construction	10	3	2
or style for years, others change frequently. The buyer must	23	8	5
have up-to-date information about product developments to	34	11	7
obtain suitable products. A new idea in hand tools may take	46	15	9
several years to become popular, and for many more years the	58	19	12
retailer will have to provide both the traditional tool and the new	71	24	14
one.	72	24	14
In fashion goods, the speed of change is generally much	11	28	17
faster. The novelty may become popular in a matter of weeks	23	32	19
and be in widespread demand for many months, even for sev-	35	36	21
eral years. The buyer must know how new a product is and use	47	40	24
that information as a guide for selecting merchandise.	58	43	26
For example, if an innovation is just beginning to spread,	11	47	28
the buyer may want to select only limited quantities of merchan-	23	51	31
dise using the new idea. If it is thought that customers shy away	37	55	33
from new products, a buyer may even delay for several months	49	59	36
before bringing the new merchandise into the store. Likewise, a	61	64	38
buyer may wish to avoid selecting any product that would have	74	68	41
characteristics of a declining style.	81	70	42
The buyer should know the steps in the fashion cycle and	11	74	44
the speed with which a given type of merchandise typically	23	78	47
moves through the cycle. The buyer, knowing the customers,	35	82	49
the store, the stock, and the market trends, can judge if a	46	86	51
product with particular qualities would be a good choice for the	59	90	54
store.	60	90	54

Timed Writing No. 8

SI	1.37
HFW	87%
AWL	4.8
TW	273

SI	1.42
HFW	85%
AWL	5.1
TW	73

SI	1.35
HFW	88%
AWL	4.5
TW	58

SI	1.44
HFW	90%
AWL	4.8
TW	81

SI	1.24
HFW	85%
AWL	4.6
TW	61

1' 1 | 2 | 3 | 4 | 5 | 6 | 7 | 8 | 9 | 10 | 11 | 12
3'   1 | 2 | 3 | 4
5'   1 | 2

ALPHABETIC SENTENCES

II.2 Your typewriter should be set for a 60-space line. Each sentence contains all letters of the alphabet and is designed to develop confidence in alphabetic key selection.

1 The Japanese ox quickly gave a withered carrot to the famished zebra.

2 All existing joists of every size supplied by this new company are of junk quality.

3 I would query the suggestion from experts that jackknives can be as old as the adze.

4 Leafy vegetables are not injured when exposed quickly to temperatures below zero.

5 Raspberry juice, when mixed with lime juice and stirred with a swizzle stick, has quite a good flavor.

6 Long ago the axe and the javelin were two of the weapons utilized by man to kill his luckless quarry.

7 Requests for extra zippers should just have been channelled through the main clerk in the usual way.

8 An experienced English speaker realizes that jargon is the very quintessence of bad form in writing.

9 The liquid lava oozed through the barren rock wastes and extended on to the plains adjoining the forest.

10 Quartz crystals are often transparent, but an exception is evident when a gem like jasper is considered.

11 Just now we know gauging the extent and size of the avalanche to be merely a question of procedure.

A rejector ring that can be put in the fuse socket and will allow only the proper amp fuse guards against the wrong fuse being used.

CSA certifies fuses and circuit breakers, which perform similar functions. Prototype fuses must undergo temperature, overload, and short circuit tests to provide this safety protection before they receive CSA Certification.

67	55	33
79	59	35
81	59	36
92	63	38
104	67	40
117	71	43
125	74	44

PLAN BEFORE BORROWING

	1'	3'	5'

Every time you use your telephone or turn on a light switch you are "borrowing" money. The phone or electricity company lets you use their service until the next billing date, when you will pay for the service. This kind of credit makes life a great deal more bearable than if you had to carry cash for everything. Imagine having to put a coin in a meter every time you want to use hot water, to get some light for reading, or telephone a friend!

1'	3'	5'
10	3	2
22	7	4
34	11	7
48	16	10
60	20	12
72	24	14
84	28	17
88	29	18

Sometimes the only way to cope with an emergency is to borrow money. A short-term loan well within the ability of the borrower to pay when the emergency is over can put a person back on his feet. However, the largest debts any individual is likely to acquire in his lifetime involve long-term planning — financing a car or purchasing a mortgage on a house. Similarly, borrowing to take advantage of a special price on an item you need or would buy anyway in the near future—a new refrigerator or a stereo set — are examples of planned borrowing.

1'	3'	5'
11	33	20
23	37	22
35	41	25
48	45	27
60	49	30
73	54	32
85	58	35
98	62	37
108	65	39

Planned borrowing involves careful consideration. For example, should you buy an item—perhaps ski equipment—on an instalment plan when it won't outlast the payments? It might

1'	3'	5'
11	69	41
22	73	44
35	77	46

1'	1	2	3	4	5	6	7	8	9	10	11	12
3'		1		2		3		4				
5'			1			2						

12   If you examine the records, you will perceive that the justice department requires all large blocks to be razed.

13   When brought to analyze the situation, experts often vary when stating the kinds of adjustments which are required.

14   When beginning to make an adjustment to life, it is extremely important to recognize that actions have consequences.

15   When I examined the requisition, I had a hazy notion that the buyer of the checked goods had not applied for a joint voucher.

16   They knew he suffered from Xenophobia, which is an abject fear of strangers, but it would be questionable to classify him as crazy.

17   When a man has a zest for living, when he enjoys his job, when he has a keen interest in people, does he need tranquilizers as extra crutches?

18   Max delivered, quite by accident, the wrong size package of cigarettes to Jeff.

19   Every expert jumper dazzles people by jumping from airplanes with a quick dive.

20   Quizmasters expect attendance by every class member, whether or not they are passing, failing, or just killing time.

SI	1.18
HFW	91%
AWL	4.2
TW	35

SI	1.42
HFW	89%
AWL	4.7
TW	71

SI	1.26
HFW	74%
AWL	4.2
TW	104

usually sixty-five. The age of retirement is gradually being re- 69 | 23 | 14
duced, and it is likely to come down still further in the future, 82 | 27 | 16
because of the need to make space at the executive or super- 94 | 31 | 19
visory level for an increasing number of younger people. 104 | 35 | 21

At the same time, however, advances in medicine have 10 | 38 | 23
helped people to live for much longer than they ever did before. 23 | 42 | 25
From 1931 to 1961 the expectation of life (from birth) for a man 36 | 47 | 28
rose from 60 years to 68 years, while for a woman it increased 48 | 51 | 31
even more — from 62 years to 74 years. Moreover a man who 60 | 55 | 33
had survived to age 65 in 1961 had a further life expectancy of 72 | 59 | 35
13.5 years, and a woman at 65 could expect to live another 16 85 | 63 | 38
years. Of course these average figures do not indicate the wide 97 | 67 | 40
individual variations. 102 | 69 | 41

Timed Writing
No. 6

SI	1.32
HFW	65%
AWL	4.6
TW	227

SI	1.08
HFW	74%
AWL	4.1
TW	40

SI	1.36
HFW	66%
AWL	4.7
TW	59

SI	1.19
HFW	68%
AWL	3.7
TW	57

DON'T BLOW A FUSE!

	1'	3'	5'

Next time a fuse blows in your home don't curse the fuse 11 | 4 | 2
—thank it—for it may have saved your life! The household fuse 24 | 8 | 5
is a safety measure designed to cut power off once a circuit is 37 | 12 | 7
overloaded. 39 | 13 | 8

A washing machine that is crammed with too many 48 | 16 | 10
clothes will blow a fuse. Why? Because the motor is overworked 61 | 20 | 12
causing the circuit to overload. If the fuse doesn't blow and cut 74 | 25 | 15
the electricity off, the machine may heat up or burst into flames 87 | 29 | 17
causing considerable damage and possible injury. 97 | 32 | 19

Make sure you know WHY a fuse blew before you replace 11 | 36 | 22
it. Most houses contain 15 A fuses, but the common mistake is 23 | 40 | 24
to replace a 15 A fuse with a 30 A fuse. This is a definite "no-no!" 37 | 45 | 27
The 30 A fuse will allow the wiring to heat up to a danger- 48 | 48 | 29
ous level and could cause a fire. 55 | 51 | 30

```
1' | 1 | 2 | 3 | 4 | 5 | 6 | 7 | 8 | 9 | 10 | 11 | 12
3' |   1   |   2   |   3   |   4
5' |     1     |     2
```

CAPITALIZATION EXERCISES

II.3 Your typewriter should be set for a 60-space line. Each sentence contains a number of capital letters and is designed to develop confidence in using the shift keys.

1 Mr. Jacobs attended a meeting of the Board of Directors of the St. Albert Real Estate Company Limited.

2 Write to R. F. Gotlieb, Chief, Information Services, Northern Mortgage and Housing Corporation, Toronto, Ontario.

3 He has been appointed to the Active Consulting Staff Group of the Prince Edward Island Crippled Children's Centre.

4 The letter was addressed to His Honor, Chief Judge Malcolm Smith, District Court of the District of Northern Alberta.

5 She works for Messrs. Harvey, Thomas, Hicks, Seville, Swanson, and Hayworth, Barristers and Solicitors, Hamilton, Ontario.

6 Healthy Canadians who eat a variety of foods as recommended by Canada's Food Guide obtain all the vitamins except Vitamin D.

7 The Customs and Excise Division administers the Customs Act, the Customs Tariff Act, the Excise Tax Act, and the Excise Act.

8 Harold M. Stinson and Margaret F. Young are attending a Seminar on University Service Supervision in Halifax, Nova Scotia in May.

9 Mr. Newman Zuk, Administrator of the Kelowna District X ray Clinic and Hospital, is a graduate of the College of Commerce, Saskatoon, Saskatchewan.

10 Branch offices are maintained in Charlottetown, Prince Edward Island; Halifax and Sydney, Nova Scotia; Quebec, Montreal, Sherbrooke, and Rouyn, Quebec; Ottawa, Kingston, Belleville, Toronto, Hamilton, and Kitchener, Ontario.

card file of information on customers who return to the store | 48 | 29
frequently will be helpful. Some customers like to be called when | 52 | 31
special merchandise arrives, so telephone numbers should be | 56 | 34
kept. Any special courtesy that will save customers time will be | 60 | 36
appreciated and make them loyal to the particular salesperson. | 64 | 39

Timed Writing
No. 4

SI	1.29
HFW	91%
AWL	4.4
TW	189

SI	1.18
HFW	82%
AWL	4.0
TW	23

SI	1.30
HFW	92%
AWL	4.4
TW	166

MONEY IN YOUR DREAMS

	1'	3'	5'

All of us dream and wish for things. The happy, successful person is the one who knows how to fulfill his dreams.

Now is a good time for you to stop and reflect upon your
dreams. Are they attainable, and how? Let your mind lazily drift
for a few minutes. Perhaps you thought about your career, a
coming date, a new record, new clothes, a car for yourself.
Some of these things are attainable now because you have the
necessary money or can rely on getting it soon; others can be
obtained with a little planning and saving; still others will have to
be rejected. However, you may think: If I only had more money, I
could have everything I want. Study after study indicates that
this is not so. The person who has financial difficulties on a salary
of six thousand dollars will probably have difficulties on a salary
of ten thousand dollars. Any increase in salary is likely to be
absorbed into a new living standard within six months.

1'	3'	5'
11	4	2
23	8	5
34	11	7
47	16	9
59	18	12
71	24	14
83	28	17
95	32	19
109	36	22
	41	24
	45	27
	50	30
	54	32
	58	35
	62	37

Timed Writing
No. 5

SI	1.30
HFW	82%
AWL	4.4
TW	210

INCREASING LONGEVITY

1'	3'	5'
12	4	2
24	8	5
34	11	7
44	15	9
56	19	11

Few people are able to predict just how long they will live,
but the chances are that they will need an income for several
years after their regular earnings come to an end.

In a modern economy such as Canada's, most people
are expected to retire from active employment at a fixed age,

1' | 1 | 2 | 3 | 4 | 5 | 6 | 7 | 8 | 9 | 10 | 11 | 12
3' | 1 | 2 | 3 | 4
5' | 1 | 2

WORD DIVISION EXERCISES

II.4 Your typewriter should be set for a 60-space line. Each sentence is designed so that the last word must be divided. When you hear your typewriter bell, quickly decide where to correctly divide the last word. (Refer to page 340 for a summary of word division rules.)

1   You will understand that each province has a provincial legislature.

2   With all plants operating at capacity we provide service efficiency.

3   They will include folders which thoroughly describe the traditional.

4   Our company must quickly clarify its policy in regard to gratuities.

5   Only by spending many thousands will we procure necessary materials.

6   Consultants were appointed to discuss the situation with management.

7   They shall certainly consider implementing that in the organization.

8   Seriously, we expect that they will examine my testimony thoroughly.

9   We shall spare no effort to give our customers complete satisfaction.

10   Each recipient has been asked to complete the attached questionnaire.

11   The new garage will provide the necessary covered parking facilities.

12   Several executive decisions made from day to day are very repetitive.

13   There is no reason why all your clients would not be very successful.

14   We have a complete list of all outstanding debentures and certificates.

15   Were they given to understand that such innovations occur infrequently?

SI	1.52
HFW	83%
AWL	4.9
TW	167

SI	1.54
HFW	82%
AWL	5.0
TW	61

SI	1.41
HFW	82%
AWL	4.9
TW	41

SI	1.58
HFW	84%
AWL	4.8
TW	65

OUTDOOR ADVERTISING

	1'	3'	5'
Throughout the country examples of the medium of	10	3	2
outdoor advertising can easily be seen in the form of billboards,	23	8	5
posters, and displays. Outdoor advertising is not one of the	35	12	7
major retail advertising media, but it is a form of promotion to	48	16	10
which retailers have paid increased attention in recent years.	60	20	12
The outdoor advertising message necessarily must be	10	23	14
brief. The reader must get the thought quickly, at a glance. For	23	28	17
some lines of business, this form of advertising can be used to	36	32	19
supplement other media.	40	33	20
The cost of outdoor advertising is based upon circula-	11	37	22
tion. Just as the newspaper rate is based upon the number of	23	41	25
potential readers, the outdoor advertising rate is based on the	35	45	27
number of people who are potential viewers. Outdoor advertis-	47	49	29
ing circulation is made up of the number and type of people who	59	53	32
will see the message.	63	55	33

SI	1.44
HFW	85%
AWL	4.9
TW	198

BUILDING A CLIENTELE

	1'	3'	5'
Men tend to be loyal to particular stores as well as to	11	4	2
particular salespeople. They prefer to be helped by a salesper-	24	8	5
son who knows their general needs and tastes and who can	35	12	7
save them time in selecting merchandise. The alert salesperson	47	16	9
can build up a repeat business, especially valuable to the store.	60	20	12
One should learn the names and the preferences of regular	72	24	14
customers. Business cards may be given to customers who	83	28	17
appear satisfied with the service they have received, and they	95	32	19
may be encouraged to ask for the same salesperson on their	107	36	21
return. If the store does not provide such cards, a salesperson		39	24
may take the initiative in having some printed. A notebook or		44	26

1'	1	2	3	4	5	6	7	8	9	10	11	12
3'		1		2		3		4				
5'		1			2							

SPEED ESCALATORS (SENTENCES)

II.5 Based on your typing speed record, select a sentence from the list below which matches or slightly exceeds your speed level. When you hear the instructor's signal to return the carriage, do so immediately. If you did not complete the sentence re-type it. If you did complete it, move on to the next sentence. Return your carriage only on the signal. Try to increase your speed.

		20″	30″	60″
1	Your rent is due today.	14	9	5
2	The workman looks tired.	14	10	5
3	He was about half my age.	15	10	5
4	She moved a little faster.	16	10	5
5	Many boys came to the game.	16	11	5
6	Be sure to answer your mail.	17	11	6
7	They still had hours to ride.	17	12	6
8	He flung open the office door.	18	12	6
9	The child ate three hamburgers.	19	12	6
10	A living room is to be lived in.	19	13	6
11	A friend is hoping to go with me.	20	13	7
12	The first cage door closed safely.	20	14	7
13	Joan mailed the letters I had here.	21	14	7
14	Few cars were parked on that street.	22	14	7
15	The blind girl answered with a smile.	22	15	7
16	There is just one chance in a million.	23	15	8
17	He watched as another carload returned.	23	16	8
18	Several men thought the contractor left.	24	16	8
19	The view from where we stood was immense.	25	16	8
20	You steam in at dawn among the outriggers.	25	17	8
21	A song sparrow sings in a woodland opening.	26	17	9
22	Old-timers say she used to be an opera star.	26	18	9
23	Some cruises are jamborees, and sold as such.	27	18	9
24	Our front desk people are agreeable hoteliers.	28	18	9
25	They came back into the living room right away.	28	19	9
26	He told me earlier that he enjoyed orienteering.	29	19	10
27	I have a compass in one hand, a map in the other.	29	20	10
28	Task forces have organized a vast array of events.	30	20	10
29	The cost of car leasing varies in a number of ways.	31	20	10

CONSUMER AND CORPORATE AFFAIRS

	1'	3'	5'

SI 1.61
HFW 83%
AWL 5.5
TW 141

If Canadians are to get the best results from the market system, they must feel confident that they are making an intelligent, effective, and satisfying choice when they exercise their purchasing power. To further this result, the Department of Consumer and Corporate Affairs has set the following consumer goals: protection against fraud and deception; protection against accident and health hazards; assurance that the market system is competitive; assistance to the consumer so that one can make valid choices and judge true prices; provision of a means for receiving and answering consumer complaints, queries, and suggestions; and representation of the consumer in the councils of government.

1'	3'	5'
11	4	2
24	8	5
36	12	7
48	16	10
61	20	12
72	25	14
84	28	17
97	32	19
109	36	22
	40	24
	44	26
	46	27

DETERMINING WORDS PER MINUTE

1. Read the scale at the right of the page opposite the last _complete_ line typed. If the timing was for one minute, use the first column; if for three minutes, the second column; if for five minutes, the third column.

2. Read the scale at the bottom of the page below the last word of a _partly_ finished line. Use the first row for one minute timings; the second row for three minute timings; the third row for five minute timings.

3. Add the extra words typed to the number of words typed at the end of the last _complete_ line. The sum gives the number of words typed per minute.

NOTE: If the length of the timed writing is other than one, three, or five minutes; follow the above procedure using the 1' scales. To calculate the number of words typed per minute, divide the total number of words typed by the number of minutes.

EXAMPLE: In a one-minute timed writing of "Consumer and Corporate Affairs," the last word typed was "fraud." By reading "61" opposite the last _complete_ line typed, and by reading "6" from the first row at the bottom of the page beneath "fraud," you will determine that the number of words per minute typed is "67."

1'	1	2	3	4	5	6	7	8	9	10	11	12
3'		1		2		3		4				
5'		1			2							

SPEED ESCALATORS (PARAGRAPHS)

II.6 Your typewriter should be set for a 60-space line. Select a paragraph from the series below which approximately equals or slightly exceeds your typing speed. Your instructor will give you a five-minute timed writing on the paragraph. Your objective should be to reach the appropriate number (in color above the words) before or as the instructor calls it. For example, if you were typing at approximately 9 words per minute, you would select paragraph 1 for practice. When the instructor calls "1," you should be typing the word "prompt."

SI 1.37

10 words per minute

Our new plant is in full operation to give you prompt and efficient
service at low prices. Please review your needs and forward
your order today to get a jump on spring business. Our spring
catalogue will be ready to mail to customers early next June.

SI 1.40

12 words per minute

If wheat is taken in for some other agent, please write the name
of the agent at the top of each storage ticket to show ownership.
When special bin storage tickets are issued for wheat that
belongs to other agents, the wheat of each agent must be
binned separately. We are held responsible for all the wheat.

SI 1.39

14 words per minute

If the whole scheme is still in the planning stage, would it not be a
good idea to determine how many summer replacements you
will need in the various departments, and add one or two extra to
give room to manoeuvre in a training program. When you get it
established, you will be in a position next year to say we can
handle seven, or whatever number.

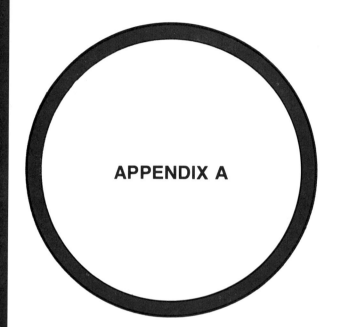

APPENDIX A

TIMED WRITINGS

THOUGHTS DURING A TYPING TEST

Get set! Go!
Even and slow
Gliding, striding
Terror hiding;
Fifty a minute —
No errors in it;
Queer looking letters
Hard to spell
One little strikeover —
Who can tell!

Zip flip
My fingers slip;
Height, tight
Do it right;
Squeeze, freeze
I have to sneeze;
Ketchup, ketchup
Try to stretchup;
Cage, rage
Turn the page!

Pace along
Sing a song
Nothing to it
I can do it;
To the show — tallyho!
To the game I'll go!
Time is flying
Speed is dying
Hurry, worry
Eyes are blurry.

Fizz, whizz
Reel and dizz
Flush, rush
Crack and crush;
Ding, zing
I've typed the thing!
Breathe and sigh,
Groan and cry —
But I did my best
With the typing test!

SI 1.39

16 words per minute

What the family physician lacks in depth, the knowledge
which requires an expert, he more than makes up for in
breadth. He deals ably with the ailments of children to the
rheumatism afflicting the aged. He sees the patient as a person,
not as a case in his appointment book. He judges the nature and
the seriousness of the patient's illness, and gives him the
correct treatment or refers him to an expert.

SI 1.37

18 words per minute

Your long November letter has just now been brought to my
attention and I am indeed sorry to learn of your displeasure with
your policy. It is a practice of our Company to value the goodwill
of all of our clients. If a new client decides that he is unhappy with
his policy and we are unable to make satisfactory changes, then
we are willing to refund the money which he may have paid. I
hope that you will call at our office soon to talk it over.

SI 1.42

20 words per minute

In order to assist us in the planning of our work, it would be
appreciated if you would contact the farmers to ascertain which
ones intend to have their houses wired in the near future. We
would like to mention that the wiring on each farm must be seen
by the local building inspector before service can be begun. In
addition, I will also require the mailing address for each of the
farmers listed for service. This will be required for billing purposes. Please write to us if you wish more information.

DEPENDING UPON THE EQUIPMENT AND FACILITIES IN YOUR SCHOOL, COMPLETE THE FOLLOWING PROBLEMS USING ONE OR TWO OF THE FOUR METHODS OUTLINED FOR PREPARING A MASTER FOR DUPLICATING.

IX.1 Type the following simplified form letter for Mr. H. A. Inwood, Controller, Saint John Lumber Company Limited, 1086 Union Street, Saint John, NB E3A 1C8.

ACCOUNT NO. (¶) At the close of business on.... your account required $.... to bring it within the minimum margin requirements. (¶) Please let us have a cheque for this amount, or provide us with additional collateral to cover this shortage. (¶) Failing receipt of the additional margin requested, we reserve the right to sell a sufficient quantity of your securities to fully margin your account without further notice to you. HOWARD A. INWOOD, CONTROLLER.

IX.2 Type the following agenda.

GERVAIS COMPANY LIMITED / Meeting of the Board of Directors / 19__ 04 25 / Board Room / Call to order / Approval of minutes of the previous meeting / Reports / New Business: (a) Product lines (b) Revision of affiliation with parent company (c) Disposal of building (d) Acquisition of land in adjacent district (e) Expansion of plant facilities (f) Dividends

IX.3 Using the following information, design an attractive form for duplicating on to a sheet of P5 paper.

Duplicating Process:

Typing	___	No. of copies required	___
Offset	___	To be collated	___
Stencil	___	To be stapled	___
Spirit	___	Working papers to be returned	___
Photocopying	___	Working papers to be destroyed	___
Other (Specify)	___		

Further Instructions: _____
_____
_____

Date Received _____ Date Required _____
Requested by _____ Approved by _____

IX.4 Attractively centre the following announcement for duplicating on P4 paper.

Announcement / The official opening of our new premises on Laurentian Circle will take place next Saturday, June 14. (¶) All facilities will be in full operation. Ladies attending will receive orchids. All visitors will be eligible for a Grand Prize to be drawn at 18:00. (¶) A guided tour for staff has been arranged for Thursday, June 12 at 20:00. A charter bus will leave at 19:45 from the north door of our present location.

22 words per minute

First, I think it should ¹/₄ be clear that the management ¹/₂ policy regarding overtime ³/₄ is that it be kept ¹ to an absolute mini-mum. ¹/₄ I feel that the time and a half ¹/₂ and double time rates are ³/₄ in the nature of penalties ² against the company for having ¹/₄ to work people beyond the ¹/₂ normal work day or week. As ³/₄ such, I believe these penalties ³ are more than sufficient to ¹/₄ discourage the use of overtime ¹/₂ except where if cannot be ³/₄ avoided. As was mentioned ⁴ by one of your agents at the ¹/₄ meeting held last June in ¹/₂ Quebec City, the nature of our ³/₄ industry makes overtime ⁵ necessary.

24 words per minute

As far as rate base is concerned, ¹/₄ the term itself is subject ¹/₂ to several interpretations. ³/₄ It would probably answer your ¹ question, however, if I say that ¹/₄ we plan to continue spending ¹/₂ about a million a year on ³/₄ system improvement and expansion ² during the next five years. ¹/₄ We predict that sales of natural ¹/₂ gas will continue to increase ³/₄ but, again, I cannot be specific. ³ You can get a good idea of ¹/₄ what to expect by simply ¹/₂ projecting the sales history ³/₄ of the past few years. ⁴ If you would like information on sales, ¹/₄ please write for our sales ¹/₂ booklets and brochure. They ³/₄ will be sent to you as soon as ⁵ possible.

8. Type with an even, normal stroke.

9. Correct errors using stencil correction fluid. Follow the instructions on the container.

10. Special tools are available for drawing diagrams and writing on stencils.

Typing a Direct Image Offset Master

1. Thoroughly clean the typewriter keys, cylinder, and paper-bail rolls.

2. Only typewriters equipped with carbon or special grease ribbons can be used for typing on an offset master.

3. Follow the typing instructions printed on the master.

4. Insert the master into the machine being careful to avoid fingerprints in the production area.

5. Type the copy.

6. Correct errors as follows:

   a. use a special grit-free "offset" eraser;
   b. avoid touching the master with your fingers — place a protective paper over areas of contact;
   c. with a circular motion, remove the carbon image by erasing slightly until a ghost image remains; (Caution: Do not destroy the surface of the master by trying to remove all traces of the image.)
   d. type the correction.

Increasingly, business offices are using the typist's original copy to produce masters for duplicating purposes.

Typing an Original for Master/Stencil Preparation

1. The typewriter keys should be clean.

2. The ribbon should be black; a carbon ribbon is recommended.

3. White paper is recommended.

4. Errors on the original copy may be corrected by using self-adhesive correction tape, white liquid correction fluid, or paste-over paper patches.

5. Type the correction on the new surface.

6. Once the original is typed and depending upon the number of copies required, a thermal copier may be used to prepare spirit or offset masters and stencils; an electronic scanner may be used for preparing stencils; and electrofax, electrostatic, and xerographic copiers may be used for preparing offset masters.

26 words per minute

I would like to take this opportunity to express my very sincere $^{1/4}$ $^{1/2}$ gratitude for the contribution made by the members of the $^{3/4}$ Hamilton Women's Hospital Aid to the smooth functioning of this ^{1} $^{1/4}$ hospital. Large as the recent donation you made to us was, $^{1/2}$ $^{3/4}$ over double what we had hoped for, it is overshadowed by the ^{2} $^{1/4}$ hours of labor given so willingly by your members in the various $^{1/2}$ $^{3/4}$ areas of the hospital's operations. In these days of government ^{3} $^{1/4}$ controls, labor unions, and high wages, it is difficult to operate $^{1/2}$ $^{3/4}$ without the help of groups such as yours. All of us at the hospi- ^{4} $^{1/4}$ tal, patients and staff, are indeed grateful to you for your gift $^{1/2}$ $^{3/4}$ and for your services. ^{5}

28 words per minute

It is our opinion that the strike was not necessary. The company $^{1/4}$ made an offer to the union on the day before the strike. Con- $^{1/2}$ $^{3/4}$ sidering our wages and fringe benefits at the time, the com- ^{1} $^{1/4}$ pany's offer was more generous than the pattern of settlement $^{1/2}$ $^{3/4}$ made by the unions in many other areas. This offer was com- ^{2} pletely rejected by the union. Because of the hardship to all $^{1/4}$ $^{1/2}$ those concerned, every effort was made to avoid a strike. $^{3/4}$ ^{3} One of the key issues in the strike is the matter of union security. $^{1/4}$ $^{1/2}$ The union has demanded that all employees pay union dues $^{3/4}$ whether they belong to the union or not. The company would not ^{4} $^{1/4}$ agree to union membership as a condition of employment for $^{1/2}$ $^{3/4}$ anybody. Soon the strike was on. ^{5}

DUPLICATING PROCESSES

Every office worker today needs to know how to make copies of correspondence, memorandums, and reports. Manual copying at the typewriter is too slow and too costly. The answer is machine copying and duplicating. Outlined below are guidelines for preparing spirit masters, stencils, and direct image offset masters.

Typing a Spirit Master

1. Thoroughly clean the typewriter keys with a type-cleaning brush, cleaning solvent, or gum preparation.

2. Slide the paper-bail rolls to left and right so that they will not rest on the master.

3. Remove the slip sheet from the master set; avoid handling the carbon.

4. Insert the open end of the master set into the typewriter.

5. Do *not* disengage the ribbon.

6. Type with a firm, even touch. Note that the carbon image appears on the back of the original.

7. Correct errors by removing or obliterating the carbon image as follows:

   a. pull original sheet forward and turn the cylinder until the error appears;
   b. with a razor blade, scrape away the error or cover the error with a self-correcting adhesive tape;
   c. snip off a piece of the unused carbon sheet and position it behind the error; and
   d. type the correction, then remove the piece of carbon.

Typing a Stencil

1. Thoroughly clean the typewriter keys with a type-cleaning brush, cleaning solvent, or gum preparation.

2. Set the ribbon control on stencil lock.

3. Place a pliofilm sheet over the waxed surface of the stencil, or decrease the printing pressure.

4. Follow the typing instructions printed on the stencil.

5. Do *not* remove the carbon sheet which enables the typist to read the copy.

6. Insert the stencil and pliofilm sheet, stub first, with the backing sheet facing you.

7. Slide the paper-bail rolls to the edges of the stencil or completely off — whichever gives you better results.

MASTER PAPER
SLIPSHEET
CARBON

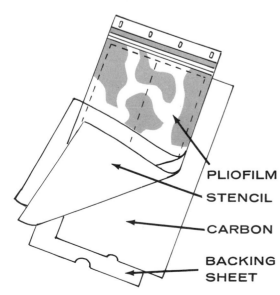

PLIOFILM
STENCIL
CARBON
BACKING SHEET

SI	1.49

30 words per minute

Thank you for the copy of the letter [1/4] from Muriel Roly regarding a meeting [1/2] to be held in Montreal next April in connection with the [3/4] formation of a lumber exporting group. This is news to [1] me and I [1/4] have no plans to attend the meeting [1/2] but it sounds as if it is something [3/4] in which we should be interested. [2] Some of our employees may attend the [1/4] meeting but, if not, I think you should [1/2] attend as our representative and report [3/4] back at our meeting early next [3] July. The formation of a group of this [1/4] nature could greatly affect the export [1/2] trade. We certainly should be aware [3/4] of what they are planning. Please [4] let me know immediately if you are prepared [1/4] to attend the meeting. Our company [1/2] will reimburse you for air fare, hotel [3/4] accommodation, and incidental expenses. [5]

SI	1.58

32 words per minute

An example of such compound errors, particularly [1/4] with regard to timing, is provided [1/2] by a company that introduced a product [3/4] in two test cities with a special offer of two packages for the price of [1] one. After [1/4] four months, factory sales were so good [1/2] that distribution was rapidly expanded. [3/4] However, the next year's sales [2] did not measure up to the level indicated [1/4] in the tests. The company concluded [1/2] it had made errors in the test process; [3/4] the main one being cutting the time so [3] short that the effects of the two for one [1/4] offer and of consumer buying were not evaluated. [1/2] The error was compounded, of course, [3/4] by using factory sales as an indicator, [4] thereby not taking into account [1/4] heavy trade stocking created by the special [1/2] offer. At our meeting next month in [3/4] Vancouver, we shall discuss cases of a [5] similar nature.

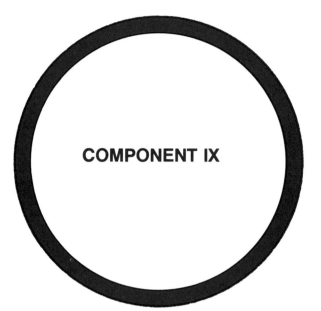

COMPONENT IX

MASTERS FOR DUPLICATION

STUDENT OBJECTIVES

1. To type in acceptable form an original copy to be used in producing a duplicating master, a spirit master, a stencil, and a direct image offset master.

2. To use appropriate correcting devices for each type of master or stencil.

DAILY ACTIVITIES

1. Current date typing. Type three lines of the current date as illustrated:

	↓ tab set	↓ tab set
19__ 05 21	19__ 05 21	19__ 05 21
19__ 05 21	19__ 05 21	19__ 05 21
19__ 05 21	19__ 05 21	19__ 05 21

2. Paragraph typing or a five-minute timed writing. Select a paragraph from Component II or III to further develop speed OR accuracy; or take a five-minute timed writing selected from Appendix A to prepare for employment tests.

3. Proceed through Component IX.

CONTENTS

Component IX introduces the student to the basic techniques used by the typist in the preparation of materials for duplicating.

Component IX / Masters for Duplication

ERROR-ELIMINATION SENTENCES

II.7 Your typewriter should be set for a 60-space line. Each sentence has been developed to provide additional practice in the selection of often-confused key locations.

R and T

1 The fur traders centred their business there.

2 There is no great price difference between different types.

3 The labor relations record in this great area is not excellent.

4 This system has proved to be most satisfactory to those who have property in rural areas.

5 These departments were most concerned about parts and services for our radio and our television set.

G and H

6 I thought these might be good for them.

7 Long ago they thought that it was a good accounting method.

8 A long time ago they threshed grain with the threshing machine.

9 This is a good time for high schools to be looking at what they should be getting.

10 After writing thoughtfully and correcting critically, you will have to read what you have written to ascertain that it is free from ambiguity, that the message is right, the words right, and the tone right.

M and N

11 The one hundred men must improve in many more of the mundane methods.

12 The morning meeting or conference should end on a note of general recommendation.

Fill-in Forms	**ITA 11**
	Compose and type ten fill-in postal cards which your school library might use as reminders of overdue books.
	ITA 12
	Design a registration card for a local motel/hotel.
Application Form	**ITA 13**
	Obtain an Application for Employment form from a local business. Fill-in the required personal information using the typewriter. (A sample Application for Employment form is provided in the Workbook that accompanies this text.)
	ITA 14
	Design a fill-in application form for the position of clerk in a local retail store.
Index Cards	**ITA 15**
	Type ten index cards in proper form, for the addresses of the parents to whom you sent postal cards in ITA 9.
Financial Reports	**ITA 16**
	Ask permission of the Treasurer of a Service Club to type in proper form their balance sheet and income statement.
Itinerary	**ITA 17**
	Prepare and type an itinerary for your summer vacation.

13 One theme that runs through your planning is the need to communicate many dynamic ideas.

14 Many sentimental things have been written in poems about a smile. Smiles win friends and customers.

15 By all means reach out your hands for all the learning you can grasp, and give your minds to mastering it.

T and Y   **16** They did their duty yesterday and today.

17 They painted the toys a pretty yellow color.

18 They will try to attach the top immediately and carefully.

19 They went slowly by your yard twice each day throughout the year.

20 You live in a time when you need to know about many things that were not even in the dictionary when your father was a youth.

S and D   **21** Sue did not do what she was told to do today. She said she had to go to school.

22 We surely shall depend on David to ease the difficult situation when he responds to the daily notes.

23 Sam said that he had delivered several solid, dry, dilapidated bundles to the six independent sellers.

24 He dreamed a dream; the sojourners set off and sailed the deep, dark sea to seek assistance for the stranded sailors.

25 So often sailboats do not seem to do what we demand they do. We assume they will do what we intend them to do without direction.

Programs	**ITA 4**
	Compose and type a program for an up-coming school function.
	ITA 5
	Compose, design, and type a Thanksgiving Dinner Menu for a restaurant.
Agenda	**ITA 6**
	Ask permission of the Principal of your school to type the agenda for the next Staff Meeting.
	ITA 7
	In consultation with the President of a school club, of which you are a member, compose and type the agenda for the next club meeting.
Minutes	**ITA 8**
	Ask permission of the President of a local Service Club to take notes at a meeting. From your notes, compose and type minutes of meeting.
Postal Cards	**ITA 9**
	Compose a postal card message inviting parents to attend an art exhibit, music festival, science fair, or other event which might take place in your school.
	Type ten postal cards bearing this message and address them to the parents of ten of your classmates. Use the school address as the return address.
	ITA 10
	Prepare ten postal cards which might be addressed and used as reminders of a Service Club meeting date.

V and B 26 We made a visit to the big park to view the beavers and the brown bears.

27 The boy beat the boat in the race to save the big sinking vehicle from a watery grave.

28 No vehicle can be as valuable as the big, black automobile in which you have invested.

29 Berries, beetles, and briars combine to make berry picking a very vital vexatious, and venturous experience.

30 We sell very good varnish and veneer at bargain prices. You have to begin saving for the big November sale of better building materials.

31 Bob vigilantly watched the village from the villa as vapor rose over the vents from the basements of battered boarding establishments.

32 As requested verbally by you, I have enclosed a revised bill. I advise you to have a bigger battery put in the vehicle because it will give better service.

E and I 33 This adds up to seeing life steadily and seeing it whole.

34 I recommend that he begin his course of studies at his leisure.

35 I intend to have them review every order received in the past year.

36 We will ship the steel springs ten weeks after receipt of his order, providing the order is received within the next year.

37 The density of the sheet which I have been receiving is about half that which I normally receive from my suppliers.

U and Y 38 The early results of the study were unbelievably unusual, but clearly valuable.

39 The youth slowly and carefully used the glue on the upper part of the ugly yellow stud.

INCOME STATEMENT
(2-Column)

VIII.66 Type a copy of the following income statement. Centre the information horizontally and vertically on a sheet of P4 paper.

KING TAXI

Income Statement

For the Month Ended 19____ 08 31

Fares Earned		$2 000.00
Operating Expenses:		
Wages Expense	$550.00	
Supplies Expense	400.00	
Depreciation Expense	200.00	
Rent Expense	50.00	
Utilities Expense	25.00	
Miscellaneous Expense	75.00	
Total Operating Expenses		1 300.00
Net Income		$ 700.00

INDIVIDUALIZED TYPEWRITING APPLICATIONS (ITA's)

VIII.67 Now that you have completed Component VIII you should experience little difficulty in performing any of the following ITA's.

Use good techniques when composing and typing each application.

News Release

ITA 1

Compose and type a news release for an event taking place in your school. Use one of the two formats presented in this Component.

ITA 2

Find out news-worthy information about a member of your business community and compose and type a news release.

ITA 3

If a group or club in school is planning a summer group tour, interview the chairperson of the group and from your notes compose and type a news release.

40 Use the words unbelievably, unavoidably, unconditionally, understandably, and unjustifiably in sentences.

41 In your letter you certainly did not tell us about the lines of furniture and heavy equipment usually sold by your company.

42 Put the words courteously, wisely, soberly, impartially, objectively, and curiously in a sentence and underscore them. Use the underscore correctly.

I and O   **43** It has not been our practice to fill senior positions from outside our organization.

44 You should find out how many you will need in the various operations of your construction firm.

45 The company would not agree to union membership as a continuing condition of employment.

46 In any job, a person should show that he is conscious of the possibility of improvement. It is not difficult to do this.

47 But if the effort you make appears to be too tedious or irksome, recall your purpose. Then the vexations of daily life will seem trivial.

Z and X   **48** You realize our next task is complex. You cannot be lazy.

49 In the next six days we shall take the exact number in a box to the zoo.

50 The next load of sixteen gauge is expected to be shipped to another zone.

51 We were amazed by the exact zero temperature. We did not realize it was so exhilarating.

52 We recognize the expansion experienced by those who realize the strength of their organization.

Although many business organizations use one-write systems or data processing equipment to produce cheques, some organizations prepare all their cheques manually on the typewriter. Problems VIII.62 - VIII.64 will give you practice in typing cheques and corresponding cheque stubs. The cheque and cheque stub are both forwarded to the payee.

If you are not using the Workbook that accompanies this text, blank cheques may be obtained from most banks.

VIII.63 Refer to the statement of account prepared in Problem VIII.59 and as typist for Laura's Steno Services type a cheque payable to Livingstone Distributors Ltd. for the statement amount.

VIII.64 Refer to the statement of account prepared in Problem VIII.60 and as typist for Killarney Collegiate Institute type a cheque payable to Livingstone Distributors Ltd. for the statement amount.

BALANCE SHEET
(2-Column)

VIII.65 Type a copy of the following balance sheet. Centre the information horizontally and vertically on a sheet of P4 paper.

KING TAXI

Balance Sheet

As at 19___ 08 31

Assets

Cash		$2 100.00
Supplies		250.00
Equipment	$7 400.00	
Less Accumulated Depreciation	200.00	7 200.00
Total Assets		$9 550.00

Liabilities

Accounts Payable		$ 350.00

Capital

John King, Capital		9 200.00
Total Liabilities and Capital		$9 550.00

DIFFICULT REACH SENTENCES

II.8 Your typewriter should be set for a 60-space line. Each sentence has been developed to provide additional practice in making difficult and awkward reaches. Practice of selected sentences will aid in developing stroking continuity.

1 In a democracy, personal effort is significant.

2 The best executives have moments of doubt and weariness.

3 To one who is bored by the routine of vacation resorts, the national parks beckon.

4 On a national scale, we waste the bounty and lay waste the beauty of our country.

5 The first virtue of writing style is brevity, and brevity is aided by use of the active verb.

6 We know much more about health protection than we apply individually or collectively.

7 In writing about a complaint you are obligated to give a full, understandable, civil explanation.

8 In some plants, all material that is damaged in any way is collected by a regular salvage department.

9 Like all business correspondence, answers to complaints should be courteous, cheerful, tactful, clear, complete, and brief.

10 The computer seems a long way from abacus, on which one counted by moving beads along wires, but the line of descent is obvious.

11 The parcel was sent C.O.D. We received it in the evening.

12 The boxes were packed so that the books would arrive in good condition.

13 Mr. L. W. Zarks, Mrs. Q. B. Schultz, and Dr. P. N. Sawyer attended our graduation banquet.

VIII.61 Use the information below to prepare a statement of account for Mrs. L. Dreisen.

```
19__ 03 31

MRS. LOUELLA DRIESEN          F  NORTHERN LIGHTS EXCHANGE LTD
608 WEST 52 AVENUE            R       1205 ARLINGTON AVENUE
VANCOUVER, BC                 O            SASKATOON, SK
V6P 1G2                       M                  STH 2X5

01 03  BALANCE FORWARD                                    150.00
   05  INV. NO. 45678-N                   50.00           200.00
   10  PAYMENT RECEIVED THANK YOU                150.00    50.00

02 15  INV. NO. 45690-N                  100.00           150.00
   20  PAYMENT RECEIVED THANK YOU                 50.00   100.00

03 31  CURRENT BALANCE                                    100.00
```

CHEQUES   VIII.62 Type a copy of the cheque below.

DUNCAN HARDWARE LTD.
432 Ninth Avenue, Brandon, MB R7A 4B1 _____ April 4 _____ 19 __77__ No. __834__ $\frac{13-34}{420}$

Pay to the Order of _____ Livingstone Distributors Ltd. _____ $ 149.00

_____ One hundred forty-nine _____ XX/100 Dollars

THE ROYAL BANK OF CANADA
742 Rosser Avenue, Brandon, MB R7A 0K9

_____
Duncan Hardware Limited

⑆0420⑈0034⑆ 797⑈550 ⑈

- -

Detach this stub before cashing cheque

_____

TO

Livingstone Distributors Ltd.
P. O. Box 121
Oakbank, MB R0E 1J0

IN PAYMENT OF THE FOLLOWING INVOICES:

Date	Invoice	Amount
19__ 03 10	1456	149.00

DUNCAN HARDWARE LTD.
432 Ninth Avenue, Brandon, MB R7A 4B1

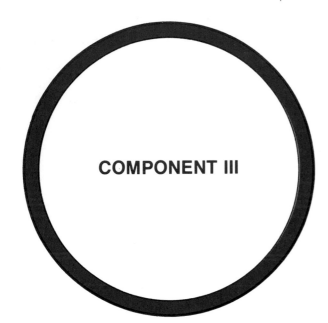

COMPONENT III

OPERATING THE NON-ALPHABETIC KEYBOARD

STUDENT OBJECTIVES

1. To establish the typing patterns for numbers and symbols.

2. To use correct techniques in striking keys; i.e., quick, sharp finger movements.

3. To type in correct form sentences containing numbers and symbols.

4. To increase stroking and copying skills.

DAILY ACTIVITIES

1. Adjust the margins for a 50-space line.

2. Select and type several times an alphabetic sentence from pages 53 to 54.

3. Select and type one or two error-elimination sentences from pages 63 to 66 or one or two difficult reach sentences from page 67.

4. Review selected exercises from the previously covered pages of Component III.

5. Proceed through Component III according to flow chart instructions.

6. Select and type a number of paragraphs from pages 37 to 52 to further develop typing continuity.

7. Select one or two paragraphs from pages 39 to 52 for one-minute timed writings.

8. Individualized Typewriting Applications. Select ITA's from pages 107 to 111.

CONTENTS

Component III introduces the student to the number and symbol keys. Sentences containing numbers and symbols are used to provide meaningful practice.

Supplementary skill-building materials include consecutive number drills, postal code drills, number speed escalators, and sentences and paragraphs containing numbers and symbols.

Individualized Typewriting Applications called ITA's which give students practice in expressing their thoughts in typewritten form.

*A **credit memorandum** is a business form sent to advise a customer that an adjustment in his favor has been made to his account.*

VIII.56 On a prepared form type a credit memorandum to Laura's Steno Services (see Problem VIII.52) for 1 dozen steno pads and 1 dozen 3H, GP pencils.

VIII.57 On a prepared form type a credit memorandum to Killarney Collegiate Institute (see Problem VIII.53) for 5 cases potato chips.

STATEMENTS

VIII.58 Type a copy of the Statement of Account for Duncan Hardware Ltd. which is illustrated below.

Livingstone Distributors Limited

P.O. BOX 121 OAKBANK, MANITOBA R0E 1J0
TELEPHONE (204) 681-9311

STATEMENT OF ACCOUNT

In account with: Duncan Hardware Ltd.
432 Ninth Street
Brandon, MB
R7A 4B1

Date: _____ 19__ 03 31 _____
Please return this stub with your cheque.

Amount enclosed: _____

Date	Reference	Charges	Credits	Balance
19__ 02 28				00.00
19__ 03 10	Invoice 1456	181.00		181.00
19__ 03 28	Credit Memo 4564		32.00	149.00
↑ Left margin set	└─── Payable on Receipt ──── tab set ───	↑	↑	↑

---

*A **statement** is a business billing form which summarizes a customer's account transactions during a given period of time.*

Forms for problems VIII.58-VIII.61 are provided in the Workbook that accompanies this text.

VIII.59 Using the information provided in Problems VIII.52 and VIII.56 prepare a statement of account for Livingstone Distributors Ltd. with Laura's Steno Services.

VIII.60 Using the information provided in Problems VIII.53 and VIII.57 prepare a statement of account for Livingstone Distributors Ltd. with Killarney Collegiate Institute.

DAILY ACTIVITY

If you are beginning a new class period, refer to page 68 and follow the suggestions for improving and developing your typing continuity.

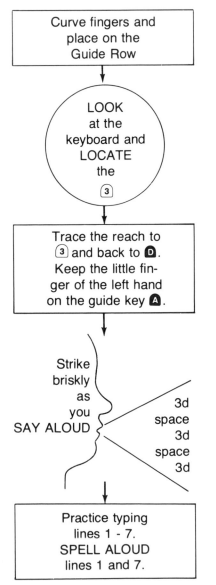

THE NUMBER ③

Curve fingers and place on the Guide Row

↓

LOOK at the keyboard and LOCATE the ③

↓

Trace the reach to ③ and back to **D**. Keep the little finger of the left hand on the guide key **A**.

↓

Strike briskly as you SAY ALOUD
3d
space
3d
space
3d

↓

Practice typing lines 1 - 7. SPELL ALOUD lines 1 and 7.

III.1 USING THE ③

1   3d 3d 3d 3d3 3d3 3d3 d3 d3 d3 d3d d3d d33 3d 3d 3d
2   Please make 33 copies of form number 33.

> *When typing numbers, type as words numbers ten and under except when used with numbers above ten.*

3   There were three accidents during January.
4   Send 3 to John, 33 to Mary, and 333 to Joseph.

> *A space should be used to indicate thousands when grouping numbers of four or more digits.*

5   At least 3 333 people will attend the next concert.
6   The interest was paid on May 3, June 3, and July 3.

7   3d 3d 3d 3d3 3d3 3d3 d3 d3 d3 d3d d3d d33 3d 3d 3d

VIII.53 On a prepared invoice form, type the following information:

Sold to Killarney Collegiate Institute, Box 490, Killarney, MB R0K 1G0 /
Invoice No. 1458 / Customer Order No. 3221 / Shipped by Livingston
Truck / Terms n/30: 1 dozen cases potato chips @ $1.60; fifteen 24-bar
boxes assorted candy bars @ $2.40; 1 box oranges @ $2.00.

VIII.54 On a prepared invoice form, type the following information.

Lorenz General Store in Deer Horn, Manitoba R0C 0T0 used Purchase Order No. 1425 to order 10 only fence stretchers #923 @ $15; 20 rolls barbed wire fencing #333-765 @ $25.50; 25 boxes staples #008 @ 85 cents; 20 boxes insulators (electric fence) #00678 @ $1.25; 80 kg nails, 65 mm, #555-67-88, $0.50/kg. This order was delivered by Livingstone Distributors on invoice number 1459. Terms 2/10, n/45.

CREDIT MEMORANDUMS   VIII.55 Type a copy of the credit memorandum illustrated below. Prepare a carbon copy for your files.

Livingstone Distributors Limited

CREDIT MEMORANDUM

P.O. BOX 121 OAKBANK, MANITOBA R0E 1J0
TELEPHONE (204) 681-9311

To: Duncan Hardware Ltd.
    432 Ninth Street
    Brandon, MB
    R7A 4B1

tab set
↓

Date:	19 03 28
Credit Memo No:	4564
Order No:	946
Invoice No:	1456

Your account has been credited as follows:

Quantity	Description	Unit Price	Amount
2 rolls	Wallpaper, 455-90	16.00	32.00 CREDIT

DAILY ACTIVITY

If you are beginning a new class period, refer to page 68 and follow the suggestions for improving and developing your typing continuity.

THE NUMBER 8

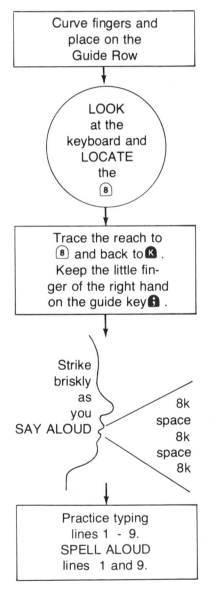

III.2 USING THE 8

1   8k 8k 8k 8k8 8k8 8k8 k8 k8 k8 k8k k8k k88 8k 8k 8k
2   We shall arrive in Toronto on March 8.

3   He ordered 3 desks, 38 tables, and 83 chairs.
4   There are eight boys and three girls in the room.

> *The metric symbol for day/days is d. When typing the number of days (a measured period of time) use the metric symbol if the number is typed in numerals. A single space separates the symbol from the number.*

5   The tour of three countries will last 83 d.
6   Invoice number 38 is packed in box 88.

7   A new order is required for size 38 dresses.
8   Approximately 3 388 people live in Chandler.

9   8k 8k 8k 8k8 8k8 8k8 k8 k8 k8 k8k k8k k88 8k 8k 8k

VIII.51 Type a copy of the invoice shown below. Make a carbon copy for your files. Note: Clear tabs and margin stops. Set left margin and tabs as indicated. (Prepared invoices are available in the Workbook that accompanies this text.)

Livingstone Distributors Limited

P.O. BOX 121 OAKBANK, MANITOBA R0E 1J0
TELEPHONE (204) 681-9311

INVOICE

tab set

Sold To: Duncan Hardware Ltd.
432 Ninth Street
Brandon, MB
R7A 4B1

Date: 19___ 03 10
Invoice No: 1456
Customer Order No: 946
Shipped By: Livingstone Truck
Terms: 2/10, n/30

Quantity	Catalogue No.	Description	Unit Price	Total
6 ℓ	146-33	General Purpose Paint, red	1.50	9.00
1 doz.	146-59	Brushes	1.00	12.00
10 rolls	455-90	Wallpaper	16.00	160.00
		TOTAL		181.00

Left margin set

tab set

---

*An **invoice** is a bill for goods sold. Formats vary from organization to organization, but most contain columns (ruled or unruled) for quantity, description, unit price, and amount.*

Terms indicate discounts offered according to payment date.

For example: 2/10, n/30 — A 2% discount will be allowed if the bill is paid within 10 days. The total amount is due within 30 days.

VIII.52 On a prepared invoice form, type the following information:

Sold to Laura's Steno Service, 123 - 25 Street, Brandon, MB R7B 1Y7 / Invoice No. 1457 / Customer Order No. 89 / Shipped by Greyhound Parcel / Terms 2/10, n/30.

Quantity	Description	Unit Price
10 bx.	P4 Carbon paper, light	6.00
12 M	Bond paper, white, No. 456	4.10
1 doz.	Steno pads, spiral	0.20
48	Pencils, 3H, GP	0.10

DAILY ACTIVITY

If you are beginning a new class period, refer to page 68 and follow the suggestions for improving and developing your typing continuity.

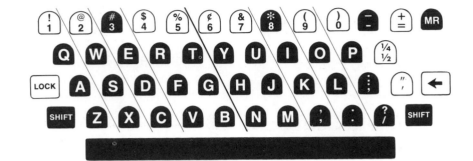

THE NUMBER ④

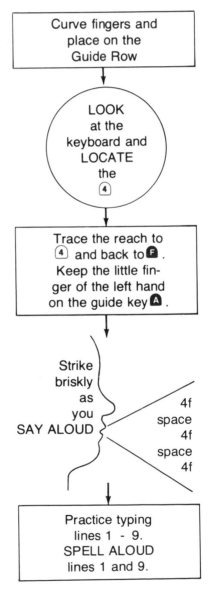

Curve fingers and place on the Guide Row

LOOK at the keyboard and LOCATE the ④

Trace the reach to ④ and back to **F**. Keep the little finger of the left hand on the guide key **A**.

Strike briskly as you SAY ALOUD

4f
space
4f
space
4f

Practice typing lines 1 - 9. SPELL ALOUD lines 1 and 9.

III.3   USING THE ④

1   4f 4f 4f 4f4 4f4 4f4 f4 f4 f4 f4f f4f f44 4f 4f 4f
2   The St. Lawrence Seaway may open on March 4.

3   Each unit will have 44 pages for case discussion.
4   His office extension number is 348.

5   Al quickly advised all 84 passengers of the delay.
6   Nearly 3 484 people live at 43 Oak Road.

7   I worked four days in June and eight days in July.
8   She took a telephone order for 843 books today.

9   4f 4f 4f 4f4 4f4 4f4 f4 f4 f4 f4f f4f f44 4f 4f 4f

PURCHASE ORDERS

*A **purchase order** is used by an organization to order goods from another. Formats vary from organization to organization.*

VIII.49 Type a copy of the purchase order shown below. Make a carbon copy for your files. Note: Clear tabs and margin stops. Set left margin and tabs as indicated. (Prepared Purchase Order forms are available in the Workbook that accompanies this text.)

Eastern Seaboard Electrical Appliances Limited
19 Green Belt Drive, Don Mills, ON M3C 1L9 Phone (416) 449-8828

PURCHASE ORDER

tab set

To: Kelly Distributors Co., Ltd.
    37 Peel Street
    Barrie, ON
    L4M 3L1

Order No: 79645
Date: 19 __ 03 06
Terms: 2/15, n/30
Ship Via: Bilnor

Quantity	Cat. No.	Description	Unit Price	Amount
6	77A	Perfection toasters	20.88	125.28
3	96C	Economy 10-cup percolators	35.49	106.47
2	41E	Combination Griddle and Waffle Irons	26.50	53.00
6	146T	Hagar immersible fry pans	31.98	191.88
2	27F	Hagar Dishwashers	485.50	971.00
				1 447.63

— Left margin set

— tab set —

Purchasing Agent:

VIII.50 On a prepared purchase order form, type the following information.

In problem VIII.50 did you remember to total the amount column?

To Miller's Stationery Limited, Box 907, Berwick, ON K0C 1G0 /Order No. 79646 / Terms n/30 / Ship Via Parcel Post.

Quantity	Catalogue No.	Description	Unit Price
48	HG405	File Folder, 20 mm cut left, P4	0.04
12	HF530	Mucilage, 30 ml glass bottle	0.11
12	HB522	3-ring, loose-leaf binders, P4	0.41
6	HC560	P4 clip boards	0.40

DAILY ACTIVITY

If you are beginning a new class period, refer to page 68 and follow the suggestions for improving and developing your typing continuity.

THE NUMBER ⑤

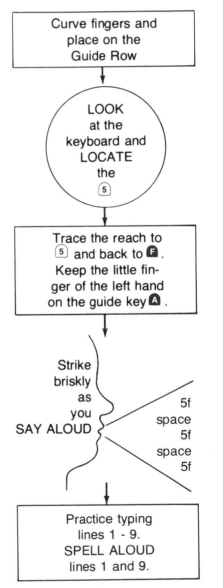

Curve fingers and place on the Guide Row

LOOK at the keyboard and LOCATE the ⑤

Trace the reach to ⑤ and back to **F**. Keep the little finger of the left hand on the guide key **A**.

Strike briskly as you SAY ALOUD

5f
space
5f
space
5f

Practice typing lines 1 - 9.
SPELL ALOUD lines 1 and 9.

III.4 USING THE ⑤

1 5f 5f 5f 5f5 5f5 5f5 f5 f5 f5 f5f f5f f55 5f 5f 5f
2 Number 5 is the bus I take to work.

3 There were 55 calls from Mr. Smith yesterday.
4 The beauty salon is located at 538 Dalbrent.

5 Invoice number 3854 covers that large shipment.
6 He lives at 4544 Crescent Drive in Regina.

7 Dial 484-4538 for information on flight arrivals.
8 Number them: 34, 35, 38, 45, 48, 58, 83, and 85.

9 5f 5f 5f 5f5 5f5 5f5 f5 f5 f5 f5f f5f f55 5f 5f 5f

Telegram
Télégramme

CNCP
Telecommunications

send this message subject to the terms on back
dépêche à expédier aux conditions énoncées au verso

19__-06-21-10:30

Mr. Kenneth Ottwell
45 St. Peters Road
Charlottetown, PE
C1A 5N1

Board meeting April six satisfactory. Arrive noon April fifth for

preliminary meeting.

Andrew Foster
Quilley Finance Co. Ltd.

check mots	12	full rate plein tarif	X	night letter lettre de nuit		tolls coût
charge account no. numéro de compte	5927	cash number numéro de caisse				
sender's name nom de l'expéditeur	Quilley Finance Co. Ltd.					
address and telephone adresse, téléphone	1121 - 100 Street, North Battleford, SK S9A 0V4 306-423-6185				CN—6106—B(11—72) 48—42—725	

NOTES ON TELEGRAMS

Style

1. Either block or modified block style is acceptable.
2. The material may be typed in ALL CAPITALS or in upper and lower case.
3. Double-spacing (depending on length) is usual.
4. Each telegram should include the time and date filed, the telegram address, the body, and the sender's name (signature).
5. The reference portion of the telegram form should be completed in full: check — the number of words in message, centred; class of service—"X" full-rate or night letter; charge account no.—if provided by telegraph company, two spaces to the right of printing; cash number—only if assigned to firm; sender's name—repeat of signature line; and address and telephone number.

Chargeable Words

1. Dictionary words in English, German, French, Italian, Dutch, Portuguese, Spanish, or Latin languages are counted as one word each, regardless of length.
2. Dictionary words from languages other than those enumerated above may be used in messages provided they are expressed in letters from the English alphabet, but they are counted at the rate of one word for every five letters.
3. Initials are counted as one word each.
4. Common abbreviations are counted as one word if they are written as a unit. For example, COD is counted as one word.
5. No charge is made for punctuation symbols.
6. Each digit of a number is counted as a word. For example "11" is counted as two words; "eleven" is counted as one word. Suffixes attached to numbers increase the word count. For example, "1st" is charged as two words.
7. Each special character is counted as one word. For example, $, %, #, are each counted as one word.
8. One signature with accompanying title is transmitted without charge.

DAILY ACTIVITY

If you are beginning a new class period, refer to page 68 and follow the suggestions for improving and developing your typing continuity.

THE NUMBER ⑥

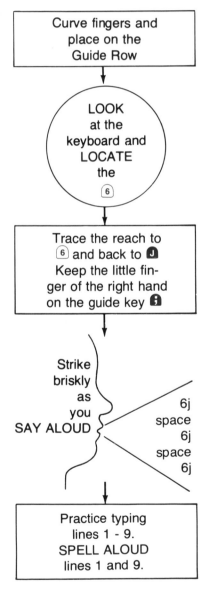

Curve fingers and place on the Guide Row

LOOK at the keyboard and LOCATE the ⑥

Trace the reach to ⑥ and back to **J** Keep the little finger of the right hand on the guide key **J**

Strike briskly as you SAY ALOUD

6j space 6j space 6j

Practice typing lines 1 - 9. SPELL ALOUD lines 1 and 9.

III.5 USING THE ⑥

1 6j 6j 6j 6j6 6j6 6j6 j6 j6 j6 j6j j6j j66 6j 6j 6j
2 How much is due if it is paid on October 6?

> *Express percentages in figures.*

3 The buyer may save 6 per cent if he pays in 33 d.
4 He will only save 3 per cent if he pays in 66 d.

> *Metric symbols are never pluralized, and are typed without a period except at the end of a sentence.*

5 Review frames 36, 64, 66, 68, 365, 386, and 684.
6 Toronto is approximately 3 454 km from Calgary.

> *Express in figures numbers that follow a noun.*

7 Problem 4 requires one to multiply six by eight.
8 Table 6 may be used in solving the problem.

9 6j 6j 6j 6j6 6j6 6j6 j6 j6 j6 j6j j6j j66 6j 6j 6j

09:30 Appointment with Mr. G. Garnham, of Eastern Canada Sales Limited, 2070 Chartier Avenue, Dorval (papers in folder 3). Travelling time by taxi approximately 5 min.

18:20 Leave Dorval Airport on CP 75 (ticket in air transportation folder). Dinner Flight.

21:45 Arrive Winnipeg.

TELEGRAMS

Notes: On telegrams —

*In business offices, **telegrams** are usually submitted by telephone to the telecommunication company. Occasionally they are submitted on a telegram form obtainable from the telecommunications company. The office copy may be typed on stationery or on the telegram form. Usually three carbon copies (file, addressee, and accounting department) are prepared.*

*There are two classes of telegrams: **full-rate** and **night letter**. Full-rate telegrams receive top priority in transmission and delivery. The standard charge is for a minimum of 15 words. Night letters are transmitted overnight for delivery the next morning. The standard charge—for a minimum of 50 words—is about 80 per cent of the cost of the full-rate message.*

VIII.46 Type a copy of the telegram illustrated on page 279. Prepare three carbon copies—file, one to be mailed to Mr. Ottwell, and one for the accounting department.

VIII.47 From the following information, provided by Andrew Foster, Quilley Finance Co. Ltd., prepare a full-rate telegram with three carbon copies. Try to use no more than 15 words.

Mr. Clint Weber, 43 Underwood Street, New Glasgow, NS B2M 3H4, 902-648-0352. Contact Vinnie Koenig of Fredericton concerning his damaged stock. Offer a six-month extension on the loan. It can be repaid from insurance proceeds.

VIII.48 From the following information, provided by Andrew Foster, Quilley Finance Co. Ltd., prepare a night letter with three carbon copies. Try to use no more than 50 words.

Mr. Vinnie Koenig, Today's Record Shop, 602 York Street, Fredericton, NB E3B 3R5, 506-395-8774. We were distressed to hear of the recent disastrous flood damage to your store from our representative, Clint Weber. We will be glad to extend your current loan for an additional six months, and as well can offer an additional loan for the same value until the insurance proceeds are received. We are sending additional information and application forms by airmail. Simply indicate your needs and return as soon as possible. Provide the name of your bank — if different from that on file — so that the necessary funds can be transferred within 24 h of receipt of your application. We have asked Clint Weber to make a trip to Fredericton to assist you in any way possible. You will be hearing from him very soon.

DAILY ACTIVITY

If you are beginning a new class period, refer to page 68 and follow the suggestions for improving and developing your typing continuity.

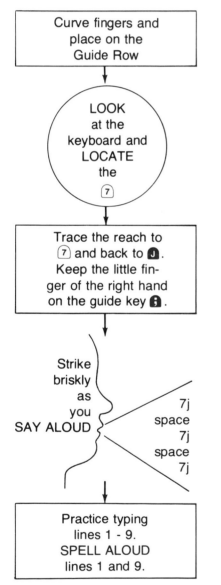

THE NUMBER 7

Curve fingers and place on the Guide Row

↓

LOOK at the keyboard and LOCATE the 7

↓

Trace the reach to 7 and back to J. Keep the little finger of the right hand on the guide key J.

↓

Strike briskly as you SAY ALOUD

7j space 7j space 7j

↓

Practice typing lines 1 - 9. SPELL ALOUD lines 1 and 9.

III.6 USING THE 7

1 7j 7j 7j 7j7 7j7 7j7 j7 j7 j7 j7j j7j j77 7j 7j 7j
2 Room 7 contains an earth science laboratory.

3 I will take 77 d to complete the tour this year.
4 Coach number 676 is a through coach to Vancouver.

5 Juanita brought 75 baskets of blueberries.
6 His average mark on the seven weekly tests was 77.

> *Postal Codes contain six characters—three alpha (A) and three numeric (N) — in ANA NAN sequence. A space separates the second alpha and numeric characters.*

7 The postal code for 7 Duke Street is E3A 4J4.
8 Subtract 5 635 from 74 378 to obtain 68 743.

9 7j 7j 7j 7j7 7j7 7j7 j7 j7 j7 j7j j7j j77 7j 7j 7j

50 mm

ITINERARY FOR JANICE CURRIE

←25 mm→ WEDNESDAY, MAY 6: WINNIPEG TO TORONTO

17:10 Depart Winnipeg on AC 196 (ticket in air transportation folder).
       Dinner flight.

20:15 Arrive Toronto. Guaranteed reservation at Royal York Hotel (confirma- ←25 mm→
       tion in travel folder). Bus transportation every 20 min to hotel.

THURSDAY, MAY 7: TORONTO TO HALIFAX

09:00 Breakfast in Tudor Room 9 with Mr. M. Wallace, of Direct Mail Services,
       re monthly mailings (papers in folder 1).

12:30 Luncheon, Bulk Mail Advertising Association, Royal York Roof Garden.
       Mrs. Terry Dowding is speaking on "Rising Costs versus Declining
       Circulation." A copy of her speech has been mailed to your attention
       at the hotel. It is marked, Hold for Arrival. Chairperson: Mr. Theo
       Logier, Ad-Search Limited.

18:45 Leave Toronto on AC 622 (ticket in air transportation folder). Bus
       transportation to airport leaves Royal York from York Street entrance
       every 20 min. Dinner Flight.

22:20 Arrive Halifax. Guaranteed reservation at Chateau Halifax (confirmation
       in travel folder). Bus transportation direct to hotel leaves 20 min
       after flight. Travel time from airport to hotel is approximately 40 min.

FRIDAY, MAY 8: HALIFAX TO MONTREAL

09:30 Sales Conference for Atlantic Region in Kesagosee Room (conference
       reports in folder 2).

19:00 Leave Halifax on EP 133 (ticket in air transportation folder).
       Transportation leaves hotel 1½ h before flight departure time. Dinner
       Flight.

20:20 Arrive Dorval Airport. Guaranteed reservation at the Grand Motor Hotel
       (confirmation in travel folder). Taxi from airport to hotel
       approximately $4.

(Problem continues on page 278.)

DAILY ACTIVITY

If you are beginning a new class period, refer to page 68 and follow the suggestions for improving and developing your typing continuity.

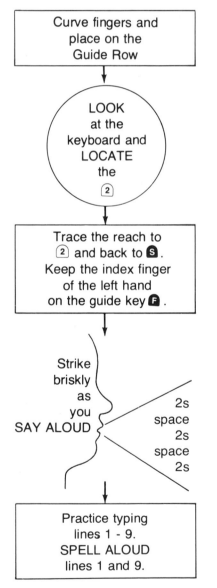

THE NUMBER ②

Curve fingers and place on the Guide Row

↓

LOOK at the keyboard and LOCATE the ②

↓

Trace the reach to ② and back to Ⓢ. Keep the index finger of the left hand on the guide key Ⓕ.

↓

Strike briskly as you SAY ALOUD { 2s space 2s space 2s

↓

Practice typing lines 1 - 9. SPELL ALOUD lines 1 and 9.

III.7   USING THE ②

1   2s 2s 2s 2s2 2s2 2s2 s2 s2 s2 s2s s2s s22 2s 2s 2s
2   Problem 2 is difficult; problem 22 is easy.

3   The chart on page 272 shows the monthly sales.
4   Take Air Canada flight 624 from Toronto to Gander.

5   The size of the master bedroom is 2.7 m by 5.4 m.
6   A total of 6 227 people attended the first rally.

> *Express sums of money in figures. Even sums are written without decimals and zeros.*

7   The stock is quoted at 22 cents.
8   I bought two cans for 63 cents. I saved 2 cents.

9   2s 2s 2s 2s2 2s2 2s2 s2 s2 s2 s2s s2s s22 2s 2s 2s

ADDITIONAL INFORMATION

For further information and registration contact the following individuals:

Family Skating	Paul Harrison Local 241
Belly Dancing	Bev Almond Local 263
Duplicate Bridge	Irene Camps Local 233
Family Gym & Swim	Don Hamilton Local 262

ITINERARY

VIII.44 Using a sheet of P4 paper with wide edge inserted, centre the following itinerary for Dr. Morris Luchowich.

Notes: On itineraries —

An **itinerary** *is usually prepared by a businessperson prior to the commencement of a business trip. It serves as a record which can be referred to by office personnel should it be necessary to contact the travelling businessperson. In addition, it provides a concise record for the traveller of important information pertaining to travel method and times, hotel accommodations, and often prearranged appointments. Formats for itineraries vary from organization to organization. As a typist, it is important to arrange the material in a concise easy-to-read and easy-to-understand manner.*

Dr. Morris Luchowich

Itinerary

	Departure			Flight	
Date	City	Time		Airline	No.
October 2	Edmonton	09:00		AC	106
October 2	Montreal	18:45		CP	206
October 18	Athens	10:10		AZ	891
October 25	Rome	09:45		CP	207
November 4	Amsterdam	13:15		CP	381

Arrival		Accommodations	
City	Time	Hotel	Phone
Montreal	16:10	—	—
Athens	11:00	Electra	(021) 3223 222
Rome	11:00	Grand	06-489011
Amsterdam	12:00	Schiller	231660
Edmonton	14:35	—	—

> *Problem VIII.44 should be set up as a table with nine columns.*

VIII.45 Type a copy of the itinerary which appears on page 277. Treat the itinerary as an unbound manuscript.

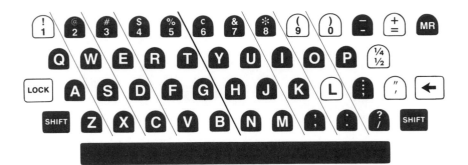

DAILY ACTIVITY

If you are beginning a new class period, refer to page 68 and follow the suggestions for improving and developing your typing continuity.

If your typewriter does not have a special key for the 1, use the small letter l for the number 1 and practice typing lines 2 - 8.

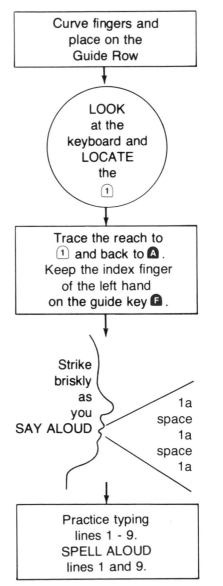

THE NUMBER ①

Curve fingers and place on the Guide Row

LOOK at the keyboard and LOCATE the ①

Trace the reach to ① and back to **A**. Keep the index finger of the left hand on the guide key **F**.

Strike briskly as you SAY ALOUD

1a space 1a space 1a

Practice typing lines 1 - 9. SPELL ALOUD lines 1 and 9.

III.8 USING THE ①

```
1   la la la lal lal lal al al al ala ala all la la la
2   The family will travel to Hawaii on July 1.

3   I have read 14 pages.  She has only read 11.
4   Lester owns 146 shares of common stock.

5   The numbers of her cheques were 21, 316, and 481.
6   A pocket book is about 11 cm wide and 18 cm long.

7   His social insurance number is 123 415 671.
8   The recipe used 125 ml flour and 1.2 ml salt.

9   la la la lal lal lal al al al ala ala all la la la
```

		Dr. Leonard Collins, Director
		Relax Limited, Calgary
Response		Dr. Elizabeth Thorn,
		Consultant
		Ontario Ministry of Tourism
21:30	Spring Serenade	Wedgewood Room
		The Carleton Trio

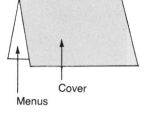

Cover

Menus

VIII.42 Fold a sheet of P4 paper in half to form a fold-over P5 size "program." Insert the folded edge into the typewriter and then using the information below, prepare an attractive Room Service Breakfast Menu for Bellevue Park Lodge. Breakfast service is available, by dialing 6, between 07:00 and 09:30.

Menu No. 1
Orange Juice
Fried Eggs and Sausages
Buttered Toast
Coffee, Tea, or Milk
$3.55

*

Menu No. 2
Grapefruit Juice
Scrambled Eggs and Bacon
Buttered Toast
Coffee, Tea, or Milk
$3.55

Menu No. 3
Tomato Juice
Hot Cakes and Bacon
Buttered Toast
Coffee, Tea, or Milk
$2.80

*

Menu No. 4
Orange Juice
Fried Eggs and Bacon
Buttered Toast
Coffee, Tea, or Milk
$3.55

VIII.43 Using the following information prepare an attractive program.

COVER

Fall and Winter Physical Fitness and Recreation Program for employees of Life Corporation Limited, 164 Commander Boulevard, Agincourt, ON M1S 3C7

PROGRAM

Mondays (Beginning October 1)
19:00 - 20:30 Family Skating   Chartwell Arena
Tuesdays (Beginning October 2)
20:00 - 21:00 Belly Dancing   Tam O'Shanter
Wednesdays (Beginning October 3)
20:00 - 22:30 Duplicate Bridge   Yelland Hall
Thursdays (Beginning October 4)
19:00 - 22:30 Family Gym & Swim
                    Stephen Leacock
                    Collegiate Institute

If you are beginning a new class period, refer to page 68 and follow the suggestions for improving and developing your typing continuity.

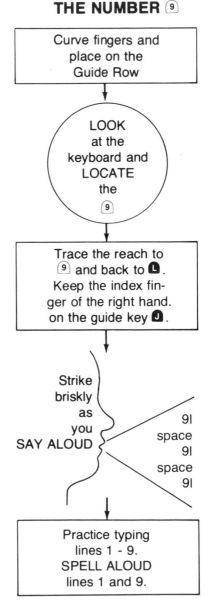

THE NUMBER ⑨

Curve fingers and place on the Guide Row

LOOK at the keyboard and LOCATE the ⑨

Trace the reach to ⑨ and back to **L**. Keep the index finger of the right hand. on the guide key **J**.

Strike briskly as you SAY ALOUD

9l
space
9l
space
9l

Practice typing lines 1 - 9. SPELL ALOUD lines 1 and 9.

III.9 USING THE ⑨

1 91 91 91 919 919 919 19 19 19 191 191 199 91 91 91
2 Interest rates now exceed 9 per cent per annum.

> *When numbers are used before other words to form compound adjectives, a hyphen is used. If the other word is typed as a metric symbol, the use of the hyphen is optional.*

3 He took a 99-d note on the unpaid invoice today.
4 There is a 99-d bus tour leaving on December 9.

5 Once every four years February has 29 d.
6 The new dictionary has 793 pages without pictures.

> *Serial, patent, and policy numbers are typed according to the style of the original source.*

7 The serial number on my machine is: C-4319897.
8 Patent No. 4345599 was issued to J. Smith in 1976.

9 91 91 91 919 919 919 19 19 19 191 191 199 91 91 91

VIII.40 Prepare business mailing labels for each of the individuals listed in Problem VIII.39. Begin the first line of type 2 line spaces below the return address, and 13 mm to the left of centre.

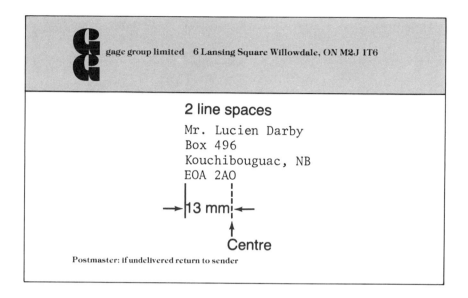

PROGRAM OF A MEETING

*The preparation of **programs** need not be difficult. Problem VIII.41 provides an opportunity to prepare and type a simple two-page (cover and program) program. Treat each page of the program as a vertical and horizontal centring problem.*

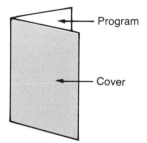

VIII.41 Fold a sheet of P4 paper in half to form a fold-over P5 size program. Insert the folded sheet into the typewriter with the fold at the left.

Using the following information, type an attractive cover page for the program.

EXECUTIVE CLUB

Spring Banquet

19___ 03 19

Glenwood Hotel
Edmonton, Alberta

Reverse the fold and re-insert the program into the typewriter. Use the following information to type an attractive program. (To pivot from the right margin, set the carriage at the margin, backspacing once for each letter and space in the line.)

P R O G R A M

18:30	Reception	Wedgewood Room
19:30	Banquet	Carleton Room
	Greetings	Gordon Muir, President
	Address	"Recreation for the Busy Executive"

If you are beginning a new class period, refer to page 68 and follow the suggestions for improving and developing your typing continuity.

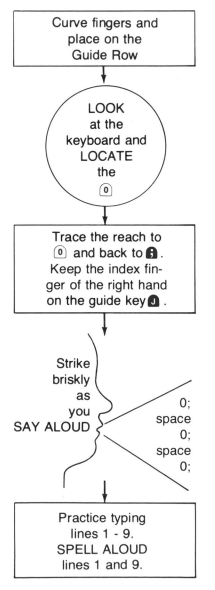

THE NUMBER ⓪

III.10 USING THE ⓪

1 0; 0; 0; 0;0 0;0 0;0 ;0 ;0 ;0 ;0; ;0; ;00 0; 0; 0;
2 September, April, June, and November have 30 d.

3 No airplane can yet carry 1 000 passengers.
4 Many airlines use the popular Boeing 707 jet.

> *When a decimal fraction of a unit is used, a zero always is placed before the decimal.*

5 Stop at the grocer and buy 0.45 kg of butter.
6 The area code for Sudbury, Ontario is 705.

> *"May 1977. New policy now rules that the official Canadian symbol for "litre" is the upper case L, both when used alone as in 4 L and when used with a prefix as in 5 mL." This policy was introduced after publication and is not reflected in this text. Students are advised to make the corrections as they occur.*

7 How much will 0.5 ℓ of milk cost next year?
8 Her father worked 40 years; her mother 30 years.

9 0; 0; 0; 0;0 0;0 0;0 ;0 ;0 ;0 ;0; ;0; ;00 0; 0; 0;

Curve fingers and place on the Guide Row

LOOK at the keyboard and LOCATE the ⓪

Trace the reach to ⓪ and back to ⑪. Keep the index finger of the right hand on the guide key ⑪.

Strike briskly as you SAY ALOUD

0; space 0; space 0;

Practice typing lines 1 - 9. SPELL ALOUD lines 1 and 9.

FILE FOLDER LABELS

VIII.38 Type file folders labels for the ten individuals listed below. If you are using individual labels (as opposed to roll-labels) use the back-feeding method for inserting the labels.

Notes: On typing file folder labels —

*When typing **file folder labels**, begin the typed line a triple-space below the fold line. Set the left margin stop 3 spaces from the left edge of the label. Type the surname first, followed by given names and/or initials.*

```
    JENKINS, Doris L.
- - - - - - - - - - - - - - - - - - - - - - - - - -
    JENKINS, Roger K.
```

Jensen, Darryl F.
Jenson, Carol Darlene
Jenssen, Steven W.
Jente, Jessie I.

Jentes, Nancy C.
Jents, Irene K.
Jentz, Peter R.
Jeoffroy, Brian F.

VIII.39 Type mailing labels for the individuals listed below. Leave a minimum of one line space between the top edge of the label and the first line of type. Set the left margin stop three spaces in from the edge of the label. If you are using individual labels, use the front-feeding method for inserting the labels.

```
Mr. Lucien Darby
Box 496
Kouchibouguac, NB
E0A 2A0
```

Mrs. L. Duxbury
52 Saint Lawrence Street
Toronto, ON
M5A 3N1

Miss Francine Parker
P. O. Box 830
Chibougamau, PQ
G8P 2K8

L. Freeman
1919 Bloomingdale Terrace
Halifax, NS
B3H 4E5

J. Singer
305 Laird Boulevard
Montreal, PQ
H3R 1Y3

Miss Cheryl Kitts
8424 - 108 Street, Apt. 4
Grande Prairie, AB
T8V 4C7

DAILY ACTIVITY

If you are beginning a new class period, refer to page 68 and follow the suggestions for improving and developing your typing continuity.

DEVELOPING TYPING CONTINUITY

Type all lines as they appear. →

III.11 REVIEWING ALL PREVIOUSLY LEARNED KEYS

1 In the last 50 years, the death rate from tuberculosis has been reduced by 80 per cent.

2 A news item said that more than 400 subcontractors work for a major aircraft engine manufacturer in constructing the 8 854 parts for a new jet engine.

3 At the last published count, Canada had 26 635 manufacturing establishments with 14 or fewer employees and 10 386 with 15 or more employees.

4 There were 61 479 new housing units started in the first half of the year, an increase of 27 per cent over the same period in the preceding year.

5 Since June of 1800, skin divers have recovered the following treasures from the wreck of La Lutine: 58 bars of gold, 33 bars of silver, 4 English guineas, and 2 half-guineas.

6 The average written sentence during the reign of Queen Elizabeth I ran to about 45 words; the Victorian sentence to 29; ours to 20 and fewer.

7 This book of 227 pages, prepared as a series of 27 lectures by the Royal Canadian Mounted Police, costs 79 cents.

When preceded by a number, use the metric symbol min for minute/minutes.

8 A 92-car train can be switched in 25 min to any of 48 tracks ready to be used again for new trains.

9 To multiply by 0.1 move the decimal one place to the left.

CHAIN FEEDING

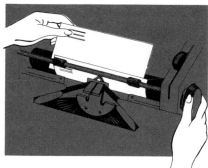

FRONT-FEEDING

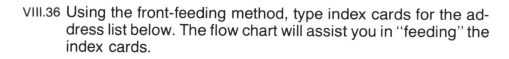

VIII.36 Using the front-feeding method, type index cards for the address list below. The flow chart will assist you in "feeding" the index cards.

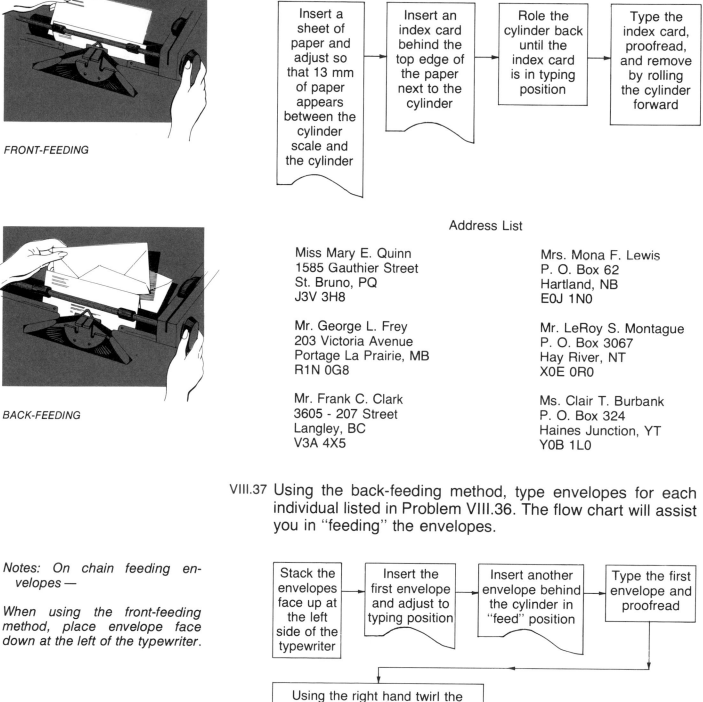

| Insert a sheet of paper and adjust so that 13 mm of paper appears between the cylinder scale and the cylinder | → | Insert an index card behind the top edge of the paper next to the cylinder | → | Role the cylinder back until the index card is in typing position | → | Type the index card, proofread, and remove by rolling the cylinder forward |

Address List

Miss Mary E. Quinn
1585 Gauthier Street
St. Bruno, PQ
J3V 3H8

Mr. George L. Frey
203 Victoria Avenue
Portage La Prairie, MB
R1N 0G8

Mr. Frank C. Clark
3605 - 207 Street
Langley, BC
V3A 4X5

Mrs. Mona F. Lewis
P. O. Box 62
Hartland, NB
E0J 1N0

Mr. LeRoy S. Montague
P. O. Box 3067
Hay River, NT
X0E 0R0

Ms. Clair T. Burbank
P. O. Box 324
Haines Junction, YT
Y0B 1L0

VIII.37 Using the back-feeding method, type envelopes for each individual listed in Problem VIII.36. The flow chart will assist you in "feeding" the envelopes.

Notes: On chain feeding envelopes —

When using the front-feeding method, place envelope face down at the left of the typewriter.

| Stack the envelopes face up at the left side of the typewriter | → | Insert the first envelope and adjust to typing position | → | Insert another envelope behind the cylinder in "feed" position | → | Type the first envelope and proofread |

Using the right hand twirl the cylinder to remove the envelope, and with the left hand "feed" another envelope

BACK-FEEDING

DEVELOPING TYPING CONTINUITY

10 If 7 113 of the patents issued went to companies and 2 568 went to individuals, how many patents went to companies and individuals jointly?

11 In 1907, a little more than ten years after introduction of the first motor car, the total number of cars registered in Canada was only 2 130.

12 All questionnaires were completed on October 15 by 3 271 secondary and post-secondary students.

13 Each year at least 24 zebras are taken into captivity and transported over 6 400 km to North American zoos.

> When preceded by a number, use the metric symbol h for hour/hours.

14 Only 35 years ago when a man left his home on Monday morning he had a 58-h work week ahead of him.

15 It takes approximately 12 h to drive the 865 km between Argentia and Port aux Basques.

16 This ritual is said to have been used by him at the coronation of King Ethelred in the year 978.

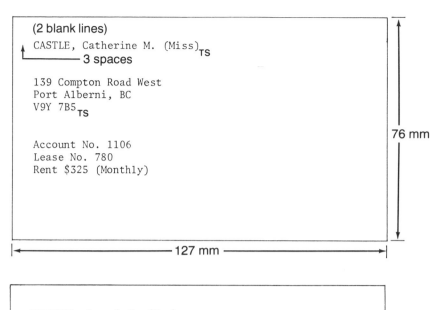

```
(2 blank lines)
CASTLE, Catherine M. (Miss)TS
         3 spaces

139 Compton Road West
Port Alberni, BC
V9Y 7B5 TS


Account No. 1106
Lease No. 780
Rent $325 (Monthly)
```

76 mm

127 mm

```
CORMIER, Joseph T. (Mr.)


601 North Crescent
Port Alberni, BC
V9Y 3B7


Account No. 30
Lease No. 93
Rent $275 (Monthly)
```

VIII.34 Prepare an index card for each salesperson enrolling in the Clinics mentioned in Problem VIII.32. For each, provide the Clinic No., and the Sales District.

VIII.35 Type the "Peach-Tomato Chutney" recipe on an index card. Triple-space after the title. Double-space between the ingredients and cooking instructions.

PEACH-TOMATO CHUTNEY

24 ripe tomatoes, peeled and sliced
12 peaches, peeled and sliced
4 diced green peppers
4 sliced onions

250 ml raisins
250 ml chopped ginger in syrup
1 ℓ brown sugar
15 ml coarse salt

Mix all the ingredients in a heavy saucepan, then bring to a boil and simmer uncovered, stirring often for about three hours or until the chutney is thick. Pour into sterilized jars and cover. Yield: 5 ℓ.

DAILY ACTIVITY

If you are beginning a new class period, refer to page 68 and follow the suggestions for improving and developing your typing continuity.

THE "DASH"

III.12 USING THE ⊡

> The dash may be formed in two ways:
> 1. By typing two hyphens without spaces before and after. (E.g. team--not)
>
> or
>
> 2. By typing a single hyphen with a space before and after. (E.g. team - not)
>
> Choose whichever method you wish, but be consistent!

Lines 1 - 4 will give you practice in typing the dash.

1 Our team--believe it or not--won the game today.
2 You will enjoy our scenic spots--Banff and Jasper.

3 Purchase the three metre length--not a shorter one.
4 He is consistent--he has scored 12 points a game.

GG gage group limited   6 Lansing Square Willowdale, ON M2J 1T6   (416) 221-0551

TWO-DAY RETAIL SALES CLINIC

Enrolment Form

DEALERSHIP _____   DATE _____

TOWN/CITY _____   DISTRICT _____

Please enroll the following salespeople
in the two-day Retail Sales Clinic. I
understand that there is a nominal
enrolment fee of twenty-seven dollars
and fifty cents (.$27.50) per person,
and I am attaching a cheque to cover
the salespeople listed below.

Signed _____

MEETING LOCATION: Parkway Hotel
                   317 Davignon Boulevard
                   Cowansville, PQ
                   J2K 1P4

CLINIC #1	CLINIC #2
DATE: February 8 and 10	DATE: February 9 and 11
TIME: 09:00 - 16:30	TIME: 09:00 - 16:30
SALESPEOPLE'S NAMES	SALESPEOPLE'S NAMES
1. _____	1. _____
2. _____	2. _____
3. _____	3. _____
4. _____	4. _____
5. _____	5. _____

DAILY ACTIVITY

If you are beginning a new class period, refer to page 68 and follow the suggestions for improving and developing your typing continuity.

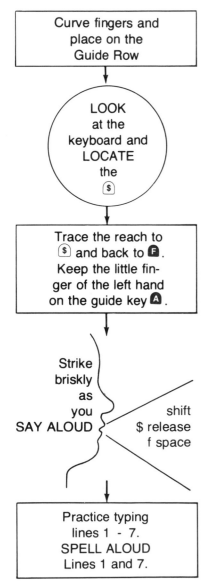

THE "DOLLAR"

Curve fingers and place on the Guide Row

↓

LOOK at the keyboard and LOCATE the $

↓

Trace the reach to $ and back to **F**. Keep the little finger of the left hand on the guide key **A**.

↓

Strike briskly as you SAY ALOUD

shift $ release f space

↓

Practice typing lines 1 - 7. SPELL ALOUD Lines 1 and 7.

III.13 USING THE $

The $ is the shift of the 4.

Even dollar sums are typed without decimals and zeros.

```
1    $f $f $f $45 $44 $67.45, an increase of $8, $1.95
2    The price of the coat is $45.  It used to be $55.

3    We received a cheque for $155.22 from your agent.
4    Last year the operation had a net profit of $700.

5    The repair bill of $56.75 is still outstanding.
6    The amount owing on your Order No. 3139 is $37.59.

7    $f $f $f $45 $44 $67.45, an increase of $8, $1.95
```

VIII.31 Make a copy of the fill-in form that appears on page 270. (If you are not using the Workbook that accompanies this text, create a suitable heading for the form from the following information: The Gage Group Limited, Management and Sales Consultants, 6 Lansing Square, Willowdale, ON M2J 1T6.)

VIII.32 Using the information below complete three enrolment forms for the Two-Day Retail Sales Clinics. (If you are not using the Workbook, prepare three additional copies of the Enrolment Form.)

A. Mr. Georges Robichaud, Manager of the Montreal North District for Circle Lincoln-Mercury Motors, 6300 Henri Bourassa Boulevard East, Montreal, PQ H1G 5W9 submitted the following names:

Clinic 1	Clinic 2
Mr. G. Robichaud	Miss L. Lisee
Ms. H. Garnham	
Mr. A. Gagnon	

B. Mr. J. Prime, Manager of the New Brunswick South district for Elm City Chrysler Ltd., 190 King Street, Fredericton, NB E3B 1C9 submitted the name of Mr. D. Middlemin for Clinic 2.

C. Mrs. M. Grives, Manager of the Annapolis District for Newer Motors Ltd., 117 Westville Road, New Glasgow, NS B2H 2J2 submitted the name of Mr. R. Cochran for Clinic 1.

INDEX CARDS

Index cards may be used for many purposes. The brief list below suggests some possible uses.

1. *Mailing Lists*
2. *Recipes*
3. *Conversion Tables*
4. *Book Reviews*
5. *Footnote Data*
6. *Bibliography Data*

VIII.33 Type a copy of each of the index cards which appears on page 271. The flow chart below will assist you in typing the index cards.

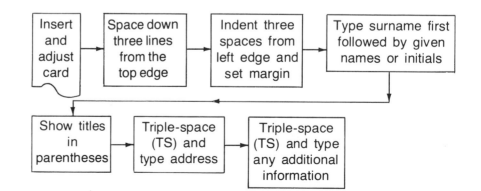

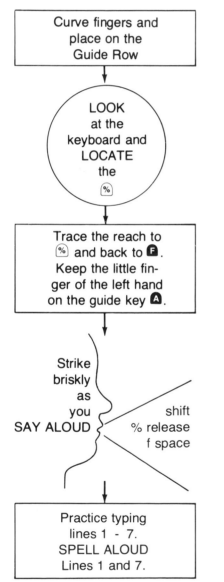

THE "PER CENT"

Curve fingers and place on the Guide Row

↓

LOOK
at the keyboard and LOCATE the %

↓

Trace the reach to % and back to **F**. Keep the little finger of the left hand on the guide key **A**.

↓

Strike briskly as you SAY ALOUD
shift
% release
f space

↓

Practice typing lines 1 - 7.
SPELL ALOUD
Lines 1 and 7.

III.14 USING THE %   *The % is the shift of the 5.*

1 %f %f %f 5% 4%, 45% were sold, 55% were not bought
2 Mr. Frank hopes to increase sales by 5% this year.

3 He also hopes to decrease expenses by at least 2%.
4 The employees received a 12.5% salary increase.

5 About 50% of the items require more than one copy.
6 The interest rate is 8%--2% higher than last year.

7 %f %f %f 5% 4%, 45% were sold, 55% were not bought

PLINKINGDON

MANUFACTURING LTD.

1185 TECUMSEH BLVD. EAST
WINDSOR, ONTARIO
N8W 1D5
(519) 256·5131

Gentlemen:

_____ has applied to us for a position.

Please take a few minutes to complete this brief questionnaire. Your opinion
of the applicant's ability and any other information which you may give us
will assist us in determining his (or her) fitness for a position in our
organization. Such information will be held strictly confidential.

Yours very truly,

4 line spaces (3 blank lines)

Personnel ·Director_{TS}

How long was applicant in your employ? From _____ to _____

Nature of work? _____

Was work satisfactory? _____

Ability: Excellent _____ Good _____ Fair _____ Poor _____

Production: Quality: Excellent _____ Good _____ Fair _____ Poor _____
             Quantity: Excellent _____ Good _____ Fair _____ Poor _____

Character: _____

Reason for leaving your employ. _____

Would you re-employ this person if you had an opportunity? Yes ____ No ____

_____
Signed

_____
Position

DAILY ACTIVITY

If you are beginning a new class period, refer to page 68 and follow the suggestions for improving and developing your typing continuity.

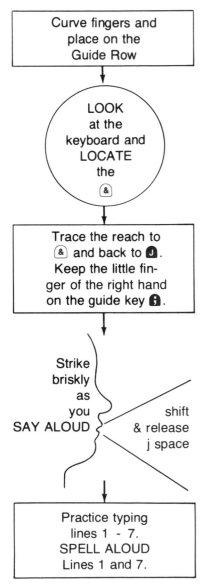

THE "AND"

Curve fingers and place on the Guide Row

↓

LOOK at the keyboard and LOCATE the &

↓

Trace the reach to & and back to J. Keep the little finger of the right hand on the guide key ;.

↓

Strike briskly as you SAY ALOUD

shift & release j space

↓

Practice typing lines 1 - 7. SPELL ALOUD Lines 1 and 7.

III.15 USING THE &   *The & is the shift of the 7.*

1 &j &j &j Boner & Rowe, C. D. Mack & Son, Hit & Run
2 She was employed by the firm of Porter & Mitchell.

3 Nancy was offered a job by Calder & Bates Co. Ltd.
4 Raskin & Leibow act as solicitors for our company.

5 I hope to buy some Whiteman & Field common shares.
6 Smith & Heath have opened a shop in Lansdowne Row.

7 &j &j &j Boner & Rowe, C. D. Mack & Son, Hit & Run

Mr. Sam King
63 Mark Street
Aurora, ON
L4G 3J4

Mr. William (Bill) J. Walker
34 Murray Street
Barrie, ON
L4N 2Y2

VIII.29 Make a copy of the fill-in form that appears on page 268. (If you are not using the Workbook that accompanies the text, use the following information for creating a 50 mm deep letterhead: Great Lakes Finance Company, 1083 Exmouth Street, Sarnia, ON N7S 1W4.)

VIII.30 Using the information below complete three separate copies of the form prepared in Problem VIII.29. (If you are not using the Workbook, prepare three additional copies of the "form" letter.)

A. The following reply was received from Mr. D. Ritchie, Personnel Manager with Marsh Bros. Construction Company Ltd., 1400 Totten Street, Windsor, ON N9B 1W9:

"Mr. King Hey has worked for Marsh Bros. Construction Co. Ltd., from 1975 08 01 through 1975 09 30 as gang-punch operator. His production was excellent both in terms of quality and the hourly quantity produced. He was prompt, conscientious, courteous, and very honest. He left our employ to return to Seneca College to pursue a career in the graphic arts industry. We would be delighted to have him as either a full-time or part-time employee."

B. The following reply was received from Mr. J. Barclay, President, Barclay Typesetters Limited, 3208 Marentetti Avenue, Windsor, ON N8X 4G4:

"Mr. P. T. Jones was employed by Barclay Typesetters Ltd., as a proofreader for two years beginning 1975 01 01. We terminated his employment with us as his work, both in terms of quality and output, did not measure up to our standards. While employed with us, we found him to be honest and trustworthy."

C. The following reply was received from Mr. R. Jones, President, Canadian Glass Co., 276 Lauzon Road, Windsor, ON N8S 3L6:

"Miss Pamela P. Price began work with Canadian Glass Co. in June, 1975. She was initially employed as a data entry operator and later promoted to supervisor of customer service. She is an exceptional employee—bright, keen, honest, and very reliable. We were sorry to see Pamela leave our firm in January, 1976, but she decided to continue with a Bachelor of Commerce program at York University. We most decidedly would be delighted to have Pamela return to our firm as inventory control supervisor upon graduation."

DAILY ACTIVITY

If you are beginning a new class period, refer to page 68 and follow the suggestions for improving and developing your typing continuity.

The "PARENTHESES"

III.16 USING THE ( )

| The (is the shift of the 9. |

| The) is the shift of the 0. |

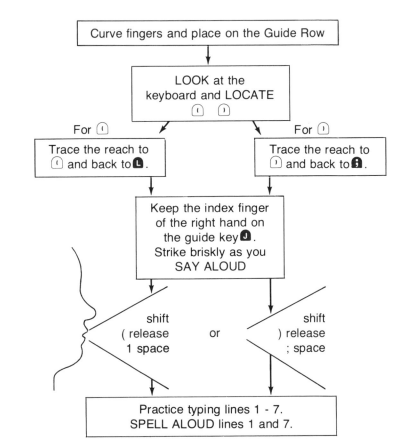

| When additional copy separates a quantity from a metric term, the metric term should be typed in words rather than symbols. |

1 (1 (1 (1););); (1) (;) due in 12 (twelve) days
2 He can (easy--easily) do the test in three hours.

3 The exam will be written next week (September 30).
4 The price of the new article ($29.75) is too high.

5 Do you have a reservation for tomorrow (April 3)?
6 The typewriter (see page 432) is fully automatic.

7 (1 (1 (1););); (1) (;) due in 12 (twelve) days

```
┌─────────────────────────────────────────────────────────┐
│     ⌂                                                     │
│  ┌─────────┐                                              │
│  │ FAMILY  │ MOTOR HOTEL                                  │
│  └─────────┘                                Telephone:    │
│  Parrsboro NS  B0M 1S0                      (902) 293-8141│
│                                                           │
│  Dear Mr. Radcliff:                                       │
│                                                           │
│       We take pleasure in confirming your reservation     │
│  for accommodation from  19__ 07 05  to  19__ 07 07       │
│  inclusive.                                               │
│                                                           │
│  Number of persons  ___1___   Daily Rate  _$16.50_        │
│                                                           │
│       Please note that we are unable to hold reserva-     │
│  tions after 18:00 unless accommodation is prepaid.       │
│                                                           │
│                                                           │
│                            _____    │
│                                Reservations Clerk         │
└─────────────────────────────────────────────────────────┘
```

VIII.27 **Prepare the following "form" as a postal card.**

```
┌─────────────────────────────────────────────────────────┐
│      ╱╱                                                   │
│     ╱╱                             PO BOX 498             │
│  ══════════════                   Collingwood, ON         │
│         Learn to SKI Limited          L9Y 4O2             │
│            Registration Form       (705) 476-7985         │
│  Name                                                     │
│  _____ │
│                                                           │
│  Address                                                  │
│  _____ │
│                                                           │
│  _____ │
│                                                           │
│  _____ │
│                                                           │
│  _____ │
│                                                           │
│  Phone                                                    │
│  _____ │
└─────────────────────────────────────────────────────────┘
```

VIII.28 **Complete both sides of the LEARN TO SKI LTD. Registration Form for each of the applicants in the list below. (If you are not using the Workbook, prepare three additional copies of the Registration Form.)**

Applicants

Ms. Denise Gorton   Miss Robin Saxton
696 Sunnypoint Drive   126 Woodward Avenue
Newmarket, ON   Thornhill, ON
L3Y 2Z8   L3T 1E9

DAILY ACTIVITY

If you are beginning a new class period, refer to page 68 and follow the suggestions for improving and developing your typing continuity.

THE "NUMBER"

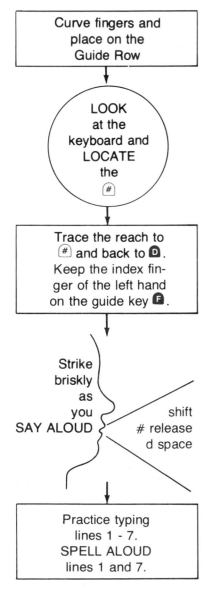

Curve fingers and place on the Guide Row

↓

LOOK at the keyboard and LOCATE the #

↓

Trace the reach to # and back to **D**. Keep the index finger of the left hand on the guide key **F**.

↓

Strike briskly as you SAY ALOUD

shift
release
d space

↓

Practice typing lines 1 - 7.
SPELL ALOUD lines 1 and 7.

III.17 USING THE #   *The # is the shift of the 3.*

When the symbol # is placed before a figure it denotes number.

1   #d #d #d #3, deed #781, the sale of lot No. 4752,
2   Will you confirm my reservation on flight #456?

3   We do not have the #890 bedroom slipper in brown.
4   I have seats #J76 and #J77 for the All-Star game.

5   Refer to Order #52 for 130 kg of modelling clay.
6   We received your cheque #2529 for $1 478.65 today.

7   #d #d #d #3, deed #781, the sale of lot No. 4752,

Centre

3 line spaces

```
The Secretary
Junior Management Club
Duffield, AB
TOE ONO
```

40 mm

15 mm

13 mm

```
Mr. Melvin Burns
Box 43
Wabamun, AB
TOE 2KO
```

15 mm

26 mm

Postal Code must appear in this area.

19 mm

This space reserved for machine sorting code.

POSTAL CARD
"Address Side"

VIII.24 Using the information provided in Problem VIII.21, type postal cards to each of the individuals on the membership list. Use your own return address.

Membership List

Mr. John Crystal	Mr. Paul Champion
Midtown Supply Co.	Champion Construction Co.
Vermilion, AB	Vermilion, AB
TOB 4MO	TOB 4MO
Miss Janet Pimm	Mr. Everett Kosta
Grandview Trust Co.	Jill's Drive-In
Vermilion, AB	Vermilion, AB
TOB 4MO	TOB 4MO
Mrs. Corinne Bailey	Ms. Helen Todd
McGregor Industries Ltd.	General Hospital
Vermilion, AB	Vermilion, AB
TOB 4MO	TOB 4MO

VIII.25 Prepare the "form" on page 266 as a postal card. Sign your name as Reservation Clerk for the Family Motor Hotel and mail the card to Mr. Carl Radcliff, 154 Genthon Street, Winnipeg, MB R2H 2J5. (For a review of "typing on a line," refer to page 127.)

VIII.26 Use the fill-in information provided in Problem VIII.25 to prepare postal cards for each person on the membership list provided in Problem VIII.24.

DAILY ACTIVITY

If you are beginning a new class period, refer to page 68 and follow the suggestions for improving and developing your typing continuity.

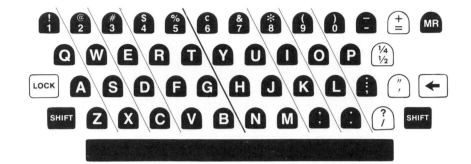

THE "DIAGONAL"

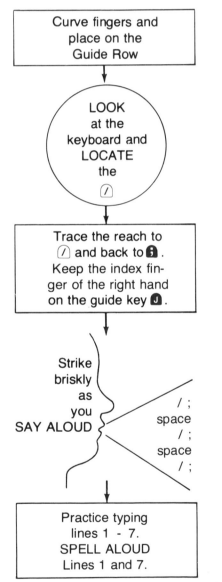

Curve fingers and place on the Guide Row

↓

LOOK at the keyboard and LOCATE the /

↓

Trace the reach to / and back to J. Keep the index finger of the right hand on the guide key J.

↓

Strike briskly as you SAY ALOUD

/ ;
space
/ ;
space
/ ;

↓

Practice typing lines 1 - 7. SPELL ALOUD Lines 1 and 7.

III.18 USING THE /

1 /; /; /; he/she; and/or; hear/here; to/too/two
2 Expressed as a fraction 0.75 is typed 3/4.

3 The reference initials on the letter are jwh/am.
4 The authors are Heffernan/Obolensky/Schumiatcher.

5 Our orders #378/379/380 have not been shipped.
6 3/4 or 0.75; 2/5 or 0.40; 3/8 or 0.375; 1/9 or 0.11

7 /; /; /; he/she; and/or; hear/here; to/too/two

POSTAL CARDS

Postal cards *(89 mm by 140 mm) are often used by organizations to send invitations or announcements of a non-confidential nature. Because of size restrictions, the messages are brief.*

Since the return /letter addresses are printed /typed on the "address side," they are eliminated from the "message side."

Notes: On card holders —

When you insert a card into the typewriter, adjust the card holders and use the paper bail to keep it from slipping.

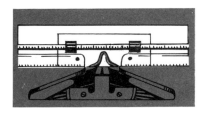

VIII.21 Type the message below on a postal card. If you do not have any postal cards, use a sheet of paper cut to 89 mm by 140 mm. The following flow chart will assist you in typing the postal card.

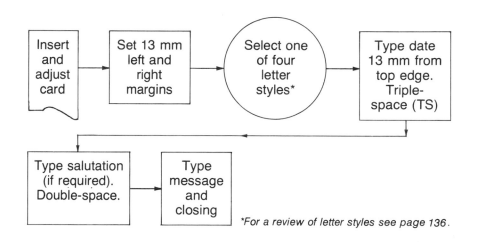

For a review of letter styles see page 136.

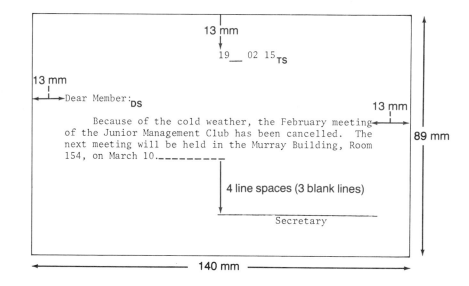

POSTAL CARD
MODIFIED BLOCK STYLE WITH INDENTED PARAGRAPHS
"Message Side"

VIII.22 Re-type the message on the postal card above, using either block or modified block style.

VIII.23 Type the postal card address shown on the following page. Since the "address side" of a postal card resembles a small envelope (89 mm by 140 mm), refer to the flow chart on page **138** for addressing instructions.

DAILY ACTIVITY

If you are beginning a new class period, refer to page 68 and follow the suggestions for improving and developing your typing continuity.

ELECTRIC TYPEWRITER

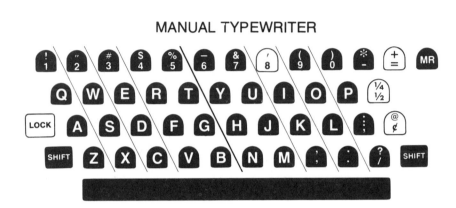

ADDITIONAL SYMBOLS

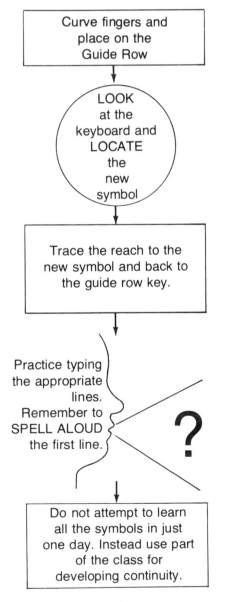

Curve fingers and place on the Guide Row

LOOK at the keyboard and LOCATE the new symbol

Trace the reach to the new symbol and back to the guide row key.

Practice typing the appropriate lines. Remember to SPELL ALOUD the first line.

?

Do not attempt to learn all the symbols in just one day. Instead use part of the class for developing continuity.

MANUAL TYPEWRITER

III.19 USING ADDITIONAL SYMBOLS LOCATED ON DIFFERENT KEYS FOR ELECTRIC (E) AND MANUAL (M) TYPEWRITERS.

The flow chart to the left should be followed when learning the location of the new symbols. It uses the same patterns as have been used throughout this Component.

Practice lines have been provided for learning each new symbol location. If you have an electric typewriter, omit the M lines (e.g. 1M). If you have a manual typewriter, omit the E lines (e.g. 1E).

THE "APOSTROPHE" ⟨'⟩

Electric: Located to the right of the semi-colon, and typed with the little finger of the right hand.
Manual: The shift of the 8.

```
1E  '; '; '; don't they're didn't, a dollar's worth
1M  'k 'k 'k don't they're didn't, a dollar's worth
```

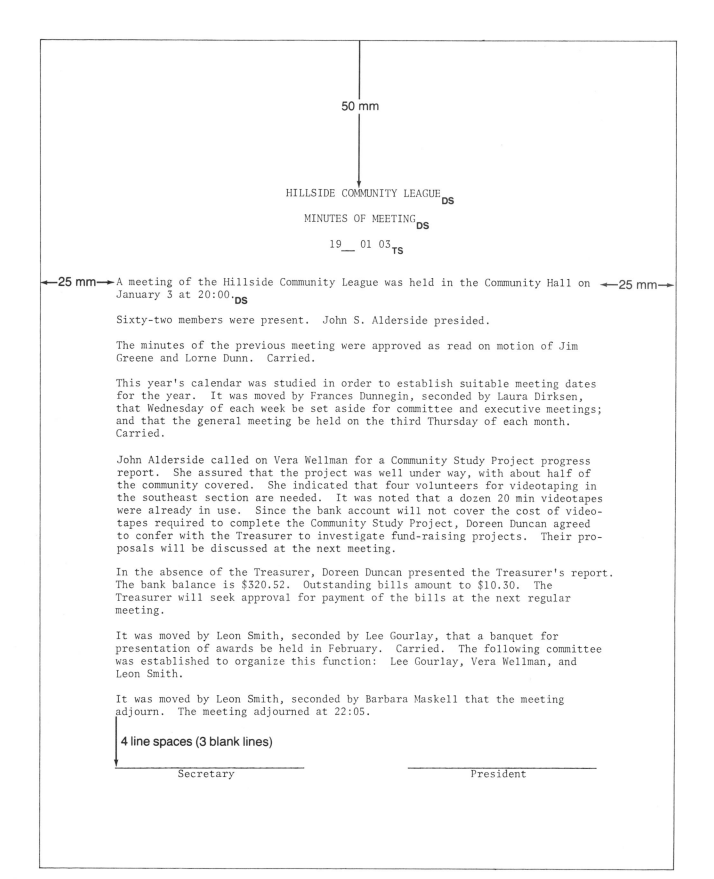

50 mm

HILLSIDE COMMUNITY LEAGUE **DS**

MINUTES OF MEETING **DS**

19__ 01 03 **TS**

←—25 mm—→ A meeting of the Hillside Community League was held in the Community Hall on ←—25 mm—→
January 3 at 20:00. **DS**

Sixty-two members were present. John S. Alderside presided.

The minutes of the previous meeting were approved as read on motion of Jim
Greene and Lorne Dunn. Carried.

This year's calendar was studied in order to establish suitable meeting dates
for the year. It was moved by Frances Dunnegin, seconded by Laura Dirksen,
that Wednesday of each week be set aside for committee and executive meetings;
and that the general meeting be held on the third Thursday of each month.
Carried.

John Alderside called on Vera Wellman for a Community Study Project progress
report. She assured that the project was well under way, with about half of
the community covered. She indicated that four volunteers for videotaping in
the southeast section are needed. It was noted that a dozen 20 min videotapes
were already in use. Since the bank account will not cover the cost of videotapes required to complete the Community Study Project, Doreen Duncan agreed
to confer with the Treasurer to investigate fund-raising projects. Their pro-
posals will be discussed at the next meeting.

In the absence of the Treasurer, Doreen Duncan presented the Treasurer's report.
The bank balance is $320.52. Outstanding bills amount to $10.30. The
Treasurer will seek approval for payment of the bills at the next regular
meeting.

It was moved by Leon Smith, seconded by Lee Gourlay, that a banquet for
presentation of awards be held in February. Carried. The following committee
was established to organize this function: Lee Gourlay, Vera Wellman, and
Leon Smith.

It was moved by Leon Smith, seconded by Barbara Maskell that the meeting
adjourn. The meeting adjourned at 22:05.

4 line spaces (3 blank lines)

_____   _____
          Secretary   President

DAILY ACTIVITY

If you are beginning a new class period, refer to page 68 and follow the suggestions for improving and developing your typing continuity.

ELECTRIC TYPEWRITER

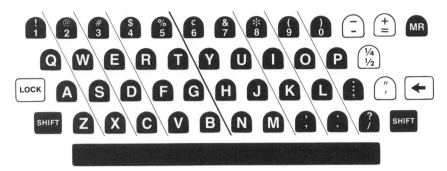

MANUAL TYPEWRITER

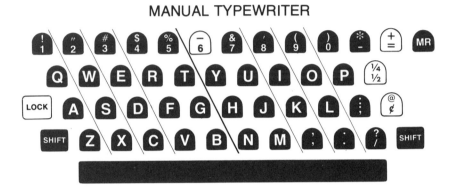

2 Your a's look like o's; your t's look like 1's.
3 The girls' and boys' coats were left in a room.

THE "UNDERSCORE" ⊖

Electric: The shift of the -.
Manual: The shift of the 6.

> *To underscore, backspace or move the carriage by hand to the first letter to be underscored, then strike the underscore once for each letter.*

4E _; _; _; think about this; don't think about that
4M _j _j _j think about this; don't think about that

> *When underscoring a group of letters, or when typing a word in all capitals use the shift lock key. It is located on the left of your typewriter. To lock the shift lock key, depress it. To unlock the shift lock key, depress either the left or right shift key.*

5 It is imperative that I have your answer today.
6 The title is The Collection Agency and the Law.

VIII.19 Re-type the minutes of meeting on page 261, using the format that follows.

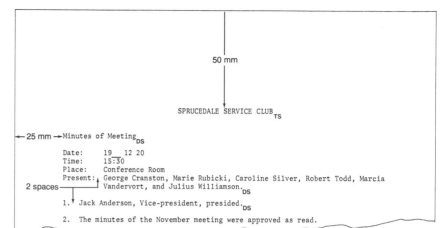

VIII.20 Type a copy of the minutes of meeting that appears on page 263. This problem illustrates a third format which is acceptable for typing minutes of meeting.

> *Now that you have typed three different styles of minutes of meeting, select one for your own personal use.*

DAILY ACTIVITY

If you are beginning a new class period, refer to page 68 and follow the suggestions for improving and developing your typing continuity.

ELECTRIC TYPEWRITER

MANUAL TYPEWRITER

THE "CENT OR CENTS" ¢

Electric: The shift of the 6.
Manual: Located to the right of the semi-colon, and typed with the little finger of the right hand.

7E ¢j ¢j ¢j 90 cents or 90¢, a two-cent or 2¢ return
7M ¢; ¢; ¢; 90 cents or 90¢, a two-cent or 2¢ return

8   The candy costs 99¢ a box. Each booklet is 25¢.
9   The auction prices were 25¢, 39¢, 89¢, and 99¢.

THE "AT" @

Electric: The shift of the 2.
Manual: The shift of the ¢.

10E @s @s @s Price 195 @ 64 cents and 150 @ 69 cents.
10M @; @; @; Price 195 @ 64 cents and 150 @ 69 cents.

11   He ordered 30 kits @ 65¢ and 25 kits @ 75¢ each.
12   Mrs. Long bought 10 m @ $2.49 and 15 m @ $3.50.

50 mm

SPRUCEDALE SERVICE CLUB **DS**

Minutes of Executive Meeting **DS**

19__ 12 20 **TS**

tab set

←**25 mm**→ Time and Place | The regular monthly meeting of the Executive of the Sprucedale ←**25 mm**→
Service Club was held on Saturday, December 20, at 15:30, in
the Conference Room. Jack Anderson, Vice-president, presided. **DS**

Attendance | Those present were George Cranston, Marie Rubicki, Caroline
Silver, Robert Todd, Marcia Vandervort, and Julius Williamson.

Minutes | The minutes of the November meeting were approved as read.

Treasurer's Report | Robert Todd, Treasurer, distributed a financial statement for
the year showing a balance of $1 536.50. The report was accepted
and placed on file.

New Business | Publicity of the Club's services was considered. It was moved
by Caroline Silver and seconded by Julius Williamson that $75
2 spaces be used to advertise the services of the club. Carried.

George Cranston and Marie Rubicki were appointed to investigate
the costs of placing an advertisement in the newspapers and of
preparing flyers for distribution at the Sprucedale Shopping
Plaza.

A proposal for increasing club membership was submitted by
Marcia Vandervort. After considerable discussion, it was moved
by Caroline Silver and seconded by Robert Todd that a committee,
chaired by Marcia Vandervort, be appointed to study the proposal
and suggest methods of implementation.

Adjournment | The meeting was adjourned at 16:30.

4 line spaces (3 blank lines)

_____   _____
Secretary   President

DAILY ACTIVITY

If you are beginning a new class period, refer to page 68 and follow the suggestions for improving and developing your typing continuity.

ELECTRIC TYPEWRITER

MANUAL TYPEWRITER

THE "QUOTATION" ⟨"⟩

Electric: The shift of the '.
Manual: The shift of the 2.

13E	"; "; "; Be careful not to type "two" for "too."
13M	"s "s "s Be careful not to type "two" for "too."

14	"I guess I was just trying too hard," he said.
15	"Yes," said Jim, "I think we certainly are lost."

THE "ASTERISK" ⟨*⟩

Electric: The shift of the 8.
Manual: The shift of the -.

16E	*k *k *k The * refers to page 2, ** to page 4.
16M	*; *; *; The * refers to page 2, ** to page 4.

17	Jackson's* article is one of the best sources.
18	*A. Jackson, "Deep Sea Diving," Comet, May, 1974.

Please give us your reaction ~~please~~ to this proposal.

AGENDA

An **agenda** lists in point form the things that are to be done at a meeting.

Formats vary from organization to organization, but basically an agenda can be treated as a vertical and horizontal centring problem.

Numbering (when used) follows the same format as used in typing outlines (see page 187) except that the numbers start with Arabic rather than Roman numerals.

When using numeric dating (19__ 01 03) with the 24 h clock (20:00), hyphens are used to separate the year from the month, the month from the day, and the day from the time.

VIII.17 Type the following agenda for a meeting.

THE HILLSIDE COMMUNITY LEAGUE

Executive Meeting, 19__-01-03-20:00

AGENDA

1. Call to order

2. Minutes of the meeting of 19__ 12 01.

3. Business arising from the minutes

    a. Reconsideration of meeting dates
    b. Progress report on Community Study Project

4. Treasurer's report

5. New business

    a. Proposed banquet for presentation of awards
    b. Financial resources for replacement of videotape used in Community Study Project
    c. Proposed participation in recreation program
    d. Appointment of delegates to convention

6. Adjournment

MINUTES OF MEETING

The **minutes of meeting** are an exact record of what took place at a meeting. Like agenda, the format and style used for recording the minutes vary from organization to organization.

Margin settings should be the same as for unbound reports.

VIII.18 Type a copy of the minutes of executive meeting that appears on page 261. Two tab stops—one at the centre point and one at a point two spaces beyond the longest marginal notation—should be set.

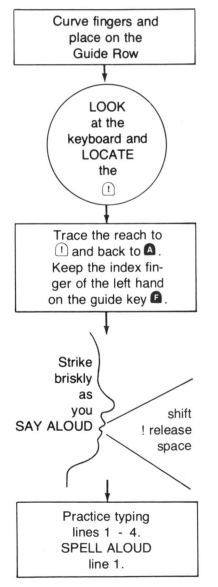

THE "EXCLAMATION"

Curve fingers and place on the Guide Row

↓

LOOK at the keyboard and LOCATE the ①

↓

Trace the reach to ① and back to Ⓐ. Keep the index finger of the left hand on the guide key Ⓕ.

↓

Strike briskly as you SAY ALOUD

shift ! release space

↓

Practice typing lines 1 - 4. SPELL ALOUD line 1.

III.20 USING THE ①

> *Leave two spaces after an exclamation mark.*

1 !a !a !a Jump! Stop thief! Stop! Help! Great!
2 Try! Type faster! Type with control! Now stop!

3 Help! Help! Fire! Fire! Is he so right? Yes!
4 Wait! We are coming. Stop! The road is blocked.

> *If your typewriter is not equipped with a special key for the "exclamation", type an apostrophe and back-space; then type a period.*

III.21 Both electric and manual typewriters are equipped with a fraction key. When using metric measurements all figures are expressed in whole numbers and decimals. Therefore, the use of the fraction key will be minimal. The following two lines will familiarize you with the location of the fraction key.

5 Joe, Al, and Ted receive $\frac{1}{2}$, $\frac{1}{4}$, and $\frac{1}{4}$ respectively.
6 Can you add $2\frac{1}{2}$, $6\frac{1}{2}$, $3\frac{1}{4}$, and $7\frac{1}{4}$? Yes, it's $19\frac{1}{2}$!

III.22 Most electric typewriters are equipped with a ⊕ and ⊖ key. If you have such a machine, locate the key and type the following sentence.

7 If you add $2\frac{1}{2}$ + $6\frac{1}{2}$ + $3\frac{1}{4}$ + $7\frac{1}{4}$ you get $19\frac{1}{2}$. Is it true that $19\frac{1}{2}$ = 19.5?

VIII.14 Type the following memorandum.

To: D. M. Metzgar, Agent
From: Mary Schroeder, Supervisor, Accounts Receivable Department

Would you please contact Mr. Jameson of Ramon's Variety Store regarding his outstanding account? It is now overdue in the amount of $4 122.60. (¶) Should Mr. Jameson be unable to suggest an arrangement for payment, it may be necessary to start legal proceedings. (¶) Will you please inform us of any progress you are able to make?

VIII.15 Type the following memorandum making the necessary corrections.

To: L.J. Kramer, Vice President
From: Grayson Meadows, Accountant

We wish to confirm that both the firms referred to in your recent memo are (Canadian incorporated) companies, both are taxable under the income tax act, and dividends from our funds are eligible for the tax dividend credit allowed to taxable Canadian corations. (¶) If you require additional information, please let me know.

Notes: On carbon copies —

Follow the same format as was used in typing business letters. (See page 145.)

VIII.16 Type the following memorandum making the necessary corrections.

To: John Pratt, Chief Engineer; cc R. Williams, President.
From: R. K. Henry, Purchasing Agent, Accounting Department.

Do you expect to order diesel generators in addition to the one mentioned in your letter to D. H. Handley? If so, we recommend that all machines be ordered be not to ensure standardization of the units and to get competition bids.

DAILY ACTIVITY

If you are beginning a new class period:

1. Adjust the margins for a 50-space line, and
2. Select several sentences from exercise III.23 to build skill in typing numbers and symbols.

DEVELOPING TYPING CONTINUITY

III.23 REVIEWING ALL PREVIOUSLY LEARNED KEYS

Before leaving Component III, select several of the following sentences and paragraphs to help build skill in typing numbers and symbols. Return to this section for periodic review.

TYPE ALL LINES AS THEY APPEAR.

1 "Recreation" is definitely a less inclusive word than "relaxation."

2 One man who went fishing frequently said: "My business requires my absence."

3 Our cheque for $6.78 in payment of the annual fees is enclosed.

4 We enclose herewith a certified cheque in the amount of $21 744.40 which represents 10 per cent of our tender.

5 We agree with the proposal to reduce the coverage to $100 000, but would not expect the premium for such a policy to exceed $1 300 for three years.

6 The break-even point for the coal mine has been set at 544 320 t.

7 While it is now relatively unimportant, a cheque for $1 593.22, which included the June charge of $674.81, was received November 30--exactly one month after our second notice to you.

8 We refer to your letter of January 8 regarding Invoice No. 10-6805-64 in the amount of $851.93.

9 Using form #357A, John B. Smith obtained his Social Insurance Card bearing number 616 100 533.

VIII.13 Type the following memorandum. Then, compose and type a reply using the reply section. (If you do not have prepared memo forms, use a self-prepared carbon pack.)

FORBES Security

1203 Retallack Street   Regina, Saskatchewan   S4T 2H8   Phone (306) 525-1122

FROM	DEPARTMENT
W. T. Carson	Accounting

	DATE	(Current Date)
J. K. Smith, Falum Agent	SUBJECT	Storage Tickets

MESSAGE

We are again asking your co-operation in regard to issuing storage tickets.

If rapeseed is taken in for some other company, please show the name of that company at the top of each storage ticket to identify ownership. When special bin storage tickets are issued for rapeseed belonging to other companies, each company's rapeseed should be binned separately because we are held responsible for the total amount of the special bin tickets issued for each account.

Please provide a list of the companies whose rapeseed is currently stored in bins 10 - 14.

WTC:yoi

USE LOWER PORTION FOR REPLY

REPLY FROM   DATE

L13-RTM-8½ GRAND & TOY LIMITED

TO ORIGINATE   **ROUND TRIP MEMO**   **TO REPLY**

L13 - RTM - 8½

Hand or type write message, remove yellow (follow-up copy) and forward balance of set. Save envelope typing. Fold form at arrows. For use in #9 or #10 window envelope.

♦ GRAND&TOY

Write reply — Retain white original and return pink copy

DEVELOPING TYPING CONTINUITY

10   We have received your letter dated August 28, and with it the invoice claiming $110.70 on the defective heels on your 45 pairs of shoes.

11   He recently shipped you Royal Blue (#99/8) and Royal Red (#99/9) to be used to print inserts for food packages.

12   I am forwarding you our Trans-Canada invoice #2752 in the amount of $7.26.

13   Thank you for your order #38137 covering two All Bronze Weave Wires for your No. 5 machine.

14   We are also attaching revised acknowledgment copies of the following pages on this sales order: pages 30, 41, 70, 78, 102, 104, 108, 110, 113, and 114.

> *Time is expressed using the 24 h clock. Four figures — two for hours and two for minutes — are used. A colon separates the hours from the minutes.*
>
> *e.g.* 08:00; 13:30; 21:57

15   I have reservations at the Hilton for arrival Tuesday, February 9 via Pan American flight #219 from New York at 19:45, departing for Bridgetown on Friday, February 12 via Pan American flight #212 at 07:00.

When preceded by a number, use the metric symbol kn for knot/knots.

16   The plane was a Cessna 172 which could be throttled back to cruise at 60-70 kn. Altogether we flew some 130-150 h.

17   When Canada's first census was taken in 1666 to measure the advancement made by this French colony since the founding of Quebec by Champlain 58 years earlier, it was found that there were 3 215 inhabitants. Two hundred years later we had nearly 3.5 million.

Did you remember to include subject, date, and reference information?

VIII.9 Type the following memorandum from Mr. R. J. Melnichuk, Controller to Mr. James T. Foster, Salesman.

We have no information on the sale of the Hamster, Serial No. 64331, to Mr. Donald Craig. Did you discuss insurance with Mr. Craig?

VIII.10 Type the following memorandum from Joan Fallman to K. T. Savage.

The Group Index Card and Certificate No. 666 for L. Mulcahy are enclosed. Mr. Mulcahy has made a request for "increased paid-up pension." (¶) Please let me know the amount of the new premium and the monthly annuity that Mr. Mulcahy can expect.

VIII.11 Type the following memorandum from Eleanor Cassidy, Secretary to the Board of Directors to Leon Benedict, Food Service.

This is official notification that the Board of Directors approved the changes which you proposed for the cafeteria at the Home Office building. It is understood that the cost of implementing the changes will be charged to your department budget. (¶) Please let us know when the project is completed.

VIII.12 Type the following memorandum.

To: Cliff Tilden, President
From: M. B. Rousseau, Secretary
Re: Annual Meeting P.N.T.F.

Because of Mr. Swanson's trip to the western branch and Mr. McNabb's sudden illness, we shall not be able to have a quorum of trustees of P.N.T.F. (¶) Attached is a copy of the Auditor's Report. I will send along the other regular reports as soon as we are able to set a date for the annual meeting.

DEVELOPING TYPING CONTINUITY

Ratchet Release

Notes: On exponential equivalents —

$10^3 = 1\ 000$
$10^6 = 1\ 000\ 000$

18 The first case weighed 56.6 kg, the second 98.2 kg, and the third 12.75 kg.

> To type an **exponent** such as **two raised to the power of three** (e.g. 2^3) operate the ratchet release, turn the cylinder backward a half space, type the figure, and return the ratchet release and cylinder to the normal position.

19 We produced 21.2×10^6 m^3 of crude oil valued at $305.5 million.

20 The area given to grain totalled 18.1×10^6 ha, of which 8.6×10^6 ha were given over to wheat. The wheat crop in the five years yielded $97\ 211 \times 10^6$ dm^3, an average per year of $19\ 442 \times 10^6$ dm^3. The yield per hectare ranged from 31.75 to 67.0, averaging $1\ 973$ dm^3/ha over the five years--a remarkable increase.

21 "Perhaps Mother was a little hasty today," he said. "No, Tom," said Mrs. Beatty.

22 How tiresome they were! Would you like to hear the story?

23 "Oh, that!" said Maggie. "That is the letter that I lost yesterday."

24 I have John's skates and Victor's gloves.

Problem VIII.8 shows an illustration of a **"round-trip" memorandum**. These forms can be obtained from most stationery outlets and consist of three sheets of paper and two sheets of carbon. The originator completes the memorandum, keeps one copy for reference, and passes two copies to the recipient. The recipient replies, keeping one copy for reference, and returns the original to the originator.

well under way. In keeping with our policy of sending our personally signed banquet invitations, may I please have a list of the guests and a supply of invitations. As soon as I have signed the invitations, my secretary will see that they are mailed.

VIII.8 Type the following memorandum. Then, compose and type a reply, using the reply section.

(If you do not have a "round-trip" memo form, prepare a carbon pack and follow the illustrated style.)

RETAIN THIS COPY FOR FOLLOW-UP

SPEEDY-MEMO

SNAP TIGHT

SEND TO:	Paul D. Gould	FROM:	Sam Booth
LOCATION:	Shipping	LOCATION:	Accounts Receivable

MESSAGE: Damage Claim--G. F. Trant   DATE: (Current)

Mr. G. F. Trant reports that the door handle and pin were returned on January 20 via parcel post, prepaid and insured. The pin was taped to the handle and tagged when shipped.

Please refer to the shipping tag returned with the parts. If the pin was not included, we should have advised Mr. Trant at least a week ago.

REPLY:

REPLY FROM: DATE:

CBL 12166

TOTAL CONCEPT SERVICE SDC SOURCE DATA CONTROL LTD 5-8166

**DEVELOPING TYPING
CONTINUITY**

25 Their order called for two @ 6¢, three @ 10¢, and four @ 15¢.

26 Two men on base – nobody out – two runs to tie the game.

27 They were in Toronto – Jack Campbell and Garth Evans – when the idea of visiting the zoo struck them.

28 Instead of a superscript, I use an asterisk (*) for footnoting.

29 If you will call me tomorrow (Monday), I can give you the information.

30 I want to read The Great Surprise, published by Price & Sloan, tomorrow. Joe says it is an exciting book.

31 Popular "how to" books of the 18th century were chiefly concerned with the subject of how to die a good death; those of the 19th century moved on to the subject of how to make a good living; and those of the 20th century are devoted to telling us how to live happily.

Interoffice Memorandum

To: Robert L. MacIntyre
      Advertising Department

From: Lorraine Dekker
      Hosiery Department

Subject: COLOR BLENDS AVAILABLE IN HOSIERY **TS**

Date: 19___ 03 05

└──── 2 spaces

└──── 2 spaces

The six new color blends in hosiery which we will put on sale on March 25 should receive coverage in a full-page ad in the evening issues of the newspaper on the weekend preceding the sale. **DS**

May I see you at once about the possibility of running color for this hosiery ad. I feel that color is necessary in order to catch the attention of the buyers we are seeking. **TS**

LD:yoi

---

paper (P5 with wide edge inserted).

Remember to make a carbon copy of all interoffice memorandums that you type.

Problem VIII.4 illustrated a format which can easily be used in offices. This format can be used for completing Problems VIII.5 - VIII.16 if you are not using the Workbook that accompanies this text.

should study Bulletin 58 regarding additional sick leave benefits available to them.

Copies of the Company policy regarding holidays and sick leave have been supplied to each Department Head. Do not hesitate to discuss your entitlement with your Supervisor.

VIII.6 Type the following memorandum.

To: Lorraine Dekker / Hosiery Department; From: Robert L. MacIntyre / Advertising Department; Subject: Ad for Color Blends; (Current Date).

I agree with you that a black and white ad for color-blend hosiery will probably be ineffective. On the other hand, our printing department finds it impossible to reproduce the "color blends" that would be needed to illustrate this hosiery. (¶) What about an eye-catching rainbow in color, dipping down into a "pot o' hosiery" at the top of the ad, and a black and white presentation of facts to follow?

VIII.7 Type the following memorandum.

To: Derrek Jones / Assistant Superintendent; From: Lawrence Drury / President; Subject: Retirement Banquet; (Current date). I understand that you have the retirement festivities for Leonard Johnston's retirement

SUPPLEMENTARY SKILL-BUILDING MATERIALS

III.24 CONSECUTIVE NUMBERS

The following lines will give you additional practice in typing consecutive numbers. Initially select and type several groups of lines to gain confidence in numeric key selection. Then re-type the lines attempting to increase the speed and accuracy with which you type numbers.

```
 1   39 40 57 69 88 19 20 43 78 98 34 19 44 80 74 34 23
 2   38 54 97 21 54 33 54 89 60 12 47 84 24 55 49 18 40

 3   44 31 17 54 90 32 08 54 67 84 50 31 54 23 54 88 20
 4   41 50 44 61 39 65 21 19 14 07 54 37 82 70 32 58 31

 5   49 17 70 54 72 31 50 49 14 88 44 01 43 60 48 20 54
 6   45 19 53 80 65 78 43 18 23 80 35 65 18 48 95 01 54

 7   431 786 309 618 541 320 455 180 777 410 800 320
 8   489 885 401 743 996 402 318 549 361 762 478 444

 9   549 360 541 296 941 823 704 580 173.274 500 050
10   340 570 650 481 389 547 299 319 586 963 243 798

11   579 450 260 410 367 489 194 230 645 788 540 432
12   789 543 170 989 342 779 430 557 319 340 438 659

13   36 678, 32 678, 465 130, 578 243, 9 843 512, 8 948
14   84 902, 91 649, 319 465, 894 503, 4 586 399, 5 779

15   236 000, 546 623, 468 849, 683 855, 891 023, 3 258
16   954 290, 368 795, 349 231, 744 914, 890 118, 4 535

17   366 000.50, 477 843.65, 389 500.93, 798 542.00, 48
18   865 766.98, 642 379.75, 584 150.77, 490 000.63, 63

19   93.74 57.39 33.32 87.43 90.45 68.70 34.50 67.00
20   94.35 89.32 70.50 37.48 34.34 68.50 29.75 88.91

21   09:00 10:00 11:00 12:00 13:25 14:39 15:46 16:52
22   17:27 18:38 19:49 20:00 21:11 22:23 23:34 00:16

23   956 834 403 913 755 304 977 243 989 107 345 987
24   234 405 887 546 203 491 984 763 401 206 405 975

25   9 775, 9 936 854, 305 498, 564 913, 94 619, 20 948
26   8 498, 2 153 489, 342 875, 301 564, 87 623, 87 663

27   19.88 57.92 50.86 43.43 84.73 50.07 23.98 53.49
28   67.00 50.43 70.68 45.90 43.87 32.33 39.57 47.93

29   1976 01 01, 1976 02 09, 1977 03 14, 1977 04 25
30   1978-05-03, 1978-06-11, 1979-07-19, 1979-08-27
```

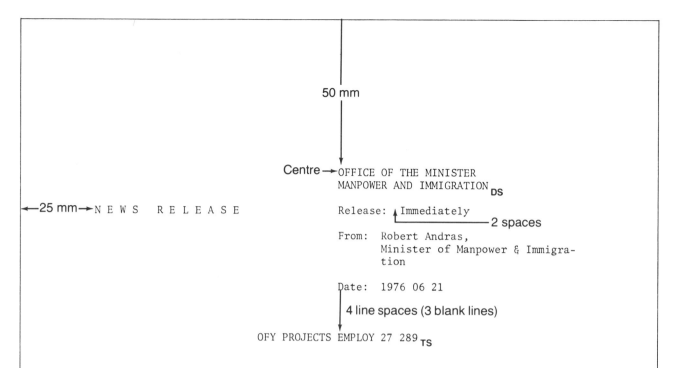

50 mm

Centre → OFFICE OF THE MINISTER
MANPOWER AND IMMIGRATION **DS**

←25 mm→ N E W S   R E L E A S E   Release: ↑Immediately
                                                          └── 2 spaces

                                              From: Robert Andras,
                                                     Minister of Manpower & Immigra-
                                                     tion

                                              Date: 1976 06 21

                                              4 line spaces (3 blank lines)

                          OFY PROJECTS EMPLOY 27 289 **TS**

        The Minister of Manpower and Immigration, Robert Andras, stated today**DS**

that 27 289 young people will have 285 623 weeks of summer employment under   ←25 mm→

the Opportunities for Youth Program.

        In all, 3 880 projects have been approved for total direct project fund-

ing of $26 653 000 by the federal government. Of these projects, 21 per cent

involve social service work and 28 per cent the provision of recreational

facilities and services. Other significant activity groupings are cultural

and artistic 14 per cent, informational 6 per cent, environment 6 per cent,

research 4 per cent, and miscellaneous categories 21 per cent.

        A provincial analysis of projects is attached and illustrates the local

importance of the various activities.

        Opportunities for Youth is a federal government program and is part of

Summer '76, the $66 million government program expected to provide direct and

indirect employment for some 390 000 students this summer.

                                    # # #

III.25 POSTAL CODES

Each line of the following drills will give you practice in typing numbers and in shifting for capitals. Initially type the line to gain confidence in numeric and alphabetic key selection. Then try to increase the speed and accuracy with which you type the lines.

1	T8G	0X9	M5W	2G6	K2P	0B6	S3J	2A5	R0S	5M1
2	K9X	3B7	A4R	8V3	C2G	1E4	B1T	5P0	E2L	6M8
3	H4K	8S1	J3V	5S3	G9P	7H5	L4V	8W1	N6N	0Z3
4	P9L	3T8	V9Y	8G2	Y5K	1M0	X2S	6R4	M6L	4Y4
5	Y8Z	6K9	X7M	5E7	V7Z	4K0	T3C	8J3	S4H	7V0
6	R0J	3L2	P8E	7L2	L1B	2C1	N7H	4N0	J3S	1W2

III.26 NUMBER SPEED ESCALATORS

Select a line from the list below which matches or slightly exceeds your speed level. When you hear the instructor's signal to return the carriage, do so immediately. If you did not complete the line re-type it. If you did complete it, move on to the next line. Return your carriage only on the signal. Try to increase your speed.

1   28 65 47 19 36 74 38

2   38 95 14 44 39 88 21 79

3   48 49 37 43 29 18 43 11 28

4   44 98 30 31 77 29 41 40 75 94

5   33 98 47 52 12 99 43 76 11 39 47

6   38 44 91 27 54 65 77 98 31 47 66 21

7   89 54 33 90 27 69 43 50 99 41 26 77 18

8   12 38 99 54 66 73 17 31 68 39 20 76 11 58

9   78 35 40 28 75 88 91 20 69 65 80 50 55 12 16

10   72 98 96 44 07 11 23 41 17 46 52 09 48 73 54 90

11   489 103 465 788 297 141

12   793 478 129 100 555 782 180

13   196 120 116 886 808 542 199 654

14   183 590 700 442 865 983 120 777 418

15   890 237 915 677 830 892 164 388 270 143

16   890 430 154 672 112 785 670 279 651 555 429

17   707 489 156 730 290 574 656 890 470 956 335 760

NEWS RELEASE

A **news release** is a formal statement made by a business or organization concerning a current event or future activity. It can be used verbatim for publication or announcement by all media.

Formats for news releases vary from organization to organization. Below are two popular and accepted formats.

FORMAT A

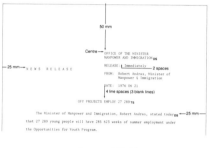

FORMAT B

INTEROFFICE MEMORANDUMS

An **interoffice memorandum** is a written message used to communicate information within a company organization.

Many business organizations prepare special forms for interoffice memorandums. Other organizations rely on efficient typists to prepare memorandums in an acceptable format.

When preparing an interoffice memorandum you should indicate the date, the recipient's name, the sender's name, the subject, and reference initials. If the memorandum is short, use a half sheet of

VIII.1 Type a copy of the News Release on page 254 in the form illustrated (Format A).

VIII.2 Type a copy of the News Release on page 254 using Format B.

VIII.3 Using the following information type a News Release. Use either format.

NEWS RELEASE from the Office of Gerald M. Conrad, President; Livingstone Distributors Ltd., Oakbank, Manitoba. Date of Release: 19___ 01 16.

TRAFFIC MANAGER APPOINTED

Mr. David Reginald Smythe of Deer Horn, Manitoba, has been appointed to the position of Traffic Manager for Livingstone Distributors Ltd. It has been the company's good fortune to have Mr. Smythe manage its Deer Horn Branch Office for the past five years. During his service, Mr. Smythe built the branch from a rented-desk space in a downtown office building to a 40-employee distribution outlet operating from comfortable offices in its own building on "L" Street.(¶) Mr. Smythe's wife, Helen, and their two daughters will be residing in Oakbank commencing January 30.

# # #

VIII.4 Using the format illustrated, type a copy of the memo which appears on page 255.

VIII.5 Type the following memorandum using the format illustrated on page 255.

To: Staff; From: Roy L. Greene, Director / Personnel Department; Subject: Holidays and Sick Leave; Date: 19___ 04 07.

Owing to some changes in holiday regulations, and some confusion among staff regarding sick leave regulations, the following Company policies are restated:

Each employee, after one year's service with the Company is entitled to two weeks' holiday with pay. Holidays must commence on a Monday. If a statutory holiday falls within a vacation period, an additional day will be granted.

One day per month sick leave is granted to every employee. Those employees who have served more than five years with the Company

III.27 The following sentences and paragraphs will give you additional practice in developing typing continuity. Select several paragraphs for practice, using correct techniques in striking all keys. Then select one or two paragraphs for timed writings.

Adjust the margins for a 60-space line. Your typewriter bell is the cue for carriage return. Word division in print is undesirable, but if you must divide a word, use only acceptable word breaks. (See Appendix B, page 340.)

		1'	3'	5'
1	"An outlaw!" I said.	4	1	
2	What did the class decide to do?	6	2	1
3	"Jan, where are you going?" called Mark.	8	3	2
4	"Hey," the hiker shouted. "Are you serious?"	9	3	2
5	"I like that," she finally said. "I like that very much."	12	4	2
6	Problems of all types are found in the book: easy, difficult, and	13	4	2
	very difficult.	16	5	3
7	Counting eight hours a working day, he spends only 2 000 h of	12	4	2
	the year's 8 760 h earning a living.	19	6	4
8	Notice that 1 metre 15 centimetres can be expressed as 1 m	12	4	2
	1 dm 5 cm, but as a decimal part of a metre it becomes 1.15 m.	24	8	5
9	Whatever becomes of the business—success or failure, growth	12	4	2
	or decline—depends on the manager. While being jack-of-all-	24	8	5
	trades, he will have his hand on the controls.	35	11	7
10	While it is true that we benefit by knowing that words have	12	4	2
	ancestors—Greek, Latin, Anglo-Saxon, and all other sorts—it is	25	8	5
	not necessary to know a word's genealogical tree before using	37	12	7
	it.	38	12	7
11	The normal life on bottom felts is about 130 d and since the dam-	13	4	3
	aged felt had been on for 67 d, the remaining life value at the	26	9	5
	time of the accident is 63/130 of its cost ($9 543) or $4 632.37.	39	13	8

```
1'  | 1 | 2 | 3 | 4 | 5 | 6 | 7 | 8 | 9 | 10 | 11 | 12
3'        |    1    |    2    |    3    |    4
5'             |        1        |        2
```

5. Proceed through Component VIII.

Supplementary:

Select and type a number of ITA's from pages 286 to 288.

SUMMARY OF COMPONENT VIII PROBLEMS

MAJOR APPLICATIONS

Agenda .... 17, ITA's 6, 7

Application Form .... ITA's 13, 14

Chain Feeding 36, 37

Cheques 62-64

Credit Memorandums ... 55-57

Fill-in Forms .... 29-32, ITA's 11, 12

Financial Reports .... 65, 66, ITA 16

Index Cards .... 33-36, ITA 15

Interoffice Memorandums . 4-16

Invoices 51-54

Itineraries .... 44, 45, ITA 17

Labels 38-40

Minutes of Meeting ...... 18-20, ITA 8

News Releases .... 1-3, ITA's 1-3

Postal Cards .... 21-28, ITA's 9, 10

Programs .... 41-43, ITA's 4, 5

Purchase Orders 49, 50

Statements 58-61

Telegrams 46-48

SPECIAL APPLICATIONS

Computer Type 61

Rough Draft Copy 15, 16

Script Copy 10, 11, 44, 47, 54, 66

Unarranged Copy 3, 5-7, 9-11, 13-17, 19, 22-25, 28, 30, 32, 34-39, 41-44, 46-48, 50, 52-54, 56, 57, 59-61, 63-66

	1'	3'	5'
12 Contributing to the fall in our inventory has been the two four-day	13	4	3
weeks we operated at Christmas and New Year, and the 16-h	25	8	5
shutdown we experienced on December 29-30 as a result of a	36	12	7
failure on the machine winder.	42	14	8
13 At the time of the 1951 census, there were 5 381 000 of Cana-	12	4	2
da's 14 009 429 people living in rural areas; that is, on farms and	26	9	5
in places of less than 1 000 population. Our rural population was	39	13	8
38.4 per cent of our total population.	47	16	9
14 Our production in manufacturing increased from $3 101 million	12	4	2
to $16 271 million, and the number of workers from 559 000 to	24	8	5
1 248 000. Figures that are easier to grasp are those showing	37	12	7
the production per worker: $5 545; $7 594; $13 043.	48	16	10
15 It is interesting to see the provincial distribution of units sold:	13	4	3
New Brunswick 71 459, Newfoundland 4 214, Prince Edward	24	8	5
Island 47 279, Nova Scotia 32 744, Quebec 148 036, Ontario	36	12	7
346 568, Manitoba 21 560, Saskatchewan 31 015, Alberta	47	16	9
32 876, and British Columbia 28 830.	54	18	11
16 Canada is rich in non-metallic minerals. It is the world's chief	13	4	3
source of asbestos, production of which is concentrated in the	25	8	5
Eastern Townships of Quebec. The value of annual production	37	12	7
increased from $24 700 in 1880 to $24.5 million in 1946 and	49	16	10
$106.5 million in 1957.	54	18	11
17 Canada's first national park was established in 1885 around the	13	4	2
mineral hot springs at Banff. Today the parks are Canada's	24	8	5
greatest single tourist attraction. From April 1 to September 30,	38	13	8
last year, they were visited by 2 520 000 persons, while historic	51	17	10
parks and sites drew an additional 240 000 visitors.	61	20	12

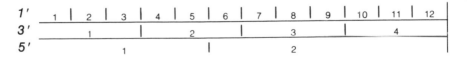

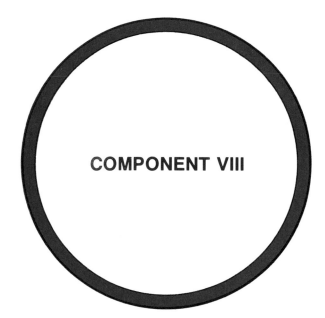

COMPONENT VIII

BUSINESS FORMS

STUDENT OBJECTIVES

1. To type in acceptable format news releases, memorandums, agenda, minutes of meeting, postal cards, index cards, labels, programs, itineraries, telegrams, purchase orders, invoices, credit memorandums, statements, cheques, and financial reports.

2. To acquire a basic knowledge of the use of and format for various business forms.

3. To learn to type information on pre-printed forms.

DAILY ACTIVITIES

Preliminary:

Current date typing. Type three lines of the current date as illustrated:

			↓ tab set			↓ tab set		
19__	05	21	19__	05	21	19__	05	21
19__	05	21	19__	05	21	19__	05	21
19__	05	21	19__	05	21	19__	05	21

CONTENTS

Component VIII introduces the student to the form and style used in typing news releases, memorandums, agenda, minutes of meeting, postal cards, index cards, labels, programs, itineraries, telegrams, and financial reports.

An introduction to purchase orders, invoices, credit memorandums, statements, and cheques is also presented.

Main:

1. Identify your work by typing your name, the name and number of the course, and the current date.

2. Select and type several number and symbol paragraphs from pages 99 to 106.

3. Select and type a table from Component VII to increase your production speed.

4. Select a paragraph from Component II or a Timed Writing from Appendix A for a five-minute timed writing.

SUPPLEMENTARY SKILL-BUILDING MATERIALS

18 Family income decreased greatly in all cases following the death of the bread-winner. In the average family the drop was 63 per cent; in families that had an income of $12 000 or more, the average drop was 80 per cent; in families with incomes of $4 000 or less, the average decline was 49 per. cent.

1'	3'	5'
12	4	2
24	8	5
37	12	7
49	16	10
59	20	12

19 In length, the Canadian National Railway is the largest in North America, and it's the only railway serving all ten provinces. To its 38 880 km of main track, about 14 500 km of secondary track, yards, sidings, and spurs must be added, making a grand total of 53 380 km. It has more than 5 000 stations, nearly 6 000 bridges, and 64 tunnels.

1'	3'	5'
13	4	3
27	9	5
39	13	8
51	17	10
63	21	13
68	23	14

20 One insurance man's records tell the story of a young man who received a raise of $1 000 a year. He bought an article for his home. Within a year he died, leaving his family of three with a $5 000 estate. Had he invested that raise in life insurance, that investment would have been enough to provide his widow with an annual income of $3 000 a year for at least 20 years.

1'	3'	5'
12	4	2
25	8	5
38	13	8
51	17	10
63	21	13
74	25	15

21 The urban libraries, serving 5.5 million people, contained 5 466 887 volumes. There were 1 230 657 registered borrowers, the circulation was 23 190 793 volumes, and the libraries were staffed by 1 454 full-time staff members of whom 563 had degrees or equivalent diplomas in library science. Current expenditures amounted to $6 773 239 or $1.30 per capita of the population served.

1'	3'	5'
12	4	2
23	8	5
36	12	7
48	16	10
60	20	12
72	24	14
76	25	15

22 In the years 1958-1963 forest consumption averaged 91 775 dm³ annually. Of this, logs and bolts for the lumber industry represented 43.7 per cent; firewood and wood for charcoal, 9.3 per cent; poles and piling, round mining timbers,

1'	3'	5'
10	3	2
22	7	4
33	11	7
46	15	9

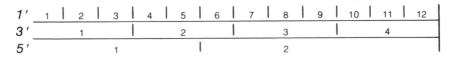

ITA 10

Do a survey of a business district in your community. In table form, list the names of 10 retail stores, the classification of goods each offers, and the store manager's name.

ITA 11

Prepare a list of 10 different occupations which might be available to you upon graduation. In table form list the starting salary, maximum salary, and the annual holiday entitlement for each.

ITA 12

Refer to Appendix A in this text. Prepare, in table form, a list of each timed writing by title, indicating the total number of words in the writing, and the page number on which the writing begins.

	1'	3'	5'
and miscellaneous products, 1.8 per cent; bolts for the pulp	58	19	12
and paper mills, 32.4 per cent. From their one-third of the con-	71	24	14
sumption, the pulp and paper mills created more national reve-	83	28	17
nue than the other forest industries combined.	92	31	18

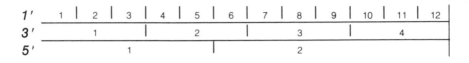

		1'	3'	5'
23	Help! Help! What shall I do?	6	2	1
24	We sat cross-legged on the grass.	7	2	1
25	"Look! What's that?" "Oh, no!" she gasped.	9	3	2
26	Miss Holmes—that was her name—found the map.	9	3	2
27	The crankshaft might have a tolerance of	8	3	2
	plus or minus 0.0001.	12	4	2
28	For the machine, we recommend one	7	2	1
	only 12.5, 550-V auxiliary load resistor.	15	5	3
29	The finished product is listed on your	8	3	2
	purchase order at 57 g, selling to the	15	5	3
	consumer at 35¢ a package.	20	7	4
30	We undertake to supply you with	6	2	1
	approximately 1 000 pieces of fir	13	4	3
	piling in lengths of 15 m to 25 m	19	6	4
	delivered to New Westminster.	25	8	5

The metric symbol for volt is V.

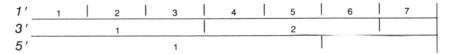

ITA 3

Create an advertisement for a sale of used cars. Plan and type the information in table form.

ITA 4

You are asked to prepare an advertisement for an auction sale of household furniture. Plan and type a table showing item names, their condition (fair, good, excellent), and minimum price.

ITA 5

Locate in a newspaper column, information which you can present in table form. Plan and type the table.

ITA 6

In table form, plan and type an order for equipment and furniture for one of the following: an office, a typewriting room, a gymnasium, a students' lounge, a kitchen. Include catalogue number, description, color, and price.

ITA 7

Prepare an inventory of household contents. Use the following headings: quantity, description, date of purchase, and purchase price.

ITA 8

You have just accepted a position in your chosen field. Estimate your yearly income and prepare a budget for one year. Present the information in table form.

ITA 9

By contacting your local Federal Member of Parliament you should be able to obtain the statistics on the number of ballots cast in your riding for each member of a major political party in the last Federal Election. Plan and type a table showing the number of ballots cast for each party and the percentage of the popular vote each attained.

	1'	3'	5'

31 Consider the percentage we find by
dividing 375 541 by 5 847 159. It is
6.4 per cent. The approximate result
would have been reached by dividing
376 by 5 847 or by dividing 38 by 585.

1'	3'	5'
7	2	1
14	5	3
22	7	4
29	10	6
36	12	7

32 We have 591 312 km² of fresh water
within our boundaries. And, our
seacoast is one of the longest of any
country in the world, with 23 860 km
of mainland sea frontage and
40 194 km of inland frontage.

1'	3'	5'
7	2	1
13	4	3
21	7	4
28	9	6
33	11	7
39	13	8

33 There is nothing derogatory about
having a mortgage on your house.
Of the 1 654 045 owner-occupied
dwellings counted in the census,
478 740 had first mortgages and
38 265 had both first and second
mortgages.

1'	3'	5'
7	2	1
13	4	3
19	6	4
26	9	5
32	11	6
38	13	8
40	13	8

34 Our Drier Model SP-18-DH has a
water evaporation rate of 1 530 kg of
water per hour and will dry
2 970 kg (dry mass) of chips per
hour from 100 per cent to 5 per
cent moisture content based on
oven-dry mass of chips.

1'	3'	5'
6	2	1
13	4	3
19	6	4
25	8	5
31	10	6
37	12	7
42	14	8

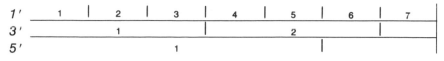

VII.47 Centre the following table attractively on P4 paper with the wide edge inserted.

WIMBLEDON TENNIS CHAMPIONS

Singles 1966-1976

Year	Men's Champion	Country of Citizenship	Women's Champion	Country of Citizenship
1966	Manuel Santana	Spain	Billie J. King	United States
1967	John Newcombe	Australia	Billie J. King	United States
1968	Rod Laver	Australia	Billie J. King	United States
1969	Rod Laver	Australia	Ann Jones	England
1970	John Newcombe	Australia	Margaret Smith Court	Australia
1971	John Newcombe	Australia	Evonne Goolagong	Australia
1972	Stan Smith	United States	Billie J. King	United States
1973	Jan Kodes	Czechoslovakia	Billie J. King	United States
1974	Jimmy Connors	United States	Chris Evert	United States
1975	Arthur Ashe	United States	Billie J. King	United States
1976	Bjorn Borg	Sweden	Chris Evert	United States

INDIVIDUALIZED TYPEWRITING APPLICATIONS (ITA's)

VII.48 Now that you have acquired a thorough knowledge of the mechanics involved in typing tables, you should be able to apply what you have learned to practical situations.

When composing and typing the tables for the following ITA's, remember to provide a suitable title and appropriate columnar headings for each.

Always use good technique when composing and typing each application.

ITA 1

Arrange the following surnames in alphabetical order. Use four columns.

Marsh, Anderson, Tilden, Smith, Poe, Benoit, McIntosh, Olson, Murdock, Atkins, Madison, Sweet, Talbot, Lewis, Miller, Benson, Vickery, Young, Lakusta, Brown, Salazar, Johnstone, Eckert, Crabbe, Pine.

ITA 2

Compile and type a list of the names of fellow students, showing the address and telephone number of each.

		1'	3'	5'

35 In 1901 the total value of machinery was $108 665 500, an average per farm of $213 and per hectare of $4.23. In twenty years the total had grown to $665 180 416, the value per farm had increased to $935, and the value per hectare was $11.68.

1'	3'	5'
11	4	2
19	6	4
29	10	6
39	13	8
48	16	10

36 Technological progress has marched hand-in-hand with territorial expansion. The number of tractors on farms increased from 47 000 in 1921, to 160 000 in 1941, and 400 000 in 1951. There were, in 1951, 526 000 automobiles and trucks on Canada's farms.

1'	3'	5'
9	3	2
18	6	4
28	9	6
39	13	8
48	16	10
49	16	10

37 On the fringe of the Great Plains region, Riding Mountain National Park occupies a vast plateau which rises 670 m above sea level. Its area of 2973 km² is heavily forested, inhabited by deer, elk, moose, and bear. There is a herd of buffalo in a fenced tract of 809 ha.

1'	3'	5'
10	3	2
19	6	4
28	9	6
38	13	8
48	16	10
53	18	11

38 Young people select the activity in which they wish to bury themselves and to perfect their knowledge. Last year's club activities showed 18 426 members interested in home economics, 23 630 in livestock and poultry, 10 383 in field crops, 9 857 in horticulture, and 2 919 in various other projects.

1'	3'	5'
9	3	2
18	6	4
27	9	5
36	12	7
45	15	9
55	18	11
58	19	12

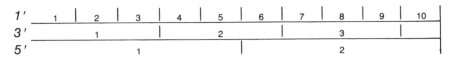

1'	1	2	3	4	5	6	7	8	9	10
3'		1		2		3	
5'		1			2	

VII.45 Centre the following information as an attractive display.

CANADIAN ELEMENTARY AND SECONDARY
SCHOOL STATISTICS*

1973-74

Province	Schools	Teachers	Pupils
Newfoundland	749	6 920	160 660
Prince Edward Island	101	1 562	29 197
Nova Scotia	667	10 190	209 541
New Brunswick	562	7 925	171 519
Quebec	3 780	79 270	1 542 283
Ontario	5 027	92 960	2 063 203
Manitoba	829	12 507	248 309
Saskatchewan	1 082	10 546	230 943
Alberta	1 355	20 793	428 302
British Columbia	1 754	24 588	561 780
Yukon and Northwest Territories	87	920	16 976
National Defence (overseas)	11	311	4 607
Total	16 004	268 492	5 667 320

*Public, federal, and private schools.

FIVE-COLUMN TABLES   VII.46 Centre the following table attractively on P4 paper.

WORLD HOCKEY ASSOCIATION CHAMPIONS

Avco World Trophy Finals
1973-1976

Year	Losing Team	Division	Winning Team	Division
1973	Winnipeg Jets	Canadian	New England Whalers	Eastern
1974	Chicago Cougars	Eastern	Houston Aeros	Western
1975	Quebec Nordiques	Canadian	Houston Aeros	Western
1976	Houston Aeros	Western	Winnipeg Jets	Canadian

SUPPLEMENTARY SKILL-BUILDING MATERIALS

39 More then 74 per cent of the wood pulp, manufactured | 10 | 3 | 2
is converted to other commodities, the remainder | 20 | 7 | 4
being shipped abroad. Newsprint accounts for | 29 | 10 | 6
about 75 per cent of all paper products manufactured | 39 | 13 | 8
but there are many other sorts of paper merchandise: | 50 | 17 | 10
bags and boxes, paperboards, building boards, | 58 | 19 | 12
and roofing. | 61 | 20 | 12

40 Benefits paid by life insurance companies | 8 | 3 | 2
totalled $337 million, a rate of $65 mil- | 16 | 5 | 3
lion a week. Of this sum, $244 million | 24 | 8 | 5
were paid under ordinary policies, | 31 | 10 | 6
$40 million under industrial policies, | 39 | 13 | 8
and $53 million under group contracts. | 46 | 15 | 9
In the same year these companies paid | 54 | 18 | 11
out $58 million under accident and | 61 | 20 | 12
sickness policies. | 65 | 22 | 13

41 Now, check this against the "general | 7 | 2 | 1
needs" previously mentioned: if less | 14 | 5 | 3
than $1 per $100 insurance is collected | 22 | 7 | 4
it will be inadequate; if more is col- | 30 | 10 | 6
lected it will be unreasonable, and if | 37 | 12 | 7
half the owners are charged $1.20 while | 45 | 15 | 9
the others pay only $1, the fund will be | 53 | 18 | 11
adequate but the rates will be discrimi- | 61 | 20 | 12
native. | 62 | 21 | 12

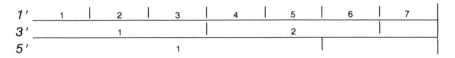

VII.43 Centre the following information as an attractive display.

```
                INVENTORY OF SUPPLIES
            BUSINESS EDUCATION DEPARTMENT

                 AS AT 1976 04 23

                                         WAREHOUSE
        CODE NO.      TITLE    QUANTITY   LOCATION

        538-018Y37    A84-3      136       86-5W
        538-029307    B93         72       85-9B
        538-063106    F31          2       86-9C
        538-076305    G63          -       87-3R
        538-087501    H75          8       88-3A
        538-113707    K37         56       84-1B
        538-131101    M11        101       90-FT
        538-181109    R11          9       90-LS
        538-195703    557         63       90-LD
        538-205407    T54        901       90-JG
```

(Tables with Footnotes)

VII.44 Centre the following information as an attractive display.

CANADA'S TOTAL LAND
AND FRESH WATER AREA*

Measured in square kilometres

Province	Land Area	Fresh Water Area	Total Area
NF	370 485	34 032	404 517
PE	5 657	–	5 657
NS	52 841	2 650	55 491
NB	72 092	1 344	73 436
PQ	1 356 791	183 889	1 540 680
ON	891 194	177 388	1 068 582
MB	548 495	101 592	650 087
SK	570 269	81 631	651 900
AB	644 389	16 796	661 185
BC	930 528	18 068	948 596
YT	531 844	4 481	536 325
NT	3 246 389	133 294	3 379 683
Total	9 220 974	755 165	9 976 139

*Source: The Statesman's Year-Book 1975/1976

Notes: On footnotes —

Footnotes to tables are typed after the last line in a table. A one-line footnote requires three lines—one for the underscore (divider line), one for the blank line following the divider line, and one for the actual footnote line.

The footnote may be typed flush with the left margin or indented 5 spaces from the left margin.

SUPPLEMENTARY SKILL-BUILDING MATERIALS

42 The leading metallic minerals produced were nickel, copper, iron, gold, uranium, zinc, and lead, valued at $1 048 million; the leading nonmetallics were coal, asbestos, petroleum, and natural gas, valued at $677 million; and in addition there were clay products and other structural material valued at $275 million. The total mineral production was valued at $2 134 million.

7	2	1
14	5	3
21	7	4
29	10	6
37	12	7
45	15	9
53	18	11
60	20	12
67	22	13
74	25	15

43 These two Canadian railroads are engaged in a country-wide service. The business done at Halifax on the Atlantic and at Vancouver, 5 600 km away on the Pacific, ends up in the same ledger. A haul of 7 254 km is possible between two points on one railway: St. John's, Newfoundland and Prince Rupert, British Columbia. The average haul between east and west is about 2 400 km; the average haul of all traffic in 1949 was over 645 km per shipment. In the United Kingdom in 1948 it was only 116 km.

6	2	1
13	4	3
20	7	4
27	9	5
34	11	7
41	14	8
48	16	10
55	18	11
62	21	12
69	23	14
76	25	15
83	28	17
90	30	18
97	32	19

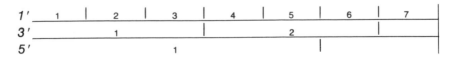

1'	1	2	3	4	5	6	7
3'		1			2		
5'			1				

VII.41 Centre the following information as an attractive display.

Hotel Accommodation
12 European Cities

City	First Class	Standard Class	Budget Class
Amsterdam	Die Port Van Cleve	Concorde	Groenhof
Brussels	Palace	Queen Anne	Herman
Copenhagen	Arthur Frommer	Globus	Sibertsen
Frankfurt	Continental	Nord	Lohmann
Geneva	Royal	Athenee	Kaufman
Lisbon	Tivoli	Roma	Caravela
London	London International	Royal National	Corton
Madrid	Palace	Breton	Asturias
Nice	Westminster	Napoleon	Little Palace
Paris	Concorde Lafayette	Amina	Phenix
Rome	Anglo American	Oxford	Forti
Zurich	Stoller	Limmathaus	Titlis

VII.42 Making the necessary corrections, centre the following information as an attractive display.

GRAND AND TOY
HOLIDAY SCHEDULE
1975 (6)

Name	Entitlement	Holiday Period
Berger, Debbie (orah)	15 working days	July 3–23 (5)
Campion, Elizabeth	15 working days	January 7–25 (5–23)
Das, Gretchan	10 ~~9~~ working days	June 19–29 (14–25)
Gracey, Helen	15 ~~10~~ working days	July 30–August 10 (26 /6)
Hanson, Patti	15 working days	May 12–21
LeBlanc, Yvette	9 ~~5~~ working days	July 23–27 (19–29)
Morrissey, Susan	15 ~~12~~ working days	August 13–27 (2)
Rivard, Michelle	15 working days	September 4–24 (7–28)
Song, Aline	15 working days	December 7–28 (6)
Suderholm, Ingrid	15 working days	June 4–23 (7–25)
Zuber, Lorri	15 working days	February 4–22 (2–20)

INDIVIDUALIZED TYPEWRITING APPLICATIONS (ITA's)

III.28 Now that you have acquired a basic typewriting skill you should be able to begin transferring some of this skill to composition at the typewriter.

Initially you might select one or two applications which only require a sentence response. Then when you gain more confidence, you can attempt the more challenging applications.

Be sure to use good techniques when typing each exercise.

ITA 1

Type an answer to each question listed below. Your answers should be in the form of complete sentences. A sample answer is given for the first question.

The typewriter that I am using is an Eaton Viking, Automatic Twelve.

A. What make of typewriter are you using?

B. What color is your typewriter?

C. Is your typewriter an electric or manual machine?

D. How long is your typewriter carriage?

E. What kind of type face does your typewriter have?

F. Who is your typewriting teacher?

ITA 2

Type an answer to each question below. Again, a sample answer is given for the first question.

The City of Ottawa is the capital of Canada.

A. What city is the capital of Canada?

B. Who is the Prime Minister of Canada?

C. What is the name of the town or city in which you live?

D. What occupation do you plan to seek after graduation?

E. What is the name of the longest river in Canada?

The next applications should be more challenging!

ITA 3

Type a paragraph about work. You may choose from the topics below, or you may select your own topic.

A. The value of work.

B. The teen-ager and work.

C. Preparation for a career.

D. Pay for work.

E. Women in the world of work.

Janet Wilson	1958 04 11	Toronto, ON
Jack Cousins	1961 02 06	Moncton, NB
Elmer Frost	1958 03 04	Winnipeg, MB
Marion Connelly	1960 08 16	Halifax, NS
Constance Roberts	1959 07 27	Camrose, AB
Wilma Webster	1960 10 14	Hamilton, ON
Fred Saunders	1959 05 03	Regina, SK

Notes: The use of the double-line underscore, as illustrated in Problem VII.39 is optional. If used, underscore the amount once. Then, operate the variable line spacer and roll the cylinder slightly forward. Using the underscore, type the second line. Return the variable line spacer to normal position.

VII.37 Arrange the information in Problem VII.36 chronologically, and type as an attractive display.

VII.38 Arrange the information in Problem VII.36 alphabetically by province, and type as an attractive display.

(Typing Double Lines)

VII.39 Centre the following information as an attractive display.

Offset Duplicating Service
Price List — Circulation 400

Item	10 pages	20 pages	30 pages
Typesetting	$ 10.00	$ 20.00	$ 30.00
Paper	8.00	16.00	24.00
Plates and negative	15.00	30.00	45.00
Collating and stapling	10.00	10.00	10.00
Addressing	4.00	4.00	4.00
Envelopes and letterhead	13.20	13.20	13.20
Printing	15.00	30.00	45.00
Total	$ 75.20	$124.20	$171.20

(Two-Line Columnar Headings)

VII.40 Centre the following information as an attractive display.

Notes: On two-line columnar headings —

Each line of a columnar heading is centred as a separate column line. If all columnar headings do not have the same number of lines, align the lines horizontally from the last line in the heading.

The first line of all columnar headings should be typed a triple-space after the title or subtitle.

SCHEDULE OF DEALERS◻ COMMISSIONS

SINGLE PAYMENT CASH ORDERS

AMOUNT	TOTAL COMMISSION	DEALER COMMISSION
UNDER $25 000	8%	6.0%
$ 25 000 TO $49 999	6%	4.4%
$ 50 000 TO $99 999	5%	3.6%
$100 000 AND OVER	4%	2.9%

ITA 4

Re-type the following limericks, providing a rhyming last line:

A. A girl who was learning to ski
   Wondered how she could miss every tree;
      She tried and she tried,
      But one day she cried,
   (Type a sentence to rhyme with tree.)

B. A man who was building a boat
   Asked his wife and relations to note
      That he filled up the cracks
      With varnish and wax
   (Type a sentence to rhyme with note.)

ROUGH DRAFT

the suden silence
shocked him. To
who could he turn.
Immediately he
realized that he
would

CORRECTED DRAFT

The ~~suden~~ *sudden* silence
shocked him. To
~~who~~ *whom* could he turn?
Immediately he
realized ~~that~~ he
would

ITA 5

Complete the following story:

At that moment Jim banged his way through the cabin door shouting, "Help! They're after me!" There was dead silence. Jim ran from room to room but found no one.

> *You may wish to prepare a rough draft at the typewriter first, correct it, and then retype it. So that you can work with your rough draft, remember to double space it. When typing, try to get your thoughts down quickly. Forget about errors. Corrections can be made after you remove your copy from the typewriter.*

ITA 6

Type suggested solutions to the following problems:

A. The car I want to buy is on a used-car lot. Having never owned a car, I feel I am not a very good judge of cars. What advice can you give me about buying a second-hand car?

B. I am going to be interviewed next Monday for a receptionist's job. I want to be successful. What should I do to prepare for the interview?

C. When shopping last week in a large department store, I picked up a $50 bill from the floor near the cashier's counter. What do you think I should have done?

ITA 7

You have just been informed that you have obtained employment—your first job—as a mail clerk in a large insurance company. Describe for a friend the type of work that you expect you will have to do.

ITA 8

The Head of the Business Education Department has asked you to write a paragraph or two describing the typewriting course you are now taking. He plans to use this information in a school handbook that contains course descriptions. Prepare the information required.

TABLES WITH SPECIAL FEATURES

VII.34 Making the necessary corrections, centre the following table attractively on P5 paper with the wide edge inserted.

(Rough Draft)

department budget

Operating budget account	estimated	Actual
causal Help	$ 250	$270
Duplicting	50ろ0	600
Equipment Replacment	9000	-
Postge	600	7,600
Printing	500	45,600
Repras & upkeep and	030	25,600
Suples plies	800	9,600.
Telephones	900	900
Vehicle rentl	44400	250

(Computer Type)

VII.35 Centre the following table on P5 paper with the wide edge inserted.

```
OVEN-TO-TABLE DINNERWARE

OPEN STOCK

ITEM DESCRIPTION  CROCUS  DAFFODIL  COSMOS  HOLLY

LUNCHEON PLATE    $ 2.81  $ 3.11   $ 3.56  $2.36
COFFEE MUG          -       3.38     3.21    2.96
SALT & PEPPER      7.46     6.40     5.70    5.62
OATMEAL            2.06     3.94     2.95    2.97
OVAL PLATTER       7.12     6.47     7.28    6.71
OPEN VEGETABLE     4.87     5.97     5.19    5.21
ROUND CASSEROLE   14.21    12.71      -       -
SUGAR BOWL         9.27     6.56     7.24    5.62
CREAM JUG          5.21     3.71     2.97    2.96
GRAVY BOAT/STAND   9.71     7.46     8.40    6.71
TEAPOT            14.96    10.87    11.20    9.88
COFFEE POT        14.96    10.87    13.65    9.50
```

(Two-line Title)

VII.36 Arrange the following information alphabetically by surname and type as an attractive display on P5 paper with wide edge inserted.

KLM
Royal Dutch Airlines
New Applicants

Name	Date of Birth	Place of Birth
Caroline Forbes	1960 01 07	Calgary, AB

Notes: On two-line titles —

Each line of a two-line or multi-line title is centred over the table. No extra space is left between lines. A double-space follows the last line of the title, if a subtitle is used. If a subtitle is not used, a triple-space follows the last line of the title.

(Continued on next page)

ITA 9

React to the following statements:

A. High school students should not be required to take a course in English.

B. Too much importance is attached to examinations.

C. Advertising benefits the consumer.

D. Cities should not be allowed to grow too large.

E. Everyone should learn how to type.

Often an individual has heard the expression: "A picture is worth a thousand words!" Type a paragraph or two about each of the following illustrations.

ITA 10

ITA 11

ITA 12

ITA 13

VII.30 Centre the following table on P5 paper with the wide edge inserted. Single-space the body.

Name	Post-Secondary Institution	Area of Study

GRAPHICS — GRADUATES OF CENTRAL HIGH SCHOOL ← Title
DS
Enrolled in Post-Secondary Education ← Subtitle
TS

Name	Post-Secondary Institution	Area of Study
Leonard King	University of Toronto	Biology
Margaret Logan	NAIT	Cooking
Mary Deleffe	University of Calgary	Education
Roger Judd	Sheridan College	Music

DS

VII.31 Centre the following table attractively on P4 paper. Double-space.

COMMUNITY INFORMATION CENTRE

Hours: 09:00 to 17:30

Committee	Convenor	Phone Number
Legal Advice	Peter Unwing	453-6205
Recreation	Roland Campbell	426-3210
Consumer Affairs	Jim Schrank	822-6197
Women's Rights	Melanie Muir	735-4100
Schools	Adelle Leibnitz	523-3619
Pre-school & Daycare	Helen Eadie	452-5181
Aldermen	Stella Mahoniuk	422-4534
Drug Counselling	Russell Demco	610-0771
Senior Citizen	Donald Versteeg	633-4589
Summer Camp Program	Estelle Poirier	645-6210
Baby Sitter	Lisa Melanchuk	462-7839
Churches	Rhona Wilson	423-8945
Health	Brenda Rowan	478-8905
Community Services	Monica Sampson	423-4277
Youth Activities	Jean Bencharsky	785-3264
Rent Problems	Ella Steinberg	892-5690
Family Planning	Ted Lucas	786-4285
Foster Children	Beth Burke	867-8795
Adoption	Paul Bennett	452-3417·

VII.32 Type the table in Problem VII.31 attractively on P5 paper with the wide edge inserted. Re-arrange the material with the committees listed alphabetically.

VII.33 Type the table in Problem VII.31 attractively on P5 paper. Re-arrange the material alphabetically by the surname of the convenor.

Using your imagination, type a short story to accompany each of the following pictures.

ITA 16

VII.28 Centre the following four-column table on P5 paper. Single-space. (Since this table is composed of two 2-column sections, you might wish to vary the space between the second and third columns. The space between the first and second columns and the third and fourth columns should be equal.)

THE FORTY MOST-USED WORDS IN BUSINESS LETTERS

Word	Rank	Word	Rank
the	1	with	21
of	2	would	22
to	3	at	23
and	4	it	24
in	5	I	25
we	6	not	26
you	7	which	27
a	8	by	28
for	9	from	29
that	10	if	30
this	11	or	31
be	12	us	32
your	13	was	33
is	14	been	34
our	15	letter	35
on	16	has	36
have	17	an	37
will	18	any	38
as	19	these	39
are	20	time	40

VII.29 Centre the following table attractively on P5 paper with the wide edge inserted.

A CODE FOR IDENTIFYING LETTERS OF THE ALPHABET

Letter	Code Word	Letter	Code Word
A	Adam	N	Norman
B	Bank	O	Ocean
C	Charlie	P	Pacific
D	Dollar	Q	Queen
E	Edward	R	Robert
F	Frank	S	Sugar
G	George	T	Tom
H	Henry	U	Union
I	Ida	V	Victor
J	John	W	William
K	King	X	X ray
L	London	Y	Young
M	Mary	Z	Zero

ITA 17

ITA 18

ITA 19

VII.26 Centre the following table attractively on P5 paper.

GRADE X RECORD — STAN TIMMINS

Course Titles	Credits	Grade
Typewriting	2	A
Shorthand	2	A
Accounting	1	B
Mathematics	1	B
English	2	A
Psychology	$^1/_2$	A
Economics	1	B

CENTRING COLUMNAR HEADINGS
(Headings Shorter and/or Longer than Column)

VII.27 Centre the following table attractively on P4 paper.

TODAY'S TEMPERATURES

City	High	Low
Brandon	24	13
Calgary	22	10
Charlottetown	19	17
Dauphin	27	14
Edmonton	20	12
Estevan	23	11
Fort Smith	26	11
Fredericton	24	15
Halifax	18	14
Inuvik	17	7
Kamloops	31	15
Kenora	26	15
Montreal	28	21
Norman Wells	27	16
North Bay	24	18
Ottawa	28	21
Penticton	29	13
Prince Albert	19	12
Prince George	27	10
Prince Rupert	18	13
Quebec City	26	19
Regina	20	13
Saskatoon	19	12
St. John's	14	9
Swift Current	17	12
The Pas	21	15
Thompson	25	13
Thunder Bay	18	17
Toronto	29	18
Vancouver	23	13
Victoria	21	10
Whitehorse	17	8
White River	27	17
Winnipeg	25	15
Yellowknife	24	14

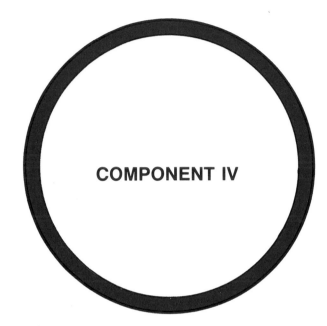

COMPONENT IV

CENTRING TYPEWRITTEN MATERIAL

STUDENT OBJECTIVES

1. To learn and apply the principles for centring copy using the typewriter.

2. To develop speed in accurately centring material.

3. To apply typing skills to the production of realistic business tasks.

4. To increase stroking and copying skills.

DAILY ACTIVITIES

Preliminary:

Current date typing. Type three lines of the current date as illustrated:

	↓ tab set	↓ tab set
19__ 05 21	19__ 05 21	19__ 05 21
19__ 05 21	19__ 05 21	19__ 05 21
19__ 05 21	19__ 05 21	19__ 05 21

Main:

1. Identify your work by typing your name, the name and number of the course, and the current date.

2. Select and type several times an alphabetic sentence from pages 53 to 54.

3. Select and type a number of paragraphs from pages 37 to 52 attempting to increase your controlled typing speed.

4. Proceed through Component IV.

CONTENTS

Component IV introduces the student to horizontal and vertical centring on a variety of standard paper sizes.

200	Excelsior Warrants	0.35	70
10	Canco 'A'	4.75	47
30	Canco 'B'	5.50	165
200	Caroway Cellulose	25.00	5000
25	Dominion Telephone	62.00	1 550
200	Dorcus Foods	12.50	2 500
50	Copper Ltd.	31.00	1 550

CENTRING COLUMNAR HEADINGS
(Headings Longer than Column Width)

VII.24 Centre the following three-column table on P5 paper with the wide edge inserted. Single-space. The flow chart below will assist you in centring the columns beneath the headings.

MEETING ROOM DETAILS

West Annex Rooms	Room Dimensions	Capacities
Gold Room	17.4 m x 9.6 m	230
Crystal Room	17.4 m x 12.0 m	320
West Salon	8.4 m x 4.8 m	40
East Salon	8.4 m x 4.8 m	40
Pioneer Hall	17.4 m x 21.6 m	550

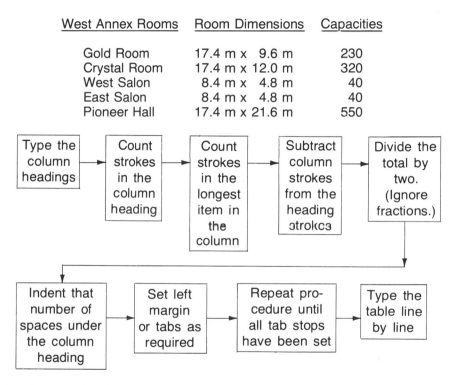

VII.25 Centre the following table attractively on P5 paper with the wide edge inserted.

TERRITORY REVISIONS

James S. Peterson	David M. Forsythe	John T. Dunsmuir
Toronto #32	Winnipeg	Stratford
Sudbury	Oakville	London
North Bay	Toronto #18	St. Thomas
St. Catharines	Cornwall	Windsor
Hamilton	Brockville	Pembroke
Kitchener	Thunder Bay	Peterborough

Supplementary:

Select and type a number of ITA's from pages 128 to 131.

SUMMARY OF COMPONENT IV PROBLEMS

MAJOR APPLICATIONS

Horizontal Centring Without Heading
General 1, 2
P5 paper (wide edge) .   3, 4, 5, 6

Horizontal and Vertical Centring Without Heading
P5 paper   8
P5 paper (wide edge) .   7, 9, 10

Horizontal and Vertical Centring With Heading
P4 paper 16, 17, 18, 19, 20, 21,
                                   22
P5 paper 12, 15, 26, 33
P5 paper (wide edge) .   11, 13, 14, 23, 24, 25,
                         29-32

SPECIAL APPLICATIONS

All Capitals in Body 9, 11, 16, 17, 23, 30-33

Centring in a Circle . . . . .   ITA's 10-13

Centring on a Line   36-38

Left Margin Set With
Heading   19

Left Margin Set With
Longest Line   21

Right Margin Set
(Pivoting)   30-33

Script Copy   24-28

Spreading 27-29, 31-33

Typing On A Line 34, 35

Unarranged Copy 1, 2, 3, 4, 5, 6, 8, 9, 10,
                              13, 14, 15, 16, 17, 18,
                              20, 22, 23, 24, 25, 26,
                              33-39

Variable Spacing
Between Lines 14, 15, 18, 30, 32, 33

Variable Spacing
Between Words 17, 30-33

VII.21 Centre the following table on P5 paper with the wide edge inserted. Single-space.

LIST OF SERVICES AND CHARGES

Services	Charges
Linen Service	$ 79.00
Cleaning Supplies	153.73
Dietary Supplies	160.88
Housekeeping Supplies	247.75
Laboratory Supplies	159.60
Drugs and Medicines	1 805.48
Medical and Surgical Supplies	1 264.94
Nursing (other than direct Nursing Care)	774.41
Maintenance and Repair Supplies	445.75
Dietary Meal Service	10 532.58
Laundry Service	1 729.64

FOUR-COLUMN TABLES

VII.22 Centre the following four-column table on P4 paper. Double-space.

ADULT EVENING CLASSES

Course	Day	Time	Fee
Fashion Modelling	Monday	19:00	$50
Personnel Development	Monday	20:30	$30
Industrial Psychology	Monday	19:00	$30
Labor Relations	Monday	20:30	$30
Native Indian Handicrafts	Tuesday	19:00	$35
Cree	Tuesday	20:30	$30
Life Drawing	Tuesday	19:00	$35
Creative Photography	Tuesday	20:30	$35
Audio-Visual Graphics	Wednesday	19:00	$30
Gregg Shorthand	Wednesday	19:00	$40
Forkner Shorthand	Thursday	20:30	$40
Pitman Shorterhand	Thursday	20:30	$40
Typewriting I	Thursday	19:00	$40
Typewriting II	Thursday	20:30	$40

VII.23 Centre the following four-column table on P4 paper. Double-space.

Stock Acquisition List

No.	Stock	Price	Value
25	R.L.K.	$ 68.00	$1 700
100	Creekside Paper	25.00	2 500
100	Amalgamated Oils	0.72	72

(Continued on next page)

Notes: Your instructor will tell you whether you are to correct errors made in typing the problems that follow.

In most typewritten work, errors should be corrected. The following information outlines three methods that may be used for correcting errors.

Typewriter Eraser

1. Choose a hard or soft eraser to match the grade of paper. The eraser chosen may be a wheel type with or without a brush; a pencil type with an eraser on one end and a brush on the other; or a pencil type with a coarse eraser on one end and a softer eraser (for carbon copies) on the other end.

2. Turn the paper up a few spaces so that the error will be at the top of the cylinder. (If the error is at the bottom of the page, roll *back* the paper until the bottom of the paper can be rested on the top of the cylinder. This prevents paper slippage.)

3. Move the carriage to the extreme right or left (use margin release) to prevent eraser crumbs from falling into the machine.

4. Remove error using light strokes of the eraser directed away from the mechanical parts of the typewriter. Brush eraser crumbs from the paper.

5. Re-position to type correction.

6. Insert correct letter by striking lightly. Backspace and re-strike if necessary.

Correction Paper

1. Backspace to the beginning of error.

2. Insert the correction paper (available in a variety of colors to match paper color) behind the ribbon and in front of the copy to be corrected.

3. Re-type the error exactly as you made it. Remove the correction paper.

4. Backspace to the beginning of correction and type the correction.

Correction Fluid

1. Turn the paper up a few spaces. (If error is near the bottom of the page, turn the paper *back* several spaces.)

2. Move the carriage to the extreme right or left (use margin release). This will prevent any fluid from falling into the machine.

CENTRING COLUMNAR HEADINGS
(Headings Shorter than Column Width)

VII.19 Centre the following three-column table on P5 paper with the wide edge inserted. Single-space. The flow chart below will assist you in centring the columnar headings over each column.

SAFETY AND LIQUIDITY OF SELECTED INVESTMENTS

Investment	Safety	Liquidity
Debentures	Fair	Good
Quality Bonds	Excellent	Good
Trust Company GICs	Excellent	Fairly good
Commercial or Finance Paper	Good	Fairly good
Quality Preferred Stocks	Good	Good
Canada Savings Bonds	Excellent	Excellent
Long-Term Canada Bonds	Excellent	Good
Medium-Term Canada Bonds	Excellent	Good
Short-Term Canada Bonds	Excellent	Good
Treasury Bills	Excellent	Good
Blue Chip Common Stocks	Good	Good
Convertible Debentures	Fair	Good
Growth Common Stocks	Fair	Good
Mutual Funds	Fair	Good

Set left margin and tab stops for columns	→	Type the title	→	Count strokes in the column heading	→	Count strokes in the longest item in the column	→	Subtract heading strokes from the column strokes

Divide the total by two. (Ignore fractions.)	→	Indent that number of spaces and type column heading.	→	Tab to next column	→	Repeat procedure until all headings have been typed

VII.20 Centre the following table on P5 paper with the wide edge inserted. Double-space.

MAXIMUM TIME PERIODS FOR STORAGE OF FROZEN MEATS

Meat	Period
Beef steaks and roasts	ten to twelve months
Lamb roasts	six to eight months
Pork and veal roasts	four to five months
Variety meats	three to four months
Ground meats	two to three months
Pork — cured, smoked	one to two months
Bacon	one month
Sausages and weiners	two and three weeks

3. Select a fluid to match the color of paper and shake the bottle. Then remove the applicator brush and daub off any excess fluid on the inside of the bottle opening.

4. Apply the fluid lightly and quickly to the outline of the stroke or strokes to be corrected. Do not "paint" the fluid onto the paper.

5. Replace the applicator brush and tighten cap.

6. Re-position paper and type correction.

CORRECTING ERRORS ON CARBON COPIES

1. Errors on carbon copies should be corrected when the paper is still in the typewriter. Place a stiff card behind the sheet on which you are erasing to prevent carbon marks from appearing on the remaining copies. Use a soft eraser. Blow eraser crumbs off the paper. When the error on all copies has been erased remove the card. Then re-position paper to type correction.

2. Corrections on carbon copies are most easily made using an eraser rather than correction paper or fluid.

CORRECTING ERRORS
AFTER THE PAPER HAS BEEN REMOVED

1. Erase the error.

2. Re-insert the paper in the typewriter.

3. Use the variable line spacer to position the paper so that the bottoms of the typewritten letters are slightly above the aligning scale.

4. Use the paper release to move the paper to left or right so that the letter "i" or "I" is lined up with a vertical line scale.

5. Test the position of the printing point by locating a typewritten period, setting the ribbon on stencil position, and typing over the period. Make any needed adjustments.

6. Return the ribbon to type position and type the correction.

7. While some typists attempt to re-insert carbon copies with the original for correction, it is recommended that errors on carbons be corrected individually. Follow the procedures as outlined above, but do not type directly onto the carbon copy. Insert a piece of carbon between the ribbon and the copy. Then type the correction.

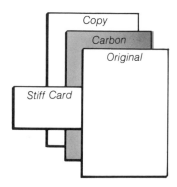

If you do not have a stiff card, use a sheet of paper inserted behind the carbon.

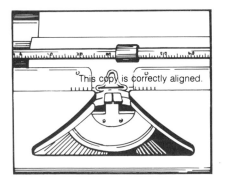

VII.15 Type the table in Problem VII.14 on P4 paper. Double-space.

VII.16 Centre the following information as a three-column table. Use P5 paper with the wide edge inserted. Single-space.

EVANGELINE DEPARTMENT STORE

Department / Floor / Supervisor
Confectionery / First / Laura Strong
Boys' Wear / First / Timothy Hold
Men's Wear / First / Donald Free
Stationery / First / Steve Manor
Notions / First / Frieda Rennie
Children's Wear / Second / Jennifer Lee
Ladies' Wear / Second / Dana McGuire
Lingerie / Second / Vera Jensen
Ladies' Shoes / Third / Don Oberholtzer
Men's Shoes / Third / Michael Rehn
Staples / Third / Lee Falconer
Sporting Goods / Fourth / John Evers
Kitchenware / Fourth / Frank Elniski
Furniture / Fourth / Ed Zaharko
Appliances / Fourth / Ted Albinston
Groceries / Basement / Larry Larsen
Cafeteria / Basement / Lisa Benson

VII.17 Type the table in Problem VII.16 on P4 paper. Double-space.

VII.18 Centre the following information as a three-column table. Use P5 paper with the wide edge inserted. Double-space.

PARKING ACCOMMODATION

Type of Facility / Location / Price
Reserved stall with plug-in / Lot "A" / $100
Reserved stall without plug-in / Lot "A" / $90
Reserved zone with plug-in / Lot "B" / $75
Reserved zone without plug-in / Lot "B" / $65
Peripheral zone / Lot "X" / $50
Evening parking only / Lot "X" / $25
Motorcycle/Scooter / Lot "X" / $15

CENTRING A LINE HORIZONTALLY

Self-check: Visually examine your work. Does it appear to be centred?

Notes: Remember that strokes include spaces.

IV.1 Centre the following line horizontally.

Business Service

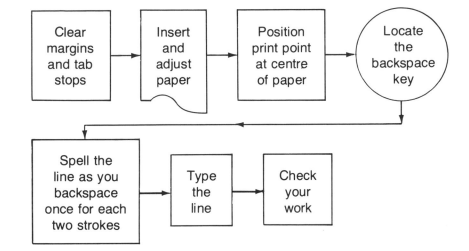

IV.2 Centre the following line horizontally.

Business Services

> *When a line does not backspace evenly, ignore the extra stroke.*

CENTRING SEVERAL LINES HORIZONTALLY

Notes: On standard paper sizes—

P4 paper *is* 21.5 cm x 28 cm.
P5 paper *is* 14 cm x 21.5 cm.
P5 paper *is half a sheet of* **P4 paper**. *One vertical line of type is approximately 0.4 cm deep.*

Notes: On metric equivalents—

```
 0.4 cm =   4 mm
 1   cm =  10 mm
14   cm = 140 mm
21.5 cm = 215 mm
28   cm = 280 mm
```

IV.3 Centre each line of the following display horizontally on a half sheet of paper (215 mm x 140 mm). Insert the wide edge of the sheet into the typewriter and leave a top margin of approximately 38 mm (9 blank lines). Single space.

```
Sale
on
IBM
Selectric
Typewriters
Lowest Prices
Easy Terms
```

Refer to the flow chart on the following page for centring displays of more than one line.

VII.12 Centre the following three-column table horizontally and vertically on P5 paper with the wide edge inserted. Leave an appropriate number of spaces between columns. Double-space the body.

CONSTRUCTION SCHEDULE

Office Buiding	Start	Complete
Tar Roof	August 4	August 7
Interior Partition Block Work	August 7	August 11
Electrical	August 7	September 8
Exterior Doors	August 15	August 30
Heating and Venting	August 21	September 15
Plumbing and Tile	August 14	September 15

VII.13 Centre the following table on P4 paper. Leave an appropriate number of spaces between columns. Double-space the body.

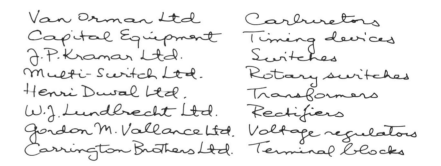

List of Suppliers

Company	Product
Van Orman Ltd	Carburetors
Capital Equipment	Timing devices
J. P. Kramar Ltd.	Switches
Multi-Switch Ltd.	Rotary switches
Henri Duval Ltd.	Transformers
W. J. Lundbrecht Ltd.	Rectifiers
Gordon M. Vallance Ltd.	Voltage regulators
Carrington Brothers Ltd.	Terminal blocks

VII.14 Centre the following information as a three-column table. Use P5 paper. Single-space.

REGIONAL SHOPPING CENTRES

Shopping Centre / Manager / Telephone
Acadia / C. V. McNab / 421-7341
Westlake / M. O. Ackland / 342-3604
Meadowbrook / S. T. Maruyama / 327-6970
Rossdale Place / R. M. Miller / 843-6214
Caribou / M. N. Schartz / 243-1659
Arbutus / W. T. Milne / 624-1673
Blueridge / C. A. Mathews / 411-7821
Parkcourt / L. D. Cather / 542-9113
Spruce Lea / V. M. MacGillivray / 923-4673
Kelsey Park / W. C. Fehr / 723-5942
Midtown / T. R. Simms / 373-4896
Silverglade / R. R. Durant / 690-4442

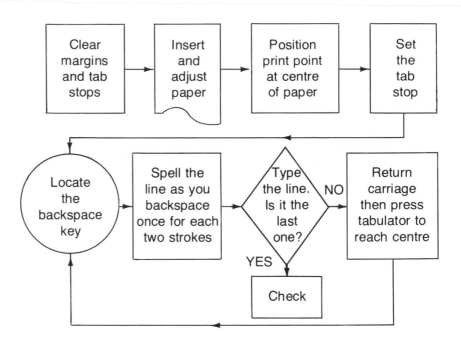

Notes: To double space the display, set your line space regulator on 2.

IV.4 Centre each line of the following display horizontally on a sheet of P5 paper with the wide edge inserted. Leave a top margin of approximately 38 mm. Double space.

P5
(Wide Edge
Inserted)

This sheet of paper can accommodate 33 vertical lines of typing.

14 cm

←—— 21.5 cm ——→

        Business Services Will Give You**DS**

        Advertising**DS**

        Interviewing**DS**

        Testing**DS**

        Fringe Benefits**DS**

        Extra Bookkeeping

IV.5 Centre each line of the following display horizontally on P5 paper with the wide edge inserted. Double space leaving an approximate top margin of 38 mm.

            Full-time employment available
            Excellent working conditions and benefits
            Sewing Machine Operators
            Service Personnel
            Personnel Assistant
            Marker or Marker Trainee
            Sewing Machine Mechanic Trainee
            Steam Press Operators

VII.10 Centre the following two-column table horizontally and vertically on P5 paper with the wide edge inserted. Leave an appropriate number of spaces between the columns. Single-space the body. The flow chart below will assist you in typing the columnar headings flush with the left margin and tab stops.

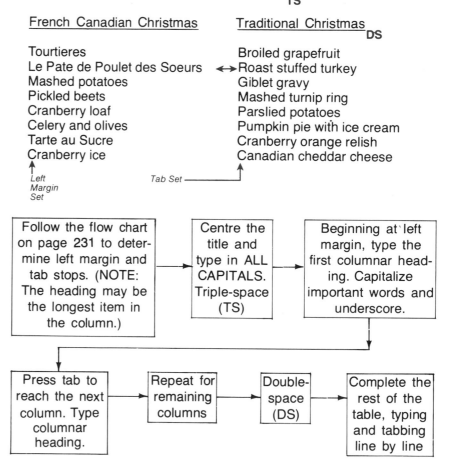

VII.11 Centre the following three-column table horizontally and vertically on P5 paper with the wide edge inserted. Leave an appropriate number of spaces between columns. Single-space the body.

CONCERT SCHEDULE_{TS}

Month	Guest Artist	Theatre
October	David Applebaum	Neptune
December	Maria Bartolli	Strand
January	Jennifer Nash	O'Keefe
February	Victor Benedickson	Windsor
March	Leontyne Price	Jubilee
May	Georges L'Hirondelle	Landsdowne

IV.6 Centre each line of the following display horizontally on P5 paper with the wide edge inserted. Single space the display leaving an approximate top margin of 50 mm.

```
Money Orders
C.O.D.
Insurance
Registration
Special Delivery
Certified Mail
```

Notes: On metric equivalents—

14 cm = 140 mm
21.5 cm = 215 mm
28 cm = 280 mm

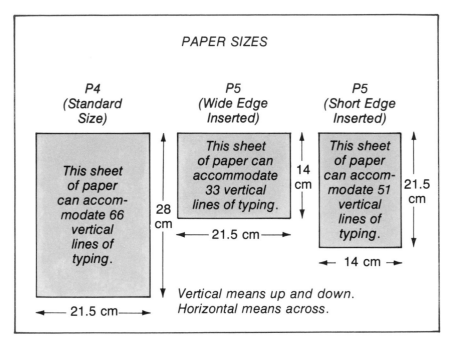

PAPER SIZES

P4 (Standard Size)

This sheet of paper can accommodate 66 vertical lines of typing.

21.5 cm

28 cm

P5 (Wide Edge Inserted)

This sheet of paper can accommodate 33 vertical lines of typing.

21.5 cm

14 cm

P5 (Short Edge Inserted)

This sheet of paper can accommodate 51 vertical lines of typing.

14 cm

21.5 cm

Vertical means up and down.
Horizontal means across.

CENTRING A DISPLAY VERTICALLY

IV.7 Centre the following display vertically on a sheet of P5 paper with the wide edge inserted. Centre each line horizontally. Double space.

Notes: On spacing—

SS means single space
DS means double space

	Return Carriage	Number of Blank lines
SS	1 time	0
DS	2 times	1

```
Corduroy Makes the Scene DS

Corduroy Pants DS

Popular Styling DS

Assortment of Brushed Medium Wale and Wide Wale DS

Assorted Colors
```

Refer to the flow chart on the following page for centring double-spaced displays of more than one line.

PERSONNEL MANUAL REVISIONS

Absenteeism	Fire Procedures	Merit Awards
Accidents	First Aid	Orientation
Benefits	Flowers	Overtime Pay
Bonus	Gifts	Promotion
Bulletin Board	Grievances	Recreation
Cafeteria	Holidays	Retirement
Car Allowances	Hours of Work	Safety
Christmas Shopping	Housekeeping	Savings Plan
Credit Union	Inspection	Sick Leave
Employee Discounts	Jury Duty	Smoking

Notes: On spacing —

P5 paper *will accommodate 51 vertical lines of typing.*

VII.8 Re-type the three-column table from Problem VII.7 on P5 paper. Double-space the body and alter the space left between the columns.

VII.9 Centre the following information horizontally and vertically on P5 paper with the wide edge inserted as a three-column table. Single-space the body.

JOB OPPORTUNITIES

1. Guard	2. Shipper
3. Garage Person	4. Teller
5. Computer Op.	6. Account Exec.
7. Taxi Driver	8. CNE Employee
9. Street Cleaner	10. Secretary
11. Usher	12. Shoe Repairperson
13. Clerk	14. Art Director
15. Auto Body Worker	16. Draftsperson
17. Model	18. Silkscreen Artist
19. Architect	20. Guide
21. Baker	22. Typesetter
23. Telephone Op.	24. News Reporter
25. Lifeguard	26. Gas Jockey
27. Announcer	28. Artist
29. Superintendent	30. Boat Builder
31. Assembly Artist	32. Teacher
33. Horse Trainer	34. Copywriter
35. Accountant	36. Editor
37. Baby Sitter	38. Factory Worker
39. Customers Clerk	40. Janitor
41. Car Jockey	42. Receptionist
43. Caretaker	44. Lumberjack
45. Gardener	

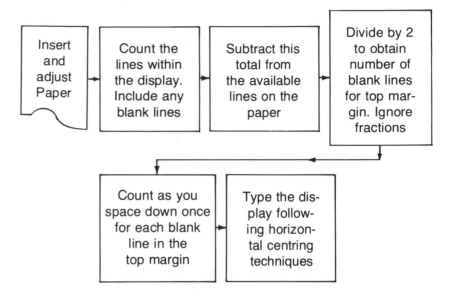

Notes: **P5 paper** means "insert short edge." See page 118.

IV.8 Centre the following display vertically and horizontally on a sheet of <u>P5 paper</u>. Single space.

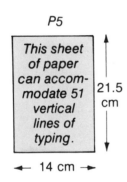

P5

This sheet of paper can accommodate 51 vertical lines of typing.

21.5 cm

← 14 cm →

```
National Choral Festival
Monday, October 12
Jubilee Auditorium
20:30
Soloists--250 Voice Chorus--Orchestra
Dora Neil (Soprano)
Sara Drew (Alto)
Cathy Cates (Alto)
Edwin Thomas (Baritone)
Tickets at Carl's News
429-8911
```

Self-check: Did you allow 13 lines for typing the display in problem IV.9?

IV.9 Centre the following display vertically and horizontally on a sheet of P5 paper with the wide edge inserted. Double space.

Notes: To type a word or group of words in ALL CAPITALS, depress the shift lock key. To release the shift lock depress either the left or right shift key.

```
Suits
Limited quantity
Broken sizes, no alterations
Thursday morning 11:00 special
THE STAG SHOP
623 Main Street
569-3456
```

VII.4 Centre horizontally the following two-column table on P5 paper with the wide edge inserted. Use ten spaces between the columns. Leave a top margin of 25 mm.

Note: In Problem VIII.4, the "key"
line is:

The Evening ReporterXXXXXXXXXXPrince George

The Albertan	Calgary
The Citizen	Prince George
The Daily Courier	Kelowna
The Evening Reporter ←10 spaces→	Cambridge
The Evening Telegram	St. John's
The Globe and Mail	Toronto
The Spectator	Hamilton
The Sun	Vancouver
The Western Star	Corner Brook

VII.5 Centre horizontally the following three-column table on P5 paper with the wide edge inserted. Select an appropriate number of spaces to leave between columns. Use a top margin of 50 mm.

January	Carnation	Garnet
February	Violet	Amethyst
March	Jonquil	Aquamarine
April	Sweet Pea	Diamond
May	Lily of the Valley ←→ Emerald	
June	Rose	Pearl
July	Larkspur	Ruby
August	Gladiolus	Peridot
September ←→ Aster		Sapphire
October	Calendula	Opal
November	Chrysanthemum	Topaz
December	Narcissus	Turquoise

Notes: On spacing —

P4 paper *will accommodate 66 vertical lines of typing.*

VII.6 Centre the table in Problem VII.5 horizontally and vertically on P4 paper. Double space.

TABLES WITH TITLES

VII.7 Centre the table on page 233 horizontally and vertically on P5 paper with the wide edge inserted. The title is centred and typed in ALL CAPITALS. Triple-space (TS) after the title. Single-space the body.

IV.10 Centre the following display vertically and horizontally on a sheet of P5 paper with wide edge inserted. Double space.

Cloverdale Estates

Truly Elegant Living!

Now Renting

Inspection by Appointment

Contact Mrs. J. Wallace

(604) 278-1169

IV.11 Centre the following display vertically and horizontally on a sheet of P5 paper with wide edge inserted. Single space the body.

BLOOD SAVES LIVES **TS**

You can help prepare for a possible emergency
by sharing your life-giving blood now
Don't Delay
CALL YOUR LOCAL RED CROSS TODAY
AND MAKE AN APPOINTMENT

Notes: On spacing—

TS means triple space

	Return Carriage	Number of Blank lines
SS	1 time	0
DS	2 times	1
TS	3 times	2

IV.12 Centre the following display vertically and horizontally on a sheet of P5 paper. Double space the body.

CAREER OPPORTUNITIES
TS

Clerk/Typist**DS**

Receptionist Typist

Bookkeeper

Secretary

Legal Stenographer

Cashier

Accounting Clerk

CENTRING COLUMNS HORIZONTALLY

VII.1 Centre horizontally the following columns. The flow chart below will assist you in centring any number of columns.

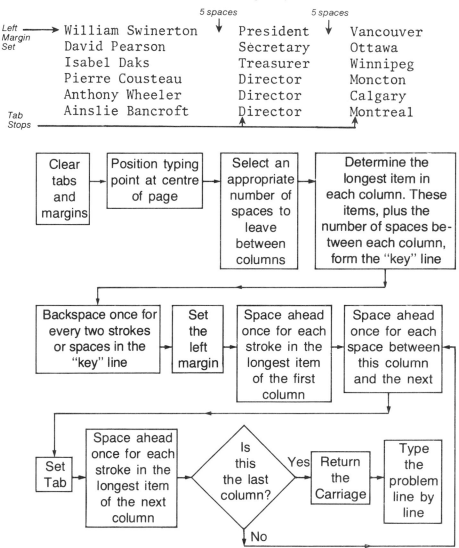

Note: In Problem VII.1, the "key" line is:

William SwinertonXXXXXPresidentXXXXXVancouver

5 spaces   5 spaces

VII.2 Centre the table in Problem VII.1 horizontally on a sheet of P5 paper with the wide edge inserted. Leave a top margin of 50 mm and 10 spaces between columns.

VII.3 Centre the table of Problem VII.2 horizontally and vertically on a sheet of P5 paper with the wide edge inserted. (For a review of vertical centring see page 119.)

IV.13 Centre the following display vertically and horizontally on a sheet of P5 paper with wide edge inserted. Double space.

```
THE GOLDEN LANTERN

18-hole Miniature Golf Course
Swimming Pool & Saunas
Tennis Court, Barbecues
Roof-top Party Room
Free Parking
Phone:   362-3330
```

*Notes: **Variable spacing between** groups of **lines** is often used for highlighting features in a display. Use judgment when selecting the number of blank lines to leave.*

IV.14 Centre the following advertisement vertically and horizontally on a sheet of P5 paper with wide edge inserted. Single space.

```
CANADA MANPOWER
SERVICES TO EMPLOYERS


Selected clients to fill your personnel needs
All-Canada Labor Source
Labor Market Information
Training-in-Industry Program
Training-on-the-Job Program
Manpower Consultative Service

For information and service
Call your
Canada Manpower Center
```

IV.15 Centre the following advertisement attractively on a sheet of P5 paper.

```
HEATED GARAGE

New High Rise
1- and 2-Bedroom Suites

William Place
```

Computer Copy 35, 40, 43

Footnotes 44, 45

Paper Sizes
   Unspecified 1, 37-45
   P4 . . . . 6, 13, 15, 17, 22, 23,
                  27, 31, 46
   P4 (wide edge) 47
   P5 . . . . 8, 14, 26, 28, 33
   P5 (wide edge) 2-5, 7, 9-12, 16, 18-21,
                  24, 25, 29, 30, 32, 34-
                  36

Rough Draft Copy 34, 42

Script Copy 13, 23, 36-39, 41

2-Line Heads 40, 41, 43, 44, 46, 47

2-Line Titles 36-38, 42-45

2-Line Subtitles 46

Unarranged Copy 2-6,8,9,11-47

IV.16 Centre the following display vertically and horizontally on a sheet of P4 paper. Double space.

Self-check: How many vertical lines of type will P4 paper accommodate?

```
ELECTION SPECIAL

Royal York Hotel Ballroom
PROGRAM
"HOT SEAT"--Election Candidates
EVERYONE WELCOME
PLEASE COME AND BRING A FRIEND
REFRESHMENTS WILL BE SERVED
```

Notes: **Variable spacing between words** *is often used to separate groups of words in a display line. For example:*

September 17   20:00

        3 or 4 spaces

Use judgment when selecting the number of spaces to leave.

IV.17 Type the following material as a display centred vertically and horizontally on a sheet of P4 paper. Use variable spacing in lines 2, 3, and 7. Double space.

```
AUDITION NOTICE

Village Playhouse
Sunday     September 16    14:00
Monday     September 17    20:00
"JOE EGG" by Peter Nichols
Director:  Keith Digby
Production Dates:  November 13 - 24 inclusive
Actors    Actresses    Production Personnel
```

IV.18 Centre the following display vertically and horizontally on a sheet of P4 paper. Use variable spacing between groups of lines.

```
BLOOR STREET COMMUNITY STORE


New & used clothing
Household items
Books
Donations needed

Craft classes

Hours:  11:00 - 20:00
        Monday - Friday
        10:00 - 18:00 Saturday
777 Bloor Street West
489-1855
```

2. Select and type several number and symbol sentences from pages 99 to 106.

3. Select and type a letter from Component V to increase your production speed.

4. Proceed through Component VII.

Supplementary:

Select and type a number of ITA's from pages 248 to 250.

SUMMARY OF COMPONENT VII PROBLEMS

MAJOR APPLICATIONS

Two-Column Tables
General 4
With Title and
Column Heads 10, 13, 20, 21

Three-Column Tables
General 1, 2, 3, 5, 6
With Title 7, 8, 9
With Title and
Column Heads 11, 12, 14, 15, 16, 17, 18, 19, 24, 25, 26, 27, 34
With Title, Subtitle,
and Column Heads . 30, 31, 32, 33, 36, 37, 38, 42
With Title, Subtitle,
and 2-line Heads ... 40

Four-Column Tables
With Title and
Column Heads 22, 23, 28, 29
With Title, Subtitle,
and Column Heads . 35, 39
With Title, Subtitle,
and 2-line Heads ... 41, 43, 44, 45

Five-Column Tables
With Title, Subtitle,
and 2-line Heads ... 46-47

SPECIAL APPLICATIONS

Column Headings
Flush Left 10-18
Mixed 27-47
Shorter Than Column . 19-23
Longer Than Column . 24-26

Notes: Problem IV. 19 illustrates an attractive method for typing a single-column display.

IV.19 Centre the following display vertically on a sheet of P4 paper. Backspace the title to centre it horizontally. Before typing the title, set the left margin stop. Type the title and each line of the body flush with the left margin. Double space.

```
                CORPORATE PERSONNEL CHART

                President
                Vice-President, Production
                Vice-President, Design
                Vice-President, Marketing
                Personnel Manager
                Information Services Manager
                Warehouse Manager
                Office Manager
                Sales Manager, Pacific
                Sales Manager, Prairies
                Sales Manager, Ontario
                Sales Manager, Quebec
                Sales Manager, Atlantic
```

IV.20 Centre the copy of Problem IV.19 vertically and horizontally on a sheet of P4 paper. Double space.

Notes: Problem IV. 21 illustrates another attractive method for typing a single-column display:

IV.21 Centre the following display vertically on a sheet of P4 paper. Centre and type the title horizontally. Backspace the longest line in the body. Set the left margin stop. Then type each line of the body, beginning with the first line, flush with the left margin. Double space.

```
                BOARD OF DIRECTORS

                Fortunato H. Aglialoro
                Eileen R. Baird
                Irene J. Camps, Chairperson
                Dr. M. O. Edwardh
                Derek Gorton
                Paul Harrison
                Mitzi J. Loughton
                Wendy Marsh
                J. K. McKnight
                Dr. Victoria Neufeldt
                Donald O. Pinsent
                Wm. S. Sloan
                Anne M. Van Ekeren
                F. John von Ompteda
                Conrad E. Wieczorek
```

IV.22 Centre the copy of Problem IV.21 vertically and horizontally on a sheet of P4 paper. Double space.

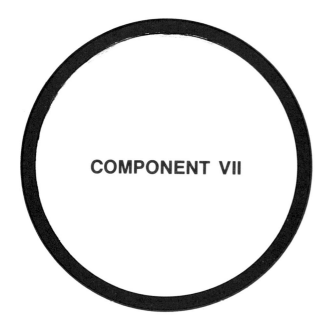

COMPONENT VII

TABLES

STUDENT OBJECTIVES

1. To learn and apply placement rules for setting up and typing tables of two, three, and four or more columns.

2. To learn and apply placement rules for setting up and typing tables with various length column headings.

3. To type tables from unarranged typewritten and handwritten copy.

4. To develop speed at typing tables.

DAILY ACTIVITIES

Preliminary:

Current date typing. Type three lines of the current date as illustrated:

				↓ tab set				↓ tab set		
19__	05	21		19__	05	21		19__	05	21
19__	05	21		19__	05	21		19__	05	21
19__	05	21		19__	05	21		19__	05	21

Main:

1. Identify your work by typing your name, the name and number of the course, and the current date.

CONTENTS

Component VII introduces the student to the typing of two, three, and four or more column tables from arranged and unarranged copy, typewritten and hand-written.

IV.23 Centre the following display attractively on a sheet of P5 paper with wide edge inserted.

> Alumnae Coffee Party
>
> You are invited to an
> ALUMNAE COFFEE PARTY
> Saturday Morning
> September 22,
> - After 10:30 -
>
> At the home of: Marian Francis
>   32 Riverside Crescent

IV.24 Arrange and centre the following information on a sheet of P5 paper with wide edge inserted.

> Typists Wanted
> The fate of this community is at your fingertips
> If you can read this, you can help!
> Meeting: November 26 at 20:00 in the
> Community Recreation Centre

IV.25 Arrange and centre the following notice on a sheet of P5 paper with wide edge inserted.

> Notice
> German Gourmet Dinner originally
> scheduled for October 2 now to be held
> on October 9 in Burton Hall.

IV.26 Arrange and centre the following notice on a sheet of P5 paper.

> Great Canadian Productions Limited
> Annual Meeting of Shareholders
> June 19 at 10:30
> Eldorado Room
> Hotel Macdonald
> 100th Street at Jasper Avenue
> Edmonton, Alberta

ITA 13

Using this typewriting text as a guide, prepare a report which outlines the content of your course. You might wish to use the Component Titles as your main headings, and "Content" and "Student Objectives" as subheadings for each division. A thorough report can be used as a guide for other students who might wish to learn of the course content.

ITA 14

Prepare and type a title page for a leftbound essay on "What is Silence?" Include your name, the name of your school, and the current date.

ITA 15

"Our laws are not primarily intended to limit the freedom of the individual." Type an essay using the quotation as the opening sentence. Type a footnote to indicate that the quotation was taken from page four of the book, Youth and the Law, Second Edition, by W. T. McGrath, Gage Educational Publishing Limited, Scarborough, 1973.

ITA 16

"The eye, more than any other member of the body, can reveal what you are thinking." Type an essay developing the thought expressed in the quotation. Begin your essay with the quotation and use a footnote to indicate that the quotation was taken from page 12 of the book, The Fundamentals and Forms of Speech, written by Andrew T. Weaver and Ordean G. Ness and published by The Odyssey Press, Inc., New York, 1963.

TYPING SPREAD HEADINGS

IV.27 Spread and centre the following headings horizontally. Double space between each heading.

ORIENTEERING

TYPEWRITING

Communications

Self-check:

O R I E N T E E R I N G

> To spread a word, backspace from the centre point once for each letter, except the last one. Type the heading spacing once between each letter.

IV.28 Spread and centre the following headings horizontally. Double space between each heading.

THE TWENTIETH CENTURY

FROM HERE TO ETERNITY

Business Applications in Typewriting.

Self-check:

To spread the heading THE TWENTIETH CENTURY, you will have to backspace 20 times.

> To spread a group of words, backspace from the centre point once for each space or letter, except for the last letter in the group. Then, type the group of words spacing once between each letter and three times between each word.

IV.29 Centre the following announcement on a sheet of P5 paper with wide edge inserted. Spread the title.

H A N D L I N G   P E O P L E

How to Establish Leadership

How to Communicate

How to Improve Employee Morale

How to Function in the Area of Human Relations

your review include at least one quotation using parenthetical source notations.

Using proofreaders' marks, edit your composition. Re-type the composition as an unbound report complete with title page and bibliography.

ITA 7

Re-type the report prepared in ITA 6 using footnote notations to acknowledge the source of quotations.

ITA 8

Bring to class an essay or report that you wrote and submitted for evaluation. Type the report in unbound form making all the corrections indicated by the instructor.

ITA9

Select a paragraph from your typewriting textbook. Type it as quickly as you can. Using proofreaders' marks, indicate the corrections that should be made. Re-type the paragraph.

ITA 10

Compose at the typewriter a paragraph or short report. Exchange your work with a classmate. Using proofreaders' marks, indicate corrections that should be made. Return the composition for re-typing.

ITA 11

Select a chapter from one of the textbooks that you are using and compose a brief, but complete outline of contents. Re-type your outline in proper form.

ITA 12

Prepare a table of contents for Appendix B in this text. Make sure each heading is descriptive of the content in each section.

SPECIAL DISPLAYS

Notes: Centre the display verti-cally. Then backspace once for every two strokes in the longest line. Set the left margin. Space as you spell out the longest line. Set the right margin. To type from the right margin back-space once for each stroke. Type the required line.

IV.30 Centre the following display on a sheet of P5 paper with wide edge inserted.

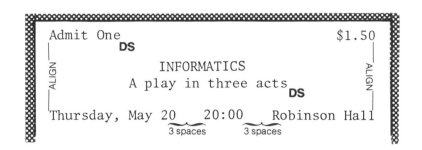

IV.31 Centre the following display on a sheet of P5 paper with wide edge inserted.

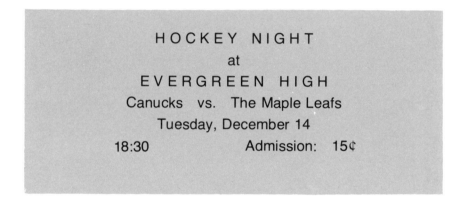

Notes: On Pivoting—

It is frequently necessary to type items in displays, tables, and pro-grams so that the last stroke in each line aligns with the right mar-gin. The technique used to align such items is known as pivoting. To pivot, position the print point at the right margin, and backspace once for every character (includ-ing spaces) except the last one. Type the item. Follow this proce-dure for each item to be aligned down the right margin.

IV.32 Centre the following display on a sheet of P5 paper with wide edge inserted.

M E M B E R S H I P   C A R D

BEDFORD BUSINESS CLUB
DARTMOUTH, NOVA SCOTIA

1976 - 78

Jim Prime   Odette Giroux
President   Secretary

IV.33 Centre the copy of Problem IV.32 on a sheet of P5 paper. Substitute your name for President and the name of your instructor for the secretary. Spread BEDFORD BUSINESS CLUB rather than MEMBERSHIP CARD.

ITA 3

Compose and type in leftbound report form, a short report on one of the following topics:

A. How to Write an "A" Essay.

B. How to Write a "D" Essay.

C. How to Type a Technically Correct Report. (This topic would serve as a comprehensive review of this Component.)

D. The Function and Structure of Student Government.

E. The Contribution of Your Community to Your Province or to Canada.

ITA 4

Compose and type in unbound form an original composition on one or more of the following topics:

A. Artists are more temperamental than other people.

B. Our society needs brains; not brawn.

C. Consumer is King.

D. A person who will not look you in the eye cannot be trusted.

E. If you had just one week to live, how would you spend it?

F. The ideal school.

G. If you were banished to a deserted island what would you take with you? Why?

H. The advantages of rural living.

I. The advantages of urban living.

J. Canada's northland.

ITA 5

Turn to the Essay "Towards Discovery in Business." (VI. 12, page 196). Read it. The author does not describe what is meant by the "discovery approach." Type a paragraph or two in proper report form describing what you think the "discovery approach" attitude might be.

ITA 6

Read a magazine article (available in your classroom, library, or from home) and compose at the typewriter a brief review. In

TYPING ON A LINE

IV.34 Follow the steps below to learn how to type on a line.

1. Type your name and underscore it.

2. Notice the relation of the underscore line to the aligning scale.

3. Type a line using the underscore.

4. Again look at the line in relation to the aligning scale.

5. Remove the paper from your machine.

6. Re-insert the paper so that the line is in the same position in relation to the aligning scale as it was before you removed it from the machine.

7. Type your name.

8. Check: Does your name now look exactly the same as you typed and underscored in Step 1?

IV.35 Draw three lines several millimetres long. Insert the paper into your machine. On the first line type your name. On the second line type your instructor's name. On the third line type the current date.

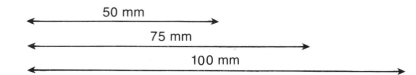

50 mm

75 mm

100 mm

CENTRING COPY HORIZONTALLY ON A LINE

1. Using the underscore, type a line approximately 70 mm long.

2. Find the centre point of the line by using one of the following methods:

    (a) Determine the number of strokes you can type on the line and divide by 2.

    (b) Use the scale on your paper bail, aligning scale, or some other suitable scale on your machine to determine the centre point.

    (c) Measure the line with a ruler, then place a light pencil dot at the centre point.

3. From the centre point of your line, backspace once for every two strokes in the word or words you wish to centre.

TABLE OF CONTENTS

LOCATION
  North America
  Western Europe
  Australasia

PHYSICAL ENVIRONMENT
  Temperature and Precipitation
  Soil and Topography

URBAN MARKETS

TRANSPORTATION LINKS
  North America
  Western Europe
  Australasia

THE LABOR FORCE
  Size of Farm
  Mechanization

CONCLUSION

VI.32 Re-type problem VI.31 as a leftbound report. Revise the footnote data and make references to the bibliography with parenthetical source notations.

INDIVIDUALIZED TYPEWRITING APPLICATIONS (ITA's)

VI.33 Now that you have acquired a thorough knowledge of the mechanics of report typing, you should be able to compose, attractively arrange, and type reports.

Remember to use good techniques when composing and typing each application.

ITA 1

Bring to class the textbooks for those subjects you are currently studying. Prepare a bibliography for these titles.

ITA 2

Select an interesting book or novel that you have read. Prepare a book review in the format of an unbound report. Your main headings might include the following:

  The Author — his/her name and a brief biographical sketch.
  The Story Setting or Plot — central theme of the book. You might include brief descriptions of each of the main characters. If you do, the names of the characters will make good subheadings.
  Interesting Incidents — those incidents which will arouse the reader's interest and make him/her want to read the book.
  Comments — your personal views about the book. Did you enjoy it? Might others enjoy it?

IV.36 Centre your name horizontally on a line approximately 75 mm long.

IV.37 Centre the name of your instructor on a line approximately 125 mm long.

IV.38 Centre the name of your community on a line approximately 70 mm long.

INDIVIDUALIZED TYPEWRITING APPLICATIONS (ITA's)

IV.39 Now that you have acquired basic centring skills you should be able to transfer these skills to individual applications. Initially you might select one or two of the beginning applications which will require the use of elementary centring skills. Then when you gain more confidence you can attempt the more challenging applications.

Be sure to use good techniques when typing each exercise.

Notes: Try to use a variety of display techniques such as:

Variable spacing between words.

Spreading of words.

Variable spacing between lines.

All capitals within the body.

Left margin set with heading.

Left margin set for longest body line.

Pivoting from the right margin.

ITA 1

Plan and type a simple menu for a community supper.

ITA 2

Plan and type a full course menu for a graduation banquet.

ITA 3

Plan and type a "For Sale" notice to sell a mini-motor bike, a car, or a boat.

ITA 4

Plan and type a bulletin board notice offering your services as a typist.

ITA 5

Plan and type a bulletin board announcement of a forthcoming meeting of your student council.

ITA 6

Plan and type a bulletin board announcement of a forthcoming social event in your school. All information including the name of the sponsoring organization, the date, time, place, fee, theme, and contact person should be centred attractively on a sheet of paper.

Conclusion

Dairying is a diverse activity. From the three major regions in the world, the industry expands in pockets to accommodate the desires of the urban settlement. But human desires are not the only factors influencing the location of the dairying industry. Physical conditions, conducive to production of a lush forage crop, play a role in the initial formulation of the dairying pattern. Supporting such a pattern are transportation systems, cultural backgrounds, and effective political intervention to ensure a just reward for the conscientious dairy farmer who spends many backbreaking days to meet demands and still maintain a minimum return on his investment

This is the dairying industry — an industry which is expanding to new regions to meet increased demands; an industry which is transitional as the urban mass pushes it toward the hinterlands. This is the industry which geographically has helped to maintain the Western World's freedom from hunger.

FOOTNOTES

[1]E. W. Zimmerman, World Resources and Industries, Revised Edition (New York: Harper & Brothers, 1951), p. 151.

[2]J. W. Alexander, Economic Geography (Englewood Cliffs: Prentice-Hall, Inc., 1963), p. 308.

[3]The Shorter Oxford Economic Atlas of the World, Third Edition (Oxford: Oxford University Press, 1965), p. 51.

[4]J. W. Alexander, Op. Cit., p. 128.

BIBLIOGRAPHY

Alexander, J. W., Economic Geography. Prentice-Hall, Inc., Englewood Cliffs, New Jersey, 1963.

Boesch, H., A Geography of World Economy. D. Van Nostrand Company, Inc., 1964.

Clarendon Press, The Shorter Oxford Economic Atlas of the World (Third Edition). Oxford University Press, 1965.

Dicken, S. N., Economic Geography. D. C. Heath & Company, Boston, 1955.

Lewthwaite, G. R., "Wisconsin and the Waikato: A Comparison of Dairy Farming in the United States and New Zealand," Association of American Geographers Annals. Vol. 54, pp. 59-87.

Thomas, R. S., The Geography of Economic Activity. McGraw-Hill Book Company, Inc., New York, 1962.

Zimmerman, E. W., World Resources and Industries (Revised Edition). Harper & Brothers, New York, 1951.

ITA 7

Plan and type a notice from the following information:

The Theatre Arts Club will hold a drama workshop on Saturday, September 15 from 10:00 until 16:30 at the Theatre Arts Building, 370 Avenue Road.

ITA 8

List as many names of businesses or organizations in your area as you can. Arrange the names alphabetically and prepare an attractive display which is centred horizontally and vertically.

ITA 9

The following advertisements appeared in a copy of a local newspaper. Type each as an attractive display:

A. Martin Watson & Company, Chartered Accountants, Toronto.

B. Pharmacist wanted for full-time position in the Muskoka area. For further information call 621-7112.

C. 25 ha for sale or trade, Commercial Industrial Property, Main Artery or Trackage, Corner of 35 St. & 17 Ave., $25 000/ha, Call 241-7129.

D. Office Space, 600 m² 5th Floor, 400 m² Main Floor, New Air Conditioned Building, Excellent Location, Edinborough Place, 1806 Upper Water Street, Halifax, 902-211-5694.

E. Excellent boarding facilities for horses, large indoor arena, modern tack room, club room, lessons, horses for sale. Richmond Hill, 884-5517.

F. Still the finest selection of Jacob Miller suits available at Alec Hamill Ltd, Fine Clothiers, 10931 Brunet Avenue, Montreal, PQ H1G 5E6, 514-521-1309.

G. Cameron Real Estate Limited (Founded in 1907), Investment Properties in Canada and the U.S.A., Suite 321, 36 King Street E., Toronto, M5C 2L9, 1-416-363-3986.

H. Rainbow Trout, famous Pine River, special weekend package, all meals and accommodation, 2 nights, min. party of 4, $35 each. Only serious fishermen accepted. Book now. Mansfield Forest Club, Mansfield, ON, 715-435-4479.

I. Real Estate Career, Become a professional real estate salesman or saleswoman, Company training program, Benefit Package, Open Territory, Canada Wide Referral System, Generous Bonus Plan, Contact your nearest branch manager for further information.

J. Electronic Service Technician to perform electrical & electric control panel service. Knowledge of solid state & relay logic essential. Car necessary, all expenses paid when travelling. Will perform panel & layout wiring when not travelling. An interesting

---

PHARMACIST
for
MUSKOKA
Full-time
Position Available
621-7112

Transportation Links

Owing to the nature of the commodities of the dairy industry, it is essential that a rapid system of transportation be available. The system may involve the use of more than one mode of transport.

North America

In the centre of the dairy industry of North America you will find some of the best systems of rural roads in the world. These are necessary to transport the fluid milk quickly to the dairies. Further from the market you will find poorer road connections because it is not as essential to gather the milk used for producing butter and cheese daily. From the factories where butter and cheese are processed, you will find rail links to the urban markets.

Western Europe

A system of roads links the fluid milk producers with the urban settlement, and the rail links from factories connect with the major shipping lanes and with other inter-country rail lines.

Australasia

In New Zealand we again find the same local road system as in North America, with rail transportation playing a minor part except in the connection of factory to shipping lanes.

The Labor Force

As can be assumed from much of the foregoing information, dairying is a type of bioculture which requires "day-after-day, week-after-week, year-after-year, unrelenting faithful attention."[4] But it is not the type of attention that requires a large labor force.

Size of Farm

In Denmark the average size of the dairy farm is 50 ha. In the United States, the farm is larger, encompassing an average 225 ha; and in New Zealand a range of varying sizes occurs—anywhere from 80 ha up. These farms are traditionally one-person farms, or as is often the case, family farms. Dairying in this respect is unlike grain farming which requires large numbers of seasonal workers to complete the annual harvesting.

Mechanization

Mechanization has also played a role in reducing the labor inputs on the dairy farm.

Milking Machines. Modern milking machines can now pump the milk right into storage tanks eliminating much of the past human handling of milk.

Automated Milking Stalls. In many instances automated milking stalls are used to control the herd at milking time and to control the consumption of food during the milking process.

It is true that dairy belts are traditionally found in heavily urbanized centres, but the dairy farmer does not have to rely on these centres for his labor.

& challenging work. Paris Automation Ltd. 2070 Chartier Ave. Dorval, PQ, 514-636-8910.

ITA 10

Centre the following line in a circle with a 50 mm diameter.

Chess Club

CENTRING COPY IN A CIRCLE

Horizontal Centring

1. *Find the horizontal centre point of a circle by using one of the following methods:*
   (a) *Determine the number of strokes you can type across the diameter of the circle and divide by 2.*
   (b) *Measure the diameter of the circle and put a light pencil dot at the centre point.*
   (c) *Use a suitable scale on your typewriter to determine the centre point.*

2. *Backspace once for every two strokes in the word or words you wish to centre.*

Vertical Centring

1. *Determine the number of lines you can type in the circle by using one of the following methods:*
   (a) *Put the paper in the machine and count down the number of available lines to the bottom of the circle.*
   (b) *Measure the diameter of the circle and calculate the number of lines you are able to type in a circle of this diameter. Remember: one line of typing requires approximately 4.2 mm.*

2. *Follow the instructions for vertical centring as found on page 118.*

ITA 11

Centre the following line as an attractive display in a circle with a 75 mm diameter.

Canada hosted The 1976 Summer Olympics!

Australasia

In Australasia, the smallest of the three major locations, we find the dairy farms scattered throughout Tasmania; on the North Island of New Zealand, particularly in the west; and on the south-eastern shores of Australia in portions of the provinces of Victoria, New South Wales, and Queensland.

Minor Pockets

Aside from the three major dairy belts, one finds pockets of dairying activity scattered throughout the world. These pockets are usually found around an urban centre, somewhat displacing the prevailing bioculture there; but they may also be found in many lowland areas.

Physical Environment

Temperature and Precipitation

Dairy animals, on the whole, appreciate and need lush grasses such as hay, oats, and alfalfa for fodder.

Temperature. To ensure the growth of luxuriant grasses the average daily temperature must be a minimum of 5°C. However, the fact that the thermometer on the average does not dip below 5°C, will not in itself ensure a healthy volume of milk.

The temperature must have an upper limit in summer of 21°C, above which milk volume per cow is known to decline.

Precipitation. The precipitation cycle for a dairy farm would ideally be one of constant drizzle, amounting to an annual precipitation slightly in excess of 75 cm.[2] Preferably this should occur during the hottest period of the growing season, since humid conditions promote a low rate of evaporation and produce a vigorous pasture.

Soil and Topography

Characteristically the dairy farm is located on grayish-brown podzolic soils,[3] over a rough terrain marked with many hills and valleys, some of which are scarred with shrubs and stones.

Urban Markets

One can generalize to state that a major region of dairying will only arise in areas near an urban market. This generalization holds for the Anglo-American dairy belt which finds its urban markets in the metropolitan areas along the Atlantic Coast, and inland through Pennsylvania, Ontario, Michigan, Illinois, and Wisconsin.

The generalization also holds for the dairy belt of Western Europe, which finds its markets in the large urban centres of Paris, Amsterdam, Rotterdam, Copenhagen, Stockholm, and London. In fact, if you carry the urbanization concept far enough, you have Moscow and Leningrad serving as urban markets. However, with New Zealand the generalization does not hold. The entire population of both islands — approximately 3 000 000 is about one-quarter the population of New York City. Yet, New Zealand produces two per cent (2%) of the world's supply of milk.

ITA 12

Centre the following advertisement as an attractive display in a circle with a 100 mm diameter.

> FREE 194-page Outdoor Catalogue. Available from THE OUTDOOR STORES. Three great locations: Oshawa, Toronto, Oakville. Open daily except Sundays, from 09:00 to 21:30.

ITA 13

You have been appointed Campaign Manager for Marcia Neeland. She is running for President of the Students' Union in your school. She has asked you to design a circular button for her election campaign. Design such a button for her approval.

ITA 14

Prepare a wallet size (80 mm by 50 mm) membership card for one of your school clubs.

ITA 15

The Drama Club is planning a production of Romeo and Juliette. Romeo will be played by Bill Lively; Juliette by Terry Martin. Tickets for adults will cost $2.00; for students $1.00. The play will run in the school cafetorium on the first Friday in May. You have been asked to design and type a sample ticket.

ITA 16

As part of a economics assignment you have been asked to prepare three tables. Table I should list the capital cities of the Canadian provinces and territories. Table II should list, in order of importance, our twelve most important export products. Table III should list, in order of importance, the twelve most important import products. Use a two line heading, double-spacing between the first and second lines; triple-spacing between the second line and the body. The first line of the heading should be typed in all capitals; the second line should be typed capitalizing only the major words.

ITA 17

Prepare and type, as an attractive display, a list of your five favorite television programs that are shown by one television station. Your display should have an effective two line heading.

Self check:
TABLE II
Canadian Exports
or
CANADIAN EXPORTS
(Decreasing Importance)

If the worse comes to the absolute worst, you may have to consider
declaring personal bankruptcy. The Bankruptcy ~~breathe~~ *Branch* of the Departm~~nrt~~ *en*
of Consumer and Corporate Affairs offers a special serv~~eic~~ *ice* to he~~o~~*lp*elessly
overburd~~n~~ed debtors who ~~dn~~*d*'t affor*d* the ~~f~~*e*es charged by private trustees. Representatives are located in the de~~½zart, emt's~~ *partment's* offices in mo~~t~~ *s* main
centres across Canada.

The impr~~lo~~tant thin*g*k, of course, is not to let yourself get into such an
unhappy position. Don't let your credit ~~c~~*n*trol you. Put a half-nelson on it.

A COMPLETE REPORT   VI.31 This exercise is provided to give you practice in typing and
organizing a report which includes a title page, a table of
contents, footnotes, and a bibliography.

Type the article as an unbound report.

AN ANALYSIS OF THE DAIRYING INDUSTRY

Dairying is the prevailing type of bioculture in three main geographic locations in the world.[1] Each location is on a different continent; one
in the Southern Hemisphere, and two in the Northern Hemisphere. In
order for the same economic activity to be carried on in such appearingly
diverse regions, there must be some common factors inherent within each
locale. Perhaps such factors can be found by analyzing the location,
physical environment, market, transportation links, and labor force in each
area.

Location

North America

The dairy region in North America spreads from the Atlantic Coast
in the New England States to the dry-land western border in the Red River
Valley of Minnesota, North Dakota, and Manitoba. On this east-west axis,
the region extends for some 2 100 km; whereas on the north-south axis it
is a short 485 km stretch at its widest point which occurs in the east of the
region between the North Forest of Southern Canada and the corn belt
and general farming area of Pennsylvania and New Jersey.

Western Europe

The dairy region of Western Europe is the largest of the three major
locations. It extends from the Atlantic Coast eastward into the Soviet
Union near Moscow, encompassing the British Isles—Ireland, Scotland,
England, and Wales—Denmark, The Netherlands, Latvia and Estonia,
and portions of Northern France, Western Germany, lowland Switzerland,
and the southern tips of Norway, Finland, and Sweden.

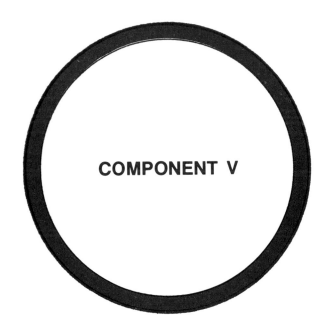

COMPONENT V

BUSINESS LETTERS

STUDENT OBJECTIVES

1. To learn and apply placement rules for typing letters and envelopes.

2. To type well-balanced, attractive letters.

3. To learn and apply placement rules for typing special letter notations.

4. To use carbon paper properly.

DAILY ACTIVITIES

Preliminary:

Current date typing. Type three lines of the current date as illustrated:

			↓ tab set			↓ tab set		
19__	05	21	19__	05	21	19__	05	21
19__	05	21	19__	05	21	19__	05	21
19__	05	21	19__	05	21	19__	05	21

Main:

1. Identify your work by typing your name, the name and number of the course, and the current date.

2. Select and type several number and symbol sentences from pages 99 to 106 .

3. Proceed through Component V.

CONTENTS

Component V introduces the student to form and style in typing business and personal/business letters. A few simple placement rules enable the student to produce properly balanced, attractive letters. Envelope addressing and the use of carbon paper are also introduced.

Component V/Business Letters

Try to keep a budget. Keep it simple and be honest with yourself when you're making it up.

You can't bank next Spring's raise into; upi get ot. Husbands and wives should sit down together to work out the details, because the budget affects the whole family.

Your budget will tell you what your borrowing limit is. That's half the battle, right there. The other half is borrowing wisely.

watch for warning signs. inability to meet current obligatins (including debt charges out of income is a clear sign that your financial position has become over-extended.

If, in spite of exercising every care, you find you can't meet your debts, it's time to seek professional advise. Some communities have credit counselling agencies which will advise you, without charbe, how to organize your indebtedness. In some cases, these organizations will prepare a repaymment plan, coupled with a family budget, If you agree to the plan and are willing to make the required amount available to the agency out of the income, they will often assume the resxponsibility of making payments on your behalf. Some banks have credit departments that can also be very helpful. But keep away from commercial debt adjusters, who perform this kind of service for profit. They often aggravate the problem instead of solving it.

And don't be afraid to face the music when you find yourself in difficulties. Go tht e credit manager of your store, if its a budget account invo volved, or to the organixation who lent you the money, and explain the situation frankly. Many firms will cooperate by rearranging your account to permit reduced payments, but they'll want you to give them the whole story first, and you must be completely frank.

Supplementary:

Select and type a number of ITA's from pages 176 to 184.

SUMMARY OF COMPONENT V PROBLEMS

MAJOR APPLICATIONS

Type of Letter
- Business 2-4, 8-30, 32-40
- Personal 47-49
- Personal/Business ... 41-46, 50

Letter Style
- Block 14-24
- Modified Block 2-4, 8-13, 30, 39, 41
- Modified Block with
   Indented Paragraphs . 25, 26, 37
- Simplified 27-29, 32
- Unspecified 33-36, 38, 48, 42-50

Punctuation Style
- No-Point 14-24
- Two-Point 2-4, 8-13, 25, 30, 37, 39, 41
- Full-Point 26
- Unspecified 33-36, 38, 40, 42-50

SPECIAL APPLICATIONS

Attention Line 30, 38

Blind Carbon Notation .. 30, 38

Carbon Copy Notation .. 30, 34, 36, 40

Carbon Packs 10-30, 32-46, 50, 51

Enclosure Notation 30, 33, 35, 37, 39, 40, 43, 44, 46

Folding Letters 6

Letter of Application 50

Letter with Enumeration . 37

Letter with Quotation ... 39, 47

Mailing Notations 30-32, 34

Personal Data Sheet ... 51

Postscript Notation 30, 44

Script Copy 20, 21, 23, 29, 35, 36, 38, 44, 45

gauged in the money markets, but no legislation can protect people from plunging into debt over their heads. Here are some points to remember that may help you to use credit wisely and keep your debts within manageable proportions.

Don't use credit just because it's easy to get. Credit costs money—yours. Consider the purpose. Does your immediate need for an article justify the cost of credit, or would it be wiser to put money aside and pay cash later? Can you afford that credit at that cost? How much of the family budget is available for repayment of principal and interest? Or will you find yourself robbing Peter to pay Paul, creating an endless circle of debt?

Compare financing costs. Credit unions usually charge the lowest rates, with banks perhaps second. If you own a life insurance policy with a cash surrender value against which you can borrow, interest rates are usually reasonable, too. If you can't tap any of these sources be prepared for higher rates if you go to a finance company. Be sure you can afford them.

Use only what credit you need. The more you borrow, the longer the repayment period is likely to be. A loan agreement is a contract that has to be repaid, job loss, strikes or sickness notwithstanding.

keep the repayment period as short as possible and make your payments on time. Late payments create additional charges that are rarely mentioned when you take out your loan.

When buying goods on the installment plan, make the down payment as big as you can afford. Pay it off as quickly as possible—and save your own money.

Don't use too many credit sources. Having to meet three or four small payments every month is like being nibbled to death by ducks.

Squeezing in Omitted
Letters 7
Subject Line 30, 32, 36
Two-Page Letters 18, 24
Typing Envelopes 5, 8-30, 31, 32-50
Unarranged Copy 8-13, 17-24, 28-29,
32-36, 38, 40, 42-49

PUBLIC. THE ADVERTISMENT SHOULD, THEREFORE,

PRESENT A WORTHY PICTURE OF THE FIRM AND A

TRUE PITCTURE OF THE COMODITY. FORM THESE A

CUSTOMER MAY FOR AN OPINION OF THE

DESIREABILITY OF THE GOODS AND THE

DEPENDABILITY OF THE COMPANY.

VI.30 Type the following article as a leftbound report, making the corrections indicated.

CREDIT — BOON OR BURDEN

There are Provincial and Federal laws to protect consumers from being

LETTER PLACEMENT, PARTS, PUNCTUATION, AND STYLE

A **business** letter is one that is written by a business firm or organization to an individual or to another business firm. A **personal/business** letter is one that is written by an individual to a business firm or organization. A **personal** letter is one that is written by an individual to another individual.

V.1 Study the illustrations below and on the following pages. This information will assist you in completing the remaining exercises in Component V. You should pay particular attention to:

1. the names and placement of the various letter parts for the four illustrated letter styles;

2. the location of the punctuation marks used in the three illustrated punctuation styles; and

3. the letter placement chart for short, medium, and long letters.

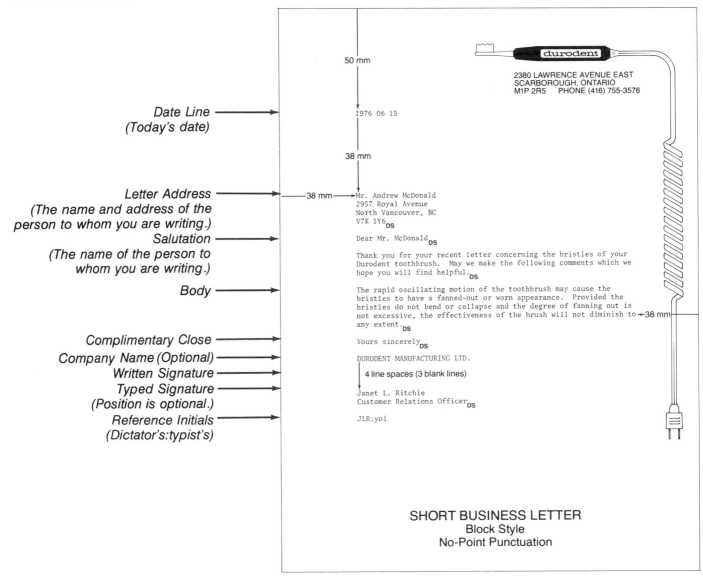

Date Line
(Today's date)

Letter Address
(The name and address of the person to whom you are writing.)

Salutation
(The name of the person to whom you are writing.)

Body

Complimentary Close
Company Name (Optional)
Written Signature
Typed Signature
(Position is optional.)
Reference Initials
(Dictator's:typist's)

50 mm

durodent

2380 LAWRENCE AVENUE EAST
SCARBOROUGH, ONTARIO
M1P 2R5   PHONE (416) 755-3576

1976 06 15

38 mm

38 mm → Mr. Andrew McDonald
2957 Royal Avenue
North Vancouver, BC
V7K 1Y6 **DS**

Dear Mr. McDonald **DS**

Thank you for your recent letter concerning the bristles of your Durodent toothbrush. May we make the following comments which we hope you will find helpful. **DS**

The rapid oscillating motion of the toothbrush may cause the bristles to have a fanned-out or worn appearance. Provided the bristles do not bend or collapse and the degree of fanning out is not excessive, the effectiveness of the brush will not diminish to ← 38 mm any extent. **DS**

Yours sincerely **DS**

DURODENT MANUFACTURING LTD.

4 line spaces (3 blank lines)

Janet L. Ritchie
Customer Relations Officer **DS**

JLR:yoi

SHORT BUSINESS LETTER
Block Style
No-Point Punctuation

VI.27 Type the following information attractively as a title page for a leftbound report. (Title page for Problem VI.13)

The Canadian Youth Hostel Association
Your Name
Your School
Current Date

PREPARING COPY FOR RE-TYPING

VI.28 Using the information on proofreaders' marks provided on page 217, type the following paragraph making the corrections indicated.

All kinds of people buy sinsurance, in widely varying amounts and at widely varying ages. Canadian's rnak third in life insurance wonership in the world and relative to national income canadians wn more life insurance then the people of anyother country. The fire and casaulty insurance premiumt writen in a year excede $,000 million, and the claims mount to some $1,350 million.

In an age when insecureity seems to be feltin some degree by every one, insurance provides a method by which large numbers of people each in some danger of a losss which he cannot prvent, or provide for single-handed, are brought to gether for mutual protection. When one of the group suffers s loss it will be made foo partly or wholy, from the contributions of the entire group.

VI.29 Type the following copy making the corrections indicated.

THE USUAL PURPOSE OF ADVERTISING, FROM THE ADVERTISERS VIEW POINT, ARE TO AFFECT SALES, TO CREATE GOOD WILL, AND TO IMPROVE UNDERSTANTING BETWEEN A BUSINESS AND ITS

Notes: On style —

Block Style: *All lines begin flush with the left margin.*

Modified Block Style: *The return address, the date line, the complimentary close, and the typed signature begin at the centre point. All other lines begin flush with the left margin.*

Modified Block Style with indented Paragraphs: *The first line of each paragraph is indented five spaces.*

Simplified: *All lines begin flush with the left margin. The salutation and complimentary close are always omitted. No-Point punctuation is used.*

Notes: On punctuation —

Punctuation within the body of a letter follows normal punctuation practices. For other letter parts, one of three styles may be used.

No-Point: *No additional punctuation is used at the end of lines.*

Two-Point: *A colon (:) is used after the salutation; a comma (,) after the complimentary close.*

Full-Point: *Use commas at the end of all lines in the letter address (except when the line ends with a Postal Code), after the complimentary close, and after the company name (if used). Use a period (.) at the end of the date and typed signature lines. Use a colon (:) after the salutation.*

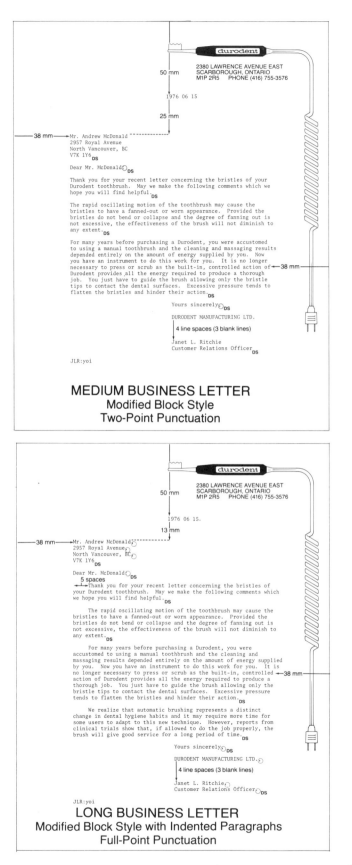

MEDIUM BUSINESS LETTER
Modified Block Style
Two-Point Punctuation

LONG BUSINESS LETTER
Modified Block Style with Indented Paragraphs
Full-Point Punctuation

TABLE OF CONTENTS

ROLE OF THE SECRETARY 1
PUBLIC RELATIONS 10
CORRESPONDENCE 19
REPORT WRITING 32
FILING 40
RECORDKEEPING 98
ARRANGING MEETINGS 125
PLANNING ITINERARIES 153
REFERENCE BOOKS 180

VI.25 The following table of contents has been prepared as part of a report on MEALS. Type it in proper form as part of a leftbound report.

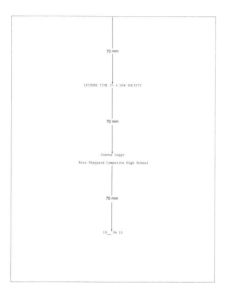

Fads and Facts	1
Health Food	1
Food Additives	3
Food Poisoning	4
Size and Shape	6
Height-Weight Tables	6
Reducing Diets	10
The Right Combination	12
Meal Planning	12
Food Shopping	15
Food Tables	16

TITLE PAGE

VI.26 A title page should show the title of the report, the name of the author, and the date. Additional information may be added as necessary. Each line is centred horizontally.

Type the following information attractively as a title page for an unbound report.

LEISURE TIME IN A NEW SOCIETY

Joanna Legge

Ross Sheppard Composite High School

19__ 06 15

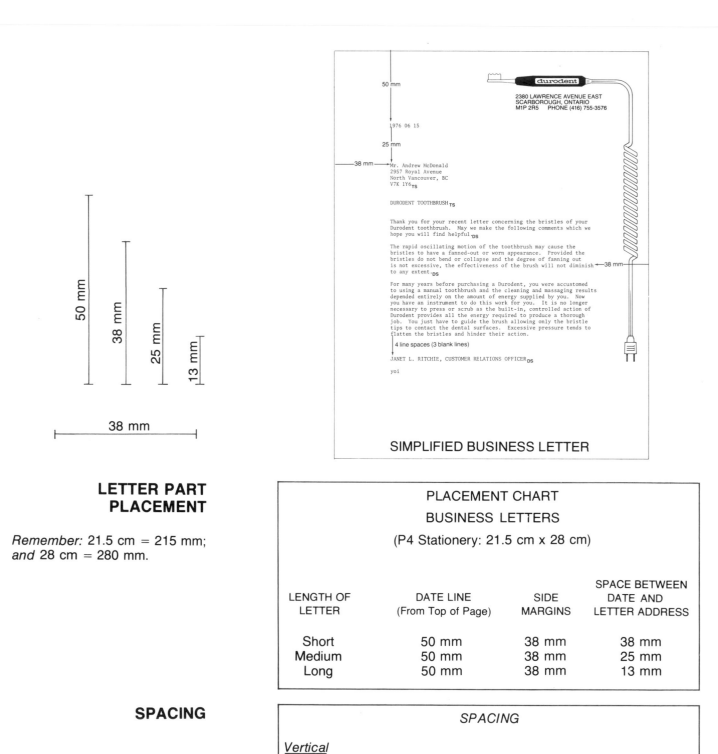

LETTER PART PLACEMENT

Remember: 21.5 cm = 215 mm;
and 28 cm = 280 mm.

SIMPLIFIED BUSINESS LETTER

2380 LAWRENCE AVENUE EAST
SCARBOROUGH, ONTARIO
M1P 2R5   PHONE (416) 755-3576

1976 06 15

Mr. Andrew McDonald
2957 Royal Avenue
North Vancouver, BC
V7K 1Y6 TS

DURODENT TOOTHBRUSH TS

Thank you for your recent letter concerning the bristles of your
Durodent toothbrush. May we make the following comments which we
hope you will find helpful. DS

The rapid oscillating motion of the toothbrush may cause the
bristles to have a fanned-out or worn appearance. Provided the
bristles do not bend or collapse and the degree of fanning out
is not excessive, the effectiveness of the brush will not diminish
to any extent. DS

For many years before purchasing a Durodent, you were accustomed
to using a manual toothbrush and the cleaning and massaging results
depended entirely on the amount of energy supplied by you. Now
you have an instrument to do this work for you. It is no longer
necessary to press or scrub as the built-in, controlled action of
Durodent provides all the energy required to produce a thorough
job. You just have to guide the brush allowing only the bristle
tips to contact the dental surfaces. Excessive pressure tends to
flatten the bristles and hinder their action.

4 line spaces (3 blank lines)

JANET L. RITCHIE, CUSTOMER RELATIONS OFFICER DS

yoi

PLACEMENT CHART
BUSINESS LETTERS
(P4 Stationery: 21.5 cm x 28 cm)

LENGTH OF LETTER	DATE LINE (From Top of Page)	SIDE MARGINS	SPACE BETWEEN DATE AND LETTER ADDRESS
Short	50 mm	38 mm	38 mm
Medium	50 mm	38 mm	25 mm
Long	50 mm	38 mm	13 mm

SPACING

SPACING

Vertical

One line of type requires approximately 4.2 mm.
Six lines of type require approximately 25 mm.

Horizontal

On an elite typewriter, 12 strokes require approximately 25 mm.
On a pica typewriter, 10 strokes require approximately 25 mm.

TABLE OF CONTENTS

VI.23 Refer to the guidelines for typing a table of contents. Then type the following table of contents in proper form as part of an unbound report.

TABLE OF CONTENTS **TS**   align
                                                             ↓
INCOME, EXPENDITURE, AND SAVINGS   1
    Setting up a Budget   1
    Solving Financial Problems   2
    Savings **DS**   3

SOURCES OF CREDIT   4
    The Cost of Borrowing   4
    Where Can You Borrow Money   5
    Retail Credit   7
    Establishing a Credit Rating **DS**   8

BIBLIOGRAPHY   10
                                                             ↑
                                                          1 space

---

GUIDELINES FOR TYPING A TABLE OF CONTENTS

A Table of Contents is prepared for reports that are very long or contain many divisions.

1. *The title is centred in ALL CAPITALS 50 mm from the top of the page. Triple-space (TS) after.*

2. *Side margins match the body of the report.*

3. *Leaders — made by alternating periods and spaces, e.g. . . . . . — are often used to align the content lines with their respective page numbers. Leaders are aligned vertically and should be preceded and followed by a single space.*

4. *Main headings are typed in ALL CAPITALS flush with the left margin.*

5. *Side headings are indented five spaces from the left margin, with important words capitalized.*

6. *Double-space (DS) after a side heading which precedes a main heading. If there are no side headings, double-space (DS) between main headings.*

VI.24 Type the table of contents on page 215 in proper form as part of a leftbound report.

TYPING ENVELOPES

V.2 Refer to the flow chart below to learn the steps to follow when typing any letter. Then type the letter on the following page using modified block style with two-point punctuation.

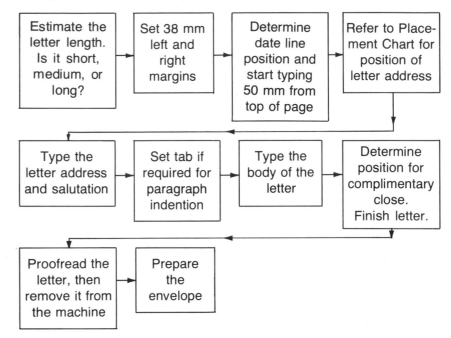

V.3 Type the letter on page 140. Use modified block style with two-point punctuation. The flow chart will aid you in positioning your letter attractively.

V.4 Type the letter on page 141. Use modified block style with two-point punctuation. Refer to the flow chart for positioning information.

V.5 Type envelopes for each of the letters prepared in Problems V.2-V.4. Follow the flow chart instructions and refer to the diagram on page 142.

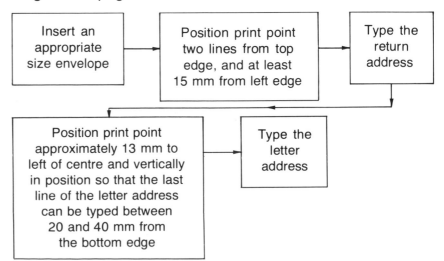

have shed. Certainly music education has been more concerned with catching up to the changing social scene than to anticipate it. Frances Andrews points out that nowhere in the literature of music education has she found reference to what we might envisage as the ideal product of music as we foresee its future emergence. She asks: "What is the living goal of our quest?"[4] (¶) Just what should be the aims of the arts in society? All seem convinced that they are a part of being 'civilized'; indeed some would claim the main part. The position paper of the Secondary School Principals stated in part:

> The arts are a subject discipline which emphasize the use of the intellect as well as the development of sensitivity, creativity, and the capacity to make reasoned aesthetic decisions in extending the range of human experience. The arts give direction to man's pattern of living, from the setting of his table to the expression of his most cherished aspirations. The arts constitute a vast communications system which complements man's cognitive word system.[5]

---

[1]H. G. Rickover, Education and Freedom (New York: Dutton and Co., 1959), p. 32.

[2]D. Reisman, "Abundance of What?" Bulletin of Atomic Scientists, 14:135 April, 1958.

[3]B. J. Muller-Thym, Changing American Population (New York: New York Institute of Life Insurance, 1962), p. 93.

[4]Frances M. Andrews, "Issues and Problems in Music Education," Music Educators Journal, 49:110, September-October, 1962.

[5]National Association of Secondary School Principals, "The Arts in the Comprehensive Secondary School," Music Educators Journal, 49:60, November-December, 1962.

BIBLIOGRAPHY

Andrews, Frances M. "Issues and Problems in Music Education," Music Educators Journal, 49:39-112, September-October, 1962.

Muller-Thym, B. J. Changing American Population. New York: New York Institute of Life Insurance, 1962.

National Association of Secondary School Principals. "The Arts in the Comprehensive Secondary School," Music Educators Journal, 49:60-66, November-December, 1962.

Reisman, D. "Abundance of What?" Bulletin of Atomic Scientists, 14:135-139, April, 1958.

Rickover, H. G. Education and Freedom. New York: Dutton & Co., 1959.

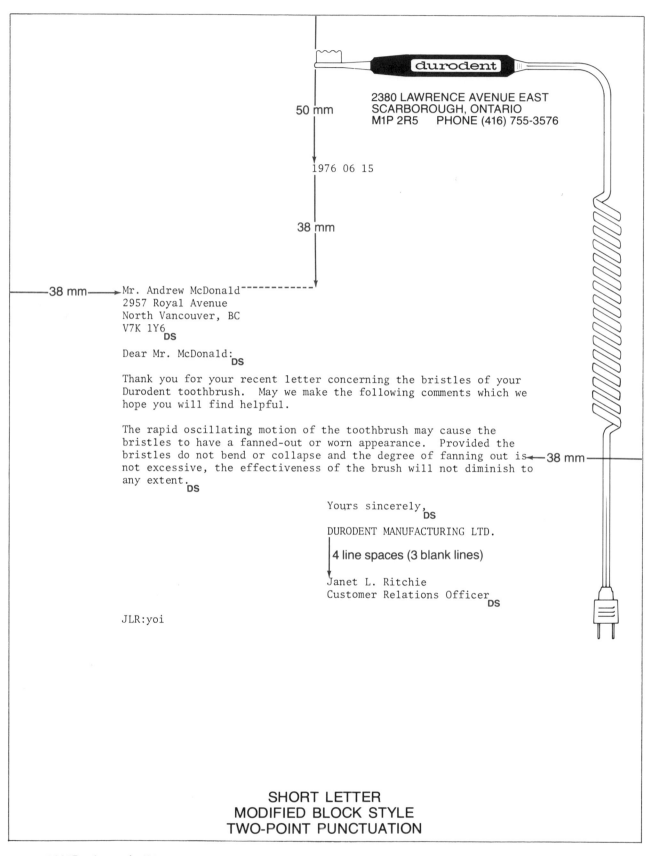

2380 LAWRENCE AVENUE EAST
SCARBOROUGH, ONTARIO
M1P 2R5   PHONE (416) 755-3576

50 mm

1976 06 15

38 mm

38 mm → Mr. Andrew McDonald
2957 Royal Avenue
North Vancouver, BC
V7K 1Y6
DS

Dear Mr. McDonald:
DS

Thank you for your recent letter concerning the bristles of your
Durodent toothbrush. May we make the following comments which we
hope you will find helpful.

The rapid oscillating motion of the toothbrush may cause the
bristles to have a fanned-out or worn appearance. Provided the
bristles do not bend or collapse and the degree of fanning out is ← 38 mm
not excessive, the effectiveness of the brush will not diminish to
any extent.
DS

                              Yours sincerely,
                              DS

                              DURODENT MANUFACTURING LTD.

                              | 4 line spaces (3 blank lines)
                              ↓

                              Janet L. Ritchie
                              Customer Relations Officer
                              DS

        JLR:yoi

SHORT LETTER
MODIFIED BLOCK STYLE
TWO-POINT PUNCTUATION

²Edward Jablonski, <u>The Flying Fortress</u> (New York: Doubleday & Company, 1965), p. 191.

³Gavin Lyall, <u>The War in the Air</u> (New York: William Morrow & Co., 1969), p. 73.

⁴Don Harron, <u>Jogfree of Canda</u> (Agincourt: Gage Publishing Limited, 1974), p. 83.

Notes: On footnotes —

If there are a number of footnotes that refer to the same source the abbreviations Ibid. *(meaning at the same place) or* Op. cit. *(meaning in the work cited) can be used.*

Ibid. is used to refer to a source in an immediately preceding footnote. Op. cit. *refers to a source given in an earlier footnote.*

Example:

⁸Barry Goldberg and George Wright, I Am A Sensation (Toronto: McClelland and Stewart, 1971), pp. 112-114.

⁹Ibid.

¹⁰Ibid., p. 117.

¹¹John Craig, No Word for Goodbye (Toronto: Peter Martin, 1969), p. 141.

¹²Goldberg and Wright, Op. cit., pp. 120-121.

VI.22 Type the following report and bibliography in proper leftbound form. Refer to the information in the box above on guidelines for typing footnotes.

LEISURE TIME IN A NEW SOCIETY

The advent of the mid-twentieth century has brought new insights into a social phenomenon which has profound importance for future educational curricula. Early industrial society regarded unproductive time as empty and wasteful. Time was for honest labor and needed rest. The cybernetic age is reducing the necessity for manual labor and consequently the amount of time necessary for the fulfilment of productive tasks. Now people do not expect to fill their lives with work. The reappraisal of human social activity has led to the awareness that leisure time is not wasted time. Yet to produce emotional satisfaction the new-found leisure time must be used wisely. This entails instruction in its use, instruction which because of its depth and intensity must be started early and continued throughout a student's school career.

> Perhaps our children — certainly our grandchildren — will have to live with fewer material possessions. It is not too early to turn to inner resources which are limitless; to art, music, literature, good conversation; to a cultivation of a more contemplative way of life . . . [1]

(¶) Indeed, with the accelerated pace of technology, many of today's students will be employed in occupations as yet unknown. Schools contemplating the future can only realistically teach basic principles which will equip their students with the tools for self-learning. The intelligent use of leisure time could conceivably become the only function of pre-university education which will remain constant for a lifetime. This may well be the most important concept in schooling yet to emerge. (¶) The mounting concern for the future by unionized workers faced with "unproductive" leisure, by management faced with production decisions involving automation, and by municipalities faced with spiralling costs, is now putting pressures on the educator to "do something." Reisman's characterization that we "live now, think later"[2] is undergoing a change. Now the scientists are quite clear about the possibilities the future holds out for us. Their problem is one of priorities and direction.[3] One would like to believe that the problem is as clearly defined in education. Unhappily such is not the case. Generally practitioners of the arts and education are still blessed with the same "live now, think later" philosophy which scientific minds

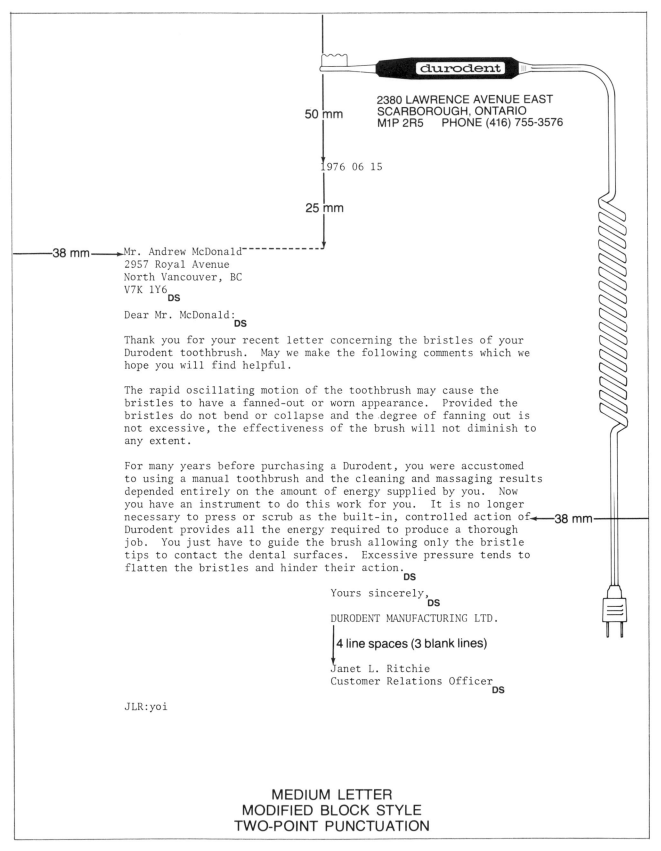

durodent

2380 LAWRENCE AVENUE EAST
SCARBOROUGH, ONTARIO
M1P 2R5   PHONE (416) 755-3576

50 mm

1976 06 15

25 mm

38 mm → Mr. Andrew McDonald
2957 Royal Avenue
North Vancouver, BC
V7K 1Y6
DS

Dear Mr. McDonald:
DS

Thank you for your recent letter concerning the bristles of your
Durodent toothbrush. May we make the following comments which we
hope you will find helpful.

The rapid oscillating motion of the toothbrush may cause the
bristles to have a fanned-out or worn appearance. Provided the
bristles do not bend or collapse and the degree of fanning out is
not excessive, the effectiveness of the brush will not diminish to
any extent.

For many years before purchasing a Durodent, you were accustomed
to using a manual toothbrush and the cleaning and massaging results
depended entirely on the amount of energy supplied by you. Now
you have an instrument to do this work for you. It is no longer
necessary to press or scrub as the built-in, controlled action of ← 38 mm
Durodent provides all the energy required to produce a thorough
job. You just have to guide the brush allowing only the bristle
tips to contact the dental surfaces. Excessive pressure tends to
flatten the bristles and hinder their action.
DS

                    Yours sincerely,
                    DS

                    DURODENT MANUFACTURING LTD.

                    4 line spaces (3 blank lines)

                    Janet L. Ritchie
                    Customer Relations Officer
                    DS

JLR:yoi

MEDIUM LETTER
MODIFIED BLOCK STYLE
TWO-POINT PUNCTUATION

London : Aldus Books Limited, 1964.

Nahm, Milton C. Selections from Early Greek Philosophy. New York : Appleton-Century-Crofts, Inc., 1934.

Pound, Ezra. The Cantos of Ezra Pound. New York : James Laughlin, 1948.

Shafer, R. M. The New Soundscape. Scarborough : Berandol Music Ltd. 1969.

TYPING FOOTNOTES   VI.21 Type the following four footnotes in correct position as part of an unbound report at the bottom of a page. The guidelines for typing footnotes given below will assist you in positioning your copy.

GUIDELINES FOR TYPING FOOTNOTES

Footnotes can be used as an alternate method for acknowledging the source of quotations and paraphrased information in a report.

1. Use consecutive superscripts to designate footnotes within the body of a report.

2. Footnotes are typed on the same page as their related superscript — above the bottom margin.

3. Usually each footnote requires 3 lines — 2 lines of type and 1 blank line. Each time you use a superscript in the body of a report, move the bottom margin mark up three lines. This will ensure sufficient space for all footnotes.

4. To type a footnote, first type a 38 mm divider line a single space below the last line of the text. Double space. (In the event that the copy on the last page of a report does not fill the page, leave sufficient space between the text and the footnotes to maintain a bottom margin of 25 mm.)

5. Indent five spaces, type the superscript and without spacing type the first line of the footnote. Begin subsequent lines flush with the left margin.

6. Single space each footnote. Double-space (DS) between footnotes.

◄— Divider line
DS
[1]Charles B. MacDonald, The Mighty Endeavor (New York: Oxford University Press, 1969), p. 59.
DS

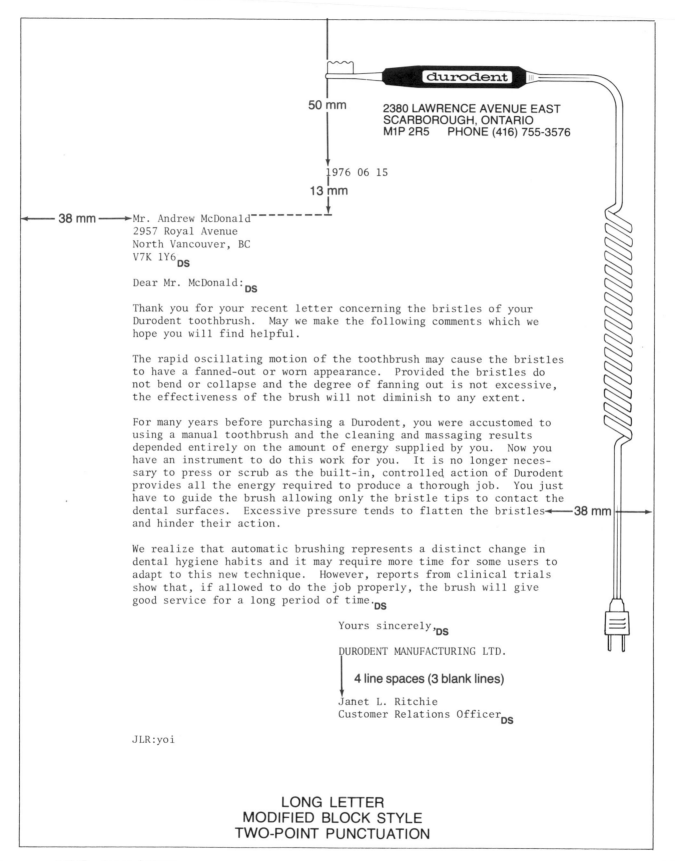

50 mm

durodent

2380 LAWRENCE AVENUE EAST
SCARBOROUGH, ONTARIO
M1P 2R5   PHONE (416) 755-3576

1976 06 15

13 mm

←— 38 mm —→ Mr. Andrew McDonald
2957 Royal Avenue
North Vancouver, BC
V7K 1Y6 **DS**

Dear Mr. McDonald: **DS**

Thank you for your recent letter concerning the bristles of your
Durodent toothbrush. May we make the following comments which we
hope you will find helpful.

The rapid oscillating motion of the toothbrush may cause the bristles
to have a fanned-out or worn appearance. Provided the bristles do
not bend or collapse and the degree of fanning out is not excessive,
the effectiveness of the brush will not diminish to any extent.

For many years before purchasing a Durodent, you were accustomed to
using a manual toothbrush and the cleaning and massaging results
depended entirely on the amount of energy supplied by you. Now you
have an instrument to do this work for you. It is no longer necessary to press or scrub as the built-in, controlled action of Durodent
provides all the energy required to produce a thorough job. You just
have to guide the brush allowing only the bristle tips to contact the
dental surfaces. Excessive pressure tends to flatten the bristles ←— 38 mm —→
and hinder their action.

We realize that automatic brushing represents a distinct change in
dental hygiene habits and it may require more time for some users to
adapt to this new technique. However, reports from clinical trials
show that, if allowed to do the job properly, the brush will give
good service for a long period of time. **DS**

Yours sincerely, **DS**

DURODENT MANUFACTURING LTD.

↓ 4 line spaces (3 blank lines)

Janet L. Ritchie
Customer Relations Officer **DS**

JLR:yoi

LONG LETTER
MODIFIED BLOCK STYLE
TWO-POINT PUNCTUATION

is symbolic of safety; the sea is symbolic of the unknown; the tension in our hearts is made audible in the crashing of breakers. (¶) Natural sounds have the most profound symbolism for people. They have endured the longest. They have been listened to attentively by poets and musicians.

> Grey peak of the wave,
> wave, colour of grape's pulp,
> Olive grey in the near,
> far, smoke grey of the rock-slide,
> Salmon-pink wings of the fish-hawk
> cast grey shadows in water ...
>   (Pound, 1948, p. 10).

The image has been replaced by the power-launch and hovercraft industry. Everywhere in the modern world the sounds of nature are being replaced, or rather obscured, by much more insistent sounds. In a recent survey, university students discovered that of the sounds heard in the contemporary sonic environment those of nature accounted for only six per cent, while 25 per cent were human sounds and 68 per cent were the sounds of tools and technology (Shafer, 1969, p. 6). (¶) Today the hard-edged throb of motors can be heard around us almost continuously. What does the motor symbolize? Two words: power and progress. Technology has given people unprecedented power, in industry, in transportation, in war, power over nature and power over other men. We are infatuated with the motor's speed, efficiency, regularity and the extensions of personal and corporate power it has afforded us.

Bibliography

Auden, W. H. *The Enchafèd Flood*. New York: Random House, 1950.

Jung, Carl G. *Man and His Symbols*.

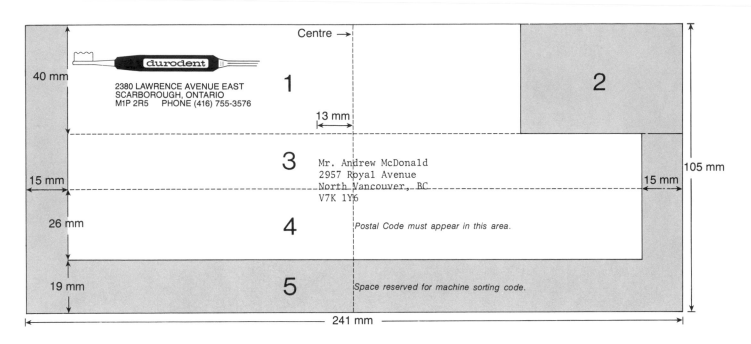

Notes: On envelopes—

Area 1 is for the return address and Post Office stickers (e.g. Special Delivery).

Area 2 is for postage stamps.

Area 3 is for the letter address. The letter address may overflow into Area 4. (Any special notations e.g. PERSONAL AND CONFIDENTIAL, will also appear in Area 3 to the left of the letter address.) The depth of Area 3 will increase as the depth of the envelope increases.

Area 4 must contain the Postal Code.

Area 5 must be left entirely blank. It's the machine sorting code band.

Notes: On Postal Codes—

When typing **addresses**, type the postal code on a separate line at the end of the address. A full space is used between the second alpha-character and the second number.

V.6 Fold each of the letters typed in Problems V.2-V.4 for insertion into the envelopes typed in Problem 5. Follow the flow chart instructions and refer to the illustration below.

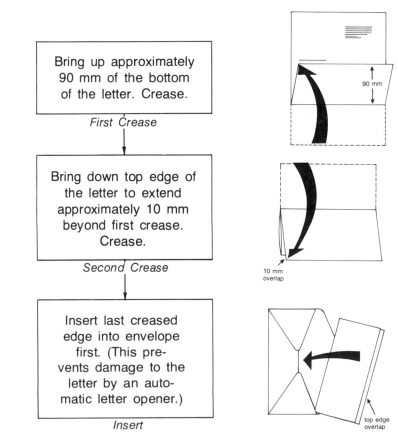

Bring up approximately 90 mm of the bottom of the letter. Crease.

First Crease

Bring down top edge of the letter to extend approximately 10 mm beyond first crease. Crease.

Second Crease

Insert last creased edge into envelope first. (This prevents damage to the letter by an automatic letter opener.)

Insert

is symbolic when it implies something more than its obvious and immediate meaning. It has a wider 'unconscious' aspect that is never precisely defined or fully explained (Jung, 1964, pp. 20-21)." A sound object is symbolic when it stirs in us emotions or thoughts beyond its actual mechanical sensations as sound. An awareness of sound symbolism will be useful in trying to decide which sounds we want to preserve in the world and which we want to suppress.(¶) The sounds of nature are mostly pleasing to people. Consider the rustling of wind in the leaves, the arabesques of birds, the bubbling of brooks. Water in particular has a splendid symbolism. Rain, a fountain, a river, a waterfall, the sea, each makes its unique sound but they share a rich symbolism. They speak of cleansing, of purification, of refreshment and renewal.(¶) The sea in particular has always been one of man's primary symbols in literature, myth, and art. It is symbolic of eternity: its ceaseless presence. It is symbolic of change: the tides; the ebb and flow of the waves. Heraclitus said, "You never go down to the same water twice (Nahm, 1934, p. 91)." It is symbolic of democracy: the magnificent democracy of waterdrops. It is symbolic of the law of the conservation of energy: from the sea, water evaporates becomes rain, then brooks and rivers and finally is returned to the sea. It is symbolic of reincarnation: water never dies. When angry it symbolizes "that state of barbaric vagueness and disorder out of which civilization has emerged and into which, unless saved by the efforts of gods and men, it is always liable to relapse (Auden, 1950, p. 7)." (¶) W. H. Auden (1950) continues: "The sea is where the decisive events, the moments of eternal choice, of temptation, fall and redemption occur (p. 7)." The shore

SQUEEZING IN

V.7 In Component IV (see pages 114 and 115) general instructions were given for correcting simple typing errors. Often an error is not discovered until the finished work is proofread. In such circumstances it is easier and quicker to insert or "squeeze in" a missed letter, than to re-type the entire copy.

On a sheet of paper type an exact copy of the following paragraph. Use a 50-space line with a 5-space paragraph indention.

Note: Do not underscore any word. The underscore is used in this exercise to highlight errors.

        Still, here are good and evident reasons for
the relativel denes population of his southwestern
land. It as good soil, reliable rainfal, and a
prosmity to consumers hat th northwest must envy.
It is pleasant, productiv, and prety rather than
remote, empty and overwhelming.

Refer to the boxed information below, then correct your copy. Some errors may be corrected by erasing, some by "squeezing in," others by erasing and "squeezing in." When you have corrected your copy it should be similar to the following:

        Still, there are good and evident reasons for
the relatively dense population of this southwestern
land. It has good soil, reliable rainfall, and a
proximity to consumers that the northwest must envy.
It is pleasant, productive, and pretty rather than
remote, empty, and overwhelming.

+---+
| *INSERTING OR "SQUEEZING IN"* |
| *AN OMITTED LETTER OF A WORD* |
| |
| *Depending on the machine used, an omitted letter may be inserted in typescript by one or more of the following methods:* |
| |
| *1. Pressing against the left end of the carriage to move to the desired typing position. (Electric or manual).* |
| |
| *2. Partly depressing the backspace key to move to the desired typing position. (Manual)* |
| |
| *3. Pressing against the right side of the carrier to move to the desired typing position. (Selectric)* |
| |
| *4. Using the half-space key. (Some electrics)* |
+---+

It is not only the teen-ager, but also the younger child who is becoming more and more of a power in decision-making in today's purchases. Satlow (1964) reports that "Current market studies have disclosed that younger children in the 10 - 14 age group are making their own decisions about colors and styles (p. 32)."

Both teen-agers and younger children are allowed much freedom in making their purchases. Edmonton stores reported that students generally buy their own clothes, sports equipment, or other merchandise without the presence of a parent.

Parents, teachers, and others charged with the responsibility of educating youth should be concerned with the increase in spending by young consumers. They should also be concerned with the increase in credit buying, the number of repossessions, the high interest rates, and certain unethical business practices. A former Alberta Minister of Public Welfare is quoted in The Edmonton Journal (1965) as saying:

> The public needs more counselling about the perils of credit buying. Young married couples are most prone to pitfalls. We will see many, many young husbands deserting intolerable situations. Much more counselling will have to be done to aid these young people in maintaining their independence.

Population figures reported by the Dominion Bureau of Statistics (1963, p. 10) show that at the present time about one-half of Canada's population is under the age of 25, and the percentage at lower age levels is increasing. A high birthrate, together with a low death rate among young children, added nearly 2 000 000 to the number of persons under 15 years of age between 1951 and 1961, an increase of 46 per cent.

The trend toward increased spending and credit buying on the part of young people makes it imperative that more emphasis be placed on education for young consumers.

BIBLIOGRAPHY

Dominion Bureau of Statistics. Canada 1963. Ottawa: Queen's Printer, 1964.

The Edmonton Journal. November 25, 1965.

International Consumer Credit Association. How to Use Credit Wisely. St. Louis: International Consumer Credit Association, 1963.

Satlow, I. David. "Consumer Economics," Business Education World, 45:32, December, 1964.

VI.20 Type the following report and bibliography in proper leftbound form.

Sound Symbolism.

Most of the sounds of our environment have symbolism. "a word or an image

Notes: On letter length —

*The number of paragraphs in the body of a letter may be used as a guide when determining letter length. A **short** letter may have three or fewer paragraphs; a **medium** letter three to five paragraphs; a **long** letter five or more paragraphs.*

Notes: On adjusting letter length—

When you have completed the body of a letter, examine its page position. If it appears high, leave more space between the complimentary close and the typed signature. If it appears low, reduce the space between the complimentary close and the typed signature.

Notes: On capitalization —

Titles of books, booklets, newspapers, and magazines may be typed in ALL CAPITALS or may be underscored with the first letter of the principal words capitalized.

Notes: On provincial abbreviations —

*When typing **letter addresses** and **envelopes**, it is permissible to spell in full the names of the provinces and territories. However, <u>Canada Postal Standards</u> recommends the use of the following two-letter designations:*

Alberta	*AB*
British Columbia	*BC*
Labrador	*LB*
Manitoba	*MB*
New Brunswick	*NB*
Newfoundland	*NF*
Northwest Territories	*NT*
Nova Scotia	*NS*
Ontario	*ON*
Prince Edward Island	*PE*
Quebec	*PQ*
Saskatchewan	*SK*
Yukon Territory	*YT*

V.8 Type the following letter using modified block style with two-point punctuation. Follow all the steps in the flowchart shown on page 138. Make corrections when necessary. Use your initials to indicate that you typed the letter. Prepare an envelope.

Letter Address: Mr. Alfred J. Madison
Ajax High School
Bayly Street
Ajax, ON
L1S 1P2

Salutation: Dear Mr. Madison

Body:

Thank you for your letter requesting a copy of <u>Telephone Voices</u>. This particular publication is no longer available because its contents have been used to produce a filmstrip for our Personnel Training Program.

If you would like to view the filmstrip to assess its value to your program, we shall be delighted to send it to you.

Complimentary Close: Sincerely

Typed Signature: Suzanne F. Shepherd

Title: Customer Relations

V.9 Type the following letter using modified block style with two-point punctuation. Follow all the steps in the flowchart shown on page 138. Make corrections when necessary. Use your initials to indicate that you typed the letter. Prepare an envelope.

Letter Address: Mr. F. T. Midgley
Baker Advertising Agency
53 Airport Road
Winnipeg, MB
R3H 0V5

Salutation: Dear Fred

Body:

We have decided to enter into the business of selling used parts for motor graders. This is a whole new phase of business for our Company, and we are anxious to promote the venture in the most effective way.

May we discuss ideas and suggestions for a promotion campaign designed to develop a market for used parts for every make of motor grader? We shall be pleased to meet with you at your earliest convenience.

Complimentary Close: Yours sincerely

Typed Signature: Benjamin Harper, President

PARENTHETICAL SOURCE NOTATIONS

VI.19 Type the following report and bibliography in proper unbound form. Refer to the boxed information for guidelines on typing quotations and parenthetical source notations.

REFERENCES IN A REPORT

Quotations: *Place in a separate paragraph quoted information which exceeds three lines. Indent the quotation five spaces from the left and right margins, and single-space. In this case quotation marks are not required.*

Acknowledge the source of quotations and paraphrased information by using either footnotes or references to a bibliography. Use parenthetical source notations to designate reference to a bibliography.

Parenthetical Source Notations: These notations appear in the text and include the author's name, year of publication, and page references. Examples:

A recent study (MacDonald, 1972)...
Saunders (1970) claimed...
The statement made by Green (1973, p. 10)

When a quotation is typed, the page number is placed at the end of the quotation. It precedes the period and the quotation marks when used. Example:

Jacobs (1974) referred to his invention as "the greatest accomplishment of the century (p. 68)."

The report, Young Consumers, is adapted with permission from the Master's thesis of Melvin R. Bakken, "Money Management Understandings of Tenth Grade Students," University of Alberta, Edmonton, 1966, pp. 4-7.

YOUNG CONSUMERS

In Canada, charge accounts are available to a large number of young consumers. Although each application for credit is considered on its own merit, there are necessary conditions for the establishment of teen-age charge accounts:

1. Approval of parent.
2. Steady income, from either employment or allowance.
3. Acceptance of credit terms, limits to credit, and repayment period.

Three large department stores which were surveyed in Edmonton indicated general satisfaction with teen-age accounts and stressed that, in their opinion, the young people were learning good buying habits. In the International Consumer Credit Association publication, How to Use Credit Wisely (1963), a similar opinion is stated as follows:

Experience shows that these young people take their credit responsibilities seriously. The money-management experience which they acquire through teen-age accounts trains them ultimately to become wise, sound, and reliable customers (p. 32).

CARBON PACKS

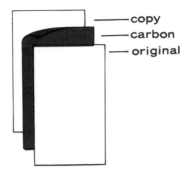

— copy
— carbon
— original

Notes: On complimentary closes —

*The selection of a **complimentary close** is determined by the tone of the letter and by the salutation.*

In informal situations you may wish to use:

Sincerely
Yours sincerely
Sincerely yours
Very sincerely yours
Yours very sincerely

In formal situations you may wish to use:

Very truly yours
Yours very truly

Other personal complimentary closings include:

Cordially
Cordially yours
Yours cordially

V.10 Type the following letter in modified block style with two-point punctuation. Make a carbon copy for your file. Make corrections when necessary. Prepare an envelope.

ASSEMBLING A CARBON PACK

Place copy sheet on desk	→	Place carbon paper (carbon side down) on copy sheet	→	Place sheet for original copy on the carbon paper	→	Insert carbon pack in machine so that the original is in typing position

Letter Address: Vancouver Manufacturers' Association
572 Howe Street
Vancouver, BC
V6C 2E3

Salutation: Gentlemen

Body:

Thank you for your letter of January 16 outlining a proposal for a one-day workshop to consider ideas for the expansion of secondary industry in the Lower Mainland. We are interested in the proposal and would like to participate.

Our primary interest is to promote sources of supply for our particular industry. The agenda for the workshop seems to encompass our concern.

Please keep us informed of further developments.

Complimentary Close: Yours sincerely

Typed Signature: A. V. Howell

Title: General Manager

V.11 Type the following letter in modified block style with two-point punctuation. Make a carbon copy for your file. Make corrections when necessary. Prepare an envelope.

Letter Address: Mr. John D. Wallbridge
326 Beaver Avenue
Banff, AB
T0L 0C0

Salutation: Dear Mr. Wallbridge

Body:

Because of an incomplete envelope address, your letter has taken several days to reach my desk. I am sorry for the delay in replying.

The Right Combination — A Guide to Food and Nutrition, Elizabeth Chant Robertson, Agincourt: Gage Educational Publishing Limited, (1975).

Nutrition and Physical Fitness, L.J. Bogert, G.M. Briggs, and D.H. Calloway, Toronto: W.B. Saunders Co. Canada Ltd., (1966).

The Science of Nutrition, M.T. Arlin, Toronto: Collier-Macmillan Canada Ltd., (1972).

Food Hygiene and Food Hazards, A.B. Christie and Mary C. Christie, London: Faber and Faber, (1971).

VI.18 Type the following bibliography as part of an unbound report.

BIBLIOGRAPHY

BARNHILL, J. A. SALES MANAGEMENT CONTEMPOR-
ARY PERSPECTIVES. AGINCOURT GAGE EDU-
CATIONAL PUBLISHING LTD., 1970.

JOHNSON, H. W. CREATIVE SELLING. AGINCOURT
GAGE EDUCATIONAL PUBLISHING LTD., 1971.

KIRBY, J. K. ESSENTIALS OF MARKETING MANAGE-
MENT. CINCINNATI SOUTH-WESTERN PUBLISH
ING CO., 1975.

KIRKPATRICK, C. A. SALESMANSHIP. SIXTH EDI-
TION. CINCINNATI SOUTH-WESTERN PUBLISH
ING CO., 1976.

LOTT, RICHARD W. PROBLEMS IN DATA PROCESSING
SCARBOROUGH PRENTICE-HALL OF CANADA
LTD., 1967.

MCGEACHY, J. B. NEW VARIETY OF NORTHERN
LIGHT, FINANCIAL POST, DECEMBER 4,
1965, P. 7.

SAXON, JAMES AND WESLEY STEYER. BASIC PRIN-
CIPLES OF DATA PROCESSING. SECOND EDI-
TION. SCARBOROUGH PRENTICE-HALL OF
CANADA LTD., 1970.

SHILT, BERNARD, KENNETH EVERARD, AND JOHN
JOHNS. BUSINESS PRINCIPLES AND MANAGE-
MENT. SIXTH EDITION. CINCINNATI SOUTH-
WESTERN PUBLISHING CO., 1973.

We firmly believe that we manufacture the best ski socks in the world. We stand behind our guarantees and we resolve all customer complaints. To ensure the continued excellence of our product, our company requires that customers return both socks of a pair even though one sock was the culprit. We then make an analysis to determine the cause of the defect so that we can correct any weakness in the manufacturing process.

If you will return the ski socks to us, I can assure you that they will be replaced without charge.

Complimentary Close: Yours sincerely

Typed Signature: S. L. Dewar

Title: Sales Manager

V.12   Type the following letter in modified block style with two-point punctuation. Make a carbon copy for your file. Make corrections when necessary. Prepare an envelope.

Letter Address: Mr. J. W. Dumont
Maritime Shoe Findings Ltd.
173 Euston Street
Charlottetown, PE
C1A 1W7

Salutation: Dear Mr. Dumont

Body:

We would like to react to the following statement in your letter of October 28: "It has always been our understanding that in this type of heel the grain of the wood should run perpendicular to the base of the heel instead of parallel to it."

It would not be practical to have the grain of the wood run perpendicular to the base of the heel because of the risk of breakage in applying the heel to the shoe. Furthermore, when buying lumber we order 50 mm and 65 mm thick planks which we cut into two metre strips. The only way we could have a perpendicular grain would be to buy thick lumber which would be expensive and unsuitable for handling by our ripping and blocking machines.

We would be happy to have you visit our plant to see the entire heel-manufacturing process. Please let us know when you can visit us.

Complimentary Close: Yours sincerely

Typed Signature: W. T. Saltzman

Title: Manager, Operations

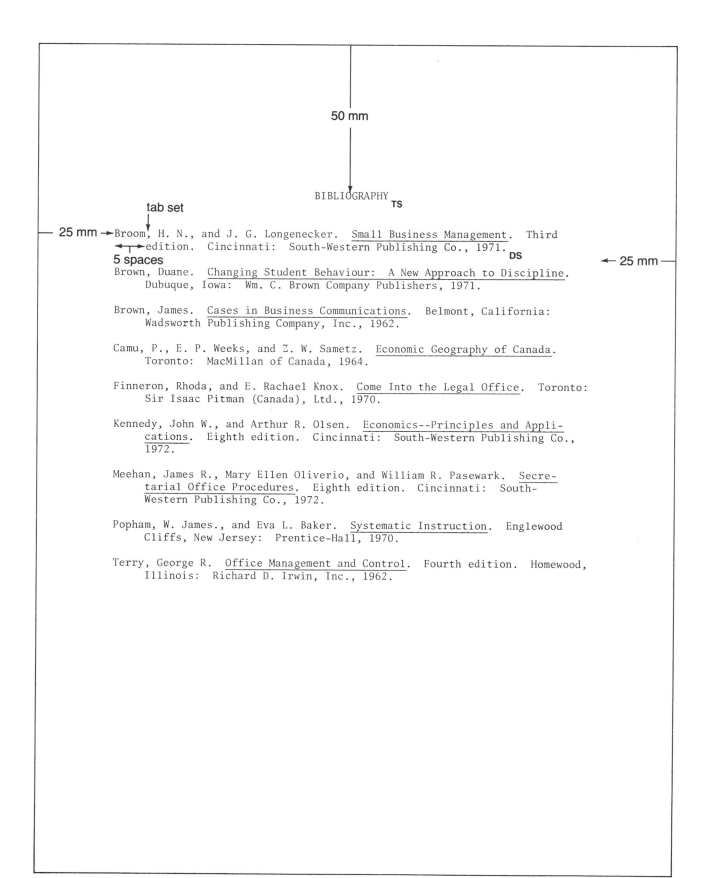

50 mm

BIBLIOGRAPHY TS

tab set

25 mm → Broom, H. N., and J. G. Longenecker. Small Business Management. Third
edition. Cincinnati: South-Western Publishing Co., 1971. DS

5 spaces ← 25 mm →

Brown, Duane. Changing Student Behaviour: A New Approach to Discipline.
Dubuque, Iowa: Wm. C. Brown Company Publishers, 1971.

Brown, James. Cases in Business Communications. Belmont, California:
Wadsworth Publishing Company, Inc., 1962.

Camu, P., E. P. Weeks, and Z. W. Sametz. Economic Geography of Canada.
Toronto: MacMillan of Canada, 1964.

Finneron, Rhoda, and E. Rachael Knox. Come Into the Legal Office. Toronto:
Sir Isaac Pitman (Canada), Ltd., 1970.

Kennedy, John W., and Arthur R. Olsen. Economics--Principles and Applications. Eighth edition. Cincinnati: South-Western Publishing Co.,
1972.

Meehan, James R., Mary Ellen Oliverio, and William R. Pasewark. Secretarial Office Procedures. Eighth edition. Cincinnati: South-
Western Publishing Co., 1972.

Popham, W. James., and Eva L. Baker. Systematic Instruction. Englewood
Cliffs, New Jersey: Prentice-Hall, 1970.

Terry, George R. Office Management and Control. Fourth edition. Homewood,
Illinois: Richard D. Irwin, Inc., 1962.

Notes: On letter addresses —

When a title follows an individual's name, it may be typed on the same line.

*e.g. Mr. E. Edward, Editor
ADVERTISING REPORTS*

If a title is particularly long, it may be typed on the second line of the address to give balance.

*e.g. Mr. E. Edward
Managing Editor
ADVERTISING REPORTS*

NEW LETTER AND PUNCTUATION STYLES

V.13 Type the following letter in modified block style with two-point punctuation. Make a carbon copy for your file. Make corrections when necessary. Prepare an envelope.

Letter Address: Mr. E. Edward, Editor
ADVERTISING REPORTS
600 University Avenue
Toronto, ON
M5G 1X5

Salutation: Dear Mr. Edward

Body:

You asked for my views on the subject of measuring the effectiveness of advertising.

Our company is budgeting a considerable sum of money for research designed to evaluate the effectiveness of our advertising. The majority of the manufacturers include an amount of money in each of their advertising budgets specifically allocated to advertising-effectiveness research. We have convinced ourselves that the evaluation task we have taken on can be completed, but we are not yet certain of the method.

Each year we add to our knowledge in the broad marketing area. At present, a workable and tested method of evaluating the effectiveness of all our advertising is still missing. Until we find this method, we shall treat the search as one of our most important projects in terms of both money and effort.

I must apologize for this brief answer to your enquiry. I am rather pressed for time but I do hope that what I have written conveys the importance we are placing on finding a way to measure the effectiveness of our advertising expenditures.

Complimentary Close: Yours sincerely

Typed Signature: S. S. Denning

Title: Promotion Chairman

V.14 Type the letter on page 148 in **block style** with **no-point punctuation**. Prepare a carbon copy and an envelope. Make corrections when necessary.

V.15 Type the letter on page 149 in **block style** with **no-point punctuation**. Prepare a carbon copy and an envelope. Make corrections when necessary.

V.16 Type the letter on page 150 in **block style** with **no-point punctuation**. Prepare a carbon copy and an envelope. Make corrections when necessary.

an employee of the Club. Complaints must be made in writing to the Manager or Management Committee. Suggestions are welcome, but should be made in writing to the Management Committee. (¶) The Executive of the Club has empowered the Manager, or designate, to conduct the total affairs of the Club in a manner consistent with the Constitution and Club Regulations, and to maintain appropriate decorum within the Club. Members are asked to co-operate with the Manager in these matters. Members disagreeing with the implementation of Club regulations, should present their case to the Club Executive in writing.

TYPING A BIBLIOGRAPHY

A **bibliography** is used at the end of an essay or report to identify the source of material or to provide the reader with additional reference material.

Notes: On bibliography entries —

The title of a book is underscored. The title of an article is enclosed within quotation marks.

Notes: On bibliography entry sequence —

Authors separated by commas, followed by a period. (Where there are two or more authors, the names of all authors other than the first are written in their natural order. Example: Bogert, L.J., G.M. Briggs, D.H. Calloway). **Title**, underscored and followed by a period. **Edition** followed by a period. **City** of publication followed by a colon. **Publisher** followed by a comma. **Year** of publication followed by a period. Normal punctuation spacing is used.

VI.16 Type the bibliography on page 205 in proper form as part of an unbound report.

GUIDELINES FOR TYPING BIBLIOGRAPHIES

Paper:	Use standard P4, paper.
Title:	Centred in ALL CAPITALS, typed 50 mm from top of page. Triple-space (TS) after the title.
Margins:	The same as for bound and unbound reports.
Page number:	The bibliography may be numbered consecutively as part of a report (13 mm from top of page) or it may be left unnumbered.
Entries:	Arranged alphabetically by authors' surnames. Each entry is single-spaced and begins flush with the left margin. Subsequent lines are indented five spaces. Double-space (DS) between entries.

VI.17 Arrange and type the following references as a bibliography for a leftbound report.

Food: Fact and Folklore, Alice Jenner, Toronto: McClelland and Stewart, (1973).

Nutrition for Today, Elizabeth Chant Robertson, Toronto: McClelland and Stewart, (1968).

(continued on p. 206)

SNAP TIGHT

Snap-Tight Couplings Limited
472 Notre Dame Avenue
Winnipeg, Manitoba R3B 1R7
(204) 943-3711

50 mm

1976 06 15

38 mm

←— 38 mm —→ Caldwell Construction Company Limited
761 Franklin Street
Brandon, MB
R7A 5R2

Gentlemen

We have noticed in the Construction Report column of the WEEKLY
BUSINESS NEWS a notification of your intention to construct a
chemical plant in Saskatchewan.

We would like to take this opportunity to introduce to you our
quality line of quick-connect couplings for use on production
lines and plant maintenance. A copy of our catalogue, which
describes in detail our complete series of industrial couplings,
has been forwarded under separate cover. Should there be any   ←— 38 mm —→
questions regarding the performance or application of these
quality couplings, please do not hesitate to write to us.

Yours sincerely

4 line spaces (3 blank lines)

Mathew J. Ingersoll
Sales Manager

MJI:yoi

SHORT LETTER
BLOCK STYLE WITH NO-POINT PUNCTUATION

wearing casual dress. Casual dress is acceptable at all hours in the downstairs area.

Club Accounts.

Purchases from the club by members will be by the chit system and the members will be billed monthly. Bills are payable ten days after the billing date. House accounts shall be limited to $300 and should be cleared within one month. Special organizational functions charged to a member's account should also be cleared within one month. Accounts which by these terms and conditions come into arrears, shall be brought to the Executive for consideration." It is agreed between the Club and each of its members that any objection to the balances or any entries on monthly statements must be made by personal application or registered letter to the manager of the Club, producing the questioned invoices. Where no such objection is made within 30 d after the mailing out by the Club of the statements (addressed to the member's last on file address), such statement and all the entries on it will be agreed conclusively to be correct and the amounts shown thereon, as owing to the Club to be owing."

Miscellaneous

No person may offer a gratuity to an employee of the Club. No person shall ask any employee of the Club to perform any private duty or errand during official working hours of that employee. No member (except a member appointed by the Executive of the Club) is permitted access to the kitchen.

Complaints and Suggestions.

No member of the Club may reprimand

McKenzie
fashions limited

27 CENTRAL STREET
SUMMERSIDE, PE C1N 3K8
PHONE (902) 293-8414

1976 06 15

25 mm

38 mm

Four Seasons Boutique
P. O. Box 1413
Summerside, PE
C1N 4K2

Ladies

It is a pleasure to welcome you as a customer of McKenzie Fashions
Limited, and to thank you sincerely for the opportunity to serve   38 mm
you.

As we take a very real and personal interest in customer satisfaction, we should greatly appreciate your letting us know, by mail
or telephone, how you would like us to handle your first order.
More than that, we want you to know that our interest does not
stop with the first delivery. If at any time our product and our
service do not merit your enthusiastic approval, we would consider
it a favor if you would call us at once.

We are ready and eager to serve you.

Sincerely yours

McKENZIE FASHIONS LTD.

4 line spaces (3 blank lines)

Jonathan K. McKenzie
General Manager

JKM:yoi

MEDIUM LETTER
BLOCK STYLE WITH NO-POINT PUNCTUATION

Club Hours

The Club opens at 09:00 Monday through Saturday and closes at 22:00 except on Friday when the closing hour is 01:00. (4) No person under the age of 19 will be served liquor at any time which contravenes the general licensing laws of the Province.

Guests

While personally present in the Club, a member has the privilege of introducing up to nine guests without prior approval of the Management Committee. A member may not authorize the use of his Club number by another person. Club members are responsible for the behavior and dress of their guests. A non-member, who is eligible for membership in the Club, may not be introduced as a guest on more than three occasions during any calendar year.

Use of Club Facilities.

Subject only to restrictions imposed by Club Hours, the Games Room and the Library are to be available for the use of members at all times. Reserved areas for large special groups and for private parties and functions will be made available only when not required for regular Club purposes. Reservations should always be made when a table is required in the Dining Room. This is important for luncheons and especially for the more formal dinner parties in the evenings. If members are unable to keep reservations, they are requested to cancel with as much notice as possible to the Manager.

Dress.

Members of the Club will not use the upper lounge and dining room while

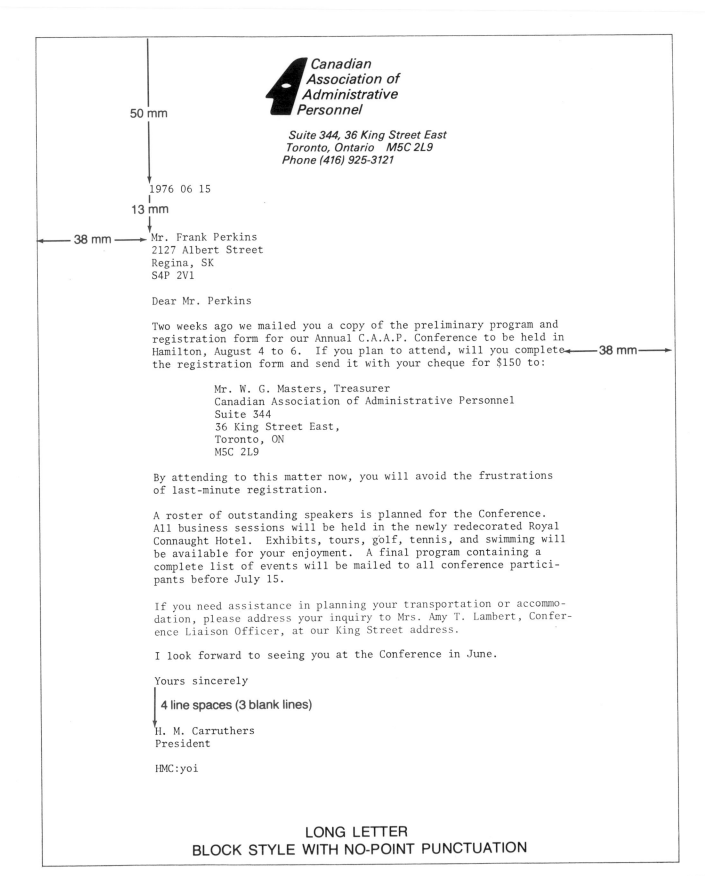

Canadian Association of Administrative Personnel

Suite 344, 36 King Street East
Toronto, Ontario   M5C 2L9
Phone (416) 925-3121

50 mm

1976 06 15

13 mm

38 mm →

Mr. Frank Perkins
2127 Albert Street
Regina, SK
S4P 2V1

Dear Mr. Perkins

Two weeks ago we mailed you a copy of the preliminary program and
registration form for our Annual C.A.A.P. Conference to be held in
Hamilton, August 4 to 6. If you plan to attend, will you complete ← 38 mm →
the registration form and send it with your cheque for $150 to:

          Mr. W. G. Masters, Treasurer
          Canadian Association of Administrative Personnel
          Suite 344
          36 King Street East,
          Toronto, ON
          M5C 2L9

By attending to this matter now, you will avoid the frustrations
of last-minute registration.

A roster of outstanding speakers is planned for the Conference.
All business sessions will be held in the newly redecorated Royal
Connaught Hotel. Exhibits, tours, golf, tennis, and swimming will
be available for your enjoyment. A final program containing a
complete list of events will be mailed to all conference partici-
pants before July 15.

If you need assistance in planning your transportation or accommodation, please address your inquiry to Mrs. Amy T. Lambert, Conference Liaison Officer, at our King Street address.

I look forward to seeing you at the Conference in June.

Yours sincerely

4 line spaces (3 blank lines)

H. M. Carruthers
President

HMC:yoi

LONG LETTER
BLOCK STYLE WITH NO-POINT PUNCTUATION

<u>Tellers' Wickets:</u>   The tellers' wickets are poorly set up. They do not allow the tellers to move out of their areas to up-date pass books. The partitions and the bars on the tellers' wickets should be removed immediately and a counter installed.

<u>Work Areas:</u>   There does not appear to be maximum utilization of space. The work areas should be efficiently planned to eliminate the problems created by the present arrangement.

<u>General:</u>   The premises are dingy and drab and require redecorating.

Equipment and Furniture

<u>Machines:</u>   The equipment appears old, obsolete, and rundown. If increased efficiency is expected, the staff must be provided with the tools to do the job. (¶) There seems to be a shortage of adding machines and calculators to accommodate the amount of computational work involved.

<u>Telephones:</u>   The telephones have six or seven locals on each line. A direct-dial intercom system would better serve the needs of staff.

<u>Furniture:</u>   Most of the furniture which is poorly arranged is the same uninteresting color and the chairs do not match. The old furniture does not reflect a progressive operation.

Personnel

<u>Senior Personnel:</u>   There appears to be an overlapping of responsibilities and a duplication of effort by several of the senior people. An organization chart should be developed to show who does what.

<u>Supervisory Personnel:</u>   The supervisors appear to be performing much detailed clerical work, leaving little time for considering revision of duties, work flow, and performance.

<u>Orientation and Training Program:</u>   An orientation and training program should be established for young employees coming into the organization.

VI.15 Type the following article as a leftbound report.

Four Winds

The Four Winds Club was organized two years ago to serve members of the local business community and their guests. Among the services and benefits offered are meals, snacks, recreational facilities, meeting room facilities, and a library. So that members will derive maximum benefit and satisfaction from these services, the Club has established a number of regulations.

V.17 Type the following letter in block style with no-point punctuation. Prepare a carbon copy and an envelope. Make corrections when necessary.

Letter Address: Ms. Sally Mitchell
1327 Pine Street
Wolfville, NS
B0P 1X0

Salutation: Dear Ms. Mitchell

Body:

Thank you for your recent letter of inquiry. Unfortunately, we cannot answer your questions without seeing the ring that you want repaired. If the ring is very old, it would lose some of its value by being reset. We could make the gems secure simply by changing the mount. However, if you want the ring restyled, we would be pleased to design a new setting.

We suggest that you send the ring to us by registered mail so that we can assess its value and give you our recommendation.

Complimentary Close: Yours sincerely

Company Name: Sheridan Jewellers Limited

Typed Signature: Thomas V. Holt

Title: Manager

TWO-PAGE LETTER

V.18 Study the information on page 152 for "Typing A Two-Page Letter." Then, type the following two-page letter in block style with no-point punctuation. Prepare a carbon copy and an envelope.

Letter Address: Mr. Andrew McDonald
2957 Royal Avenue
North Vancouver, BC
V7K 1Y6

Salutation: Dear Mr. McDonald

Body:

Notes: The (¶) symbol indicates the beginning of a new paragraph.

Thank you for your recent letter concerning the bristles of your Durodent toothbrush. May we make the following comments which we hope you will find helpful. (¶) The rapid oscillating motion of the toothbrush may cause the bristles to have a fanned-out or worn appearance. Provided the bristles do not bend or collapse and the degree of fanning out is not excessive, the effectiveness of the brush will not diminish to any extent. (¶) For many years before purchasing a Durodent, you were accustomed to using a manual toothbrush and the cleaning and massaging results depended entirely on the amount of energy supplied by you. Now you have an instrument to do this work for you. It is no longer

Centre ⟶ Senior (three year)	25.00
longest line· Family	15.00
Leader	10.00
Life	50.00 **TS**

Accommodation **DS**

Charges for overnight at the hostels vary with the type of accommodation, but the usual charge is $1 for adults and 75 cents for juniors at mountain hostels. In cities like Montreal and Vancouver the charges may be $2 or $2.50.

There are hostels in Europe, Japan, and even Canada which provide many of the comforts of a hotel: hot showers, cafeterias, rest and recreation rooms. A few are in old castles and manor houses, but in the mountains, hostels are simple huts with an outdoor john.

Each hut consists of a dormitory for men, one for women, and a common room for cooking. Most hostels have insulated walls, and all of them have wood-burning stoves and propane heaters. There are beds with mattresses and blankets, but it is advisable to bring your own sleeping bag. In the winter it is essential. **TS**

Companionship **DS**

The bulletin boards in CYHA offices are crammed with requests for people for canoe trips, mountaineering, cycling, and just plain hikes into some beautiful wilderness.

For those who lack equipment, and are not sure they want to take up hostelling, more information is available from CYHA offices in all provinces of Canada.

VI.14 Type the following article, as an unbound report.

NEW IMAGE FOR BARNHARD LOAN COMPANY

A preliminary examination of the premises and facilities of Barnhard Loan Company has been made, and the following observations and recommendations for improving the image of the Company are offered for your consideration.

Premises

Entrance: The entrance should be relocated to provide easier access to the main offices. A corner entrance should be considered.

Front Office: The front office gives an appearance of an old, conservative, and stuffy company. Renovations should be made.

necessary to press or scrub as the built-in, controlled action of Durodent provides all the energy required to produce a thorough job. You just have to guide the brush allowing only the bristle tips to contact the dental surfaces. Excessive pressure tends to flatten the bristles and hinder their action. (¶) We realize that automatic brushing represents a distinct change in dental hygiene habits and it may require more time for some users to adapt to this new technique. However, reports from clinical trials show that, if allowed to do the job properly, the brush will give good service for a long period of time. (¶) You may be interested in knowing that a second, firmer texture brush is available through your pharmacy. If your gums are in a normal, healthy condition, you may prefer the firmer texture. (¶) Under separate cover, we are sending you two of the regular brushes, with our compliments. We believe that these new brushes, used in conjunction with the above suggestions, will enable you to continue using your Durodent with greater satisfaction.

Complimentary Close: Yours sincerely

Typed Signature: Janet L. Ritchie

Title: Customer Relations Officer

TYPING A TWO-PAGE LETTER

1. *Follow the same placement guidelines as used for typing a long letter. (See flow chart page 138.)*

2. *With a pencil make a light mark approximately 38 mm from the bottom of the page. (A manuscript frame can also be used. See Appendix B, page 357.)*

3. *The last paragraph on the first page should contain at least two lines of type. The last word of the last line should not be hyphenated.*

4. *At least two lines of the body should be carried to the second page.*

5. *Allow for a top margin of approximately 25 mm before typing the "second page heading." Triple-space between the heading and the body.*

6. *Either of the following headings may be used for the second (or subsequent) page.*

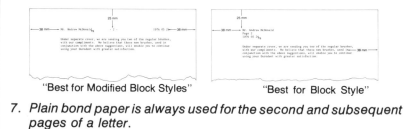

"Best for Modified Block Styles"   "Best for Block Style"

7. *Plain bond paper is always used for the second and subsequent pages of a letter.*

VI.13 Type the following article, which illustrates the placement of headings, as a leftbound report.

THE CANADIAN YOUTH HOSTEL ASSOCIATION **TS**

5 spaces

|←——→|For those who feel the urge to wander, cycle, or canoe over the **DS** countryside, hostelling may be the answer.

In 1972, more than 30 000 Canadians travelled around the countryside and enjoyed the privileges of the Canadian Youth Hostel Association. By 1980, 60 000 Canadians are expected to take advantage of and enjoy the privileges of membership in the Canadian Youth Hostel Association. **TS**

Origin **TS**

The Canadian Youth Hostel Association is an international organization initiated in Altena, Germany, by a school teacher who felt his students needed to know and understand the beauties of the country. There are now more than 4 500 youth hostels in virtually every country in the world.

In 1968 over twenty million nights were used in hostels, and of these, 19 600 were used by Canadians.

Hostelling in Canada

Hostelling came to Canada in 1936 and was first established in Alberta in the Rockies. There are now six regular hostels in the Banff and Jasper areas—fourteen during the summer. There are 46 across Canada. A comprehensive guide to all youth hostels throughout the world is published annually and is available from all CYHA offices. **TS**

Membership **DS**

Membership in the CYHA is not just for the young, but also for the young in heart. There is no age limit, and families are encouraged to take out memberships and travel together. A membership card is valid from January to December inclusive, and can be used at any youth hostel in Canada or abroad.

Fees vary with the type of membership:

↓ *Tab Set*   ↓ *Tab Set*

Junior (under 18) $ 5.00

Senior   10.00

V.19 Type the following letter in block style with no-point punctuation. Prepare a carbon copy and an envelope.

Letter Address: Mr. George Unwin
All Boys Drum and Bugle Band
One Grove Street
Dartmouth, NS
B3A 3C5

Salutation: Dear Mr. Unwin

Body:

Last week we sent you a pamphlet prepared by the Canadian Music Publishers' Association which will answer most of your questions concerning the use of copyright materials. You will see from the pamphlet that you cannot use any copyright material without the permission of the copyright owner. Many copyright owners do not grant permission and those who do, often want a fee or royalty. (¶) The duration of copyright is 50 years after the death of the author or composer. In the case of joint authorship—a composition having the music composed by one person and the words by another—the duration of copyright is 50 years after the death of the author or composer who died last. (¶) For a small fee our copyright department will be pleased to assist you.

Complimentary Close: Yours sincerely

Typed Signature: K. C. Calder

Title: Manager

V.20 Type the following letter in block style with no-point punctuation. Prepare a carbon copy and an envelope.

Letter Address: Red River Community College
2055 Notre Dame Avenue
Winnipeg, MB
R3H 0J9

Salutation: Gentlemen

Body:

Much as we should like to comply with your request for one of our plastic heart models, we regret that we are unable to do so. Our supply is exhausted because we distributed our models to almost every nursing school across Canada. We have tried on several occasions to obtain a further

Although you might say this is an unusual approach, an extreme approach, it is not. (¶) If I describe the characteristics of the "head-in-sand" approach, you will see that it is not unusual. (¶) The individual who is attracted to a career in business solely or primarily for steady employment, regular working hours, paid vacation, prestige, pleasant and clean surroundings is demonstrating the "head-in-sand" approach. The individual who works completely and implicitly under direction, who will do what he is directed to do but nothing more, is demonstrating this approach. The person who learns only that which is required for the tasks to be done is demonstrating this approach. Now how do the people who demonstrate this "head-in-sand" approach fare in business? Are they acceptable? Are they successful? Are their performances satisfactory? I would like to answer with this statement: If persistence of employment, or length of employment, is an indication of satisfactory performance, then the "head-in-sand" individuals can be giving satisfactory performances. In fact, they may be giving commendable and valuable service if those with whom they are compared also have a "head-in-sand" approach. (¶) But much more interesting, much more exciting is another approach to business which I shall call the "discovery approach." In contrast to the "head-in-sand" approach, the discovery approach is characterized by a mind-set towards discovery in business and this is the approach that I wish to dwell on at some length.

supply, but we have been unsuccessful. It is possible that one of the many clinics in Winnipeg to whom we supplied models might be willing to lend theirs to you for your project.

Complimentary Close: *Yours sincerely*

Typed Signature: *D. J. Barber*

Title: *Western Sales Representative*

V.21 Type the following letter in block style with no-point punctuation. Prepare a carbon copy and an envelope.

Letter Address: *Mrs. Germaine LeClerc
120 Fairford Street W.
Moose Jaw, SK
S6H 1V6*

Salutation: *Dear Mrs. LeClerc*

Body:

Thank you for your letter complimenting us on the packaging of our Choice Cheddar Cheese. I can assure you that those responsible for our packaging will appreciate your kind remarks. It is always a pleasure to hear from one of our good customers.

Complimentary Close: *Sincerely yours*

Typed Signature: *Patrick Murphy*

Title: *President*

Notes: On salutations —

*When writing to an individual whose name you know use **Dear Miss, Ms., Mrs.** or **Mr.** followed by the surname. If you know the individual on a first name basis use **Dear** and the **first name**.*

*When writing to a firm or organization composed of men and women, use either **Gentlemen** or **Ladies and Gentlemen** as the salutation.*

*When writing to a firm employing women only, use **Ladies**.*

*When writing to a woman whose marital status is unknown, use **Ms**.*

V.22 Type the following letter from M. R. Steele, Ontario Zone Manager, Century Canada Ltd. in block style with no-point punctuation. Prepare a carbon copy and an envelope.

Letter Address: Mayfair Department Store
9 Fisher's Hill
Corner Brook, NF
A2H 1A8

Towards Discovery in Business

I am delighted to have the opportunity of participating in the graduation ceremonies of the Holgerson Secretarial School. I am particularly happy to be able to address you on this great occasion — the culmination of a period of concentrated learning, self-discipline, disappointments, and accomplishments. I offer my warm congratulations to you, graduates, on the achievement of your goal, and to your teachers for the creation and surveillance of the environment for learning to which you have been exposed. Indeed, you are being graduated from an institution that is highly respected among the business colleges of Canada, an institution which has contributed to the business education of students for a period of 59 years. (¶) Now that you have successfully completed your period of training, you will be taking employment in business. I hope you are looking forward with excitement to the experience; and I hope that you will enjoy, in good measure, the advantages that business offers. (¶) When one first takes employment in business one has, whether aware of it or not, an approach or a mind-set towards business. Likewise, the employee who has worked for a number of years has an approach or a mind-set towards business. Now the approach adopted by one individual might differ considerably from that adopted by another. One approach I shall call the "head-in-sand" approach; its nature is indicated by the title.

Body:

In recognition of the unprecedented sales momentum generated by Century Canada Ltd., and in acknowledgment of the requests from many customers, we are pleased to inform you that a two-day Sales Clinic has been planned for the Toronto area, May 1 and 2. (¶) The clinic is designed to train sales people in basic retail selling. Considerable emphasis will be placed on methods of prospecting, presenting, demonstrating and closing, and on methods of up-to-date merchandising. (¶) A modest fee of $50 has been established for participation in the Sales Clinic. A cheque for the appropriate amount should be attached to your enrolment form. (¶) We urge you to take full advantage of this excellent opportunity. A well-trained salesperson is the greatest asset you have in your pursuit of a profitable operation. We look forward to your enthusiastic support in this forthcoming Sales Clinic.

Self-check: Does your letter contain a date line, letter address, salutation, body, complimentary close, typed signature, dictator's title, and reference initials?

V.23 Type the following letter from R. J. Rogers, Superintendent in block style with no-point punctuation. Prepare a carbon copy and an envelope.

Letter Address:

Mr. D. J. Hodges, Agent
Federal Grain Limited
Spruce Grove, AB
T0E 2C0

Body:

We wish to impress upon you the importance of selling as much registered or certified seed as you possibly can in order to maintain a high standard of quality in grains grown in your area. (¶) As you know, the strains of popular grains have been developed through cross-fertilization. The continued use of successive generations of grain for seed, results in the grain taking on the original characteristics of one of the parents. Such grain declines in germination and yield, and deteriorates in resistance to plant disease. (¶) The progressive farmer recognizes the importance of good seed. In order to maintain a high standard of quality in his field crops, he is receptive to the idea of purchasing, occasionally, either certified or registered seed from which he is able to produce his entire seed requirements for the next

Notes: When typing a leftbound report, the centre point is moved three spaces to the right. Refer to manuscript frame on page 357.

VI.11 Type the following article as a leftbound two-page report.

REFUNDS

The customer is always right! (¶) Satisfaction guaranteed or money refunded! (¶) Tom Thumbs in the retail merchandising business have grown to Goliath size delivering on those kinds of promises and matching them with quality and service. That's not the total recipe for merchandising success but those ingredients have helped. (¶) But consumers, weaned on such retail service, have come to expect it from all stores. And heat is generated when a merchant declines to extend refund and exchange privileges to his customers. Consumers become angry and confused when they can't "take it back." (¶) Unless the article is defective in some way, there's really no "right" involved. There is no law that compels a merchandiser to exchange goods or give refunds to a customer. It's wrong to believe in automatic cash refunds, or to expect to have goods exchanged just for the asking. (¶) Some stores do it, as an investment in customer goodwill. To keep customers happy, many retailers are willing to take back, either by refund, exchange, or for a credit note, goods that have been bought and have been found to be not satisfactory. Some stores bend over backwards in this direction; they take back rugs that don't fit or match, clothing, furniture, household items, products that really can't be afforded, or things bought on impulse. (¶) Unfortunately, some customers abuse the privilege and then wonder why the retailers who promise satisfaction and give exchanges and refunds are a diminishing band. (¶) It is reasonable to expect that a retailer who states that he makes refunds to dissatisfied customers will honor his own undertaking, especially when he advances this promise as part of the terms under which he sells. (¶) The law says that contracts are binding on buyers and sellers. And when you agree to buy something from someone, you are making a contract. There are laws that compel a seller to refund money in particular circumstances, but there is no requirement that this be done at the customer's whim. (¶) Trouble can be avoided in this area of retail purchasing if the buyer will first establish what the store's practice is in the matter of refunds and exchanges. More care can then be used in buying, and it becomes more satisfying. (¶) Shop with care, get precisely what you want and then you won't be one of those disappointed consumers who can't "take it back." Look for the sign that says "all sales final" and realize the merchant means it.

few years. (¶) You should make sure your growers know that you are in a position to supply almost any variety of seed grain that they require. Spring will soon be here and it is not too soon to contact your farmer friends and solicit orders for quality seed.

V.24 Type the following letter from James M. Jenkins, Foreperson, Printing Plant, Canprint Company Limited in modified block style with no-point punctuation. Prepare a carbon copy and an envelope.

Letter Address: Mr. Brian T. Sanderson, General Manager
Carlton-Blackburn Company
600 Dorchester Blvd. West
Montreal, PQ
H3B 1N4

Body:

You recently advised me that the purchasing agent of the Carlton-Blackburn Company had requested written assurance from us, your printer, that any envelopes which cannot be delivered because of spoilage will be destroyed. I checked with Jerry Lennon of your Company and discovered that the Carlton-Blackburn Company had an unfortunate experience when an envelope with the Company's corner card was returned by the Post Office because the addressee could not be located. On examining the content of the letter, it was discovered that the envelope had not been mailed by the Carlton-Blackburn Company, but by someone whose business was, to say the least, rather shady. A police investigation disclosed that the envelopes had been purchased from some jobber dealing in defective merchandise. The original corner card may have been covered with a sticker but, if so, it had dropped off. (¶) I assured Jerry that it was our strict policy not to sell to others the envelopes printed for a customer. I advised him that we could not guarantee that all spoiled envelopes would be mutilated, but I did tell him that they were baled and sold as waste paper. The possibility of their being retrieved and sold as useable envelopes was very remote because they would almost certainly be crumpled or twisted. (¶) I asked Jerry to try to find out who had produced the envelope in question. If by some remote chance it happened to be ours, we should very much like to know. In the meantime, I hope that your Company is quite satisfied with our assurance that we do not sell any defective printed envelopes for use as envelopes. All such defective merchandise is disposed of as scrap.

NEW LETTER AND PUNCTUATION STYLES

V.25 Type the letter on page 157 in **modified block style with indented paragraphs** and **two-point punctuation.** Prepare a carbon copy and an envelope.

was happening and tried to carry the barbecue out of the trailer. She died at the doorway. The other two died where they sat. (¶) To equip Canadians with the knowledge of the danger of improper use, the Department of Consumer and Corporate Affairs, through its product safety program, is taking steps to require manufacturers of charcoal briquets to put cautionary statements on the bags. (¶) So during and after cookouts, be sure to leave the grill and the charcoal embers outside in the open air.

TWO-PAGE REPORT
(Unbound)

Notes: Planning the bottom margin —

Leave a 25 mm bottom margin. This may be marked with a pencil, or a manuscript frame can be used.

Notes: On second and subsequent page headings —

Notes: An example of a manuscript frame appears on page 357. It is useful when typing reports of two or more pages.

VI.10 Type the following student essay in proper form as an unbound two-page report.

TO BE PRESIDENT IN A SCHOOL-RUN COMPANY

The duties and responsibilities that are required of the president in a company are many. He or she must: (¶) 1. Make sure that every motion that has been passed at meetings is attended to promptly. (¶) 2. Work in close cooperation with the Production Manager and his department. (¶) 3. Delegate jobs to the members of the company. (¶) 4. Be well informed on business matters at all times. (¶) To build a well-organized company, the president is involved in much detailed work. It is most interesting and worthwhile for the person who loves working with people. (¶) The purpose of a company is to offer goods and services for profit. (¶) The jobs within a company can be very rewarding in many ways. First of all, one will get satisfaction out of doing a job well. Second, he will learn a lot about conducting a business. Third, he will find that the teachers are not as hard to get along with as he might think. They are actually human. With the right attitudes, the company man will find himself loving the work that he is doing because it is interesting. He will learn to work and cooperate with other members of the company. Most important of all, he will learn how to sell other people on his ideas and win them to his way of thinking. (¶) After considering my own experience, I feel that the training I received will be very valuable to me in the future. I feel that I am better equipped to meet any kind of situation or emergency. I have learned much about production problems, purchasing problems, staff problems; not to mention the usual office routines connected with invoices, order blanks, bank transactions, and many other items. (¶) Personally, I would hope another school-run company would be set up next year so that others might learn about business experiences.

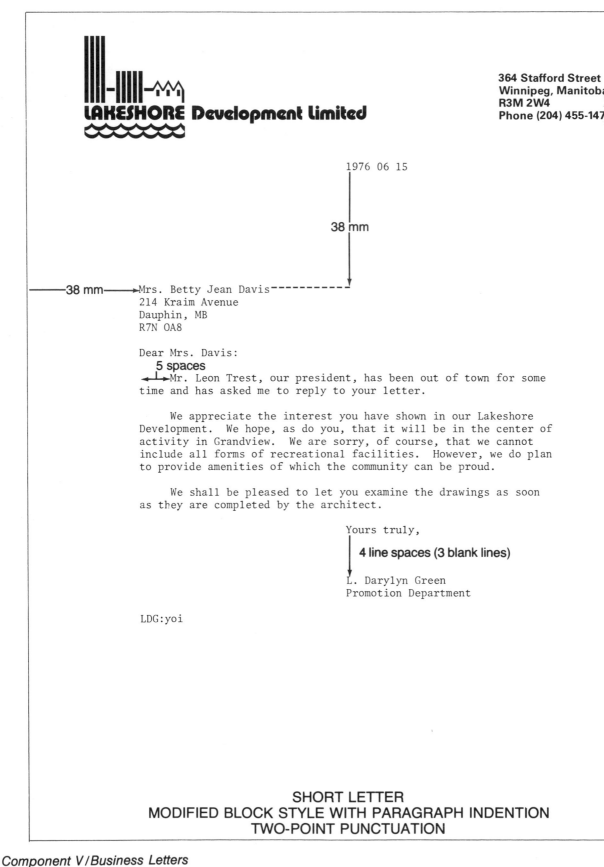

LAKESHORE Development Limited

364 Stafford Street
Winnipeg, Manitoba
R3M 2W4
Phone (204) 455-1470

1976 06 15

38 mm

38 mm → Mrs. Betty Jean Davis
214 Kraim Avenue
Dauphin, MB
R7N 0A8

Dear Mrs. Davis:

5 spaces

Mr. Leon Trest, our president, has been out of town for some time and has asked me to reply to your letter.

We appreciate the interest you have shown in our Lakeshore Development. We hope, as do you, that it will be in the center of activity in Grandview. We are sorry, of course, that we cannot include all forms of recreational facilities. However, we do plan to provide amenities of which the community can be proud.

We shall be pleased to let you examine the drawings as soon as they are completed by the architect.

Yours truly,

4 line spaces (3 blank lines)

L. Darylyn Green
Promotion Department

LDG:yoi

SHORT LETTER
MODIFIED BLOCK STYLE WITH PARAGRAPH INDENTION
TWO-POINT PUNCTUATION

VI.8 Type the following article as an unbound one-page report.

HOW TO CHOOSE PEARS

Canned fruit is a common item on the shopping list the year round. When buying canned fruit, notice that they are all labelled with the grade — Canada Fancy, Canada Choice, or Canada Standard. Canada Fancy is the top grade; the fruit is as nearly perfect as possible. Canada Choice grade fruit may have slight variations in size, color and maturity, but is still a good selection for the majority of times canned fruit is on the menu. Canned fruit graded Canada Standard is of good quality but may not be uniform in size. This fruit is usually best used where appearance is the least important consideration, such as in puddings or chopped in jellied desserts. These grade standards are established by the Canada Department of Agriculture and are enforced by their inspectors. (¶) Dessert pears and Bartlett pears can usually be seen on the store shelf. Bartletts are usually considered the best pear for canning because they are fine-grained and flavorful. Bartletts are canned in a 35% sugar syrup and may be a little higher priced than dessert pears such as Flemish Beauty or Kieffer. The latter are usually coarse and firmer than Bartletts, so only a 25% sugar syrup is needed. The amount of fruit would be the same in cans of both types. The percentage syrup refers only to the strength of syrup and not the amount in the can. Look for both kinds when you're shopping and buy and compare.

VI.9 Type the following article as an unbound one-page report.

Lethal Fumes

Charcoal briquets are dandy for outdoor cookouts. They are convenient, inexpensive, generate heat quickly, and have no detectable odor. Left outdoors to cool and die, They are safe. But warm, flameless briquets may produce a dangerous accumulation of carbon monoxide if brought indoors in a confined space and used as a source of heat. Most people don't do this. But some do and the result is, all too often, death. (¶) Three people living in a trailer in an Ontario trailer camp, decided to have a barbecue over the July 1 weekend last year. But it rained, so they moved the barbecue into the trailer to finish cooking their meal. Before they realized it, all three had partially succumbed to carbon monoxide poisoning. One realized what

V.26 Type the letter on page 159 in **modified block style with indented paragraphs** and **full-point punctuation.** Prepare a carbon copy and an envelope.

SIMPLIFIED LETTER

V.27 Study the information on "Typing A Letter In Simplified Style." Then type the letter on page 160 in **simplified style.** Prepare a carbon copy and an envelope.

TYPING A LETTER IN SIMPLIFIED STYLE

1. *Refer to the placement chart on page 137 for positioning the date line and the letter address.*

2. *The salutation, complimentary close, and company name are omitted from the letter.*

3. *Punctuation marks are not used at the ends of special letter part lines.*

4. *All lines begin flush with the left margin, except for unnumbered enumerated items which are indented 5 spaces.*

5. *A subject line follows the letter address and is typed in ALL CAPITALS with a triple space above and below it.*

6. *The typed signature and title is typed in ALL CAPITALS.*

V.28 Type the following letter from Lorene Durant, Controller in simplified style. Prepare a carbon copy and an envelope.

Letter Address: Mr. Gerald Kennedy
Atlantic Food Processors Limited
460 Water Street
St. John's, NF
A1E 1B1

Subject: Invoice Form

Body:

Our invoice form, in use across Canada since last May, was the outcome of a recommendation of the Committee on Invoice Standardization established by the Food Products Manufacturers' Association of Canada of which your Company is a member. (¶) Since May of last year our accounting procedures have been adapted to this particular form of invoice. Because it has become standard throughout the entire country, and because it is designed for machine use, it is impractical to make an exception for one area. (¶) We thank you for giving us this opportunity to comment on our form of invoice.

Self-check: Does your letter contain a date line, letter address, SUBJECT, body, TYPED SIGNATURE AND TITLE, and your initials?

Component V/Business Letters

158

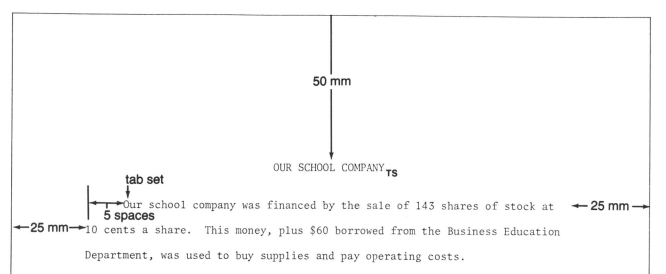

OUR SCHOOL COMPANY TS

Our school company was financed by the sale of 143 shares of stock at 10 cents a share. This money, plus $60 borrowed from the Business Education Department, was used to buy supplies and pay operating costs.

During the first half of the year, our company undertook various jobs for which we received a commission. Our money-making project at Christmas was to design and manufacture Christmas cards. These cards were sold to the Students' Union at a profit. In the last half of the year, we continued our work on a commission basis and also produced a school directory which sold at a profit.

About January, a subsidiary company, Prospectus Limited, was established. It was financed by the sale of shares at 10 cents per share. In order to retain controlling power in the subsidiary, our company bought 52 per cent of the shares. Prospectus Limited sponsored advertising to raise money. It was liquidated at the beginning of June and, as the main company, we received the profits.

Our company paid off the $60 debt in the first half of the year. No wages were paid within our company, but a dividend was declared when the shares were bought back from the stockholders. Profits made through the year are being spent on equipment for the duplicating division. This company is not being liquidated because there are plans for its continuation next year.

Dividends declared were 5 cents per share.

ONE-PAGE REPORT
(Elite Type)

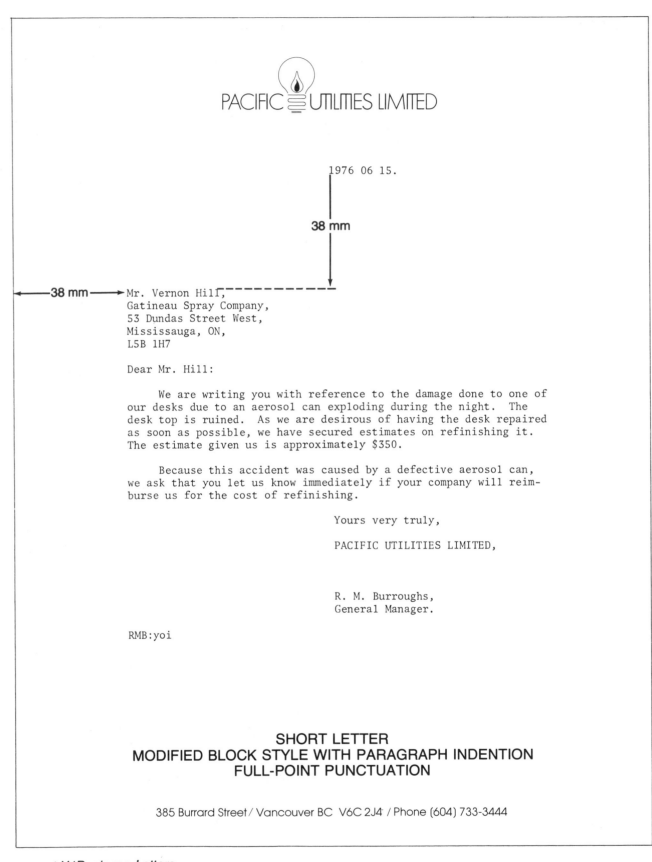

PACIFIC UTILITIES LIMITED

1976 06 15.

38 mm

←—— 38 mm ——→ Mr. Vernon Hill,
Gatineau Spray Company,
53 Dundas Street West,
Mississauga, ON,
L5B 1H7

Dear Mr. Hill:

    We are writing you with reference to the damage done to one of
our desks due to an aerosol can exploding during the night. The
desk top is ruined. As we are desirous of having the desk repaired
as soon as possible, we have secured estimates on refinishing it.
The estimate given us is approximately $350.

    Because this accident was caused by a defective aerosol can,
we ask that you let us know immediately if your company will reimburse us for the cost of refinishing.

                        Yours very truly,

                        PACIFIC UTILITIES LIMITED,

                        R. M. Burroughs,
                        General Manager.

RMB:yoi

SHORT LETTER
MODIFIED BLOCK STYLE WITH PARAGRAPH INDENTION
FULL-POINT PUNCTUATION

385 Burrard Street / Vancouver BC V6C 2J4 / Phone (604) 733-3444

**TYPING ONE-PAGE
REPORTS**

VI.7 Refer to the flow chart below to learn the steps to follow when typing the body of any essay or report. Then type the information on page 193 as an unbound one-page report.

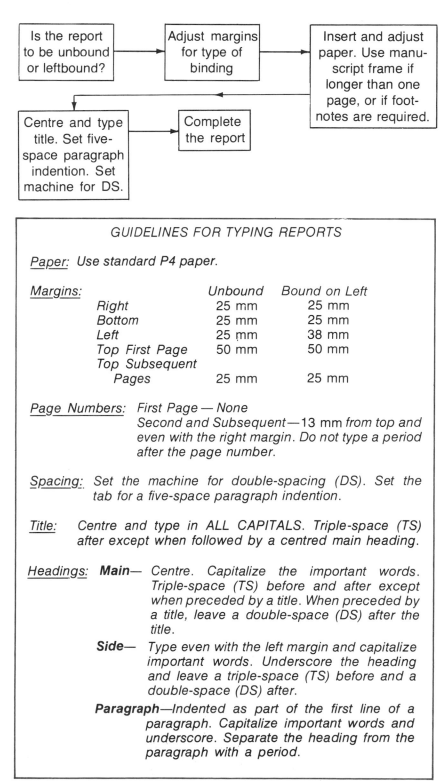

GUIDELINES FOR TYPING REPORTS

Paper: *Use standard P4 paper.*

Margins:

	Unbound	Bound on Left
Right	25 mm	25 mm
Bottom	25 mm	25 mm
Left	25 mm	38 mm
Top First Page	50 mm	50 mm
Top Subsequent Pages	25 mm	25 mm

Page Numbers: *First Page — None*
Second and Subsequent—13 mm from top and even with the right margin. Do not type a period after the page number.

Spacing: *Set the machine for double-spacing (DS). Set the tab for a five-space paragraph indention.*

Title: *Centre and type in ALL CAPITALS. Triple-space (TS) after except when followed by a centred main heading.*

Headings: **Main—** *Centre. Capitalize the important words. Triple-space (TS) before and after except when preceded by a title. When preceded by a title, leave a double-space (DS) after the title.*

Side— *Type even with the left margin and capitalize important words. Underscore the heading and leave a triple-space (TS) before and a double-space (DS) after.*

Paragraph—*Indented as part of the first line of a paragraph. Capitalize important words and underscore. Separate the heading from the paragraph with a period.*

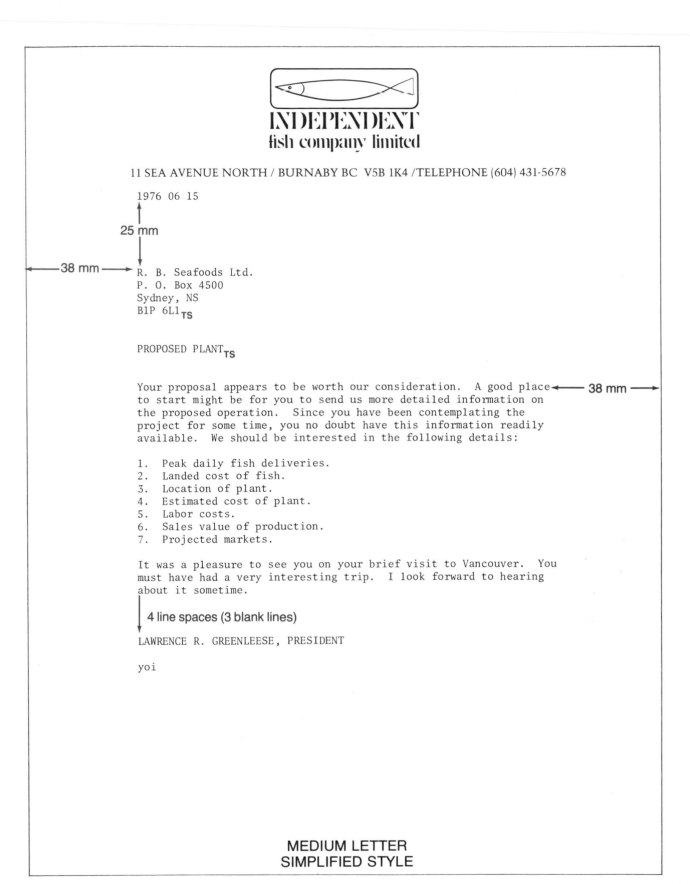

INDEPENDENT
fish company limited

11 SEA AVENUE NORTH / BURNABY BC V5B 1K4 /TELEPHONE (604) 431-5678

1976 06 15

25 mm

38 mm

R. B. Seafoods Ltd.
P. O. Box 4500
Sydney, NS
B1P 6L1 TS

PROPOSED PLANT TS

Your proposal appears to be worth our consideration. A good place ← 38 mm →
to start might be for you to send us more detailed information on
the proposed operation. Since you have been contemplating the
project for some time, you no doubt have this information readily
available. We should be interested in the following details:

1. Peak daily fish deliveries.
2. Landed cost of fish.
3. Location of plant.
4. Estimated cost of plant.
5. Labor costs.
6. Sales value of production.
7. Projected markets.

It was a pleasure to see you on your brief visit to Vancouver. You
must have had a very interesting trip. I look forward to hearing
about it sometime.

4 line spaces (3 blank lines)

LAWRENCE R. GREENLEESE, PRESIDENT

yoi

MEDIUM LETTER
SIMPLIFIED STYLE

```
        2. 10-20
        3. 21-30
        4. 31-40
        5. 41-50
        6. 51-60
        7. 61+
    B. Sex
        1. Male
        2. Female
V. Analysis of Employment Structure
    A. Mining
    B. Government
    C. Other
```

VI.6 Type the following information as an outline.

NHL Hockey

Players
    Six Men Per Team one goalkeeper, two defencemen, three forwards.
    Rules for Player Substitutions: no time-outs for substitutions; no substitutes for players serving penalties.
Rink
    Size: 60.96 m x 25.9 m
    Lines and Zones: Two blue lines dividing rink into three zones — defending neutral and attacking. Centre red line dividing rink in half.
Game
Object: To score the greater number of goals, and to prevent the opposition from scoring.
Length: Three 20 min periods of play, average game length 2.5 h.
Scoring: One point per goal; no overtime for tied scores, except in playoffs.

V.29 Type the following letter from Henry T. Hodges, Service Manager in simplified style. Prepare a carbon copy and an envelope.

Notes: Unusually long business, government, and organization names may be typed on two lines. The second line should be indented two or three spaces.

Letter Address:
Mr. Ed. Leibow Manager
Canadian Wholesalers and
    Distributors
166 rue St - Laurent
Quebec City, PQ
G1R 4N6

Subject: Grayson Proposal, Shipping
And Receiving Area

Body:

The exhaust outlet from your air-conditioning unit is located close to the ground and approximately in the centre of your building in the shipping and receiving area During cold weather the exhaust from the unit forms vapor clouds which are sufficiently large and dense to reduce visibility in this area. As a result of poor visibility there have been three accidents in the past month caused by truckers driving into this area and colliding with moving or parked vehicles. (¶) Mr. Tom Grayson, who has investigated the matter, indicates that relocating the vent by installing additional ducts would be expensive. He has suggested the installation of a flashing light which would warn truckers to proceed with caution in the shipping and receiving area. (¶) Please let me know when you would like to have the light installed.

Notes: On special notations —

All special notations on envelopes should be typed in Area 3 (see page 142) to the left of the address and above the postal code.

Many employers prefer these notations to be typed in ALL CAPITALS, and Canada Postal Standards illustrates these notations in ALL CAPITALS. However, it is permissible to type them in lower case capitalizing the important words.

V.30 Type a copy of the letter which appears on page 162. This letter illustrates the proper placement of the **additional letter parts** which are occasionally used in business and personal affairs.

Business Growth and Development
  Present industries
  Proposed industries
  Competition
  Rental charges
  Proximity to supplier

Location Within a Community
  Central Shopping District
  Central Shopping District Fringes
  Secondary Shopping District
  Suburban Shopping Centres
  String Streets
  Neighborhood Shopping District

The Building

Physical Details
  Size
  Construction
    Soundproof
    Fireproof
    Weather secure

  Heating
  Windows
  Entrances and exits
    Main entrance
    Employee entrance
    Fire escapes
    Loading dock

Customer Appeal
  Wide aisles
  Floor coverings
  Well lighted
  Air-conditioned

VI.5 Type the following outline.

The Demography of Yellowknife.

I. History of the Population
II. Analysis of Growth Rates
III. Present Distribution of Inhabitants
    A. New Town
    B. Old Town
    C. Con Mine
    D. Giant Mine
    E. Indian Village
IV. Analysis of Age and Sex
    A. Age
        1. 0-9

(Continued)

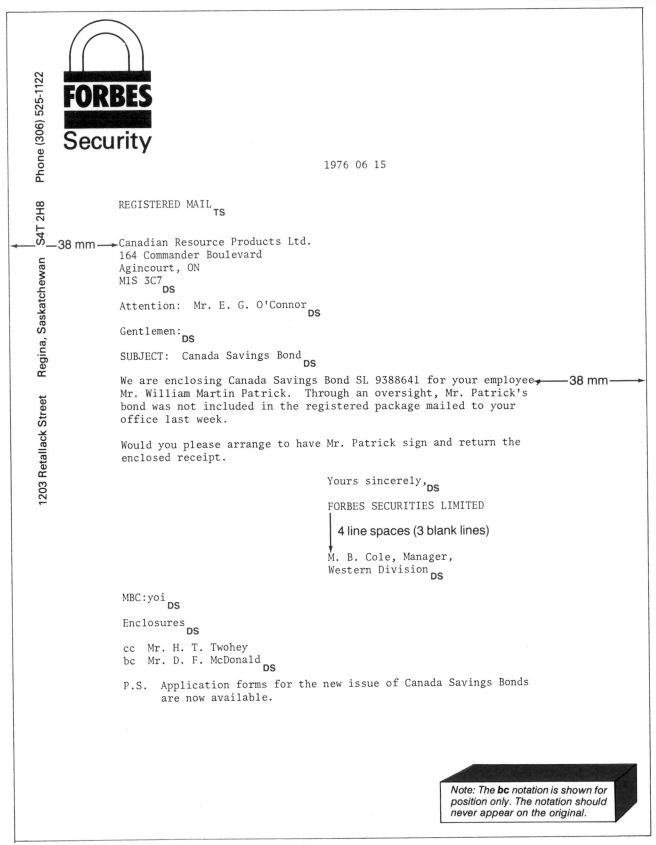

Phone (306) 525-1122

S4T 2H8

Regina, Saskatchewan

1203 Retallack Street

FORBES
Security

1976 06 15

REGISTERED MAIL TS

←—38 mm—→ Canadian Resource Products Ltd.
164 Commander Boulevard
Agincourt, ON
M1S 3C7 DS

Attention: Mr. E. G. O'Connor DS

Gentlemen: DS

SUBJECT: Canada Savings Bond DS

We are enclosing Canada Savings Bond SL 9388641 for your employee ←—38 mm—→
Mr. William Martin Patrick. Through an oversight, Mr. Patrick's
bond was not included in the registered package mailed to your
office last week.

Would you please arrange to have Mr. Patrick sign and return the
enclosed receipt.

                                        Yours sincerely, DS

                                        FORBES SECURITIES LIMITED

                                        │ 4 line spaces (3 blank lines)
                                        ↓
                                        M. B. Cole, Manager,
                                        Western Division DS

MBC:yoi DS

Enclosures DS

cc Mr. H. T. Twohey
bc Mr. D. F. McDonald DS

P.S. Application forms for the new issue of Canada Savings Bonds
      are now available.

Note: The **bc** notation is shown for
position only. The notation should
never appear on the original.

                    2. Secondary
                        a. Documents
                        b. Comments by critics
                    B. Reliability of Sources
                        1. Informed Observation
                        2. Written Information
                            a. The Writer
                            b. The Work
            IV.   <u>Do the Writing</u>
                    A. Completeness
                    B. Conciseness
                    C. Clarity
                        1. Semantic clearness
                        2. Intellectual honesty
                    D. Readability
                        1. Simple
                        2. Short paragraphs and sentences

VI.3   Type the following information as an attractively arranged outline.

Instruction on Basic Swimming

Swimming Strokes

1. Breast Stroke: Legs, Arms, Coordination
2. Side Stroke: Legs, Arms, Coordination
3. Elementary Back Stroke: Legs, Arms, Coordination
4. Trudgen: Legs, Arms, Coordination
5. Front Crawl: Legs, Arms, Coordination

Life Saving Strokes and Kicks

1. Inverted Scissors Kick
2. Regular Scissors Kick
3. Frog/Rotary Broad Kick

VI.4   Type the following information as an attractively arranged outline.

ESTABLISHING THE NEW STORE

<u>Selecting a Location</u>

The Community
    People of the Community
        Population
        Income
        Family size

    Community Services
        Banking
        Advertising
        Parking and transportation
        Law enforcement and protection

(Continued on next page)

Type envelopes for the following three addresses. If necessary refer to the information on page 142 for typing the special notations.

Address	Special Notation
Mr. Brian T. Sanderson, General Manager c/o The Palisades Hotel 1277 Robson Street Vancouver, BC V6E 1C4	HOLD FOR ARRIVAL
Mr. Henry T. Jacques, President Allwynn Transport Limited 14 St. Lawrence Avenue Kingston, ON K7L 3T6	PERSONAL AND CONFIDENTIAL
Security National Bank 444 Tremont Street Boston, MA 02112 U.S.A.	ATTENTION: MR. E. G. O'CONNOR

Notes: On American Addresses—

*The **American Zip Code** (e.g. 45227) is typed on the same line as the community and State. Two spaces must separate the State and Zip Code. The country abbreviation (U.S.A.) is typed separately on the last line of the address. A complete list of the two-letter State abbreviations is provided in Appendix B, page 343.*

MAILING NOTATIONS AND SUBJECT LINE

***Mailing notations** such as SPECIAL DELIVERY, REGISTERED, and AIRMAIL are typed in ALL CAPITALS flush with the left margin, centred between the date line and the letter address.*

Notes: On Subject Lines —

*In letters, other than simplified letters, a **subject line** may be used to indicate the content of the letter. Generally, the word SUBJECT is typed flush with the left margin in ALL CAPITALS followed by a colon (:). The subject is then typed in lower case letters with the most important words capitalized. The subject line is always typed a double space below the salutation.*

V.32 Type the following letter from C. V. McLean, Manager in simplified style. Prepare a carbon copy and an envelope. (The Special Delivery notation may be typed in Area 3 on the envelope or a Canada Post Special Delivery sticker may be affixed in Area 1.)

Notations: Special Delivery

Letter Address: Union Transport Limited
130 Fox Farm Road
Saint John, NB
E2H 1J4

Subject: Shipment of Fish

Body:

You stated in your letter of December 19 that 61 cases of Atlantic salmon and 25 cases of dressed sturgeon were not received by your express office in Montreal. (¶) According to our records, the cases are still in our storage awaiting shipment. May we please have shipping instructions as soon as possible?

NOW THAT YOU HAVE HAD AN OPPORTUNITY TO TYPE FOUR DIFFERENT LETTER STYLES WITH THREE DIFFERENT PUNCTUATION STYLES, YOU SHOULD SELECT ONE FOR TYPING THE REMAINING EXERCISES IN THIS COMPONENT.

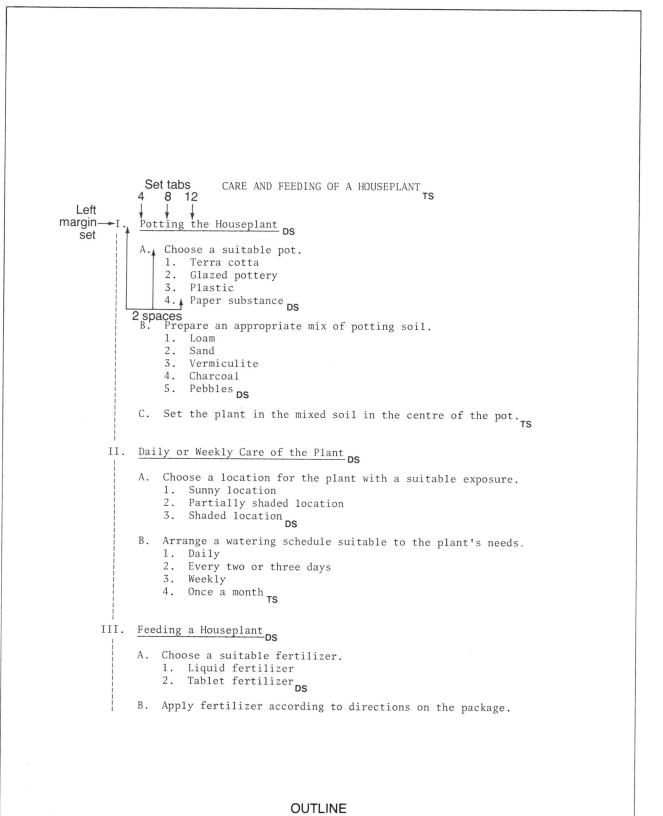

Set tabs   CARE AND FEEDING OF A HOUSEPLANT **TS**

4   8   12

Left
margin →I.   Potting the Houseplant **DS**
set

     A.   Choose a suitable pot.
         1.   Terra cotta
         2.   Glazed pottery
         3.   Plastic
         4.   Paper substance **DS**

2 spaces
     B.   Prepare an appropriate mix of potting soil.
         1.   Loam
         2.   Sand
         3.   Vermiculite
         4.   Charcoal
         5.   Pebbles **DS**

     C.   Set the plant in the mixed soil in the centre of the pot. **TS**

 II.   Daily or Weekly Care of the Plant **DS**

     A.   Choose a location for the plant with a suitable exposure.
         1.   Sunny location
         2.   Partially shaded location
         3.   Shaded location **DS**

     B.   Arrange a watering schedule suitable to the plant's needs.
         1.   Daily
         2.   Every two or three days
         3.   Weekly
         4.   Once a month **TS**

III.   Feeding a Houseplant **DS**

     A.   Choose a suitable fertilizer.
         1.   Liquid fertilizer
         2.   Tablet fertilizer **DS**

     B.   Apply fertilizer according to directions on the package.

OUTLINE
(Centred Vertically and Horizontally)

ENCLOSURE NOTATION

An **enclosure notation** is always typed at the left margin a double space below the **reference initials**. If reference initials are not used, as in the case of personal and personal/business letters, the enclosure notation is typed a double space below the typed signature.

```
(Body) → I shall be in your city next m
         matter over lunch. DS
(Complimentary → Yours very truly,
Close)
         4 line spaces (3 blank lines)
(Typed → L. J. Drury,
Signature)   Executive Assistant DS

         LJD:yoi

(Enclosure → Enclosure
Notation)
```
Enclosure Notation
Block Style Letter

CARBON PACKS

A **carbon copy notation** (usually abbreviated **cc**) and the name of the recipient is typed a double space below the reference initials. If the letter has an enclosure notation, the cc notation is typed a double space below the enclosure notation.

```
                financially responsible.
(Body) I shall be in your city next m
       matter over lunch. DS
(Complimentary Yours very truly,
Close)
       4 line spaces (3 blank lines)
(Typed Signature) L. J. Drury,
                  Executive Assistant DS

       LJD:yoi

       cc  Mr. W. Syme
```
Carbon Copy Notation
Block Style Letter
(No enclosure)

```
           I shall be in your city next m
(Body) → matter over lunch. DS
(Complimentary → Yours very truly,
Close)
       4 line spaces (3 blank lines)
(Typed → L. J. Drury,
Signature)   Executive Assistant DS

       LJD:yoi DS

(Enclosure → Enclosure DS
Notation)
       cc  Mr. W. Syme
```
Carbon Copy Notation
Block Style Letter
(Enclosure)

V.33 Type the following letter from L. J. Drury, Executive Assistant. Prepare a carbon copy and an envelope.

Letter Address: Chamber of Commerce
1247 Hollis Street
Halifax, NS
B3J 1T7

Body:

We would very much appreciate knowing if you can give us any information regarding potential distribution outlets in your area for our line of jewellery. (¶) As the enclosed brochure indicates, we manufacture a complete line of sterling silver jewellery consisting of necklaces, earrings, bracelets, and brooches. Many of these are in matching sets but, of course, are sold either in sets or individually. We sell to large firms such as Meridian Jewellers and MacFarland's Jewellery Ltd., as well as to small firms across Canada. We naturally seek firms which are well established, well known in the trade, and financially responsible. (¶) I shall be in your city next month. Perhaps we could discuss the matter over lunch.

V.34 Type the following letter from R. T. Holmquist, Acting Manager. Prepare a carbon copy for Northland Trust and for your file. Type an envelope.

Notations: Airmail; cc Northland Trust

Letter Address: Mr. Randolph Gillen, Manager
Security National Bank
444 Tremont Street
Boston, MA 02112
U.S.A.

Body:

Thank you for your letter of March 16. We have informed Northland Trust, our transfer agent, of the loss of your certificate. We have also forwarded a copy of your letter to the Northland Trust and they will be contacting you concerning the requirements for the replacement of your lost certificate.

V.35 Type the following letter from Manfred T. Rease, Controller. Prepare a carbon copy and an envelope.

Letter Address: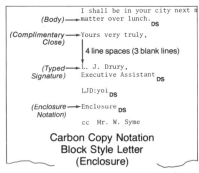

TYPING OUTLINES

An **outline** is often used to summarize information about a particular topic or to present information in a concise and easy to understand format.

Notes: On punctuating outlines —

If a heading, subheading, or subpoint is a sentence, use a final period. If headings and points are not sentences, do not use a final period.

Notes: On numbering outlines —

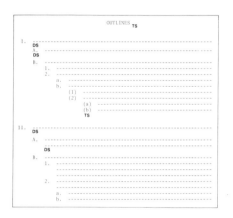

(Do not create a division or subdivision unless two or more points are required.)

VI.1 Type a copy of the outline on the CARE AND FEEDING OF A HOUSEPLANT that follows on the next page.

Treat the outline as a display which is centred both horizontally and vertically. (The flow chart on page 119 provides the procedures for horizontal and vertical centring.)

TYPING OUTLINES

1. *Centre the outline vertically and horizontally. Include the first Roman numeral when centring the longest line.*

2. *Set the left margin at the first Roman numeral.*

3. *Centre and type the title in ALL CAPITALS. Triple-space (TS) after the title.*

4. *Main headings are typed two spaces after the Roman numeral period. Capitalize important words and underscore the entire heading. Triple-space (TS) before and double-space (DS) after each main heading.*

5. *Align columns of numerals (Roman and Arabic) to the right. Use the margin release and backspace key to type outside the left margin. Type a period after each numeral and letter, and space twice after each period.*

VI.2 Type the following outline.

WRITING A REPORT

I.   <u>Define Your Objective</u>
   A. Information
   B. Policy Making
      1. With diagnosis of conditions
      2. With recommendations for action
II. <u>Determine the Form</u>
   A. Narrative
      1. Chronological . . . (causes, origin, successive stages of development, results, conclusions from the study)
      2. Episodic . . . (in story form)
   B. Analysis (research)
      1. Case Study
      2. Genetic
      3. Comparative
      4. Appreciation
   C. Compilation
III. <u>Search Your Sources</u>
   A. Kinds of Sources
      1. Primary
         a. Observation
         b. Experimentation

(Continued)

To **assemble a carbon pack:**

1. place copy sheet on desk,
2. place carbon paper (carbon side down) on copy sheet,
3. add an additional copy sheet and carbon sheet for each extra carbon required,
4. place original copy on top of last carbon sheet, and
5. insert carbon pack so that the original is in typing position. (When inserting hold the carbon pack with one hand to prevent slippage; turn the cylinder with the other.)

Body:

Our records indicate that you have recently acquired 100 shares of Class "A" stock. It is a pleasure to welcome you as a new shareholder. (¶) In the past few years, the Company has been vigorously reorganized. Unprofitable product lines have been dropped, marketing methods and facilities have been modernized, and eleven new companies have been acquired. The management of the Company is dedicated to operating in the best long-range interests of all shareholders. Unlike many companies, the management itself owns a substantial number of shares. (¶) The enclosed booklet gives a profile of our present-day operations. We hope you will find it interesting and informative. If you have any questions or suggestions, we shall be pleased to hear from you.

V.36 Type the following letter from Thomas Gifford, Administrative Assistant. Prepare carbon copies and an envelope.

Notations: *cc Personnel Manager*

Letter Address: *Ms. Darlene French*
1056 Dahl Street
Swift Current, SK
S9H 3C7

Subject Line: *Application for Employment*

Body:

Your letter addressed to the Personnel Manager has been handed to me for reply. (¶) While new operations are quite extensive, the number of our office employees and the opportunities are quite limited. At the present time we do not know of any future openings. However, if you will complete the enclosed application form, we will keep it on file for one year.

3. Select and type a paragraph or two from pages 37 to 52 to develop further typing continuity.

4. Proceed through Component VI.

Supplementary:

Select and type a number of ITA's from pages 224 to 227.

SUMMARY OF COMPONENT VI PROBLEMS
MAJOR APPLICATIONS

Bibliography	16-20, 22, 31, 32
Footnotes	21, 22, 31
Multi-Page Reports	10-15, 19, 20, 22, 30-32
One-Page Reports	7, 8, 9
Outlines	1-6
Parenthetic Source Notations	19, 20, 32
Table of Contents	23-25, 31, 32
Title Page	26, 27, 31, 32

SPECIAL APPLICATIONS

Binding Left	11, 13, 15, 17, 20, 22, 24, 25, 27, 30, 32
Unbound	7-10, 12, 14, 16, 18, 19, 21, 23, 26, 31
Computer Type	18, 24, 29
Enumerations	13, 20
Headings	13-15, 31, 32
Rough Draft	28-30
Script Copy	5, 6, 9, 12, 15, 20, 25, 27
Unarranged Copy	2-6, 8-12, 14, 15, 17-20, 22, 24-27, 30, 31, 32

LETTER WITH ENUMERATION

BLIND CARBON COPY NOTATION AND ATTENTION LINE

Notes: On Attention Lines —

When writing to a firm or organization, individuals often direct their letter by an **attention line** *to a department or particular position within the firm. Generally, the word Attention followed by a colon (:) and the name of the department, position, or person is typed flush with the left margin a double space below the letter address. When using an attention line, the salutation must agree with the letter address:*

e.g.   Heffring, Johnston …

> ATTENTION: Mr. H. J. Heffring

> Gentlemen **not** Dear Sir

Blind Carbon Copy Notation: *A notation that is of no importance or significance to the recipient of the letter is typed at the left margin a double space below the last typed line on the carbon copy only. To do this, insert a heavy piece of paper between the ribbon and the original. Type the notation. It will then appear on the carbon copy, but not on the original.*

LETTER WITH QUOTATION

V.37 Type the letter on the following page. Prepare a carbon copy and an envelope.

V.38 Type the following letter from P. L. Leonard, Manager, Business Properties. Prepare carbon copies and an envelope.

Notations: bc Legal Department

Letter Address: Heffring, Johnstone, Maryberries and Sloan Suite 201 Toronto Dominion Bank Building 55 King Street West Toronto, ON M5K 1A2

Attention Line: Mr. H. J. Heffring

Body:

We have advised Mrs. Tedini in our recent telephone conversation that it was not our intention to develop the leased property in the immediate future. The lease, which expires on July 13, could be extended for a period of two years with the understanding that a further year would then be granted if, at the expiry of the two years, we had not made any plans for development. (¶) The two-year extension will be granted provided a monthly rental of $275 is acceptable. (¶) Please let us know if Mrs. Tedini wishes to have the lease renewed.

V.39 Type a copy of the letter on page 168. Prepare a carbon copy and an envelope.

V.40 Type the following letter from E. T. Malone, Personnel Manager. Prepare carbon copies and an envelope.

Notations: cc Mrs. T. P. Toner

Letter Address: Mr. Scott Reid
1357 Collingwood Avenue
London, ON
N6K 2H2

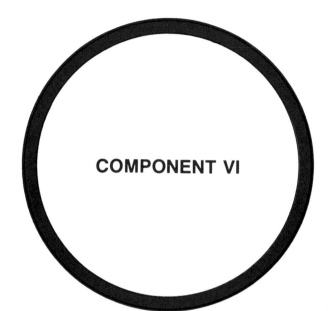

COMPONENT VI

OUTLINES, REPORTS, AND MANUSCRIPTS

STUDENT OBJECTIVES

1. To learn and apply placement rules for typing outlines, essays, reports, and manuscripts.

2. To learn to acknowledge the source of quotations and paraphrased information by using footnotes or references to a bibliography.

3. To type headings properly.

4. To type from rough draft copy making the changes indicated by proofreaders' marks.

DAILY ACTIVITIES

Preliminary:

Current date typing. Type three lines of the current date as illustrated:

	↓ tab set	↓ tab set
19__ 05 21	19__ 05 21	19__ 05 21
19__ 05 21	19__ 05 21	19__ 05 21
19__ 05 21	19__ 05 21	19__ 05 21

Main:

1. Identify your work by typing your name, the name and number of the course, and the current date.

2. Select and type several number and symbol sentences from pages 99 to 106.

CONTENTS

Component VI introduces the student to form and style used in typing outlines, essays, reports, and manuscripts.

MANAGEMENT
information & services
CONSULTANTS

305 DORCHESTER BLVD. W.   MONTREAL, PQ H2Z 1A6   (514) 636-0198

1976 06 15

Mr. Barry Laughton, President
Côte St-Luc Hockey Association
5610 Blossom Avenue
Côte St-Luc, PQ
H4W 2T1

Dear Mr. Laughton:

The enclosed booklet states that the order of business on the agenda for a meeting is not absolutely fixed. The agenda varies with the needs of the organization, and the business to be handled. ←—38 mm—→ The following order is recommended for the meetings of your organization:

5 spaces   **5 spaces**

1. Call to order. (The secretary will record all the names of those present at the meeting.)**DS**

2. Approval of the agenda.

3. Minutes of previous meeting.

4. Treasurer's Report.

5. Business arising from the minutes.

6. New Business.

7. Adjournment.**DS**

I was happy to receive your request for information in this regard. Please call on me again at any time.

Yours very truly,

4 line spaces (3 blank lines)

James B. Price
Public Relations Manager

JBP:yoi

Enclosure

LETTER WITH ENUMERATIONS
(The information to be enumerated should be indented five spaces from the left margin. All items should be five or more spaces from the right margin.)

ITA 22

Mr. W. P. Spinks of 1343 Georgia Street, Vancouver, BC V5L 2A9, has written to the firm where you work requesting information about franchise arrangements for a burger drive-in chain which a Vancouver paper reported was to be established in British Columbia. Write a letter to Mr. Spinks advising that the local office does not have this information but that his letter will be forwarded to the Head Office in Montreal.

ITA 23

Write a letter to the reservation clerk at the Chateau Halifax, 1990 Barrington Street, Halifax, NS B3J 1P2 reserving a room for your boss, Mr. J. L. Woodhouse, for the night of April 17. Mr. Woodhouse will arrive at the hotel about 20:00 and will leave at noon on April 18.

ITA 24

Mr. Paul M. Ritz has requested a copy of the speech given by your supervisor, Mr. C. V. Scott, at the Canada Club meeting of January 14. Mr. Scott has asked you to send the copy. Write a letter to Mr. Ritz enclosing the copy of the speech. Mr. Ritz' address is 34 Coronation Street, St. John's, NF A1C 5C1.

P.O. BOX 9 PQ G6G 5S1
C.P. 9

TOWN OF

THETFORD MINES

(418) 453-3500

1976 06 15

Jewelson Bus Service Limited
P. O. Box 390
Thetford Mines, PQ
G6G 5T1

Gentlemen:

←——38 mm——→ I direct your attention to the provincial regulation governing bus ←——38 mm——→
operations. The following statement appears on page 85 of the
enclosed booklet:

      10 spaces   10 spaces

         No public vehicle is to be operated unless a
         Public Utility Plate has been obtained for such
         vehicle. The plate that has been assigned to
         such vehicle must be attached to that vehicle.

Will you please complete and file with the Board your application
for a Public Utility Plate?

                       Sincerely yours,

                        4 line spaces (3 blank lines)

                       Rene A. Langlois
                       Chairperson

RAL:yoi

Enclosure

LETTER WITH QUOTATION

ITA 18

Compose and type a personal letter to a friend or relative. You may wish to describe some recent school activities, a recent vacation, plans for your next vacation, the last NHL or WHA hockey game you attended or watched on television, or any one of a great number of personal events. The length and subject of your letter will only be limited by your imagination.

ITA 19

Compose and type a personal letter of invitation to a friend or relative. You may choose an event from the list below, or you may select your own event.

A. A school basketball, volleyball, or hockey game.

B. The Annual School Awards Night.

C. Your graduation/commencement exercises.

D. A local performance by a well known recording star or by a famous "pop" group.

E. A weekend hiking and camping trip.

ITA 20

Mr. T. L. Love, the Business Editor of the Downtown News in your city or town has written to Mr. K. O. Cavanaugh who is Manager of the firm where you work. In his letter Mr. Love has asked Mr. Cavanaugh to give some financial predictions for the year ahead. Mr. Cavanaugh is out of town for two weeks. You are to write to Mr. Love acknowledging receipt of his letter and advising that Mr. Cavanaugh is out of town and will reply to Mr. Love's letter on his return.

ITA 21

You are employed as a typist in the Personnel Department of a local firm. Write a letter to Mrs. Lisa Sirois, 357 Edgewood Apartments, your town or city, enclosing an application form which Mrs. Sirois requested in a letter to the Personnel Department.

Body:

Thank you for your recent letter requesting information on employee qualifications required by Independent Telephone Services Ltd. Had you indicated your area of interest, or the department in which you would like to work, I could have supplied you with specific job requirements. However, the following information might be of some help to you. (¶) A High School Diploma is a basic requirement for employment in our Company. Additional training or experience may be necessary depending on the position and the department. For example, our Plant Department which looks after the installation and repair of telephone equipment, central office equipment, pole lines, cables, et cetera, must look for people who have had training in electricity or electronics. On the other hand, our Accounting Department must look for people with bookkeeping experience or an accounting course from a technical institute or university. Other departments may look for engineering, arts, science, or business administration graduates. (¶) From time to time we have openings in various departments within the Company. If you will let us know your interest, and your qualifications, we shall advise you on a course of study to best equip you as a qualified applicant. However, if you wish to complete the enclosed application and return it to us, we shall be happy to place it on file for future consideration.

PERSONAL/BUSINESS LETTERS

All the preceding exercises required the typing of business letters — letters from a business firm or organization to an individual or to another business firm. The next few exercises will give you practice in typing personal/business letters — letters from you, an individual, to a business firm or organization.

Letter Parts

The format for typing personal/business letters differs only slightly from that used in typing business letters. A return address (rather than a letterhead) is typed, beginning 50 mm from the top of the page, and followed immediately by the date line. If the letter is short leave approximately 38 mm between the date and the salutation; if medium, leave approximately 25 mm between the date and the salutation; if long, leave approximately 13 mm between the date and the salutation. Simplified letters are not usually used. Reference initials are omitted since the typist and the dictator (writer) are the same person.

Punctuation

No-point, two-point, or full-point may be used. However, full-point punctuation is not recommended.

V.41 Type a copy of the letter on page 170. Prepare a carbon copy and an envelope.

E. Switchboard Operator

Knowledge of 2-position cord board; knowledge of long distance operations; Telex skill useful.

F. Sales Person

Career-minded; service conscious; sales-oriented; ability to deal with customers over-the-counter.

G. Electrical Assembler

Ability to read schematic wiring diagrams; knowledge of motor control centres and customer control panels; ability to work with electrical panel salespeople.

H. Manager Trainee

Must be well groomed, personable, ambitious; ability to make decisions; knowledge of business procedures; willing to re-locate upon completion of initial training course.

ITA 16

Prepare and type a personal data sheet to accompany the letter of application typed in ITA 15. Remember that your data sheet helps to sell you to the organization with whom you are applying for a position.

Be sure to state any special skills you have acquired. They may not be pertinent to the position for which you are applying, but they may serve as a guide for future advancement if you obtain initial employment.

List any full-time or part-time jobs that you have had, even if you did not receive any pay for them.

When listing references — a present or former teacher, a former employer, your minister, or an acquaintance — be sure to ask permission to use the individual's name before you list it as a reference. Three references are appropriate.

ITA 17

Compose and type three personal letters to the individuals whose names you wish to use as references on the personal data sheet prepared in ITA 16.

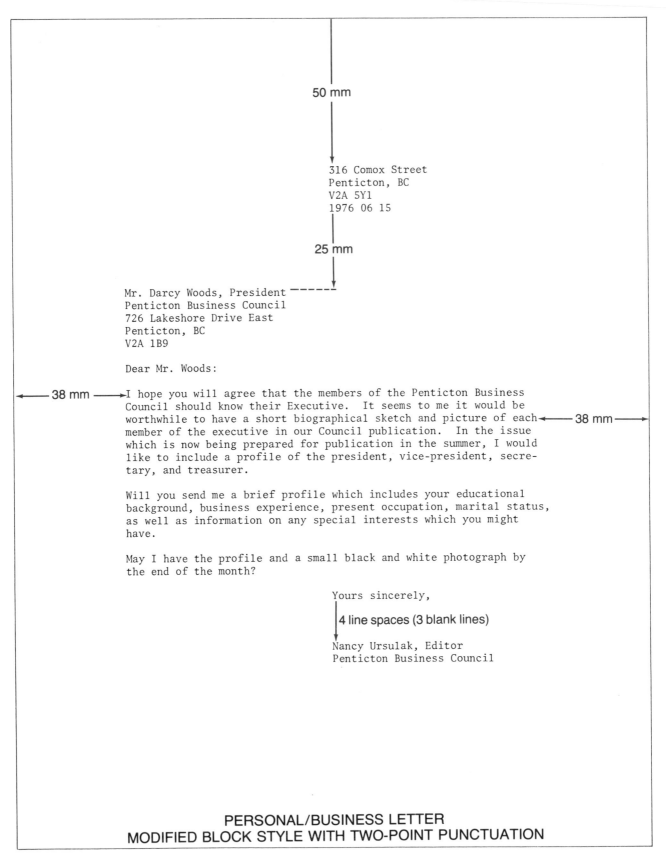

50 mm

316 Comox Street
Penticton, BC
V2A 5Y1
1976 06 15

25 mm

Mr. Darcy Woods, President
Penticton Business Council
726 Lakeshore Drive East
Penticton, BC
V2A 1B9

Dear Mr. Woods:

38 mm

I hope you will agree that the members of the Penticton Business
Council should know their Executive. It seems to me it would be
worthwhile to have a short biographical sketch and picture of each
member of the executive in our Council publication. In the issue
which is now being prepared for publication in the summer, I would
like to include a profile of the president, vice-president, secretary, and treasurer.

38 mm

Will you send me a brief profile which includes your educational
background, business experience, present occupation, marital status,
as well as information on any special interests which you might
have.

May I have the profile and a small black and white photograph by
the end of the month?

Yours sincerely,

4 line spaces (3 blank lines)

Nancy Ursulak, Editor
Penticton Business Council

PERSONAL/BUSINESS LETTER
MODIFIED BLOCK STYLE WITH TWO-POINT PUNCTUATION

outstanding deeds. You think a friend of yours merits the Award for Bravery.

Compose and type a letter to Mr. J.S. Rankin, Deputy Minister, nominating your friend. Give reasons for your nomination.

ITA 15

The Capital Construction Company of Canada has eight job openings in each of its 12 "Capital City" plants and offices. Compose and type a letter of application for one of the jobs in the "Capital City" closest to your present residence. Letters should be addressed to the Personnel Manager.

REGIONAL MAILING ADDRESSES FOR THE CAPITAL CONSTRUCTION COMPANY OF CANADA

Victoria — P.O. Box 4001, Postal Station "A", V8X 3X4
Edmonton — P.O. Box 6001, Postal Station "C", T5B 4K5
Regina — P.O. Box 2001, S4P 3E6
Winnipeg — P.O. Box 3501, Postal Station "B", R2W 3R4
Toronto — P.O. Box 1101, Postal Station "D", M6P 3K2
Ottawa — P.O. Box 4501, Postal Station "E", K1S 5G2
Quebec — P.O. Box 3001, St. Roch Postal Station, G1K 6X9
Fredericton — P.O. Box 5001, E3B 5G7
St. John's — P.O. Box 8001, Postal Station "B", A1B 3M7
Halifax — P.O. Box 7001, B3K 5J4
Charlottetown — P.O. Box 1501, C1A 7N3
Yellowknife — P.O. Box 101, X0E 1H0

JOB OPENINGS

Customs Traffic Clerk

A. Grade 11; good typing; good telephone manner; ability to deal with public.

B. Accounting Clerk

Grade 11 education; knowledge of computerized accounting applications; aptitude for figures.

C. Typist

Knowledge of general office procedures; ambitious; congenial; ability to deal with other office employees.

D. Statistical Clerk

Ability to prepare statistical data; mathematical aptitude; minimal typing skills; excellent command of English; overtime work essential.

SELECT YOUR FAVORITE LETTER STYLE — BLOCK, MODIFIED BLOCK, MODIFIED BLOCK WITH INDENTED PARAGRAPHS — AND PUNCTUATION STYLE — NO-POINT, TWO-POINT — FOR COMPLETING EXERCISES V.42 - V.46 USE YOUR OWN ADDRESS FOR THE RETURN ADDRESS.

Notes: On envelopes —

Refer to the illustration on page 142. Your name and **return address** should be typed in **Area 1,** 3 spaces from the edge of the envelope, starting on line 4 (3 blank lines).

V.42 Type the following letter. Prepare a carbon copy and an envelope.

Letter Address: Ms. Janis Jakubec, Editor
Business Barometer
341 Mountain Road
Moncton, NB
E1C 2M5

Body:

In the latest edition of BUSINESS BAROMETER there is an article on the development of business in our community. The article praises the contributions made by my late father, Mr. Patrick Soley. (¶) Would it be possible to obtain an additional copy of this edition of your magazine? If there are charges involved, I shall be pleased to reimburse you.

V.43 Type the following letter. Prepare a carbon copy and an envelope.

Letter Address: Alberta Power and Electric Company
2513 Third Avenue South
Lethbridge, AB
T1J 0M1

Body:

I am enclosing a photocopy of the bill which I received yesterday showing an amount due of $43.75 for utilities for the months of June, July, and August. I am enclosing, also, photocopies of my cancelled cheques for $12.40, $16.30, and $15.05. These cheques are dated June 30, August 1, and August 30. (¶) I hope you will take steps to correct the error immediately.

V.44 Type the following letter as Secretary to the Recreation Society. Prepare a carbon copy and an envelope.

Letter Address: Mr. & Mrs. John Shaeffer
848 Saskatchewan Crescent East
Saskatoon, SK
S7N 0L4

Body:

Charter Night for the Recreation Society is November 25. This will be a social

ITA 10

Most radio stations have a program announcing community or club events. This service is provided free of charge. Compose and type a letter to your local radio station, asking them to include in their program of club activities an announcement about a forthcoming event sponsored by your school, church, or club. The announcement should be set apart (similar to a quotation) in the body of the letter. The announcement should be brief but should include the essential information about the event; that is, what, where, when, why, and how.

ITA 11

Compose and type a letter to your local newspaper requesting that the editor accept a news item describing a recent event in your school. Describe the event in your letter.

ITA 12

Compose and type a letter to the teacher-advisor of your Students' Council outlining areas of concern which you think the Council should investigate. Make suggestions for improvements.

ITA 13

Type a letter-to-the-editor of your local newspaper or to the editor of a magazine. You may choose from the topics below, or you may select your own topic.

A. Our school graduation diploma is not worth the paper it is printed on.
B. There are too few National Parks in Canada.
C. The personal advantages of metric conversion.
D. The local, provincial, or federal systems of Government in Canada.
E. Canada's role in international trade.

ITA 14

The Ministry/Department of Youth and Recreation in your Province has asked for nominations for youth awards for

evening with greetings from officials, a buffet supper, and dancing. Tickets are $5 each. Be sure to come and bring your friends. (¶) Minutes of the Executive Meeting held on October 27 are enclosed. You will find that your Executive has been very active. A first priority item for the Society's attention is artificial ice for the arena in the Sports Complex. An outline of the proposal and the estimated cost will be found in the minutes. You will be notified of a meeting at which the proposal will be placed before the membership for approval.

Refer to page 161 for typing the postscript.

Postscript:

The ladies of the Recreation Society have agreed to cater for the Charter Night buffet. Can you help?

V.45 Type the following letter. Prepare a carbon copy and an envelope.

Letter Address: Professor L. B. Mitchell
Faculty of Law
University of Toronto
Toronto, ON
M5S 2E6

Body:

The members of the Business Club of Seneca College recall the valuable contribution you made to their seminar "Law and the White Collar Worker." On January 16 we are having a seminar, "Ethics in the Business World." Will you accept our invitation to participate in a panel discussion on the topic? The panel is scheduled to begin at 09:00 in the Students' Lounge, Central Academic, Building (¶) We hope you will accept our invitation.

magazine, type the following letter-to-the-editor of your school newspaper.

Recently a friend and I went to see the movie <u>Earthquake</u> at the local theatre. We went to pay the cashier children's fare (15 and under) and she asked us for school identification. We are both 15 and, expecting to pay children's fare, did not bring enough money for the adult fare. (¶) As we were talking, two ladies (in the finest sense of the word) overheard our plight and offered to give us the money we needed. We wanted the money, but did not want to take charity from people we didn't know. They gave us the money anyway. (¶) When we again went to the cashier, she kindly decided to allow us in for children's fare. We looked for the ladies to return the money but we didn't find them. (¶) I've written this letter to show that there are still some kind people in this world and we appreciate the ladies' gesture.

ITA 8

As an interested citizen, write a letter of response to each of the correspondents of the "letters-to-the-editor" that you typed for ITA 7. You may either agree or disagree with the views they have taken.

If you typed the letter-to-the-editor of your school newspaper in ITA 7, compose and type a similar letter describing a personal occasion.

ITA 9

The advertisment below appeared in your local newspaper. Compose and type a letter, ordering two of the advertised items. Be sure to obtain the correct mailing address for your local "fine luggage shop or department store."

Lady Afrique:—Golightly bags a bargain!

Samsonite Safari II Luggage
Beauty Case Reg. $54.00 Sale $45.00
21″ Overnight Reg. $62.00 Sale $52.00
24″ Wardrobe Reg. $76.00 Sale $65.00
Men's Carry-on One-Suiter Reg. $64.00 Sale $57.00
Men's Two-Suiter Reg. $79.00 Sale $70.00
Men's Three-Suiter Reg. $84.00 Sale $75.00

Open stock, soft-sided luggage for men and women. In Ivory, Gold, Red and Brown. All with our special guarantee for cleaning and repair.
Available at all fine luggage shops and department stores in Canada.

V.46 Type the following letter. Prepare a carbon copy and an envelope.

Letter Address: Mr. Aaron Dodds
Fairview, AB
T0H 1L0

Body:

I would very much appreciate it if you would review my Grass Incentive application with the following information in mind. (¶) Prior to 1975, I had 225 ha of land in hay, but in 1975, I sold a large part of my livestock and plowed down 105 ha of it. When applying for my grain permit book in July, 1975, I asked the agent if I should list that 105 ha separately as summerfallow or just include it with the previous hay land, and he said it didn't matter. That 105 ha was then listed along with the hay land in error. If it had been listed as the summerfallow that it was after July 1, 1975, I would have received the benefit from it in grass incentive payments in the years following. (¶) I feel that this error in the permit book should be considered and that the 105 ha should be figured in with the rest that is eligible for the grass incentive payment. I have been raising hogs and feeding all my grain for years rather than selling any to the elevator. (¶) My 1975 and 1976 permit books are enclosed for your information. May I have them back as soon as you are finished with them. Your help in this matter will be very much appreciated.

PERSONAL LETTERS

All the preceding exercises required the typing of business or personal/business letters. The next few exercises will give you practice in typing personal letters — letters from you to friends and acquaintances.

Letter Parts

The format for typing personal letters differs only slightly from that used in typing business or personal/business letters. No letter address is typed, and generally a carbon copy is not prepared. If your personal letter is short leave approximately 38 mm between the date and the salutation; if medium, leave approximately 25 mm between the date and the salutation; if long, leave approximately 13 mm between the date and the salutation.

Punctuation

The only difference between the punctuation styles of personal and personal/business letters, is that the colon (:) after the salutation — in two-point punctuation — is changed to a comma (,). Full-point punctuation is not recommended.

V.47 Type the following letter. Prepare an envelope. (Joan Snow lives at 191 Somerset Street, Saint John, NB E2K 2Y1.)

Body:

I am glad that you enjoyed the week in Hamilton. Beth and I hope that you will spend another week with us next July. (¶) Mother is

ITA 4

Compose and type a letter to the Registrar, Ministry/Department of Education in your Province, requesting a transcript of your school record.

Remember to enclose the necessary fee with your letter.

ITA 5

Assume that you are working part-time as a typist for the local Chamber of Commerce. The President of the Chamber has asked you to reply to the following letter from Mrs. Jane Hildebrand, 3601 Franklin Drive, Yellowknife, NT X1A 2B5.

"I have been offered a position to teach in your local Central high school. Since the subjects that I am to teach and the salary offered are attractive, I am strongly considering accepting the position. Before making a decision, however, I would like to know more about your area.

"Could you reply to the following questions?

1. What is the population of your city?
2. Is public transportation available in your city?
3. What types of living accommodations are available within walking distance of the high school?
4. What types of recreational facilities are available in your city?

"If I could have the above information within two weeks, it would be very helpful to me."

ITA 6

Compose and type a reply to the following letter from Mr. Joseph Daks, Secretary Students' Council, Atikokan High School, Atikokan, ON P0T 1C0.

"Our Students' Council is making a study of the organization of high school clubs in Canada. We are interested in the variety of clubs in high schools, whether they are supported by the Students' Union, and when they meet — noon, after school, et cetera.

"We would be grateful if you would give us a list of the clubs in your school with a brief outline of their operation."

ITA 7

From your local newspaper, or from a favorite magazine, select and type a number of letters-to-the-editor. Use your favorite letter and punctuation style.

If you do not have immediate access to a local newspaper or

delighted to give you her recipe for Pineapple Pork. She asked me to copy it for you.

PINEAPPLE PORK

2 kg boneless lean pork shoulder, cut in 25 mm cubes
15 ml salad oil
1 medium sized onion, chopped (0.5 kg)
1 can (about 0.75 kg) pineapple chunks
30 ml brown sugar
3 ml salt
110 ml water
80 ml vinegar
30 ml catsup
15 ml soy sauce
1 large green pepper, sliced thin
30 ml cornstarch

Brown pork cubes, a few at a time, in salad oil in a large frying pan; remove. Add onion and saute just until soft, then return pork to pan. Drain syrup from pineapple into a bowl; set fruit aside. Mix brown sugar, cornstarch, and salt in a small bowl; blend in water slowly until mixture is smooth. Then stir in pineapple syrup, vinegar, catsup, and soy sauce. Stir in pork and onion in frying pan. Cook, stirring constantly, until mixture thickens and boils three minutes; cover. Simmer one hour, or until meat is tender. Stir in green pepper and pineapple; cover. Cook three minutes longer or until bubbly hot. Serve with Chinese fried noodles or hot cooked rice. Serves six.

When you visit us next July, we'll have you make Pineapple Pork. I'll make the Baked Alaska!

V.48 Type the following letter. Prepare an envelope. (Mrs. Mary Martin, your Aunt, lives at 258 Assiniboine Drive, Saskatoon, SK S7K 4A2.)

Salutation: Dear Aunt Mary

Body:

Yesterday I received the book that you sent about floods. I took it to school today, and everyone said that it was just what we needed. Somehow you always manage to find the right book for me. Thanks so much. (¶) Larry, my friend who lives in Winnipeg, wrote me last week describing his summer holiday in Saskatchewan. He spent much of his time visiting relatives in Lumsden and Fort Qu'Appelle. They were able to provide him with statistics on the flood damage in the Lumsden area in 1974. He even provided me with the number of sandbags used to protect the town. (¶) Just recently I wrote Aunt Bessie in Regina. I hope she can tell me about the floods they have experienced there. (¶) I'll write a longer letter in a few days and let you know how my report turned out. I really appreciate your help. Thanks again.

Self-check: You may wish to centre the recipe using the longest line to establish a left margin. The cooking instructions might then be indented from the left and right margins.

Notes: The closing used in a letter to a friend or relative is a matter of personal choice. It is usually very informal, such as "Regards," "With love," or any closing considered suitable by the writer.

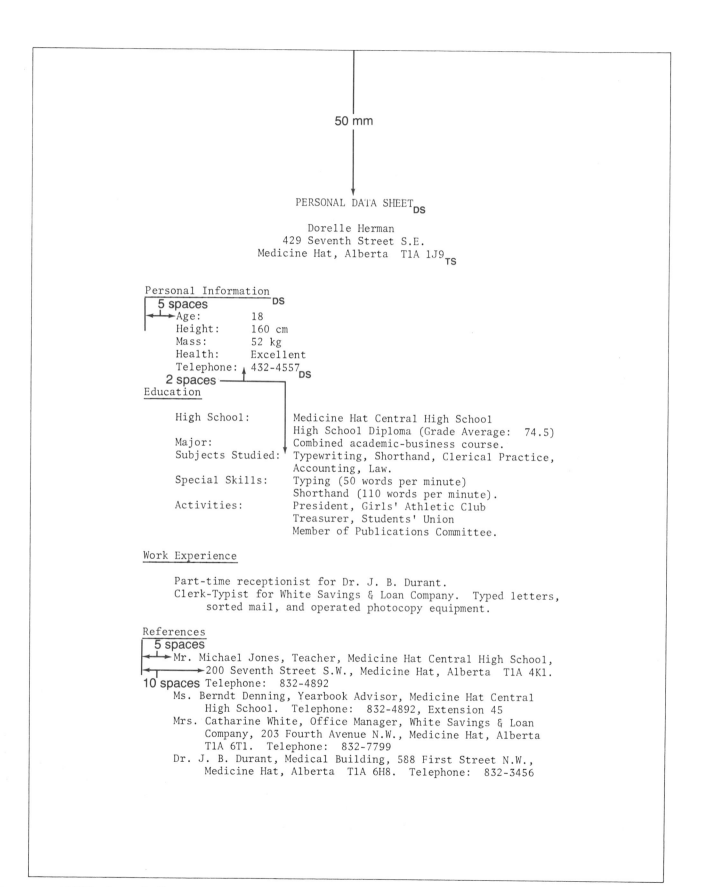

50 mm

PERSONAL DATA SHEET**DS**

Dorelle Herman
429 Seventh Street S.E.
Medicine Hat, Alberta T1A 1J9**TS**

Personal Information
5 spaces————**DS**
Age: 18
Height: 160 cm
Mass: 52 kg
Health: Excellent
Telephone: 432-4557**DS**
2 spaces
Education

High School: Medicine Hat Central High School
                    High School Diploma (Grade Average: 74.5)
Major: Combined academic-business course.
Subjects Studied: Typewriting, Shorthand, Clerical Practice,
                    Accounting, Law.
Special Skills: Typing (50 words per minute)
                    Shorthand (110 words per minute).
Activities: President, Girls' Athletic Club
                    Treasurer, Students' Union
                    Member of Publications Committee.

Work Experience

Part-time receptionist for Dr. J. B. Durant.
Clerk-Typist for White Savings & Loan Company. Typed letters,
    sorted mail, and operated photocopy equipment.

References
5 spaces
Mr. Michael Jones, Teacher, Medicine Hat Central High School,
200 Seventh Street S.W., Medicine Hat, Alberta T1A 4K1.
10 spaces Telephone: 832-4892
Ms. Berndt Denning, Yearbook Advisor, Medicine Hat Central
    High School. Telephone: 832-4892, Extension 45
Mrs. Catharine White, Office Manager, White Savings & Loan
    Company, 203 Fourth Avenue N.W., Medicine Hat, Alberta
    T1A 6T1. Telephone: 832-7799
Dr. J. B. Durant, Medical Building, 588 First Street N.W.,
    Medicine Hat, Alberta T1A 6H8. Telephone: 832-3456

V.49 Type the following letter. Prepare an envelope. (Mr. Gordon McCalla lives at 6432 Ash Street, Vancouver, BC V5Z 3G9.)

Salutation: Dear Gord

Body:

A good many months have passed since I received your last letter, and I am feeling a bit guilty for not having written sooner. I could blame my delay on the heavy assignments which my teachers give me or on the chores that my parents ask me to do, but that would be dishonest. I'm just plain lazy. (¶) Since many exciting things have happened recently I thought I should let you in on a few of them. Perhaps most important is the fact that my parents have just bought a cottage on Maple Lake. It is a fully furnished three-bedroom cedar cottage on lake-front property. The sandy beach and shallow water in front of the cottage will make an ideal summer swimming hole. The fishing in the deeper lake waters is also reported as excellent. Just as soon as school is out, I plan to leave for the cottage to spend the entire summer. (¶) My sister Marg, her husband Bob, and their three kids are coming from Spruce Grove to visit us this summer. Bob has six weeks of holiday time—some of which will be spent with his parents in Ajax; the rest just relaxing at the cottage. (¶) Joan telephoned me last week to let me know that your Dad has been transferred to Ottawa. When will you be moving? Will you be stopping in Toronto on the way? Please let me know so that I can see you and extend a personal invitation to visit our summer retreat.

LETTER OF APPLICATION

V.50 Type the following letter of application. Prepare a carbon copy and an envelope.

Return Address: 429 Seventh Street S.E.
Medicine Hat, AB
T1A 1J9

Letter Address: Mrs. R. H. Duncan, Personnel Officer -
Central Finance Corporation
1366 Fifth Avenue N.E.
Medicine Hat, AB
T1A 6C4

Salutation: Dear Mrs. Duncan

Body:

Please consider me an applicant for the stenographic position advertised in the Medicine Hat Courier on Saturday, November 14. I am particularly interested in the variety of work which your advertisement suggests and feel confident that my high school program has given me the necessary preparation. (¶) My business courses at the Medicine Hat High School included Typewriting. 10 and 20, Accounting 10, Shorthand 31, Law 20, and Clerical Practice 20. My speed in taking dictation was 110 words per minute. In all courses, I received above-average grades. (¶) As a special project during my Grade XII year, I set up a bookkeeping system for the students' store and acted as the store accountant. (¶) My high school program included 125 h of supervised work experience as a clerk-typist with the White Savings and Loan Company in Medicine Hat. During my final year of high school, I served as receptionist for Dr. J. B. Durant on Saturday afternoons. This experience has increased my knowledge of office procedures and my confidence in working with others. Further information regarding my work experience is provided in the enclosed personal data sheet. (¶) May I have a personal interview at your convenience? My telephone number is 432-4557.

Complimentary Close: Very sincerely yours

Typed Signature: Dorelle Herman

Notations: Enclosure

DATA SHEET

V.51 There are many acceptable formats for a Personal Data Sheet. The Personal Data Sheet for Dorelle Herman, as shown on the following page, is one format.

Type a copy of the Data Sheet on page 177 for Dorelle Herman. Make a carbon copy for your file.

INDIVIDUALIZED TYPEWRITING APPLICATIONS (ITA's)

V.52 Now that you have acquired a thorough knowledge of the parts of a letter, and have selected a favorite letter and punctuation style, you should be able to compose and attractively arrange letters at the typewriter.

Prepare carbon copies of each application for your file. Remember to use good techniques when composing and typing each application.

ITA 1

Compose and type a letter to the National Film Board, 150 Kent Street, Ottawa, ON K1P 5P4, requesting a copy of their 35 mm film catalogue.

ITA 2

Compose and type a letter to the Canadian Labor Congress, 100 Argyle Avenue, Ottawa, ON K2F 1B6, asking for their booklet "The Structure of Labor in Canada."

ITA 3

Compose and type a letter to the Registrar of a college or university of your choice, requesting a calendar for the school or faculty that you wish to enter.

P, control of, 19
P.S., to indicate postscript, 162, 172, 349
Page-end reminder, 152, 195
Page numbers of manuscripts, 192, 352
Paper, assembling for carbon pack, 115, 145, 165, 357; facts about, 116, 118, 346; horizontal centre of, vii; inserting, vii; size of, 116, 118, 346
Paper guide, setting the, vii
Paper guide placement, vii
Paragraph headings, 192, 200, 352
"Paragraph" symbol, 151, 217, 358
Paragraphs, block, 37; handwritten, 46; indented, 43; number and symbol, 99; speed escalator, 58
Parentheses, control of, 85
Parenthetic source notations, 207, 353
Per cent sign (%), 83
Percentages, expressing, 73, 341
Period (.), after abbreviations, 17; after initials, 17; at end of sentence, 9; control of, 9; in exclamation mark, 92; placement with quotation mark, 91; spacing after, 9; use as decimal point, 75; with initials, 17; with quotation mark, 91
Periodicals, titles of, 144, 339
Personal data sheet, 177, 350
Personal letter, complimentary close, 174; definition, 135; illustrated, 350; notes on, 173
Personal notation, on envelope, 142, 351
Personal/business letter, definition, 135; illustrated, 169; notes on, 169
Pica type, vii, 346
Pivoting, 126
Plays, titles of, 144, 339
Plus symbol (+), 92, 345
Poems, titles of, 144, 339
Points of compass, 339
Postal cards, 264, 352; form message on, 266
Postal Codes, 74, 342; exercises, 98
Postscript, 162, 172, 349
Posture, ix
Pound Sterling symbol, 345
Professional titles without name of person, 339
Program of a meeting, 274
Proofreaders' marks, 217, 358
Proofreading, 138, 335
Punctuation, styles, 136, 347
Purchase orders, 280

Q, control of, 23
Question mark, after direct question, 31; control of, 31; placement with quotation mark, 91; spacing after, 31
Quotation marks ("), 91
Quotations, capitalization in, 91; colon before long, direct, 168, 207; fragments of, 91, 352; long, in manuscript, 207, 352
Quoted material in manuscripts, 207, 352, 353

R, control of, 16
Ratchet release, See Automatic line finder
Reference initials, 135, 348
Reports, See Manuscripts
Return address, envelopes, 142, 351; personal/business letter, 169, 349; postal card, 265
Ribbon, changing, 334; control, v, vi
Right parenthesis ()), control of, 85
Right shift key, control of, 13
Roman numerals, aligning, 188; in topic outline, 188
Rough draft, 108, 217, 358
Ruled lines, drawing on the typewriter, 335; typed and nontyped, 280

S, control of, 2
Salutation, business letter, 135, 348; notes on, 154; personal/business letter, 169, 349; personal letter, 173, 350; placement of, 135, 348; postal card, 264
Seasons of the year, 339
Second-page heading for letter, 152, 349
Semicolon, control of, 2; spacing after, 6
Sentences, alphabetic, 53; difficult reach, 67; error-elimination, 63; speed escalator, 57
Seven (7), control of, 74
Shift key, control of left, 8; control of right, 13
Shift lock, use in typing ALL-CAP words, 119; use in underlining several words, 89
Side headings, 192, 199, 352
Signature, business letter, 135, 348; personal/ business letter, 169, 349; personal letter, 173, 350; postal card, 264; simplified letter, 158, 348
Signer's name on letter, 135, 348
Simplified letter, 158, 348; illustrated, 160
Simplified style, 136
Six (6), control of, 73
Space bar, control of, 4
"Space" symbol, 217, 358
Spaces (horizontal), to a full line of elite type, vii; to a full line of pica type, vii; to 25.4 mm of elite type, 137, 346; to 25.4 mm of pica type, 137, 346
Spaces (vertical), on P4 paper, 118, 232, 346; on P5 paper, 118, 231, 233, 346; to 25.4 mm, 137, 346
Spacing, bibliography, 205, 353, 354, 356; envelope addresses, 138, 142, 351; footnotes, 211, 212, 353, 354, 355; letters, 137, 348; manuscripts, 192, 352, 356, 356; outlines, 187, 354, 356; summary of paper, 116, 346; table of contents, 214, 353, 355; title page, 215, 353, 355
Spacing (horizontal), above and below divider line for footnote, 211, 353, 355; after comma in sentence, 22; after colon, 32; after exclamation mark, 36, 92; after period at end of abbreviation, 17; after period at end of sentence, 9; after period used with an initial,
17; after period within an abbreviation, 17; after question mark, 31; after semicolon, 6; before and after "at" sign, 90; before and after "cent" sign, 90; in serial, patent, and policy numbers, 77, 342; to indicate thousands (000's), 69; with cent sign, 90; in Postal Codes, 74; in Postal Codes, 74; in serial, patent, and policy numbers, 77, 342; to indicate thousands (000's), 69; with cent sign, 90; with dollar sign, 82; with metric symbols, 70, 344; with number sign, 86
Spacing, summary of rules, 338, 339
Spacing (variable), between lines, 121; between words, 122
Spacing (vertical), after heading lines, 120, 192, 352; after main heading, 120, 192, 352; between headings and columns, 234; between lines of title page, 215, 353, 355; between main and columnar headings, 234; between main and side headings, 192, 352; between main, side, and paragraph headings, 192, 352; double, 3, 347; single, 3, 347; triple, 3, 347
Special characters and symbols, 345
Spread headings, 125, 346
Spreading letters, 125, 346
Squeezing letters, 143, 337
Statements, 283; income, 286
Street names, abbreviations in, 342
Subject, in simplified letter, 158, 348
Subject line, in letter, 163, 348
Subtitles, 242; spacing between columnar headings and, 242; two-line, 247
Superior figures, 95, 353
Superscript, 95, 353
Syllable intensity (SI), 38

T, control of, 7
Tab stops, clearing, 334; in columnar material, 199, 231, 237, 239, 240; setting, 43; setting for columns, 231, 237, 239, 240; use in paragraph indentions, 43; use in typing date and closing lines of letters, 139; use in typing outlines, 188; use in typing invoices, 281
Table of contents, 214, 353, 355
Tables, aligning figures, 199; centring by columnar headings or entries, 242; dollar sign in, 199; five-column, 247; four-column, 238; grouped data, 241; in manuscripts, 199; three-column, 232; with footnotes, 246; with subtitles and columnar headings, 242; with titles, 233; with titles and columnar headings, 234
Tabulation summary, 358, 359
Telegrams, 278; notes on, 279
Three (3), control of, 69
Three-column tables, 232
Time, how to express, 94
Title page, 215, 353, 355
Titles, articles, 144, 339; books, 144, 339; magazines, 144, 339; manuscripts, 192, 352; newspapers, 144, 339; plays, 144, 339; poems, 144, 339; of signer of letter, 135, 348; solid underline for, 89; two-line, 243

"Transpose" symbol, 217, 358
Twenty-four hour clock, 94
Two (2), control of, 75
Two-letter abbreviations, provincial and territory, 144, 343; state, district, and territory, 343
Two-page letters, 151, 349; heading for second page, 152, 349; second page paper, 152
Two-point punctuation, 136, 347
Typewriters, facts about, 334, 335
Typing position, ix

U, control of, 14
Unbound manuscript style, outline of, 192, 352, 353
Unbroken line, shift lock used to type, 89, 335
Underline, continuous for series of words, 89, 335; solid, under several words, 89, 335; symbol, 217, 358; to introduce footnotes, 211, 353, 354; unbroken, below several words, 89; use with columnar headings, 234
Underlining, bibliography, 204, 353, 354; in footnotes, 211, 353, 354; paragraph headings, 192, 200, 352; side headings, 192, 199, 352; titles of books, 144, 211, 339; titles of magazines, newspapers, and periodicals, 144, 339
Underscore, control of, 89

V, control of, 24
Variable line spacer, v, vii, 335
Vertical centring, See Centring (vertical)
Vertical ruled lines, drawing, 335

W, control of, 20
Word counts, in copy, 38
Word division, exercises, 56; hints on, 33, 46, 340
Words, average length of (AWL), 38; counting typewritten, 10; high-frequency (HFW), 38
Wrist position, 3
Writer, name of, on business letter, 135, 348

X, control of, 29
x, symbol for multiplication, 345

Y, control of, 27

Z, control of, 30
Zero (0), control of, 78; before a decimal, 78
ZIP Code, 163, 342, 343